D1106138

A SHADOW OF RED

A SHADOW
OF RED

COMMUNISM AND THE BLACKLIST
IN RADIO AND TELEVISION

David Everitt

IVAN R. DEE

CHICAGO 2007

www.ivanrdee.com

Library of Congress Cataloging-in-Publication Data:
Everitt, David, 1952–
  A shadow of red : communism and the blacklist in radio and television /
David Everitt.
      p. cm.
  Includes bibliographical references and index.
  ISBN-13: 978-1-56663-575-2 (cloth : alk. paper)
  ISBN-10: 1-56663-575-6 (cloth : alk. paper)
1. Broadcasting—United States—History. 2. Broadcasting—Political aspects—United States—History. 3. Blacklisting of entertainers—United States. 4. Anti-communist movements—United States—History—20th century. I. Title.
  PN1990.6.U5E84 2007
  384.540973—dc22
                                                        2006031926

For my wife Laurie and my sons Anthony and Gregory

Contents

	Acknowledgments	ix
	Foreword	xi
1	Communist Squad	3
2	Something in the Air	20
3	Cultural Work	42
4	Comrades of the Comrades	71
5	Confronting an Institution	93
6	The Boys from Syracuse	116
7	Congressional Oversight	142
8	The Passion	158
9	Renewed Vigilance	184
10	The Middle of the Road	211
11	Backlash	235
12	A Case of Libel	259
13	Verdict	283
14	End of an Era	318
	Notes	351
	Bibliography	379
	Index	385

Acknowledgments

MY RESEARCH for this book has brought me into contact, either personally or electronically, with many invaluable document collections and
many outstanding archivists and librarians who made these collections accessible to me. My thanks to Peter Filardo and his associates at the Tamiment Library and Robert F. Wagner Labor Archives at New York
University; Daniel J. Linke and the staff at the Seeley G. Mudd Manuscript Library at Princeton University; Ellen Kastel at the Ratner Center
for the Study of Conservative Judaism at the Jewish Theological Seminary; George Abbott at the Media Services Department at Syracuse University Library; Steve Siegel at the 92nd Street Y archives; Ed D'Onofrio
at the Science, Industry and Business Library in New York City; and the
staffs at the Center for American History at the University of Texas at
Austin, the Special Collections and Archives at George Mason University,
the Special Collection Library at the University of Sussex, the Hoover Institution Library and Archives at Stanford University, the Onondaga Historical Association, the Manuscripts and Archives Division of the New
York Public Library, the Special Collections Division of the New York
Public Library for the Performing Arts, and the Scholars Room at the Museum of Television and Radio in New York City. For those libraries far
from home I relied on some excellent researchers. My heartfelt appreciation to Milanne Hahn, Michael Sangervasi, and John Mason. Thanks also

to Bob Thompson and David Marc for their help in accessing the Steven H. Scheuer Television History Collection at Syracuse University, and to William Dungey for allowing me to peruse the treasure trove of papers left behind by his father. In addition, Ronald D. Cohen and Robert M. Lichtman were a great help in finding and sharing an especially hard-to-find document from their personal collection.

Another important part of my research entailed interviewing participants in the political broadcast struggles of the 1950s. They were all cooperative and generous with their time, and they are all listed among my sources at the back of the book. Special thanks go to Vincent Hartnett, who not only agreed to an interview but answered all my written followup questions and graciously lent me his copy of the transcript for the Faulk vs. Hartnett, Johnson and Aware libel trial, an absolutely essential source. Thanks also to George Berger for patiently explaining fine points of the legal process, to Leslie Barrett for allowing me access to his correspondence, and to John Earl Haynes, Harvey Klehr, Herb Romerstein, and Ronald Radosh for fielding questions on the American Communist movement.

Although I concentrated on examining primary source material, I would like to acknowledge as well the efforts of authors who, from various perspectives, have previously delved into this subject, principally Michael C. Burton, Howard Blue, Ronald D. Cohen, Robert M. Lichtman, Stefan Kanfer, Paul Buhle, David Wagner, Patrick McGilligan, Kenneth Lloyd Billingsley, Rita Morley Harvey, Joseph Persico, and A. M. Sperber.

Throughout the project I relied on my wife Laurie, not only for her patience and understanding but for her indispensable services as my in-house editor.

Finally, I would like to thank my literary agents, Loretta Barrett and Nick Mullendore.

D. E.

Huntington, New York
January 2007

Foreword

IN 1949 the historian Arthur Schlesinger turned his attention from explaining the past to analyzing his own troubled times, a period when the cold war confronted America with a new crisis. His book *The Vital Center* stressed the importance of opposing the Soviet Union—the great threat to American democratic, civil libertarian principles—while at the same time counseling caution. He argued that the United States must resist Soviet expansion overseas. As for Communists and Communist sympathizers at home, he believed they were a cause for concern, but he insisted they could be defused "by the traditional democratic methods of debate, identification, and exposure."[1] At all costs, he said, Americans must avoid irresponsible Red-baiting that could compromise the spirit of the Bill of Rights.

The idea that the United States must strike a balance between vigilance and restraint was shared by President Truman and other moderate anti-Communists in his administration. Pursuing that course, Truman instituted a policy of containment against Communist forces in Europe, a response to Soviet aggression and destabilizing tactics that was both forceful and measured. But even as this strategy was being formulated, some constituencies in the country were already moving in other directions. Repudiating the containment policies were those on the left who saw no reason to resist Soviet expansion, as well as some who outright supported it.

On the right, the administration's opponents in the House Un-American Activities Committee had already responded to these sentiments by embarking on a grandstanding campaign against suspected subversives, while the committee's efforts would soon be reinforced by the anti-Red vigilantism of other groups and demagogues. Genuinely alarming developments fueled fears of communism in the opening years of the cold war—the discovery of Soviet espionage rings in the United States, the shock of the Soviet-backed invasion of South Korea—but much of the anti-Communist purge began to thrive on little more than its own headlong momentum and often exceeded the genuine domestic threat.

For the next ten years the anti-Red crusade continued to provoke suspicions and denunciations in schools and government agencies, in businesses and trade unions. The phenomenon was especially acrimonious in the broadcast industry. There a blacklist affected scores of performers, writers, and directors, triggering the most intense period of political crisis in the history of the electronic media. It also served as a vivid reflection of the country's larger free-speech debate.

From the beginning of my research for this book, I felt the need to put this story of the radio and TV blacklist in its proper place within the context of early cold war politics. In the past, I found, historians tended to treat the phenomenon merely as an adjunct to the movie-industry purge of the 1950s; but I believe it is a story apart, and in certain ways more crucial and compelling.

First is the matter of sheer size. Radio and television provided a livelihood to many more people than the movie studios did and reached a wider audience. Second, the nature of the medium itself made it more contentious. Broadcasting was not just a supplier of entertainment but a major source of information. This information pipeline, connecting directly into people's homes, was a vital concern for both the government and a wide array of civic groups, on both the right and the left. For many it carried an insidious potential for propaganda.

The blacklist in broadcasting also differed from its Hollywood counterpart in another significant way. The movie-industry purge was essentially imposed from above, prodded by congressional investigations into Communist influence in Hollywood. In radio and TV, though, the driving force was cultivated from below, a grassroots phenomenon led by a small group of zealots.

Taking it upon themselves to cleanse the airwaves were three ex-FBI agents, one former naval intelligence officer, and one supermarket owner. Various collaborators joined their cause—from clergymen and lawyers to American Legionnaires and New England matrons—but to a great extent the radio and television industry was cowed by these five men. Many media executives of the day were convinced they could not challenge the right of this handful of watchdogs to determine who could and who could not work.

Setting the broadcast blacklist apart in yet another way is the dramatic arc of its narrative. In Hollywood the ban on alleged Reds faded gradually over the years, the process sometimes imperceptible to the public eye. Never was there a definitive reckoning. In broadcasting, though, the growth of the blacklist eventually led to a legal confrontation when one victim by the name of John Henry Faulk succeeded in bringing the anti-Red watchdogs to court, where the two sides of the issue finally clashed, in the open, and brought the historical episode to a dramatic climax.

My belief in the distinctiveness of this experience remained constant throughout my research. What changed as I dug deeper into the subject was how I perceived the conflict. More and more I saw that the broadcast blacklist was not the simplistic morality tale that had been the theme of many previous accounts of the period. This was not merely the story of persecutors and the persecuted, the standard witch-hunt narrative of right-wing fanatics hounding political innocents that they insisted were agents of the Communist devil. Although clearly excessive and destructive, the blacklisters were not necessarily deluded hunters of an imaginary menace. The broadcast purge was the culmination of a long-standing ideological struggle in which advantage had shifted from one side to the other, from radical leftists to right-wingers. It was a time when neither side was willing to engage in reasonable discourse. Many of those, in fact, who decried the repressive tactics of the early 1950s had previously advocated similar measures against *their* enemies in an earlier period of emergency.

Targets of the blacklist, even those who admitted being part of the Communist movement, have often been portrayed as nothing more than idealistic progressives, their politics characterized as essentially vigorous opposition to bigotry and fascism, as if communism in the age of Stalin were nothing more than liberalism with attitude. Often they have been touted as political and cultural heroes, worthy of inclusion, as the broadcast historian Erik Barnouw claimed, on a "roll of honor."[2] Too little attention has been paid to the implications of their ideology, both within the broadcast industry and on the wider political stage. And too little credit has been given to those, like Arthur Schlesinger, who avoided both extremes and opposed both communism and the blacklist.

In discussing this project with friends over recent years, one question has frequently come my way: Do you see a parallel to what's going on today? As a rule, my short answer has been, "No." Not that there have been no parallels at all. The Danny Glover–MCI incident, for instance, certainly echoed some of the elements of the blacklist period. After the radical activist Glover delivered a harsh, public criticism of President Bush at the beginning of the Iraq War, conservative MSNBC commentator Joe Scarborough denounced the actor on the air and organized a protest among his viewers, demanding that Glover be fired as the spokesman for MCI on the phone company's TV commercials. The campaign had its effect. By May 2003, MCI announced it would let Glover go. The tactics spearheaded by Scarborough were clearly reminiscent of methods used by pressure groups to remove suspected Communists from the airwaves in the early 1950s, but there was a difference. Unlike many of those branded as Communist sympathizers in the 1950s, Glover continued to work regularly as an actor both in films and on TV. The same held true for other anti-war performers. Sean Penn, for one, not only continued to appear in films after taking an outspoken stand against the Iraq War in 2003, he even went on to win an Oscar. More important, despite predictions after the MCI incident of a new age of McCarthyism, no organized blacklist emerged. This is a critical distinction. What made the 1950s blacklist troubling were not individual firings but the institutionalized nature of the industry purge.

All that said, my longer answer is that, in other less direct ways, the early cold war purge is still relevant. First, it serves as a cautionary tale about measures taken in any time of war or emergency, on the need to distinguish between justified and unjustified responses and to monitor the extent of even warranted measures. Second, it provides a commentary on the temptations of extremism, on both sides of the political spectrum, and the mischief created by irresponsible accusations that poison the public discourse. And third, it offers a vivid illustration of the battle between political factions to control the media, a battle that continues to this day.

To my mind, the best way to understand the blacklist period in radio and TV, as well as the political skirmishing that preceded it, is to focus on those five figures most responsible for orchestrating the phenomenon, who have also typically been, in previous accounts, the people examined the least.

The three ex-FBI agents who published a paperback book called *Red Channels* in 1950 caught a tiger by the tail, releasing a list of suspected Communist sympathizers just as the cold war heated up into outright military conflict. Within just a few months, as the Korean War raged, their book would be regarded as the blacklister's bible in the broadcast industry. It also served as the springboard for the career of Vincent Hartnett. A former naval intelligence officer and a key contributor to *Red Channels*, he soon set out on his own to become the most prominent clearance consultant for radio and television, a Red hunter who compiled dossiers on broadcast talent that could determine whether or not an entertainer was fit to appear on the airwaves. His work made him a lightning rod of controversy as the debate over the broadcast purge intensified. And then there was the supermarket owner from Syracuse named Laurence Johnson. At the age of sixty-two, when others might have been planning retirement, he began an ideological crusade to rid the airwaves of any Red taint. Armed with only a limited number of business contacts and an alliance with his local American Legion post, he succeeded in making media moguls dance to his tune.

Too often the portrayals of these blacklisters have failed to rise above the depths of caricature, reducing them to little more than political bogeymen in a partisan political melodrama. Only by constructing a more complete picture of these people and their times can we understand how something like the blacklist could occur in a free society. And only by raising certain questions about their careers can we come to grips with the issues of their time. What did they get right? And where did they go wrong? How were they able to acquire such influence, and why were so many willing to grant them such power? And who was willing to stand up to them?

Some who opposed the blacklist did so out of self-interest because they themselves were targeted by the Red hunters. Others were driven by reflexive ideological bias and ignored the excesses and inconsistencies of those on their side of the political fight. And there were those who acted as a matter of nonsectarian principle, both anti-totalitarian and civil libertarian, people who supported resistance to Soviet aggression abroad and defended fair play at home. Their perspective, coming from the vital center, offers a vantage point for observing the flaws in politics and human nature at a time of peril and uncertainty.

A SHADOW OF RED

Communist Squad

MOST OF THEIR DAYS were spent churning out weekly scripts or reading aloud lines of dialogue into a radio microphone, lending their talents to a great media machine that catered to a massive, often nondiscriminating audience. While some explored radio's potential for artistry and social commentary, many more occupied themselves in featherweight comedies and escapist soap operas and pulp-fiction adventures. But behind the scenes a large contingent of creative players in the broadcast industry dedicated themselves to higher-minded pursuits. From obscure writers and actors to such stars as Edward G. Robinson and Orson Welles, they conferred in union caucuses and congregated at rallies in midtown hotels to grapple with issues that extended far beyond the confines of their profession, issues that pitted one faction against another in bitter debate.

The conflict had been gathering momentum since the Great Depression, when many writers, directors, and actors first began to gravitate toward opposing political camps. Whatever the specific dispute at the time, their greater concerns often related not to developments in their immediate experience in the entertainment business but to extraordinary events unfolding on the other side of the world. At the eye of the political storm were clashing perspectives on the Soviet Union. Some who had championed the New Deal and opposed the rise of fascism found it only natural to support a Russian experiment that might solve the problems of poverty and war. Forming a loose alliance with them were others, not quite so radical. They might not be outright advocates of communism, but they viewed the Soviet system as at least a tolerable alternative to the American way. Together, they found themselves at loggerheads with all those in broadcasting who believed Soviet tyranny to be the great enemy of political liberty around the world. In one respect, the two sides had something in common. Both were determined and ready to discredit their adversaries whenever possible.

Few of these disputes reached the larger public. Arguments over the Russo-Finnish War or internal union regulations were unlikely to galvanize those outside a small circle of die-hard partisans. But with the end of World War II and new questions about relations between Washington and Moscow, the controversies within broadcasting threatened to escalate and attract outside scrutiny.

The debates intensified at a time of great uncertainty in the industry. The new technology of television promised to transform broadcasting by adding an unprecedented visual dimension to the programs transmitted over the airwaves, a potentially seismic change that preoccupied many who worried about how to adapt old radio habits to a new medium. This was not a time when executives were eager to welcome additional turmoil, but others in the field, more politically inclined, remained impatient with parochial concerns. Their gaze was focused abroad, where they saw vexing developments they were certain would press upon their lives at home.

The first indication of trouble arose in eastern Europe. Despite promises he had made at the end of the war, Stalin blocked free elections in Poland and soon installed subservient Communist regimes throughout the region. Bringing the situation to a crisis in 1948 were Soviet actions in Berlin, where the USSR blockaded the sector of the city controlled by the West. The Truman administration responded by airlifting food to West Berlin's beleaguered residents. The cold war had begun.

In broadcasting as in other areas of American life, many individuals entered the debate over this spiraling confrontation. As events accentuated the differences between the two sides, some saw the need now more than ever to resist a new totalitarian hegemony while others strove with greater urgency to foster peace and cooperation between the United States and its new adversary—or rival, as they chose to characterize the Soviet Union. Partisans staked out their ideological turf through groups with such names as the Voice of Freedom Committee, the Artists Committee, and the People's Radio Foundation. The political rift succeeded in importing cold war tensions into the business of transmitting news and entertainment.

To most Americans, political skirmishes among writers, directors, and actors did not seem terribly important. Here were issues, after all, best decided by those in government. As intriguing as radio personalities might be, for most people they did not loom large in the national debate. But there were exceptions. For three men in particular, the implications of ideology on the airwaves became especially acute, and they were determined to make the public aware of how insidious those implications could be. Their concerns had been percolating for some time, going back to the desperate days of the recently concluded war.

A hatred of communism united the three FBI agents in a common cause. In this they were little different from fellow agents at the time. What set them apart was a mounting sense of frustration that propelled them to take extraordinary measures, to devote themselves to a life of eternal vigilance in the face of creeping subversion.

Their names were John G. Keenan, Kenneth M. Bierly, and Theodore C. Kirkpatrick, and they all joined the FBI within a twenty-month period between December 1940 and August 1942. Little in their background at the time suggested they were ever likely to be consumed by political passion. Unlike many of the radicals they would later denounce, the three future watchdogs of the airwaves originally entered adulthood along a path that had nothing to do with ideology.

John Keenan, the most privileged of the three, was the son of a successful Manhattan attorney and lived his early years as if ready to follow his father's conventional example. Moving from prep school to undergraduate work at Fordham University and law school at St. John's, the Brooklyn-bred Keenan began his legal career in 1938 by litigating negligence cases for the Brooklyn, Manhattan Transit Corporation. For the time being he was unable to join his father's firm. The Great Depression had diminished its roster of clients and had left no room for new employees. In 1939, though, he took a step toward becoming a part of Alexander & Keenan's staid business of personal estates, bankruptcy sales, and incorporation charters when he took an office at the firm for freelance legal work.[1]

Keenan's future partner Kenneth Bierly grew up in Peoria, Illinois, where he generally impressed his elders as a methodical, diligent young man, absorbed primarily with bucking the odds presented by hard economic times. He worked his way through college by taking jobs as a clerk and a watchman in spare hours between class and study, and after graduating from the Chicago-Kent College of Law found a way to make a living by taking a position in the legal department of a Midwestern insurance company.[2]

The third of the group, Theodore Kirkpatrick, another son of the American heartland, grew up first in Campbellstown, Ohio, then Richmond, Indiana, just ten miles away. Handsome, industrious, and a tireless joiner, he presented the persona of a young man destined for a comfortable Rotarian future. He earned a scholarship to nearby Earlham College, played on the school's football team, performed in the dramatics society and glee club, and went on to weather the depression by taking a job with a loan corporation.[3]

Ordinary as their first years of manhood might have been, all three young men seemed to itch for something different. In assessing these applicants, the FBI was impressed with their clean-living resourcefulness, what the Bureau considered model Americanism as envisioned by its image-conscious director, J. Edgar Hoover. Beneath their veneer, though, beyond their determination to seek success in the private sector, they were all eager to find something their civilian lives could not offer.

Broad-shouldered and square-jawed, Jack Keenan was described by contemporaries as rugged and hard-nosed, "all man." He had been a three-letter athlete at Fordham, especially renowned for his play on the football field, an experience that drilled young men to be tough in both body and mind. In the classroom, meanwhile, his Jesuit instructors had stressed the importance of sublimating oneself to a greater good. Once out on his own, Keenan might have been frustrated by the lack of opportunity at both the New York transit authority and his father's firm, but as an educated man of action he had not been likely to embrace the sort of sedentary, insulated livelihood he found at those places. Bierly had also been restless with the legal work he encountered after entering the bar. He lasted only a year at the Continental Casualty Company of Chicago before he tired of wrangling over surety issues; a subsequent job as an insurance investigator had not held his interest any longer. For his part,

Kirkpatrick had seemed intent to leave his Hoosier confines behind as soon as he could, something that his job with the Beneficial Industrial Loan Corporation had helped him accomplish: over nine years he had worked a series of seven field-office assignments, ranging from West Virginia to Arizona. A secretary to one of his supervisors observed that he had "not progressed as rapidly as others in the company." The problem might have been a certain lack of enthusiasm for the work. As one supervisor put it, Kirkpatrick was "not tough enough in finance collections." After America entered World War II, he was ready for a bolder move.[4]

Ten years before the crisis they would later instigate, Keenan, Kirkpatrick, and Bierly were all prepared to plunge themselves into something larger than their own private pursuits. Helping determine the direction they took was a sense of patriotism that the Bureau considered beyond reproach. As an FBI telegram on Kirkpatrick summed it up, "Americanism unquestioned."

The FBI offered a taste of their future cause during their time at the Quantico training center. There they received formal instruction about totalitarianism, both Communist and fascist; but this was only a prelude. Most likely Keenan was the first to put this instruction to use when he investigated Communists at the FBI's Philadelphia office in the fall of 1941 and went on to the Internal Security Section in Washington the following year. The true immersion in the totalitarian threat for all three began after they met during their later assignment to the Bureau's New York Communist Squad.

Of the thousand FBI agents stationed in New York City during World War II, only some twenty-five were assigned to this unit. Separate from those agents investigating Soviet espionage, the group focused on the infiltration of domestic organizations and businesses and the potential of Reds to overturn the American system. Like the rest of the squad members, Keenan, Kirkpatrick, and Bierly received intensive instruction in the ideology of the Communist Party of the USA (CPUSA), studying in particular Karl Marx's *Communist Manifesto* for its practical application in the real world of Soviet governance and foreign policy. The unit operated in a world mostly invisible to the public eye. As long as the country's official enemies posed the most immediate threat, it was only natural that headlines would seize upon the capture of Nazi saboteurs, not the investigation of Soviet-inspired infiltration. Even so, despite their lack of public recognition, the agents formed a cohesive, inspired group, remembered squad member Charles Blaisdell. "The feeling for one another and the dedication," he said, "were very similar to that which is so revered among the Marine Corps."[5]

Headquartered in downtown Manhattan's Foley Square, the squad investigated Communists, fellow travelers, and the organizations they sought to control, especially those that could play a role in transportation, unions, politics, and communications. By gaining influence in these four areas, the agents surmised, Communists could sabotage the country's vital functions in time of emergency or perhaps form a power base for an eventual putsch. In this the squad members reflected the ideas of their director, whom, even years later, retired agents would still refer to as "Mr. Hoover." They saw him as a man devoted to protecting America's democratic institutions against totalitarian dangers that assumed their most seductive and deceitful form in the Communist party's promise of a classless workers' paradise.[6]

The squad's perceptions set the men apart from prevailing attitudes of the day, just as it would distance them from the conventional wisdom of later years. Certain cases underscored this disparity more than others, especially the investigation of the veterans of the Abraham Lincoln Brigade, the voluntary military force that had been organized by the Communist International to fight the armies of Franco in the Spanish Civil War. The popular culture of the era, particularly such Hollywood films as *For Whom the Bell Tolls* and *Fallen Sparrow*, portrayed members of the brigade as courageous anti-fascists, and for many the passage of time has only added to the romantic aura surrounding these men. The Communist Squad, though, saw them as something entirely different. The brigade, from the squad's perspective, had been a tool in Stalin's strategy to dominate the anti-fascist coalition in Spain, and was now a battle-hardened cadre ready to take the lead if there should ever be an attempted Communist coup in America.[7]

As part of the Bureau's World War II service, Keenan acted against the fascist variety of totalitarianism by investigating the German-American Bund and assisting the roundup of Nazi saboteurs who landed on Long Island in the summer of 1942. Once in the Communist Squad, though, he spent most of his time investigating the possible infiltration of New York City unions, including the Transport Workers Union and the American

Communications Association. He also assisted on other cases when agents needed help with especially difficult assignments. His fellow agents regarded him as skillful and intrepid, "the type of fellow you'd want as a partner, and to rely on," as agent Gino Fopp put it. At a time when the Roosevelt administration allowed the FBI considerable latitude, thorny assignments could include unauthorized entries and searches. In a particularly memorable instance, a message from Washington made it clear exactly how dissatisfied the director was with the New York office's efforts to assemble an authoritative list of members of the Communist party, whose national office was a short distance uptown from the Foley Square headquarters.[8] Keenan was recruited to help get hold of the requested information. In later years the agents involved would describe the mission as a complete success, but they would refuse to reveal any details. When carrying out this sort of work, agents were mindful of what were known as the eleventh and twelfth commandments. The eleventh commandment was, "There's no excuse for not having an excuse" (meaning, be ready with a cover story if you get caught). The twelfth commandment: "Don't get caught."

Bierly and Kirkpatrick specialized in recruiting and handling informants within the Communist party who could relay inside information about the organization's leadership as well as shifts in party doctrine and tactics. Their most notorious spy was a young photographer named Angela Calomiris. Bierly persuaded her to pass herself off as a Communist and use her contacts in the leftist Photo League to infiltrate the party. For seven years she passed along information, first to Bierly, then to Kirkpatrick and others, until she finally revealed her undercover status by testifying in the prosecution of Communist party leaders in 1949. A year later she published an account of her experiences in a book entitled *Red Masquerade*. Kirkpatrick, like Keenan, might also have carried out black-bag jobs. As a Bureau report cryptically stated it, Kirkpatrick "participated in quite a large number of highly confidential surveillances which resulted in the obtaining of information which would not have been available to an ordinary confidential informant."[9]

The investigations conducted by Keenan, Kirkpatrick, and Bierly had a powerful influence upon their views of American security, and their observations of the Communist movement reaffirmed for them the urgency of their work. This commitment crossed partisan political lines. Keenan was a registered Democrat, though his voting pattern would become increasingly Republican and conservative; Kirkpatrick would describe himself as a liberal Republican; and Bierly would eventually register with the Liberal party.[10] Anti-communism provided the common purpose between them. In time, what united them even more was a disheartening realization.

"We used to talk," Kirkpatrick would later say, "about how little the public, as a whole, knew of some of the details of the Communist movement and some of the facts that were routine to us; facts being brought in by us and others day to day and actually being buried in files." This, Kirkpatrick said, was especially vexing "to any individual who is impatient."[11]

The military alliances born of necessity during World War II accounted for much of the agents' frustration. As long as the Soviet Union was a partner in the war against the Nazis, American officials treated Stalin's police state with the same respect they extended to allies that were democratic. They also encouraged the media to promote the same view, or at least did nothing to discourage it. The entertainment industry praised the Soviets in such films as *Mission to Moscow* and on radio programs like *Passport for Adams* and "Concerning the Red Army." For all that, the public was not necessarily as gullible as the three agents might have thought. In 1942 two-thirds of Americans polled by the Gallup Organization looked ahead to the end of the war and stressed the importance of containing Soviet aggression.[12]

Even if Keenan, Kirkpatrick, and Bierly were aware of this fact, it still might not have altered their basic complaint. They believed that the public did not understand the specific techniques that Communists used to gain influence in America. They admired efforts in the press to expose these machinations—in the columns of labor writer Victor Riesel, for instance, or in issues of the *New Leader*, the social democrat weekly that opposed totalitarianism on both the right and the left—but they didn't think this was enough.[13] And their sense of urgency could only have been intensified by events following the close of the war in Europe. In June 1945, FBI agents discovered secret government documents in the offices of the left-wing magazine *Amerasia*, and in September Soviet agent Igor Gouzenko defected in Canada and revealed details of a Russian spy network in the Western Hemisphere.

As long as Keenan, Kirkpatrick, and Bierly worked in the FBI, they were not allowed to disseminate information to the public. Outside the Bureau, they conjectured, they might be able to address the issue in an important way. They discussed the possibility of publishing an exposé-style magazine that would correct the situation.

The first to leave the FBI was Kirkpatrick. Bloomingdale's department store offered him a job in store security, with the promise that he would soon be promoted to manager of the department. Enticed by the increase in pay, he resigned from the Bureau in November 1945 to take the job. Later that month an illness in the family convinced Keenan to make a similar move. His father, who had for some time been pressuring Keenan to return to the family's law firm, was now suffering from glaucoma and was unable to handle matters on his own. Keenan returned to the firm to assume his father's day-to-day responsibilities. Bierly, the first of the three to join the FBI, remained in the Bureau for now, but he stayed in touch with Keenan and Kirkpatrick and continued to talk with them about a private anti-Communist venture.[14]

Their desire to find some way to exploit the potential of the media underscored in a very practical way their belief in the vital nature of the communications industry and the need to guard it against subversive influence. Also shaping their ideas at this time were international developments. The Soviets were tightening their grip on those countries they had occupied at the end of the war and were beginning the process of installing puppet regimes. In March at Westminster College in Fulton, Missouri, Winston Churchill had declared that these developments signaled the descent of an Iron Curtain across Europe. If the three ex-FBI agents needed further incentive for action, these events provided the final impetus.

FBI reports indicate that Keenan took the lead in finding backers for the proposed publishing enterprise, beginning as early as January 1946 to recruit allies, especially within the ranks of Catholic clergy. An early partner was Father John F. Cronin of the National Catholic Welfare Conference, who agreed with Keenan that the country needed a forceful anti-Communist publication and helped coordinate the project. He may have been instrumental in enlisting the unofficial cooperation of New York Archbishop—soon to be Cardinal—Francis Spellman as well as the very tangible aid of Samuel Cardinal Stritch of Chicago, who contributed one thousand dollars. A far more important investment came from outside Catholic circles, helping to bring a multi-faith dimension to the venture.

The Jewish anti-Communist Alfred Kohlberg, a textile importer who had been doing business in China since 1916, was a staunch advocate of Chiang Kai-shek and the Nationalist Chinese in their fight against Mao's Marxist rebellion. He believed enough in the publication outlined by Cronin and Keenan that he was willing to contribute fifty thousand dollars. By the time Kohlberg became involved, a more detailed, three-part plan for the project had begun to emerge.

A monthly magazine would be the most visible part of the scheme. Early proposed titles were *Alert* and *On Guard*, but eventually the partners selected the name *Plain Talk*. Editing the publication would be Isaac Don Levine, a journalist and former leftist who had turned against the Soviets after witnessing their excesses following the Russian Revolution. A second unit would provide research for the magazine, and a third would produce confidential reports for clients seeking information on Communist influence within their businesses or unions. The last two units would be run by Keenan and any other ex-FBI agents he could enlist.

Keenan, who had left his father's firm to join the Bureau, felt obligated to stay with the practice and was not about to abandon it yet again. In arranging terms with the *Plain Talk* outfit, he agreed to work in the research and confidential-report units on a part-time basis. He recruited another former agent, William F. Higgins, but Higgins too would be no more than a part-timer because of a familial obligation to work in his father's real estate company. Bierly, who was making arrangements to leave the FBI, was toying with the idea of practicing law when the *Plain Talk* venture presented another possibility. The issue of "whether this other thing could be practical," he later said, "and whether or not I could feed a family and do this type of work was a paramount question." Ultimately he decided the *Plain Talk* gamble was worth the risk. Kirkpatrick, meanwhile, had no such difficulties in deciding to come aboard. He had grown restless with his work at Bloomingdale's where, he said, he was consumed with the perils of shoplifting "when here the Communists were trying to take our country." He joined Bierly as one of the two ex-agents who would work for *Plain Talk* full-time.[15]

The research unit set up shop in offices accessible only by freight elevator at 240 Madison Avenue in Manhattan, a building owned by Kohlberg. While organizing their files, the ex-FBI agents also laid the groundwork for the confidential-report service, a nonprofit venture called John Quincy Adams Associates. Expanding upon the original concept, the unit went beyond compiling reports to include a lecture program to offer the public information on the Communist movement. The organization's purpose, as outlined in its promotional literature, was "to assist in changing emotional dislike of Communism to informed and documented knowledge."[16]

Much of their effort concentrated on labor issues. They produced reports on suspected Communist union officials and provided similar information to Jesuit labor schools—principally the Xavier Institute of Industrial Relations in Brooklyn—that were attempting to provide a non-Communist alternative for workers seeking better job conditions. While assembling incriminating information on suspect labor and civic leaders, they also made a point of exonerating those they considered non-Communist—merely "tolerant liberals of various faiths," as one report phrased it. To help get their message out, to propagate "informed and documented knowledge" to as wide an audience as possible, they contacted radio commentators who shared a similar perspective, providing information that could be included in upcoming broadcasts.[17]

It was in this sector of broadcasting that the three ex-FBI agents first grappled with the issue that would soon envelop them in so much notoriety. In February 1947 they drafted a five-page paper entitled "Communist Pressure on the Radio Industry." The report examined a recent controversy over the firing of left-wing news commentators, including Quentin Reynolds, Johannes Steel, and, as an adjunct to his acting and directing career, Orson Welles. Although the authors conceded that only some of these radio personalities were pro-Communist, they argued that Communists orchestrated "an all-out campaign" against the dismissals as part of a cynical effort to smear the entire radio industry as reactionary while also promoting those commentators who were likely to take a pro-Soviet line. Considering the reputation that Keenan, Kirkpatrick, and Bierly would later acquire, the report is surprisingly circumspect—no outright alarmism, no Red-baiting hysteria. Still, it concludes by warning of a campaign—allegedly masterminded by Reds—to secure a license for a left-wing FM station.[18]

The ex-agents drew upon their Bureau contacts to fill the staff of their new operation, hiring four clerical workers who had formerly been employed by the FBI. They also hired two people to take on more executive responsibilities. One of them was a man named Jack Wren.[19] During the blacklist period, this short, balding, unimposing-looking man would go on to play an influential and controversial role in the anti-Red purge in broadcasting, and in later accounts of the period would become something of a mystery man, his personal background only vaguely defined. More immediately, during his time as head of research for the *Plain Talk* outfit, he became a focal point for a growing acrimonious dispute between the ex-agents and the FBI.

Several writers have described Wren as a former naval intelligence officer, a claim that is based on a suspect source. In fact, according to FBI reports, he was employed by another branch of the federal government. During World War II he was a confidential informant for the FBI's New York Communist Squad, supervised by Bierly from 1943 to 1944, then by Kirkpatrick until the fall of 1945. The reports explain that Bierly convinced Wren to handle research for *Plain Talk* in April 1946 at a time when Wren had just left a job at an advertising agency. When FBI officials later found out about this arrangement, they were not pleased. For them, the first problem was that Bierly recruited Wren while he was still a special agent, a month before he left the Bureau. The second and more distressing problem was that Bierly and his associates were exploiting their Bureau contacts to further a private enterprise. Wren later assured the FBI that, as a *Plain Talk* employee, he was using no material he had gathered while an informant, that he based his current research solely on a study of other publications. This failed to mollify Bureau officials. As far as they were concerned, FBI informants could not "serve two masters," and once they took on a second employer they were no longer fit to serve the Bureau. They made this exceedingly clear to Wren when they fired him at the end of September 1946.[20]

The problem, though, was far from over. Other informants had also been used by the ex-agents at *Plain Talk*, and in some cases FBI officials believed that they too had to be dismissed. And it was not just FBI informants that the ex-agents were using but FBI techniques as well. Kirkpatrick approached a former informant who was the superintendent for the building that housed the Queens Communist party headquarters and persuaded him to allow a search of the party's trash. "Kirkpatrick also requested and secured keys for the premises for the purpose of conducting a black-bag job." Whether Kirkpatrick actually carried out the job is not clear.[21]

Also not clear is how much FBI information people like Wren actually passed to *Plain Talk*. Perhaps Hoover and his lieutenants were merely being territorial. Kirkpatrick, at least, tried to respect the boundaries between his old and new employers, but Keenan undermined that effort and infuriated his old bosses by claiming he had no idea Wren had been working for the Bureau, when in fact two of his partners had been the informant's handlers.[22] What is beyond question, though, is that Bureau officials would have taken a more forgiving view were it not for another contentious issue: they believed the ex-agents had stolen secret FBI reports.

Over the summer a special agent in the New York headquarters noticed that copies of ten reports were missing from the office files. Five had been written by Keenan and one each by Kirkpatrick and Bierly, and all ten concerned Communist influence in unions, a special focus of the ex-agents at *Plain Talk*. While no proof of the ex-agents' guilt ever surfaced, the circumstantial evidence was clearly incriminating, and Bureau investigators were convinced that Keenan in particular was responsible and perhaps Bierly as well. By September the Bureau decided against further action because, officials believed, Keenan and Bierly knew they were under suspicion and had probably eliminated any trail of physical evidence by destroying the documents. Whatever the factual basis for the charges, the Bureau's resentment continued. FBI reports repeatedly blasted the ex-agents' integrity, characterizing them in one instance as "unethical, mendacious, and consequently, untrustworthy."[23] Other allegations of questionable conduct would dog the ex-agents in years to come.

Rancor of another kind began to develop within the *Plain Talk* operation itself. Kirkpatrick and Bierly were concerned about the magazine's modest circulation, its inability to reach a sufficiently wide section of the public with its anti-Communist message, and they had no doubt about the source of the problem. They argued with editor Levine that the magazine was taking too intellectual an approach. They wanted *Plain Talk* to deal more directly with practical issues faced in America by business and labor rather than examining broad policy questions. What they had in mind was a sort of anti-Red muckraking publication that would drag not only Communists but all their defenders out into the light. But Levine would not budge from his loftier, more cerebral ideas.[24] Their inability to change the magazine's course spurred Kirkpatrick and Bierly, and Keenan as well, to consider other options.

Early on at John Quincy Adams Associates they had considered publishing a newsletter to bring their information to a wider section of the population. Now they put that plan into action. At a time when the organization was beset by bureaucratic problems—the government was questioning its nonprofit status—the threesome decided to correct the limitations they faced by striking out on their own.[25]

Once again, Kohlberg played a key role. He provided a loan of fifteen thousand dollars, and even though the three partners were severing their ties to *Plain Talk*, he agreed to let them retain the files they had assembled for the magazine's research unit and keep them in his building at 240 Madison Avenue. For their editorial offices, Keenan, Kirkpatrick, and Bierly leased a small two-room suite several blocks uptown at 55 West Forty-second Street, across from Bryant Park. The three men each bought shares and incorporated the new company in April 1947 under the name American Business Consultants.[26]

The venture required some immediate on-the-job training. Except for Bierly's stint as an editor at his college paper and the Chicago-Kent *Law Review*, the partners had no background in publishing. Their first order of business was to hire an experienced staff writer and editor. They chose a journalist named Sam Horn, who, under the pseudonym of Andrew Avery, had recently written a twelve-part exposé of communism for the *Chicago Journal of Commerce*. Here was someone who had a crisp writing style they appreciated, and who saw the problem as they did: Horn's series of articles had focused on the issue of Americans being recruited, sometimes unwittingly, into supporting causes that served Communist purposes.[27]

The title the three partners chose for their new venture left no doubt as to the militancy of their stance. They called their newsletter *Counterattack*.

While Horn took charge of the editorial side of the business, the three partners settled into their own specialized tasks. Keenan, who carried the title of president, devoted most of his time to administration. As part of his responsibilities, he solicited subsidies for *Counterattack* by persuading business executives to place mass subscriptions for their firms. He could sometimes project a brusque manner, not necessarily ideal for the role of salesman, but his man's-man demeanor could nonetheless make a strong impression upon similarly hard-driving captains of industry and convince them of the importance of his newsletter's cause. Secretary-treasurer Kirkpatrick, serving as the newsletter's managing editor, shepherded leads for stories and also spent much of his time as the company's front man. He handled a great deal of the correspondence with outside contacts, including allies such as Kohlberg and leading anti-Red columnists, while also lecturing to civic groups and acting as spokesman with the press. The studious Bierly, taking the post of vice president, was most responsible for supervising research. The firm gathered information by combing through periodicals and pamphlets, both mainstream and Communist, and relied on researchers in the field, some of them, to the Bureau's continuing chagrin, undercover informants with ties to the FBI. At times the company's outside sources were capable of passing along reports on closed Communist party meetings.[28]

During this formative stage, while preparing to launch their crusade against domestic communism, Keenan, Kirkpatrick, and Bierly were forced unexpectedly to confront another ideological peril residing at a different point on the political spectrum. The incident arose while they were still pursuing funding for their company. A real estate agent, who happened to be a staunch anti-Communist, told Kirkpatrick that he could introduce the American Business Consultants partners to a potential investor at a ceremonial dinner at the Seventh Regimental Armory on Park Avenue in Manhattan. "After I talked to him for about five minutes," Kirkpatrick later said, "I knew there was something wrong with him, but I did not know what." Setting aside whatever doubts they might have had, the three partners showed up at the event on the off-chance that something positive might come of it. As they sat down for dinner, Kirkpatrick later explained to Merle Miller, they were told that thousands of dollars would be theirs—provided they agreed to one stipulation. Their newsletter, they were told, would have to inform readers that communism was more than a Soviet scheme for world supremacy; it was, at its core, a worldwide Zionist conspiracy. The three partners finished their dinners quickly, "got out as soon as possible," and had nothing more to do with this rabid crowd.[29] But the underlying issue would remain. This would not be the last time that their anti-Communist cause would bring them into contact with the dark, anti-Semitic recesses of right-wing extremism.

The three partners were not immune, certainly, to the provincial, ethnocentric attitudes of the day. In one of their early promotional flyers, for instance, they promoted the idea that Kirkpatrick possessed the virtues of an "average American." To underscore the point, the caption under his picture identified him as of "Scotch-Irish descent, Protestant, married, two children" (only the accompanying photo made it unnecessary, apparently, to mention that he was also white). At the same time, though, in his public addresses Kirkpatrick would tell his audiences to make sure they "do not support anti-Communists who are at the same time pro-fascist," that the country faced the danger of right-wing extremism "if we allow ourselves to listen to those people who keep telling us that all Jews are Communists and all negros [sic] are communists, and other such lies."[30]

Their four-page weekly first appeared on May 16, 1947, with its full title—*Counterattack: The Newsletter of Facts on Communism*—printed over a red hammer and sickle. The text was grouped into short paragraphs headlined by capitalized or underscored sentences, a punchy, telegraphic style that clearly conveyed the publishers' pugnacious attitude. In an introductory section, Horn encapsulated the newsletter's credo. The Soviet Union, he wrote, was attempting to burrow inside the United States. "To prevent war," he concluded, "we must crush the Communist Fifth Column."[31]

The first issue included one mention of an entertainer—an item accusing singer-activist Paul Robeson of being a Communist and stirring up anti-American sentiment—and the second installment linked prominent radio writer Norman Corwin with fellow-traveling activities. But contrary to its later reputation, *Counterattack*'s earliest issues treated subversion in show business as just one part—and a small part at that—of a much larger problem. The concerns of Keenan, Kirkpatrick, and Bierly far exceeded any one single industry, spanning instead the entire gamut of business and labor, from manufacturers and financiers to factory workers and department store clerks. It was here, among company executives and union officials, that *Counterattack*'s publishers initially sought most of their subscribers. Their concern extended even to the realm of organized religion, as the newsletter often warned its readers about such Protestant clergymen as William Howard Melish and Guy Emery Shipler, whose fellow-traveling speechifying was all the more insidious, *Counterattack* maintained, because it was camouflaged in the vestments of piety. For several months the newsletter bombarded the opposing lines of domestic subversion with a wide range of fire before it began to adjust its sights to more specific targets.

Even though Keenan, Kirkpatrick, and Bierly had never shown any particular interest in entertainment, they were bound eventually to see the necessity of monitoring radio and television. Their days in the Communist Squad had trained them to regard communications as an industry to be protected from enemy influence. No other medium communicated to more people than broadcasting, an electronic pipeline, for good or ill, to millions of American homes. In a time of crisis it could transmit valuable information. As for its potential to sow panic, there could be no doubt: Orson Welles's 1938 broadcast of "War of the Worlds" had already made that quite clear. A great many people, both supporters and critics of *Counterattack*, would agree on the importance of the airwaves, particularly at such a critical point in history, at a time when the medium was poised on the brink of a new era.

TWO

Something in the Air

MANY IN the broadcast industry might have been loath to admit it, but they had something very much in common with the three *Counterattack* partners. For them, too, the Second World War had served as a crucible that forged their political zeal.

While Keenan, Kirkpatrick, and Bierly were molded by their FBI training, many writers, actors, and directors in radio had been shaped by their response to the Great Depression. While the *Counterattack* publishers were inspired by the principle of anti-communism, these broadcast artists were alarmed by the rise of fascism and invigorated by the alternative offered by the New Deal. While one group spent the war investigating enemies within, the other advanced its ideas through activist organizations and dramatized those ideas over the air through a special breed of programs. For these creators, and for later historians, this period of broadcasting was best described as radio's Golden Age. Others saw germinating in these programs the seeds of anti-Americanism.

Today the most celebrated shows from the early 1940s tend to be the commercial entertainment series, from the comedic antics of Jack Benny and Fred Allen to the pulp adventures of the Green Hornet and the Shadow. But at the time the most renowned shows belonged to a more sober, early-broadcast species, considered by many to be the most genuine, most glistening nuggets of this so-called Golden Age: sustaining programming. Without it, an impassioned contingent of broadcast talent would not have had a true voice.

Commercial networks in those days set aside a significant portion of their schedules to so-called sustaining programs, shows that aired without the benefit of a sponsor. Much of this category consisted of news and information, fashioned by a remarkable generation of on-air journalists who established their reputation during the war, among them Charles Collingwood, Howard K. Smith, William L. Shirer, Eric Sevareid, and, most prominent of all, Edward R. Murrow, the great doyen of broadcast news. Another form of sustaining fare was the handiwork of a select group of playwrights and directors who orchestrated a unique brand of radio that incorporated, in various combinations, drama, poetry, music, and pseudo-documentary. More than any others, these broadcast creators were most clearly identified with progressive politics.

The substance of the sustaining shows took various forms, from educational (*American School of the Air*) and spiritual (*The Eternal Light*) to experimental anthology (*The Columbia Workshop*). Somewhat similar were those shows that, despite commercial sponsorship, devoted themselves to a high-minded purpose, such as *Cavalcade of America*, underwritten by DuPont to dramatize episodes from American history. Taken together, all these programs, aired over different networks, served the same purpose assumed years later by public broadcasting.[1]

The shows cultivated an impressive collection of talent, including such broadcast pioneers as William Robson, Robert Lewis Shayon, and Arch Oboler, as well as a young playwright named Arthur Miller. But one stood out as its true standard-bearer, both for his critical acclaim, which set him apart, and for his belief in using radio to promote social and political ideals, which cast him as a representative of the whole.

Admirers have designated producer-writer-director Norman Corwin as radio's poet laureate. Some of his shows he literally wrote in verse, but even his prose work was often imbued with a lyrical quality, a style applied to a wide range of formats. Beginning with his earliest programs for *The Columbia Workshop* in the late 1930s, Corwin had produced literary adaptations, whimsical fantasies, psychological dramas, anti-war tracts, satires, operatic Bible stories, social dramas, and folk-ballad cantatas. For all the accolades these shows received, Corwin reached the height of his fame and reputation when, like similar-minded writers and directors, he devoted himself to the war effort.

The New Deal's promise of social and economic justice had galvanized Corwin and his associates, and now, seeing those principles pitted against the most barbarous form of tyranny, they were more inspired than ever to defend their beliefs on the air in such programs as *Words at War* and "An Open Letter on Race Hatred." Anti-fascism was their great passion. They believed the nation could show no quarter to the enemy, either abroad or at home. Speaking before a 1942 conference on educational radio, Corwin described domestic pro-fascists as "the equivalent of six battleships or a couple of Panzer divisions." Using a phrase that foreshadowed future controversies, he demanded to know why, at the conference, there had not been "names named."[2]

Corwin delivered this speech at a time when many considered right-wing extremists to be not only terribly wrongheaded but traitorous, a sentiment motivating the federal government early in 1943 to indict thirty-three native fascists on a charge of sedition. Although the most spectacular of these cases, this trial was hardly unique, and sedition was not the only charge. In 1942 two men were prosecuted for criminal libel for printing allegations that General Douglas MacArthur had deserted his troops in the Philippines. Using its power to regulate the mail, the federal government also shut down several publications that it charged were following the Axis line.

One of the leaders in the fight was the organization Friends of Democracy's Battle, headed by L. M. Birkhead, a liberal Unitarian minister from Kansas City. The group agitated against fascist propaganda and applauded the various sedition cases and censorship efforts as "democratic gains." In fact the group was not content with targeting only outright fascists but also attacked seemingly mainstream, isolationist newspapers like the *Chicago Tribune* and the *New York Daily News* that it claimed "fronted" for the fascist movement and acted as fellow travelers. John Roy Carlson, author of a popular book-length exposé of the Nazi underworld entitled *Under Cover*, expressed similar sentiments, warning against "dissentionist propaganda while our country is at war" and explaining that "many otherwise fine Americans were propagating the lies and the 'party-line' originally advanced by Hitler's agents and doing it sincerely in what they believed to be good Americanism."[3]

While excoriating fascism, the radio war effort could also heap praise on America's ally, the Soviet Union. Corwin indulged in this wartime deviation from usual American attitudes in his short-lived series entitled *Passport for Adams*. The show followed a fictitious Middle American newspaper editor, Douglas Adams, and his impetuous photographer, Perry "Quiz" Quisinberry, as they traveled the world and reported on America's allies. In September 1943 the series focused on Moscow. Not content to admire the bravery of the Russian people in the face of a ruthless enemy, the program went on to laud the entire Stalinized nation, describing it as a "young and powerful and amazing country." In one especially curious section, a Russian official patiently explains to the Nazi-hating Quiz why the Soviets treat German POWs in such a remarkably civilized manner. "We treat them humanely because we believe in human dignity, Mr. Quisinberry, and in international law," says this representative from the nation that invented the Gulag.[4]

The next year Corwin directed another show along these lines, "Concerning the Red Army," written by the poet Norman Rosten. Here again the program went beyond acknowledging the perseverance of a temporary military ally—which the wartime situation required—to applauding the entire Soviet system. Stalin's Russia, Rosten tells us, is "building a new life," a land of opportunity where children face an inspiring future. In the final moments the narrator intones, "Honor to the Red Army and its commander in chief, Marshal Stalin!"[5]

In dealing with the American side of the war, Corwin was at his most overtly propagandistic when directing and sometimes writing a series for the federal government entitled *This Is War*, which pulled out all stops in its effort to whip up anti-fascist sentiment on the home front. Corwin would later claim that the show helped persuade the government to shut down *Social Justice*, the pro-fascist magazine published by Father Charles Coughlin.[6] More artistically ambitious were a series of specials that mixed atmospheric music and sound effects with dramatic vignettes and lofty rhetoric: "We Hold These Truths" (a celebration of the Bill of Rights), "New York: A Tapestry for Radio" (an evocation of the melting-pot experience), and "On a Note of Triumph" and "Fourteen August" (commemorations of, respectively, the German and Japanese surrenders). In these Corwin stressed the critical importance of not only crushing fascism but building a new, more just world.

While the airwaves provided an effective means of voicing these ideas, many in the broadcast industry were not content to restrict themselves to this one avenue of expression. They also joined activist organizations—groups such as the Artists' Front to Win the War and the Joint Anti-Fascist Refugee Committee—and lent their talent to staging sketches and musical performances for political events. One organization, the Independent Citizens Committee of the Arts, Sciences and Professions, acknowledged the importance of its members from the broadcast field by forming a separate radio division, co-chaired by Corwin and including many respected members of the industry.[7] As the war ended, progressives in broadcasting saw great opportunities for the country to foster a new era of civil rights, improve working conditions, and provide services for the underprivileged. They also saw a grave danger as the country faced the prospect of yet another war, this time with a former ally. The airwaves, they believed, provided a chance to nurture forward-looking ideas during a pivotal period. Frustrating their aspirations were new attitudes evolving both within their industry and outside their profession.

The contours of broadcasting were starting to shift. For twenty years the airwaves had been the sole province of radio, but now, in the late 1940s, network executives paved the way for a new, potentially more potent outlet. During World War II, broadcasters had suspended their development of television as they concentrated instead on putting radio to use in the country's service in a national emergency. Now, with the war over, their efforts moved forward again. As the media historian Michele Hilmes has pointed out, "radio network profits were taken from that side of the business and applied directly to television's growth," making it clear that the best days of radio were over.[8]

Imminent as its decline might be, radio was still, for the time being, a vibrant medium, both creatively and commercially. From their headquarters in New York City, networks still commanded a fleet of stations across the country and offered listeners a variety of programming highlighted by both long-running hit series and ambitious new drama anthologies such as *Studio One* and the *Theatre Guild on the Air*. For writers, directors, and actors, radio might have continued to be a robust source of employment, but the content of programming was changing—constricting, some might say—while the medium labored under new pressures.

As profits were diverted and the TV market expanded, radio program-
mers resorted more often to gimmickry and commercialism to hold on to
their audiences and maintain profits. A conspicuous casualty of this
process was Fred Allen, radio's great wit, whose comedy series went off the
air after seventeen years when it proved unable to compete with a give-
away quiz show being aired on another network.[9] Also beginning to fade
was the genre of dramatic sustaining programs.

What did not diminish was the political fervor of those most closely
identified with the genre. Although their opportunities to craft socially relevant drama might be declining, they continued, off the air, to advocate
liberal causes. While the names of the organizations changed, the principles that motivated the broadcast activists remained the same. The Independent Citizens Committee of the Arts, Sciences and Professions, for
instance, merged with another group in 1946 to form a larger entity known
as the Progressive Citizens of America, and this in turn played a role two
years later in forming the Progressive party, a third-party movement that
coalesced around the presidential candidacy of former vice president
Henry Wallace, a campaign that stressed a planned economy, full employment, and peaceful coexistence. Through all these organizational
transformations, radio professionals like Norman Corwin and William
Robson continued their enthusiastic support for the New Deal and their
unwavering opposition to fascism, issues that had inspired them so during
the war. Their fervent anti-totalitarianism of World War II, though, did not
necessarily translate into fervent opposition to the totalitarian Soviet
Union once the war ended. This posture did not escape *Counterattack's*
attention.

Corwin encapsulated his view of cold war politics in 1946 when he
recorded his experiences touring the world for a series called *One World
Flight*, a trip that included a visit to Moscow. Following up on sentiments
expressed in *Passport for Adams*, he left the Soviet Union, "thinking it neither the best nor the worst country in the world," and stressed that America should abandon the idea of rigid opposition and instead embrace
some form of compromise with Stalin's regime. Although he took issue
with blindly loyal Soviet supporters, he had asserted years before that
"hatred of Russia was the triumph of a long and calculated propaganda of
suspicion."[10]

This opinion may have been popular, but a willingness to give the Soviets the benefit of the doubt was not universally characteristic of radio writers. One writer in particular steeped himself in controversy by giving voice over the air to an opposing perspective. By doing so, he helped bring into the open a conflict that had been agitating for years beneath the surface.

A liberal anti-Communist, Morton Wishengrad was best known for his work on *The Eternal Light* and for a brilliant, heartrending radio special called "The Battle of the Warsaw Ghetto." His opposition to communism had begun some ten years earlier when he served as educational director of the International Ladies Garment Workers Union and became familiar with the tactics used by Communists to dominate labor groups.[11] The experience now served as part of the inspiration for his program on the American Communist party that aired in August 1948.

Using a pseudo-documentary style, "Communism—U.S. Brand" tells the story of a young party recruit who helps commandeer a chemical factory union, then moves on to organize seemingly well-intentioned political action groups that bamboozle liberals into supporting the Soviet line. For the most part the program avoided melodrama and instead presented its case in a subdued, thoughtful manner, an approach that *New York Times* radio critic Jack Gould described as "brilliantly successful and provocative." Others were less impressed. More than that, they were outraged. Writing in the *New Republic*, Saul Carson took the program to task for overstating its case and complained that the Communists were not allowed to tell their side of the story. Wishengrad later pointed out that this begged the question: if he had written an anti-Nazi show, should the Nazis have been allowed a rebuttal? But this argument was not likely to sway Carson, who concluded in his review that he couldn't "see how Wishengrad can ever hold up his head again." A more personal attack came in a letter to the program's author from Anton Leader, a friend and co-worker who had directed many of the writer's earlier scripts. His letter suggested that Wishengrad was joining "the ranks of active cranks, neo-fascists, sensation-seekers and red-baiters."[12]

For those in the broadcast industry who advocated peace with the Soviet Union, either because they sympathized with the Soviets or simply dreaded another war, the international tensions of the late 1940s were profoundly disturbing. On the domestic front these individuals also believed that the New Deal was under attack, especially so when Congress curtailed the power of trade unions in 1947 by passing the Taft-Hartley Act. They saw themselves facing a double bind: not only did they find fewer chances to express themselves in noncommercial programming, but in the larger political arena their ideas now seemed to be passing out of favor as the cold war gathered momentum.

They were bitterly resentful when they saw people they considered New Deal liberals being slandered as Reds. Particularly alarming was the House Un-American Activities Committee (HUAC) investigation of the Hollywood Ten, the group of writers, directors, and producers who refused to cooperate with the committee in what would be the beginning of the anti-Red probe into the motion picture industry. All those accused by HUAC, Corwin wrote, "are mainly decent Americans who have contributed much that is worthwhile to the culture, edification or just plain entertainment of their fellow Americans." Some in broadcasting joined organizations like the Committee for the First Amendment to fight this trend and found a way to use the airwaves to address the issue in the fall of 1947 in two all-star specials, co-directed by Corwin and Robson, which attacked HUAC as an instrument of repression. The second program urged that the committee "be abolished, not merely reshuffled but voted out of existence."[13]

For many in broadcasting the situation presented a dire crisis. They watched with mounting trepidation as HUAC cited the Hollywood Ten for contempt of Congress, and as the movie studios issued a statement on November 25, 1947, that they would no longer employ Communists or other subversives. Many broadcast progressives could clearly see that the seeds of a blacklist had already been planted in Hollywood. Unless they took a firm stand, they concluded, the same thing would happen in their own industry.

The most alarmed among them regarded the words printed in *Counterattack* as the handwriting on the wall.

📻 *Counterattack*'s offensive against broadcasting, inconsistent at first, began to take shape in the latter half of 1947 when the publishers singled out one section of the industry. Keenan, Kirkpatrick, and Bierly considered the airwaves to be, first and foremost, a vehicle of public information and believed the control of information at a time of crisis to be essential.[14] The first people to watch, then, were the news commentators.

With the exception of occasional criticisms of noted reporter Howard K. Smith, most of the journalists that Counterattack targeted have since faded from public memory. Even at the time, during the late 1940s, they were not ranked at the top of their profession and were often found only on local stations; but the Counterattack publishers believed that any influence or stature they might have enjoyed was far too much. They pulled no punches in denouncing such on-air personalities as William S. Gailmor (a "Communist commentator"), J. Raymond Walsh ("the cleverest of all party-line commentators"), and Johannes Steel (a "Fifth Column propagandist").[15] Just as alarming to them was an organization called the Voice of Freedom Committee, which promoted the careers of these commentators.

At a time when the Soviets were consolidating their satellite regimes in eastern Europe, American Business Consultants believed that radio and the coming medium of television were in danger of becoming a source for anti-American propaganda that could sabotage the country's efforts to confront its new enemy. If the government and the broadcast industry could work so closely together during World War II and agree that news commentary and documentaries were critical weapons in the war of ideas, Counterattack insisted, similar thinking should apply to the new war, even if it was not yet an overt military conflict.

While most people could at least agree that information programs influenced public opinion, the argument for monitoring entertainment shows was not as obvious. The Counterattack partners themselves paid little attention to this type of programming during their first year in print, but by 1948 they began to reconsider. They alerted their readers to such shows as the Theatre Guild on the Air and Philco Radio Time, and accused the likes of Burl Ives, Abe Burrows, and John Houseman of being either Communists or associates of Communists. Some might ask: How could a writer in a drama anthology series or an actor in a weekly comedy or a musician in a variety show possibly have an effect on the march of world events? Keenan, Kirkpatrick, and Bierly had an answer. It could best be described as the third-violinist theory.

An interviewer once took issue with the extent of Counterattack's vigilance by asking the partners what possible security threat could be posed by a Communist sympathizer who, say, played third violin in a radio orchestra. Bierly, normally the most cautious of the three, argued that the presence of this musician could not be isolated from the larger, more ominous picture. "He is sitting next to the first violinist," he explained, "and he is going into the radio station and he is talking to the engineer and he has friends who are news commentators, and so forth and so on." Summing up for his partner, Kirkpatrick then insisted that anyone with access to a radio station was "a potential security problem."[16]

By formulating this idea, Keenan, Kirkpatrick, and Bierly took a fateful step. Their widely inclusive definition of the Communist threat transformed their operations from pure information gathering to an incendiary form of activism with the potential to unleash forces that would be difficult to control. If anyone in any position in broadcasting could be portrayed as a menace to the republic, few measures could be ruled out in policing the industry.

The partners began encouraging action on this theory of Red infiltration as early as September 1947, within four months of *Counterattack*'s premiere, when the newsletter announced: "Communist actors, announcers, directors, writers, producers, etc., whether in radio, theater, or movies, should all be barred, to the extent permissible by law and union contracts." To what extent this action *would* be permissible, the article does not make clear. The newsletter conceded that carrying out this purge would be difficult but added that "we may as well recognize that anything we gain by personal or business appeasement will eventually plague us, as international appeasement has already done." Within another four months, the newsletter urged its readers to get involved, instructing them to "tell radio sponsors what you think about hiring Communist entertainers."[17]

For ideas and initiatives like these, *Counterattack* would be condemned for being reckless and reactionary. To their own mind, the publishers considered themselves relatively cautious. They denounced, for instance, John Rankin, the openly racist member of HUAC, and though they themselves lambasted the committee's nemeses, the Hollywood Ten, they took issue with HUAC's excesses, supporting its continuation only "until it can be replaced with something better." Closer to home they fended off proposed alliances with such right-wing fanatics as Merwin K. Hart and Myron Fagan, and in the case of Fagan publicly repudiated him.[18] In taking these actions the publishers may have skirted the worst pitfalls of extremism, but antagonism and controversy still pressed upon them. This they guaranteed by their own words and actions.

The first lawsuit against *Counterattack* was filed on March 15, 1948, less than a year after it began publication. The plaintiffs were movie, theater, and radio star Fredric March and his wife Florence Eldridge, a distinguished actress in her own right, best known for her work on the stage. *Counterattack* first published an item about March on October 17, 1947, describing him at that time as a supporter of Communist-front causes, then quickly proceeded to raise the ante. Two weeks later the newsletter called both Marches party-liners, and after the new year went on to complain, "These Communists have acted on U.S. Steel's Sunday night program time and again."[19] It took two more references to the couple as Communists before the actors filed suit for libel and demanded $500,000 as compensation.

Before long *Counterattack* was associated with yet another legal action. In January 1949 a musical performance team of dancer Paul Draper and harmonica player Larry Adler sued a Greenwich, Connecticut, housewife for labeling them pro-Communist when they had been scheduled to appear in a concert in her hometown. The woman, Hester McCullough, had based her allegations on information she had gleaned from recent newspaper articles, one of which had appeared in *Counterattack*. The newsletter had been investigating Draper as early as the previous March and had been one of the whistle-blowers in December 1948 when it charged that both Draper and Adler had been involved with various politically suspect activities. More important, the *Counterattack* partners now consulted with McCullough's attorneys and passed along the information they had collected.[20]

As the legal furor began to encircle the *Counterattack* crusade, one controversy in particular began to dominate the debate: the Communist front. In issue after issue the newsletter cited organizations with names like American Youth for Democracy, the Congress of American Women, and the National Committee to Win the Peace. So much of what the newsletter said—whether it alleged someone was a Communist, fellow traveler, or dupe—was based on how deeply involved the person was with these so-called Communist front groups. For the *Counterattack* publishers, these organizations, taken as a whole, represented something deeply troubling. For their opponents, the very idea of citing these fronts as evidence of Communist sympathy was symptomatic of destructive paranoia. The arguments on both sides tended to generate more heat than light while the political divide over the issue would polarize people for more than a decade.

In more practical terms, the public's verdict on the significance of these groups could place people's livelihoods in peril.

֍ In their 2001 book *Red Scared!*, Michael Barson and Steven Heller debunk the culture of anti-communism by assembling a catalog of campy artifacts from the late 1940s and 1950s—pulp-novel covers, lurid magazine articles, sensationalistic movie posters, even educational anti-Red bubble-gum cards. Among the many single-page items is a list entitled "HUAC's So-Called Communist Front Organizations to Which Dashiell Hammett Was Linked." Why the authors singled out mystery author Hammett is something of a mystery in itself, but the implication of the list is clear: How could anyone other than a rabid reactionary possibly take exception to organizations with such names as the American Continental Congress for World Peace, the American Writers Congress, the Joint Anti-Fascist Refugee Committee, or the Stockholm Peace Appeal? This attitude has hardly been uncommon in recent accounts that deal with the concept of the Communist front, so much the cornerstone of anti-Red accusations at the height of the cold war. Some writers, in fact, feel obliged to mention the words "Communist front" only in quotes.

In perusing the various names of these groups, an observer would be tempted to see nothing but well-meaning intent, especially when trying to divine the subversive threat posed by such organizations as the Consumers Union or the League of Women Shoppers. Yet a look at the history of American Communist party strategy during the 1930s and 1940s reveals that the story behind these apparently benign groups is more complex.

It began twelve years before the founding of *Counterattack*, in August 1935, at the Seventh World Congress of the Communist International (Comintern), the Soviet-directed organization that supervised Communist parties outside Russia. Until then the American Communist party, like its counterparts in other countries, was a purely revolutionary organization with no interest in becoming part of the bourgeois political system which, party members insisted, was only subtly different from pure fascism. Pronouncements at the Seventh World Congress changed all that. The messenger for the new policy was Georgi Dimitrov, a Bulgarian Communist, now Comintern's general secretary, who had first gained fame two years earlier as an acquitted defendant at the Reichstag Fire trial. In his speech at the Comintern congress in Moscow, he now told party leaders from around the world that they should no longer hold themselves apart from the mainstream. Instead they should form alliances with socialists and reformers in unions, political parties, and activist organizations. In the United States in particular, Communists should direct these new partnerships, these fronts, toward issues such as unemployment insurance and civil rights, causes that could attract a wide liberal following.

The new Popular Front strategy conveyed the impression that Communists were less extreme, more willing to compromise, but Dimitrov stressed another, clearly calculating dimension to the new thinking. He related the story of the Trojan Horse and described how the ancient Greeks had employed this ruse to infiltrate their enemy's defenses. He instructed his listeners that they "should not be shy about using the same tactics."[21] American Communist leaders who attended the congress relayed the new directive to the party when they returned home.

In one sense the Popular Front was a continuation of previous policies: the CPUSA had always made use of the front technique as a way to expand its influence. As the historian Theodore Draper has pointed out, "it is best to think of Communism as a movement rather than merely a party, a movement of which the party constitutes only a part."[22] What made the new policy different was a matter of degree—a striking difference as it turned out. Never before had fronts played such a central role and so radically altered the way the CPUSA presented itself.

Before the Popular Front the party had branded Franklin Delano Roosevelt as a fascist (specifically a social fascist, the CPUSA term for a reactionary who pretended to be liberal). Now Communists portrayed the president as a progressive, and they transformed the party into an enthusiastic booster for his New Deal policies. Party literature and speeches might still mention Lenin and Stalin, but now they were more likely to invoke the legacy of revered American icons and would go on to name party-run schools after Thomas Jefferson, Samuel Adams, Tom Paine, and Abraham Lincoln. The new party motto summarized the makeover in just a few words: "Communism is Twentieth Century Americanism."[23]

Alliances with liberals could cultivate new political partners, either fellow travelers or credulous idealists, both of whom could help propagate the new party line, and some of these partners could, in turn, be converted into CPUSA members. Anti-fascist and pro–civil rights front groups attracted such luminaries as Eleanor Roosevelt and Albert Einstein, and from the field of entertainment and the arts they recruited the likes of Fredric March, Jo Davidson, Judy Garland, and Thomas Mann. Communist party officials valued the prestige and publicity these names lent to their front efforts, but that did not necessarily mean they respected the political acumen of their new allies, even the most accomplished of them. At the offices of the party newspaper, the *Daily Worker*, there would be staff meetings, a Communist official later recalled, "that rocked with laughter at the expense of famous intellectuals who pretended to think for themselves yet goose-stepped on the line we drew."[24]

Far greater respect extended to those within the front coalitions who clearly guarded CPUSA interests. Perhaps no one during these years was a more charismatic, more solicited attraction at front events than Paul Robeson. Today he is often remembered as a man of great accomplishment and political conviction. He certainly was accomplished—an All-American football player, a lawyer and a linguist, a brilliant singer and a powerful actor—and his commitment to political causes was beyond question, especially the cause of African-American rights. At the same time, though, he was a tireless propagandist for Stalin and the Soviet Union, ready to defend every Communist transgression. He regarded Stalin's Gulag state as a "land of love and happiness," a leader in the "struggle for peace and democracy," and he once commented that anyone who lifted his hand against the Soviet state "ought to be shot."[25] He might never have actually joined the Communist party, but his words and actions could not have been any more consistent with Soviet policy, and his enormous talent and presence were a boon to every front he embraced.

As energetic as the front groups could be in their support of generically progressive causes, they occasionally revealed more sectarian motives. When the interests of the Soviet Union came into question, Communists in these organizations would not stray far from the party line and would rise to the challenge of rationalizing Stalin's most egregious policies. Many Popular Front liberals found this reflex especially disconcerting.

Non-Communist front members were spared at least one vexing issue. By the time the Popular Front began, Stalin's collectivization program was already old news. Liberal progressives did not have to grapple with front officials who denied or apologized for that program's vindictive manmade famine that killed six million people. The Moscow purge trials would be another matter.

Stalin began his prosecution of the old-guard Bolsheviks in 1937, just as the American Popular Front was gaining momentum. A year later a group of 136 people, labeling themselves "American progressives," published a statement declaring their support for the Moscow trials, arguing that the defendants were dangerous conspirators plotting against the noble Soviet experiment. The signers—including bacteriologist Paul de Kruif, actor John Garfield, playwright Lillian Hellman, author Dorothy Parker, and photographer Paul Strand—urged American liberals to stay the course toward progressive democracy despite reactionary slanders of Stalin's actions.[26] Although information coming out of the Soviet Union was sparse, liberals like philosopher John Dewey insisted that the trials were an ominous sign of Stalinist repression. History would confirm their suspicions. Eventually Stalin's purge would hunt well beyond party officials, reaching down to all levels of Soviet society, and would kill nearly 700,000.

The defense of totalitarianism might have tried the patience of many Popular Front liberals, but far more disturbing were sudden policy shifts that could only be attributed to Soviet dictates. Film and TV writer Don Mankiewicz was one of many to find this experience deeply jarring.

At the age of seventeen, Mankiewicz joined the prominent entertainment-industry front known as the Hollywood Anti-Nazi League. Unlike most people in the organization who were involved in highly public activities, Mankiewicz was given a special secret assignment: he was to infiltrate the Los Angeles branch of the Silver Shirts, an American fascist group founded by the former novelist and screenwriter William Dudley Pelley. Mankiewicz attended several meetings and reported on the group's anti-Semitic plans, but soon he began to fear that the Silver Shirts would tumble to the fact that he was a spy.

He went to see the woman who was supervising him at the Hollywood Anti-Nazi League and told her he intended to quit. She informed him that his resignation was a moot point because the organization would not be investigating groups like the Silver Shirts anymore. When Mankiewicz asked why, she said, "Well, you haven't seen today's paper, have you?'"

The date was August 22, 1939. The country's newspapers had just announced that the Soviet Union and Nazi Germany had signed a nonaggression pact. "The Hollywood Anti-Nazi League, she explained to me, could no longer be anti-Nazi," Mankiewicz recalled, "because, after all, they were only National Socialists, and they were our allies. Her phrase, 'our allies,' meaning they were allies of the Russians."[27] Soon the Hollywood Anti-Nazi League would change its name to remove any anti-fascist reference, becoming the Hollywood League for Democratic Action. By then Mankiewicz had already resigned, as did other liberals confronted with the same issue in other fronts.

Some front joiners managed to toe the party line no matter how tortuous its route. Few fit this description better than Dashiell Hammett, whose front record would be so cavalierly dismissed by the authors of *Red Scared!* A week before the nonaggression pact, Hammett signed a statement that ridiculed the very idea that the Soviets and Nazis would ever come to terms and attacked the "fantastic falsehood that the U.S.S.R. and the totalitarian states are basically alike." As soon as the pact was signed, he then spun around and defended Stalin's new alliance. As late as June 6, 1941, he participated in a conference of the League of American Writers—later a frequent target of *Counterattack*—that denounced Roosevelt for trying to involve America in Britain's fight against Germany, an effort the group characterized as "an imperialist war for world markets." The next seismic change came just sixteen days later when the Nazis invaded Russia. Within a month Hammett, now serving as League of American Writers president, called on his fellow writers to rally round both Great Britain and the Soviet Union "to insure the military defeat of the fascist aggressors." If some regarded this sequence of about-faces as evidence of hidden motives, they had good reason for thinking so. Hammett, as biographer Joan Mellen has made clear, was a devout Communist, though he would never publicly admit it.[28]

Another front singled out by *Counterattack* was the Theatre Arts Committee, which clashed with the larger Broadway community over another nonaggression pact controversy. As part of his deal with Hitler, Stalin had reserved the right to annex Finland and went on to wage a brutal war to accomplish that goal. Some Broadway producers contributed proceeds from special benefit performances to the Finnish Relief Fund to aid women and children victimized by the Soviet invasion. The Theatre Arts Committee backed another group of producers who refused to donate to the fund. The Committee maintained that any theatrical benefits should help first the American unemployed, particularly out-of-work actors. For many, this argument was nothing more than a "smoke screen," an attempt to camouflage pure party-line politics. Subsequent actions by the Theatre Arts Committee seemed to confirm this assessment: in May the group picketed a performance of Robert E. Sherwood's *There Shall Be No Night*, a pro-Finnish play, and charged that the producers were "warmongers." Only the most gullible or the most unperceptive could fail to see that this was a distinct echo of the CPUSA position at the time.[29]

The dispute over the war in northern Europe intensified, clearly representing far more to each side than the single issue of Finnish independence. In a foreshadowing of things to come, two producers, deeply offended by what they considered Stalinist machinations, announced that they would employ no Theatre Arts Committee members. "No Communists, No Nazi sympathizers, No TAC members need apply at this office for appointments or interviews," a placard in one producer's office read. "It is our policy to consider for employment only good Americans."[30]

The *Counterattack* partners did not join the FBI's Communist Squad until after these controversies had subsided, but they did witness the rebirth of the Popular Front and with it another set of issues when America and Russia joined forces against the Nazis. In the case of the Independent Citizens Committee of the Arts, Sciences and Professions, founded in 1944, party influence was confined to the background as the group devoted itself to objectives that only an ideological curmudgeon could quibble with—a decisive military victory leading to a lasting peace, full employment at respectable wages, the international exchange of ideas— and recruited a wide range of non-Communists, including many eminent intellectuals and celebrities, from Yehudi Menuhin, Norman Corwin, and Bette Davis to Van Wyck Brooks and Linus Pauling. Party officials saw organizations of this kind as a great opportunity to extend their reach. What they did not foresee were the tactic's unintended consequences.

As front man for *Counterattack* and *Red Channels*, former FBI agent Theodore Kirkpatrick became the most visible agitator for the broadcast purge in its earliest years. *(Roy Stevens)*

Blurring the line between Communists and liberals might have served the party's purposes at the time, but it would soon boomerang on them and on the Popular Front allies they were cultivating. As long as Communists contrived plans to include well-meaning progressives in their activities, they created the impression that their influence was greater than it actually was, and fostered the illusion that New Dealers were part of their efforts. Some observers were able to discern the trouble that was brewing. The philosopher Sidney Hook warned that "if liberals did not themselves differentiate clearly between themselves and the Communists and fellow-travelers in their organizations (who were betraying the ideals of liberalism) a reaction would set in, which would harm others besides genuine Communists."[31] The obligation to differentiate also rested with the Red hunters. The ability of people like Keenan, Kirkpatrick, and

Bierly to carry out that obligation would determine how much havoc would ensue once the accusations began to fly.

⌐ By the time American Business Consultants had put out their first issue of *Counterattack*, the party line had changed yet again. In May 1945 a letter from the French Communist Jacques Duclos had appeared in the United States to signal the latest instructions: American Communists, recently so devoted to reform and Twentieth Century Americanism, were now to become revolutionists once again—the fourth about-face for party policy in ten years. Abrupt as this switch was, it did not repeal the front concept as a useful tactic. Communists were to continue to "agitate the masses," CPUSA official Eugene Dennis explained, by promoting mass front organizations that confronted popular issues. Among the groups Dennis held up as examples of this renewed effort were the Independent Citizens Committee of the Arts, Sciences and Professions, the National Negro Congress, and various unions within the CIO.[32]

Very much aware of this development, the *Counterattack* partners prepared to answer the libel suit of Fredric March and Florence Eldridge by assembling a comprehensive list of fronts linked to the two actors. Among them were several groups included in the attorney general's list of "totalitarian, fascist, Communist, or subversive" organizations; but the federal government, the sponsor of the list, had itself pointed out that membership in any of these groups did not mean that the individual was conspiring against the United States. To substantiate their allegations, Keenan, Kirkpatrick, and Bierly cited 1940 grand jury testimony given by former CPUSA official John L. Leech, who had identified March as a Communist party member. Soon they realized they could not rely on this. As an internal *Counterattack* memo put it, Leech's "credibility is extremely doubtful."[33] In the end their case rested solely on the front records of the two actors, and that would not be enough to prove anything other than political activism or, at worst, political naiveté. Not only did American Business Consultants have to settle with the Marches out of court, their agreement stipulated that they print a retraction.

On the first page of their December 23, 1949, issue, the publishers stated that the Marches had joined alleged front groups out of "patriotic & humanitarian" motives and even pointed out that the performers had aided Finland against Russia in 1939, contrary to the Soviet line at the time. After including a statement from the Marches that denounced all forms of totalitarianism and upheld the virtues of the American system, the publishers added, "No Communist would make such a clear & unequivocal public statement."

The retraction did not sit well with Sam Horn. As editor and writer, he had chosen the words that had originally denounced the Marches, and now those words had been repudiated. By the end of the year he quit as editor, though he would continue to help the newsletter on occasion. Also infuriated by the outcome was Keenan, who believed that March was not telling the truth about his political background and that the newsletter had been unfairly obliged to back off from an accurate characterization. But this complaint he kept private. Publicly he insisted that the settlement of the suit was "a real achievement and victory" for his firm. He instructed Horn's replacement, Francis McNamara, to explain to any allies with doubts that *Counterattack* was proud of the outcome because it had compelled the Marches to distance themselves "from all Communist front activities."[34]

Counterattack's efforts in the Adler-Draper case did not fare much better. Once more the evidence the publishers supplied amounted to a list of fronts—from the Joint Anti-Fascist Refugee Committee and the Civil Rights Congress to the Theatre Arts Committee—but Adler and Draper were unfazed. They freely admitted appearing at functions sponsored by these organizations. And why shouldn't they? the performers argued. There was no reason to believe, they said, that these groups were unpatriotic in any way.[35]

At the trial in May 1950 the *Counterattack* partners took heart at the testimony of Louis Budenz, a former CPUSA official, now a fervent anti-Communist. Budenz conceded that many non-Communists were duped into joining front organizations bearing altruistic names, but added that "after a man was fooled four times he ceases to be innocent." Less helpful was the testimony of the defendant herself, Hester McCullough, who confirmed the most negative stereotypes about anti-Communists by saying she hated liberals and by suggesting that Franklin Roosevelt might have personally profited from appeasing Stalin.[36] The trial ended in a hung jury, the jurors' indecision reflecting the country's confusion over the meaning of fronts and the motivations of those who joined them.

These two legal encounters failed to help Keenan, Kirkpatrick, and Bierly to make their broader, rhetorical case against what they saw as a dangerous campaign to camouflage Communist infiltration of the media. Although Senator Joseph McCarthy was now galvanizing the anti-Communist movement—and igniting furious opposition—the *Counterattack* partners were dissatisfied with their own progress. More and more they came to believe they needed to take dramatic steps.

They continued to issue warnings about the Voice of Freedom Committee, whose benign title, they insisted, masked insidious designs. With mounting frustration they saw the organization, and others like it, carry on without opposition, or at least without the devastating opposition they preferred. Not only was the Voice of Freedom Committee promoting what the *Counterattack* publishers considered Soviet-friendly commentators, it was also attacking those voices on radio who they believed were standing up to the Communist menace. The organization claimed to have fifteen hundred volunteers across the country acting as monitors, on the alert for what the group considered reactionary ideas transmitted over the airwaves. In the case of New York talk-show host Martha Deane, a Voice of Freedom flyer announced, "Women's programs are not as innocent as they seem," and could, indeed, "exert a very dangerous influence on millions of women." Singling out Deane as especially pernicious, the flyer urged readers to "turn the heat on" by barraging her sponsors with letters of protest. In initiatives of this kind, monitors were instructed to omit any reference to the Voice of Freedom in their letters in order to create the impression that the protests were a spontaneous response—a tactic that the organization would soon see its enemies adopt.[37]

This offensive could not be ignored, concluded Keenan, Kirkpatrick, and Bierly. Nor could other, equally bold actions. As early as 1948 the partners had received information from an actress that a small, determined core of Communists was securing a foothold in the theater industry. By 1950 they still saw no improvement in that field.

The entire issue came to a head in March when the three partners learned of a document that was circulating through offices at the networks and advertising agencies. Under the heading "Most Undesirable," it listed broadcast talent allegedly affiliated with Communist causes and suggested that the reader "protest their participation in programs by writing to the *manufacturers of the product* they advertise." Solely a collection of names, the paper included no information explaining why these people were listed. The *Counterattack* partners decided, as Kirkpatrick later put it, that they should "come out with something documented and do it publicly, lay it all on the line and sell it over the counter to try to clear the air."[38]

American Business Consultants had published special supplements before, one on the United Office and Professional Workers of America and another on the role of business in the fight against communism. Now, they believed, was the time to focus on the radio industry.

They hoped their new report would raise awareness both within the broadcasting business and among the general public. They had seen previous supplements serve their limited purpose; perhaps this new project would even inspire some form of action. They had no way of knowing how much its influence would be buoyed by the tide of tumultuous world events.

THREE

Cultural Work

THE IDEA was to put together a list. Arguing the extent of Communist influence in broadcasting, American Business Consultants decided, could accomplish only so much if the discussion confined itself to generalities. Individuals needed to be held to account. Advocating a strategy that should have been familiar to those World War II progressives who had agitated against fascists and their helpers, Keenan, Kirkpatrick, and Bierly insisted that the public should know the names of those people who aided a foreign totalitarian cause.

Listing writers, directors, and actors who were actual party members was never really an option. This might have been due partly to a certain degree of caution instilled by the March lawsuit; more fundamentally, American Business Consultants knew that assembling such a list would simply not be practical. CPUSA members didn't generally advertise their political affiliation—if anything, most were inclined to keep their membership a secret—and nothing short of breaking and entering into party headquarters, as the Communist Squad had done during World War II, was likely to yield conclusive results. One more reason was the publishers' larger vision for their new project. They were determined to reveal the full scope of communism in broadcasting, encompassing not only party members but those people gullible enough to align with them.[1] Once more, front activities would provide the ammunition for American Business Consultants in their fight against the subversive threat.

After weeks of discussing the project, the real work began when Keenan, Kirkpatrick, and Bierly acquired an extra partner for the venture. A radio writer and former naval intelligence officer named Vincent Hartnett had been exchanging information with the newsletter publishers, and now, in early 1950, he revealed that, like them, he was also working on an exposé of Red influence in radio and TV. The *Counterattack* partners could see that Hartnett would be an asset. He was an experienced writer and, just as important, had his own set of files on the subject and could assist in research. Rather than duplicate his efforts, American Business Consultants decided to combine forces with him.

Hartnett was interested in creating what was essentially an expandable data base. The printed pages would be bound in loose-leaf notebooks, and those customers who purchased the notebook would receive periodic supplements that would update the information. American Business Consultants preferred not to get involved in such an open-ended project.[2] Perhaps the partners didn't believe there would be sufficient interest to support an ongoing venture. Instead they chose to publish a single, self-contained booklet. They would call it *Red Channels*.

The seven-page introduction to the booklet, written by Hartnett, began with a warning from J. Edgar Hoover, delivered during congressional testimony three years earlier, that the CPUSA was now focusing its attention on the airwaves, rather than print, as its prime medium of propaganda. Later on in the piece, Hartnett went on to say that Communists and their sympathizers constituted only a minority in the broadcast industry, but he painted a dark picture of their intentions: to control the airwaves in a time of emergency and to play a role in a Communist party attempt to dominate the country "as the result of a final upheaval and civil war."[3]

In more immediate terms, *Red Channels* maintained that the CPUSA's concerted effort to infiltrate radio and TV would transform programming into "transmission belts," a term taken from the writings of Lenin which meant, in this case, that programs would transmit "pro-Sovietism to the American people." The Red Fascists, as Hartnett liked to call Communists, were also determined to use their influence in broadcasting to raise money for their activities. His introduction asserted that the handsome salaries of the entertainment industry allowed Communists in radio and

TV to contribute substantial party dues while the deceptively progressive fronts promoted by these same people and their allies succeeded in raising even more funds for party purposes. As part of this CPUSA strategy, the introduction alleged, Communists in broadcasting had ensured that their allies would enjoy both prominence and prosperity by boosting one another's careers and by instituting a blacklist against leading anti-Communists.[4]

In his closing paragraphs, Hartnett cautioned readers against making irresponsible accusations against "innocents and genuine liberals." But he also made it clear that drastic measures were required; he quoted a recent *Broadcasting* magazine editorial which declared that "Communists and Communist sympathizers have no place on our air."[5]

Red Channels's list consisted of 151 names, each followed by a summary of the individual's front activities. Some were quite famous, including John Garfield, Judy Holliday, Edward G. Robinson, Orson Welles, and Gypsy Rose Lee. A great many were lesser stars and character actors, or writers and directors whose reputations were known mostly within the industry. To differentiate their project from lists already making the rounds, Keenan, Kirkpatrick, and Bierly based their compilation on public records and included citations so that readers could check the sources themselves if they were so inclined. The most common sources were back issues of the *Daily Worker*, organization letterheads, and reports from the un-American activities committees of both the California state legislature and the U.S. House of Representatives.

The criteria for selecting names were not exactly clear. Nearly sixty of the individuals had listings of front associations numbering in double figures, suggesting they might have been consistently involved in this sort of activity. The name of writer Langston Hughes, in particular, was coupled with a prodigious total of forty-one citations. More than a third of the names, though, had five or fewer listings, and six of those had only one.

Bierly, the *Counterattack* partner most responsible for assembling the list, would later explain that the publishers included both serious and casual front supporters to show that both witting and unwitting broadcast personalities "lent grandeur and prestige to these party causes." The booklet itself provided another rationale. The index of names, the booklet maintained, illustrated how many "prominent actors and artists have been inveigled to lend their names" to Communist causes, and the list served as a warning to discourage others from making the same mistake. In describing those included in the list, *Red Channels* declared that many had associated themselves with Communist causes "regardless of whether they actually believe in, sympathize with, or even recognize the cause advanced."[6]

Earlier *Counterattack* supplements had been distributed solely to the newsletter's subscribers, but the publishers had detected a special interest in the issue of subversion in broadcasting among both their readers and the general public, which warranted a more expansive approach. They produced *Red Channels* as a paperback and, in addition to mailing free copies to *Counterattack* subscribers, distributed the 213-page booklet to newsstands, to bookstores, and via direct orders, to be sold for a dollar apiece.[7]

The booklet reached the public at a time when anti-Communist activists were intent upon dramatizing their cause. On May 1, just a month and a half earlier, the American Legion in the Wisconsin mill town of Mosinee had staged a mock Communist putsch, an elaborate demonstration of what life would be like under a totalitarian regime. The *New York Times* provided a detailed account of the "pageant." Beginning with the capture at dawn of the town's mayor, the Legionnaires posing as Communist invaders had nationalized all businesses, abolished all competing parties, and herded uncooperative citizens into makeshift concentration camps as they declared Mosinee a part of the United Soviet States of America. When the townwide theater piece had come to an end that evening, the Legion's state commander had announced the lesson the community should have learned: "It is our duty to guard against subversion, to be actively interested in our Government, to be eternally vigilant."[8]

In this time of growing anti-Communist fears, certain conservative journalists shared American Business Consultants' belief in the importance of *Red Channels*. "A bombshell will be dropped into the offices of radio-tv networks, advertising agencies and sponsors this week," wrote Ed Sullivan in the *New York Daily News* on June 21, 1950, a day before the booklet's release. Two days later *Counterattack* devoted half its current issue to its new supplement and trumpeted the urgency of the situation with these opening words:

IN AN EMERGENCY (at any given time)
IT WOULD REQUIRE ONLY THREE PERSONS (subversives)—
<u>one engineer</u> in master control at a radio network

<u>one director</u> in a radio studio
<u>one voice</u> before a microphone—
TO REACH 90 MILLION PEOPLE WITH A MESSAGE![9]

As impassioned as the promotion for the booklet would be—whether originating from inside or outside the *Counterattack* offices—its impact paled in comparison to the power of hard news unfolding on the other side of the world. On June 25, just three days after the *Red Channels* release, newspaper headlines reported North Korea's invasion of South Korea.

For anyone concerned about Stalin and the reach of his tyrannical ambitions, events had been carrying ominous implications for some time. In 1948 the Russians had blockaded Berlin, and Whittaker Chambers had alleged that a Soviet spy ring was operating within the federal government in Washington, D.C. A year later the Soviet Union had detonated its first atomic bomb. The one consolation throughout the period had been that the escalating cold war remained cool, and American soldiers remained out of harm's way. That consolation vanished when Communist North Korea attacked and the Truman administration responded by committing American troops to turn back the invaders. Any lingering hopes for post–World War II cooperation between Washington and Moscow dissolved. Only five years after the surrender of Germany and Japan, Americans faced the grim prospect once again of going to war against totalitarian aggression.

President Truman quickly blamed the war on the Soviet Union, asserting that North Korea was a Russian puppet state committing Soviet aggression by proxy. Recent research into declassified Soviet documents has verified that Stalin did indeed give his blessings to North Korea's invasion and fed its war machine with military aid.[10] Being correct in his assessment, though, did not ensure Truman much success in the early going. By the time American troops entered the fight at the beginning of July, Communist forces had already captured the South Korean capital of Seoul, and within three weeks had seized the city of Taejon as well. American and South Korean troops continued to fall back. Throughout August and into September they found themselves cornered in the southeastern tip of the Korean peninsula, their backs to the Japanese Strait, as they dug in for a desperate defense.

The new struggle had a sobering effect on at least one of those people listed in *Red Channels*. Irwin Shaw, the novelist, playwright, and former radio scripter, had affiliated himself in the past with such front organizations as the League of American Writers and in 1938 had gone so far as to endorse the Moscow purge trials. The war in Korea opened his eyes to perils in the new world order. Soon after the fighting began, he refused to allow an old anti-war play of his to be staged. Shaw had written *Bury the Dead* in 1935 when he believed a second world war must be avoided at all costs. The play, as he now explained in a letter to the *New York Times*, was based on the belief "that by appealing to reason and sentiment war might be forever halted." In the wake of the Communist invasion of South Korea, Shaw believed "the rulers of Russia have demonstrated that the gentle hopes of 1950 are as naive as they were in 1935." He had no patience for supporters of Communist aggression who masqueraded as advocates of peace, and he "did not wish the forlorn longings and illusions of 1935 to be used as ammunition for the killers of 1950."[11]

A more defensive response came from another *Red Channels* listee, radio actor Roger De Koven. He contacted *Counterattack* to explain the one citation attached to his name. He had been accused of acting as translator for overseas messages delivered to the Scientific and Cultural Conference for World Peace, a March 1949 meeting that had been denounced as a Stalinist propaganda event not only by conservatives but also by leftist anti-Communists such as Sidney Hook and Dwight Macdonald. After receiving a statement from the actor about his citation, the *Counterattack* publishers printed the essence of his remarks, namely that he was opposed to communism and had no idea that the peace conference was controlled by Stalinists at the time he had participated. Some viewed this development as evidence of *Red Channels*'s carelessness in making accusations, or as a demonstration of mounting hysteria that forced people to justify innocent, liberal-minded actions from their past. But *Counterattack* was not about to concede any such thing, asserting instead that De Koven's statement proved that the CPUSA "uses deception and tried to conceal the true nature of its fronts to win individual and public support for them."[12]

In the opening months of the Korean War, most Americans believed that Truman's decision to send troops was necessary, but there were other voices, too, that infuriated those who were determined to find any possible fifth-column activity on the home front. *Counterattack* noted, for example, that the Civil Rights Congress held a rally at Madison Square Garden on June 28 to advocate the Soviet position. Speaker Gus Hall, CPUSA national secretary, set the tone for the event by branding American intervention in Korea as "naked, armed struggle for the imperialist domination of the Far East." The Communist press was another area of *Counterattack* scrutiny. Over the first two months of the war, the *Daily Worker* referred to the North Korean army simply as "Koreans," clearly implying that the Communist forces represented the entire country in its fight against Americans. On July 18, when mainstream newspapers reported that the latest Communist assault was temporarily stalled, a *Daily Worker* headline announced, "Koreans Free Taejon." The accompanying article explained that the Korean People's Army had "liberated" the city despite resistance from American troops, which the article described as "murderous." Similar sentiments could be found in the August issue of the more circumspect but still Soviet-apologist *Monthly Review*, whose editors explained that the North Korean dictatorship of Kim Il Sung was a vehicle for "social and economic transformation," which gave its people "hope of a better future." Victory for North Korea, the editors concluded, "would effectively solve the Korean problem, while victory for the Americans would not."[13]

As the war intensified, *Counterattack* hammered away at the Stockholm Peace Appeal, a petition that had reportedly gathered half a million signatures in the United States, a movement that typified for American Business Consultants the sort of Soviet-inspired propaganda that Irwin Shaw had alluded to when withdrawing his anti-war play. The newsletter also followed up on the release of *Red Channels* by condemning recent appearances of some performers who were included in the booklet. Why, the newsletter demanded to know, was poet, literary critic, and *Red Channels* listee Louis Untermeyer participating on the panel of *What's My Line?*, the popular TV game show on CBS? The publishers raised similar questions about broadcast performances by actors Marsha Hunt and Howard Da Silva. More consistently now, the newsletter urged readers to write letters of protest to the sponsors and networks that hired these people.

Counterattack's efforts raised an alarm within certain sectors of the entertainment industry. Three unions—the Radio Writers Guild, the Radio and Television Directors Guild, and Actors Equity—responded to *Red*

Channels by passing resolutions condemning what they regarded as the beginning of a blacklist, similar to the one already in place in the film industry. Joining the attack on *Red Channels* was the venerable magazine the *Nation*. In a liberal publication that otherwise supported Truman's war effort in Korea, the magazine's Observer column had earlier vilified *Counterattack* as a purveyor of "back-alley gossip, second-hand slander, and wild accusation." Now it likened *Red Channels* to a 1934 book entitled *The Red Network*. The earlier book, subtitled "A Who's Who and Handbook of Radicalism for Patriots," had been written and privately published by Elizabeth Dilling, a rabid Christian Fronter and anti-Semite, whose list of subversives included not only known Communists but also Supreme Court Justice Felix Frankfurter, ACLU attorney Arthur Garfield Hays (whom Dilling helpfully identified as a "Jewish lawyer"), and New York City mayor Fiorello La Guardia ("of Italian-Jewish parentage").[14] By comparing *Red Channels* to Dilling's book, the anonymous Observer columnist was contributing to the increasingly rancorous tone of the debate by clearly implying that Keenan, Kirkpatrick, and Bierly were fascists.

Counterattack answered the charge that it was instigating a blacklist by deriding the issue as "a sham." Relying on as narrow a definition as possible, the newsletter maintained that the term "blacklisting" referred only to workers fired because of their involvement in unions. The term did not apply, *Counterattack* claimed, to people who the newsletter believed were providing "aid and comfort to Stalin."[15]

For the time being, the issue of blacklisting in broadcasting was primarily a debating exercise. But that time would soon pass.

On Saturday, August 26, Kirkpatrick returned from a trip out of town and checked into the office to catch up on work that might have accumulated in his absence. He received a phone call that tipped him off to a show-business announcement made just the day before. An actress by the name of Jean Muir was to debut the following night in the role of the mother in the NBC-TV sitcom *The Aldrich Family*. Until then Muir had been a minor leading lady in Hollywood whose career had attracted only cursory attention in the media and who had not appeared in a film since 1943. For Kirkpatrick, though, it was not her professional credentials that warranted attention. He and his partners had already publicized their concerns on pages 113 and 114 of *Red Channels*, where they listed nine alleged front activities under her name.

Several months earlier a casting announcement of this type would probably have earned nothing more than a routine mention in *Counterattack*—the newsletter had in fact briefly mentioned Muir's appearance on the *Philco Television Playhouse* the previous February—but now Kirkpatrick took a particularly dim view of the situation. To his mind there was no reason for leniency as long as American troops were locked in a do-or-die battle along the Pusan perimeter in Korea. He began contacting some associates to see what could be done.[16]

The Phone calls to the sponsor and the network began coming in that very same day. Among those protesting Muir's appearance on *The Aldrich Family* were Hester McCullough (defendant in the Adler-Draper lawsuit and a *Counterattack* ally), Alfred Kohlberg (*Counterattack*'s benefactor), Rabbi Benjamin Schultz (official of the Joint Committee Against Communism, an organization that included Kirkpatrick as a member), and Stephen C. Chess (commander of the Catholic War Veterans in Queens, where Kirkpatrick lived). The exact number of protests has never been conclusively established. Initial news articles reported twenty phone calls and two telegrams, but a spokesman for General Foods, the sponsor of the show, later claimed there had been as many as two hundred calls.[17] Two things, though, are quite clear. First, the protesters objected to Muir on the basis of her listing in *Red Channels*, and second, the sponsor and the network panicked.

Final rehearsals for *The Aldrich Family* were scheduled for the next day, Sunday, at noon. This was the era of live television, and the rehearsal was to take place just seven and a half hours before the actors would perform the show on-air that evening. But the rehearsal never happened. Cast and crew suddenly received word that there would be no broadcast of *The Aldrich Family* that evening.[18]

Michael Dann, working in the NBC public relations division at the time, recalled that he received an urgent call from the network's sales department early that Sunday and was told to come in that afternoon to NBC's offices in the RCA building in New York for a special meeting. Joining him were an NBC advertising executive and an executive from Young & Rubicam, the ad agency that represented General Foods. One item not addressed was the issue of whether Muir should be kept on the program. General Foods had already made that decision: Muir had to go.

"We certainly were going to please General Foods promptly," Dann recalled. "There was no discussion about the validity of whether or not she would be canceled, or whether or not there was any sort of injustice. It was automatic. General Foods made a decision and we certainly were going to support it." The executives were concerned exclusively with figuring out the best way to present the decision to the public.[19] That announcement came on Monday and appeared in newspapers the next day.

Jean Muir was fired, according to the General Foods statement, because the protests had rendered her a controversial personality who might "provoke unfavorable criticism and even antagonism among sizable groups of consumers."[20] The sponsor emphasized that it had not concerned itself with the accuracy of the allegations against the actress, only with the audience's perception of her. By making this distinction, General Foods tried to assure the public that it was staying above the ideological fray, that it was not conducting a political inquisition. But what the statement actually revealed was how absolutely timorous the company's executives were. The mere fact that there had been protests was sufficient reason in itself for General Foods to remove Muir from its show.

Muir immediately denied any connection to communism, which she condemned as "a vicious and destructive force," and maintained that the front activities attributed to her in *Red Channels* were either false, misleading, or meaningless. Within a week she offered to back up her claims by testifying about her background, under oath, before the House Un-American Activities Committee. None of this did anything to slow General Foods' rapid retreat. Three days after dismissing Muir, the company hired actress Nancy Carroll to take her place on *The Aldrich Family* beginning the following Sunday. The sponsor's one concession was to pay Muir for the entire run of her eighteen-week contract.[21]

Across the country the incident set off a wave of criticism directed squarely at *Red Channels* and its newfound influence. Some of the voices came from predictable sources, such as Saul Carson of the left-wing *New Republic*, but the Muir dismissal stirred indignation from the aggressively anti-Communist *New Leader* as well. Its September 9 editorial mocked the anti-Muir protesters as trivializers who had somehow convinced themselves that they were taking a stand against the international Communist conspiracy by removing an actress from a weekly sitcom. "Were Miss Muir a proven Communist and a five-day-a-week coast-to-coast news commentator," the editorial continued, "the action of the enraged citizenry might be looked upon with some degree of approval, although, Lord knows, it would hardly shake the walls of the Kremlin." Included in the piece was a testimonial by Morton Wishengrad, writer of "Communism—U.S. Brand," who pointed out that Muir had recently participated in a civil rights documentary he had written, in which she had recited—and "expressed satisfaction with"—a section that criticized Communist manipulation of divisive issues.

Another anti-Communist magazine to speak up was *Life*, which objected especially to General Foods' firing of Muir without giving her a chance to defend herself. Referring to her alleged front activities, the editorial writer explained, "We don't approve of gullibility, but we don't like to see it equated with subversion or treason in advance of a hearing." Even a former associate of the *Red Channels* publishers weighed in against them. Isaac Don Levine, editor of *Plain Talk* for which Keenan, Kirkpatrick, and Bierly had provided research, was so offended by the Muir affair that he resigned from the American Jewish League Against Communism, which, under the leadership of Rabbi Schultz, had contributed to the protests against the actress.[22]

Perhaps most forceful of all was *New York Times* radio editor Jack Gould. Going beyond the particulars of the case, Gould warned of the incident's implications for the future. He argued that General Foods, a leading and influential player in radio and TV, was setting a dangerous precedent by giving in to a small group of activists, that its actions "put a policing power behind the allegations contained in 'Red Channels.'" Fearing that watchdog groups could become "dictators of the airwaves," he urged political centrists in broadcasting to correct the situation. It was up to them to resist pressures from both the far left and the far right, and to steer the industry down a reasonable, middle course.[23]

Many protested on civil libertarian grounds, out of a concern for preserving essential rights even in a time of emergency. Others failed to see the issues as clearly. Some Popular Fronters berated repressive tactics in the war against communism but failed to see the inconsistency with their own previous support for measures that had compromised civil liberties during World War II. A few years earlier L. M. Birkhead, of Friends of Democracy's Battle, had celebrated the government's sedition cases in the fight against fascism and had railed against misguided organizations that served the enemy's cause. Now he saw no reason to become alarmed about Soviet agents and fronts. Similarly Norman Corwin was appalled by both recent HUAC hearings and the Muir incident, but during World War II he had rejoiced when the government had shut down publications that undermined the war effort.

Unifying the critics of *Red Channels* was the sense that the Muir case marked a turning point in an ongoing controversy. Rumors of a broadcast blacklist had been circulating for several years. The radio program of news commentator William L. Shirer, for instance, had been canceled in 1947 by CBS supposedly because of his liberal views. The network's decision, however, might have had more to do with failing ratings and Shirer's own professional complacency. A more compelling case involved Paul Draper, whose appearance on Ed Sullivan's *Toast of the Town* in January 1950 had been excised in repeat broadcasts of the TV show after the program received protests about the performer's alleged front activities. Another example was William Sweets, who had lost his job as director of radio's *Gangbusters* and *Counter-Spy* in August 1949 because of a letter-writing campaign that denounced him as a Communist sympathizer.[24] The Muir case, though, was more telling, an indication that a true, full-scale anti-Red purge might be imminent. Here the allegations originated with a publication that could easily become a master list for the industry—a blacklist bible, as some in broadcasting were now beginning to call it. Already other performers listed in *Red Channels*, such as Hazel Scott, Philip Loeb, and Gypsy Rose Lee, were coming under fire.

The controversy swirled around the issues of fair play and due process. Was it right, was it truly the American way, to fire someone solely on the basis of protests from a miniscule percentage of the public? For many, the answer to this question was clearly no. *Counterattack* and its allies, though, stressed another issue.

At certain times, they argued, effective opposition to a determined enemy transcended all other concerns, no matter how valid those concerns might be. As *Counterattack*'s September 13 issue put it, "GI's in Korea are being murdered by those who have been helped by the people in this country who are members of, or who have given service to, the

Communist party." But, as the *New Leader* pointed out, how does an actress in a TV comedy figure into the larger picture of the cold war conflict? Unless the *Red Channels* camp could somehow make this connection, its argument was empty.

No one, even among those on the right, claimed that Jean Muir was an indispensable Communist functionary or a vital linchpin in an anti-American conspiracy. But, in an October speech before an American Legion rally in Illinois, *Red Channels* contributor Vincent Hartnett offered another explanation for Muir's importance. He told his audience that the Muir controversy was a test case for those in the Communist-front movement. "If they lose," he said, "they stand to lose their whole elaborate underground apparatus they have built up in the past 12 years."[25]

Ultimately the argument rested on the premise that Communists had been infiltrating the broadcast industry in a secret campaign of the witting and unwitting which included Muir among many others. For the *Counterattack* partners to legitimize their third-violinist theory, they had to establish the facts of a Communist offensive in radio and TV. If true, their position could still be attacked on civil libertarian grounds, but it would at least merit serious discussion.

Was there really an organized Communist effort to infiltrate the airwaves? Or was it nothing more than a Red-baiter's fever dream?

The *Counterattack* partners certainly harbored no doubts about the answers to these questions; still, they must have welcomed the support for their position that came in December, just three months after the Muir controversy erupted. That was when the *American Legion Magazine* published an article by Louis Francis Budenz entitled "How the Reds Invaded Radio."

Budenz had been a high-ranking CPUSA official for ten years. After an early career as a labor organizer for the American Federation of Labor, he joined the party at the age of forty-three and began his service there as labor editor at the *Daily Worker*. Eventually he became the paper's managing editor as well as a member of the Party's central committee. In 1945, yielding to the moral suasion of Monsignor Fulton J. Sheen, he broke with the CPUSA, took a position as assistant professor of economics at the University of Notre Dame, and returned to his original faith of Catholicism. He also embraced the fighting faith of anti-communism. He waged his war by testifying against former Communist associates and those he considered fellow travelers, not only in the Draper-Adler libel case but before congressional committees and at the 1949 trial of CPUSA leaders.

His *American Legion* article began with a scene from the fall of 1943 at the CPUSA's seat of power on the ninth floor of its headquarters on Thirteenth Street in Manhattan. There, Budenz claimed, party official Alexander Trachtenberg revealed to him the formation of a new commission to expedite "the big red putsch" in the radio industry. The party intended to exploit Popular Front issues of the day by pressuring networks into broadcasting labor-oriented shows, to be created by Communists and their allies. The commission also planned to promote the careers of commentators and those people already producing wartime radio propaganda who could help further the party's cause. After first building a faithful core occupying important positions, Budenz wrote, the CPUSA hoped to continue infiltrating until eventually it controlled the industry.

Trachtenberg made it clear that "a good beginning had already been made." The Communists, he said, had already secured a foothold on the commercial airwaves and in the radio division of the Office of War Information (OWI), Washington's official propaganda agency. Further inroads would be made, the article said, through organized letter-writing campaigns as well as the assistance of front organizations and Communist-controlled unions.

In his article, Budenz named the members of the radio commission: Trachtenberg, Joseph Brodsky, Abraham A. Heller, and V. J. Jerome. He went on, however, to dangle tantalizing questions by not identifying two other key players in the scheme. One was a *Daily Worker* writer who was assigned to kick off the radio initiative with a series of articles. Budenz revealed only his pen name: Peter Ivy. The other was the leader of the party's forces among broadcast professionals, described in Budenz's article as the John Howard Lawson of the industry. Lawson, one of the Hollywood Ten, had often been characterized as the party's movie-industry commissar, responsible for maintaining discipline within Hollywood's Communist ranks and instrumental in advancing the careers of his comrades. As for Lawson's broadcasting counterpart, Budenz said only that his name "will undoubtedly be exposed before long in some Congressional hearing."[26]

What are we to make of this story? Those who could have directly corroborated Budenz's account—the four men on the alleged radio commission—never said anything to back up Budenz, and obviously would have had no reason to do so unless they too had a change of heart about the Communist party, which they never did. The key issue, then, is Budenz's credibility during his career as an informant.

Over the years Budenz has been attacked as a fabricator who slandered innocent people in order to foist himself into the limelight. Much of the controversy surrounded his highly contested allegations that Asia expert Owen Lattimore was a secret Communist. Budenz has been portrayed as a questionable character no better than Whittaker Chambers and Elizabeth Bentley, the two other prominent ex-Communist witnesses of the era. But in more recent years, research into Soviet documents, including the so-called Venona transcripts of secret intelligence messages between the United States and the Soviet Union, has changed the portrait of all three informants. As in the case of Chambers and Bentley, new sources have rehabilitated Budenz's reputation.

"Budenz's early testimony and writings were largely accurate, and some points that were questioned at that time have been confirmed by documents appearing from Moscow's archives in recent years," write the Communist party researchers John Earl Haynes and Harvey Klehr. Their one qualifier is that Budenz "sometimes exaggerated his direct knowledge" and could occasionally give "his accounts a melodramatic aura." Another researcher in the field, Herb Romerstein, is reluctant to make even this concession. "I think there were times when his interpretation might have been different than somebody else's," he said, "but I don't think he stretched the truth."[27]

Among the secret Soviet agents in America named by Budenz and later corroborated by decrypted Soviet communications were Zalmond Franklin, Bill Gebert, and Bernard Schuster. Budenz also implicated American Communists in the Soviet conspiracy to murder Leon Trotsky in Mexico. As Romerstein put it, this account seemed "counter-intuitive and shocking at the time—and it's all turned out to be true."[28]

This research suggests that Budenz's *American Legion* article cannot be cavalierly dismissed. Further buttressing its validity is other documentation that corroborates both certain details and the overall thrust of the story. The most compelling evidence concerns Trachtenberg's claim that the Communists had already infiltrated OWI. Decrypted communications reveal that CPUSA official Eugene Dennis informed Moscow about contacts within the agency and make it clear that such OWI employees as

Peter Rhodes and Flora Wovschin were Soviet agents. The problem at the agency quickly became serious enough to attract the attention of the FBI. As OWI radio writer Henry Denker recalled, "The FBI was very active in that office, and they were not looking for German spies."[29]

The problem appeared in the open in October 1943—around the time of Budenz's meeting with Trachtenberg—when newspapers reported the temporary shutdown of the Labor Short Wave Bureau, an AFL and CIO news service that had been providing stories on the American labor scene to OWI's radio division, which then broadcast the reports to Europe. The union outfit stopped sending material because OWI writers were allegedly distorting the stories, turning them into promotional pieces for American Communist labor leaders. Although OWI head Elmer Davis tended to be skeptical of reports of Communist activity within the agency, he felt it necessary in this case to make personnel changes to correct the situation. Ultimately he fired about a dozen OWI employees for party-line tendencies.[30]

As for radio news commentators, one has clearly been identified in the Venona transcripts. Johannes Steel, a favorite *Counterattack* target, appears in four messages between New York and Moscow that reveal he was communicating with Russian agents and, in one instance, directed their attention to a Polish journalist who was interested in contacting them. Another commentator, William S. Gailmor, is singled out in Budenz's article as a CPUSA success story, and apparently for good reason. A frequent subject of *Counterattack* pillory, Gailmor originally emerged from a colorful background that managed to include both rabbinical studies and car theft before he settled on a career in journalism. Sponsoring his show in the 1940s was the Electronics Corporation of America, owned by Sam Novick, who, Budenz claimed, had close ties to the CPUSA underground, an allegation supported by an FBI investigation. The Communist connections of Gailmor himself have not been verified by Soviet documents, but his commentaries indicate that he was, at the very least, a useful CPUSA tool. In the premiere issue of his weekly newsletter, *Now!*, published in 1946 as Russia was consolidating its domination of Eastern Europe, Gailmor sneered at those diplomats who shed "crocodile tears" over, as he mockingly called them, poor little Finland, poor little Baltics, and poor little Poland, countries that were now enjoying "the dignity of freedom," Gailmor insisted, thanks to their Soviet masters.[31]

Documented details aside, the basic thesis of Budenz's article should come as no surprise. For years the CPUSA had been hard at work establishing influence in major American industries, most often by gaining control of unions in the CIO. In the field of journalism, for example, a profession closely related to broadcasting, the party aggressively cultivated contacts and succeeded in making Soviet agents out of such reporters as Cedric Belfrage, Nathan Einhorn, Stephen Laird, and Winston Burdett.[32] It would be naive to think that Communists would not have also targeted broadcasting, the most dynamic of communications media.

As early as the mid-1930s the party made clear in its own publications how much it valued a Communist presence on the airwaves. *Party Organizer*, an internal CPUSA journal, frequently published articles with such titles as "Radio—The Voice of Our Mass Agitation" and "How Can We Secure the Use of Radio?" At this point, though, the objective was not to burrow inside the industry but to find some way to get party officials on the air to broadcast "revolutionary propaganda." Within ten years the strategy had changed. In April 1946, three years after the formation of the radio commission, the party sponsored a symposium entitled "Art as a Weapon," which outlined exactly what was expected of artists, or "cultural workers" as the Communist hierarchy was fond of calling them. Among the speakers at the event was CPUSA chairman William Z. Foster, who published his themes for the symposium in the *New Masses*. While he praised efforts to create an independent people's art outside the mainstream, he also exhorted writers, directors, and actors "to make their constructive influence felt within the scope of the great commercialized organizations of the bourgeoisie—motion pictures, radio, literature, theater, etc." To penetrate these media—a process that Foster pointed out was already in motion—creative professionals should focus on trade unions and guilds, where they "must ceaselessly teach artists the elements of Marxism."[33]

The men whom Budenz identified as members of the Communist party radio commission were all the likeliest suspects for such a venture. Alexander Trachtenberg was known within party circles as a high-ranking cultural commissar in America while publicly he was the head of International Publishers, which distributed Communist books and pamphlets and was subsidized in part by the Soviet Union. Abraham Heller, a wealthy industrialist, helped bankroll the party by donating his own money and smuggling Soviet funds into the country. Joseph Brodsky was the party's attorney, who, after his death in 1947, would be eulogized at the New York State Communist Party Convention as an honored comrade.[34] The last of the commission members, V. J. Jerome, played an especially important role in all the party's efforts in the realm of arts and entertainment.

Born Jerome Isaac Romain in Poland in 1896, he emigrated to England as a child and moved on once more to New York City at the age of nineteen. In part his expertise in the arts came from his own direct experience—he was himself a poet and novelist—but far more crucial to his career was an understanding of the arts that he devoured whole from Communist orthodoxy and imposed upon his fellow creative comrades. Beginning in the mid-1930s Jerome served as chairman of the party's national cultural commission and was responsible for enforcing cultural discipline, whether on the grand stage of Hollywood's Communist community or within obscure local party groups.[35] A bald, bespectacled man with shallow, puffy eyes, he left a trail of disgruntled creative comrades in his wake.

Budd Schulberg had an encounter with Jerome while writing his novel *What Makes Sammy Run?* A Communist at the time, Schulberg was expected to submit to a demand from John Howard Lawson that the party exercise control over the writing of the book. Lawson brought in Jerome to put on the pressure. To Schulberg the cultural commissioner was "imperious and cold," a "terrifying figure." Communist author Howard Fast offered a somewhat different but no less damning description of the man: "a horrible, rigid little monster."[36]

Within their ideological orbit, cultural officials like Jerome could be effective in browbeating playwrights and novelists into conforming to whatever party dictate was in fashion, but commanding that sort of obedience in the field of broadcasting was far more difficult. Radio and TV writers had other masters to obey, namely producers, sponsors, and network executives interested in little else except reaching the largest possible audience with as little controversy as possible. The extent to which party cultural functionaries could insert their messages in broadcast material is debatable. What is clear, though, is the sort of propaganda that Communists would have liked to disseminate.

Some of the CPUSA's cultural work from that time comes across now as little more than overly earnest foolishness, as in an effort called "Puppets for Propaganda," a drive to promote party demonstrations and election campaigns through hand-puppet shows ("We want comrades who will seriously apply themselves," admonished a recruiting flyer for the initiative).[37] Not so easy to dismiss was the party's propaganda campaign during the years of the nonaggression pact. At a time when labor strikes at defense-related factories hindered American efforts to aid Britain's resistance against Germany, opposition to the anti-Nazi fight came from such efforts as a record album entitled *Songs for John Doe*.

The songs were written and performed by the Almanac Singers, a folk group consisting of Pete Seeger, Woody Guthrie, Lee Hays, Millard Lampell, Sam Gary, and Josh White, and the album was produced by Eric Bernay, head of Keynote Recording Company.[38] The songs branded President Roosevelt as a cold-blooded, calculating warmonger who sought to throw away the lives of American boys for no other reason than to line the pockets of J. P. Morgan, DuPont, and Republic Steel. Not content to slander FDR alone, the Almanac Singers also insinuated Eleanor into their smear:

> Oh, Franklin Roosevelt told the people how he felt
> We damn near believed what he said
> He said, "I hate war, and so does Eleanor
> But we won't be safe till everybody's dead."

When it came to Britain's desperate defense against the savage Nazi blitz, the group resorted to some breathtaking moral equivalency between the two sides. In a Stalinist take on the traditional folk tune "Billy Boy," the title character repeatedly resists the call to military duty and finally clinches his argument by quipping, "You can come around to me when England's a democracy."[39]

The album was released in the latter half of May 1941. A month later the Nazis invaded the Soviet Union, and the Almanac Singers quite literally changed their tune. Within months they appeared on a Norman Corwin broadcast singing "Round and Round Hitler's Grave," harmonizing their readiness to wade into the heart of Italy and Germany to shoot and hang the fascist tyrants with bloodthirsty relish.

In some cases a party-line entertainer could use his prestige to indulge in propaganda that had truly dire implications. In June 1949, as Stalin was carrying out a murderous anti-Semitic purge, Paul Robeson chose to make one of his celebratory visits to the Soviet Union. To his credit, as re-counted by such writers as Martin Bauml Duberman and Louis Rapoport, Robseon was genuinely troubled by the disappearance of Russian Jewish artists and was especially concerned about his old friend, the Jewish poet and active Stalinist functionary, Itzik Feffer, who had seemingly vanished from the public scene. Through his contacts within the Soviet govern-ment, Robeson was able to arrange permission for Feffer to meet him at his room in Moscow's Metropole Hotel. When Feffer arrived from his prison cell in the infamous Lubyanka, Robeson had no trouble learning that something was very wrong. The poet, scribbling notes to avoid being overheard in the bugged room, informed Robeson that Jewish writers had been imprisoned and murdered. As for what he himself could expect, Fef-fer made a silent throat-slitting gesture. Even though he was disturbed by this secret conversation, Robeson continued to stick to the Soviet line upon his return to the United States, telling a journalist that reports of an anti-Semitic campaign in Russia were groundless. Thus he deprived the world of an inside account of what was really happening.[40] Stalin, free of any significant international pressure, continued his purge. Not only was the Jewish artistic community devastated during this phase of the dicta-tor's newest terror, but thousands of others were also imprisoned. In Au-gust 1952 the secret police murdered at least thirteen of the country's Jewish writers and intellectuals, including Feffer, the friend whom Robe-son had abandoned.

Throughout World War II and its aftermath, much of the party's cul-tural message was channeled to the public in slightly gentrified form through front groups that were willing to twist and turn with the move-ment's changing directives. In broadcasting, as *Counterattack* was fond of pointing out, the Voice of Freedom Committee took the lead. When not lavishing praise on the likes of Johannes Steel and William Gailmor, the group revealed its Soviet partisanship by lauding on-air attacks on the Mar-shall Plan, perhaps America's greatest postwar accomplishment that laid bare the disparity between democratic Western Europe and the Russians' totalitarian Eastern Bloc. In its publications the Voice of Freedom Com-mittee also conveyed the doctrinaire, humorless vision that the Commu-nist front movement had in mind for broadcasting, a perspective that was perhaps at its most strident when the group vilified the popular radio co-median Fred Allen for ribbing the Russians. Allen was promoting a Third

World War, the organization declared. "This is the stuff of which that war will be made," the Voice of Freedom newsletter scolded Allen, "and it's not at all funny because men, women, and children may someday pay with their lives for having laughed at just such cheap jokes as yours."[41]

Any question about what the front movement thought should be the remedy for politically incorrect media messages was answered in 1948 when 20th Century Fox released *The Iron Curtain*. The film dramatized the defection of Soviet spy Igor Gouzenko, a case that was a breakthrough in the West's understanding of the Russian intelligence network in North America, and a story that the CPUSA, itself a conduit for espionage, did not wish to see publicized. In February, even before the movie opened, the National Council of American-Soviet Friendship insisted the film be banned. To justify this blatant call for censorship, the Council made the specious claim that the movie violated a "United Nations declaration against war propaganda."[42]

In the movement's most ambitious broadcast initiative following the war, the People's Radio Foundation attempted to use the airwaves to relay an unadulterated front perspective that would not have to conform to network radio standards. At the time, many in the radio industry were exploring the new possibilities of greater high fidelity presented by FM radio. Within this new frequency spectrum the People's Radio Foundation sought to establish its own New York station, in keeping with V. J. Jerome's call to support "community-group establishment and democratic ownership of Frequency Modulation (F.M.) radio stations." As in all fronts, the organization had its share of well-meaning liberals, drawn no doubt by the group's stated objective to broadcast programs highlighting civil rights and international peace. Less moderate were such officers and stockholders as Abraham Heller, Joseph Brodsky, and the Communist-dominated International Fur and Leather Workers Union.[43]

The enhanced FM signal would have allowed the People's Radio station to broadcast across a sixty-mile radius in the greater New York City area, creating a wide potential audience for the group's political views. By March 1947 the organization had raised more than sixty thousand dollars to pursue this venture, but in November the FCC turned down its application for a license.[44] The chances of creating an independent outlet friendly to Soviet interests then evaporated as the radio industry's effort to cultivate FM began to flounder, not to be fully revived again until the

1960s. With this avenue closed, the CPUSA's best opportunity in broadcasting could be found in the established stations and networks.

Writers within the mainstream radio industry began to notice what they believed to be a Communist influence in the mid-1940s, the same period cited by Budenz as the beginning of the CPUSA's radio commission. Author and scriptwriter Ruth Adams Knight first heard about the change as early as 1943 when she returned to New York City after a year's absence and was told by fellow scriptwriter Katherine Seymour about new developments in the Radio Writers Guild. Knight attended a membership meeting of the guild to see for herself. The experience was jarring. What had once been a subdued assembly of polished professionals had now, according to Knight, turned into something more akin to a "meeting of the Steamfitters Union." While this sounds like little more than professional snobbery, another member, approaching the new developments from another direction, confirmed her appraisal. Around this time Welbourn Kelley noticed that the guild had taken on a "labor-union fighting spirit," which he thought would be useful when the time came to negotiate new contracts. Both writers would soon conclude that the new atmosphere signified something more than either simple boorishness or working-class pugnacity.[45]

Kelley began to question the direction the guild was taking when he found that there was now an unofficial ban on the word "communism" at guild meetings. If people did use the word, "they were booed down." Moreover, Knight, and others too, noticed that certain members would raise issues that seemed to have no direct bearing on guild business. Henry Denker recalled being taken by surprise at a meeting when he heard a member propose a resolution in support of Willie McGee. He had no idea who Willie McGee was. In time he would find out that McGee was a Mississippi black man sentenced to death for the rape of a white woman, a previously obscure case that the Communist party had now adopted as a cause célèbre. In another instance, guild board members attempted to collect signatures for the Stockholm Peace Pledge, a seemingly benign petition that was viewed by anti-Communists as a cynical Soviet attempt to weaken U.S. resolve in the fight against Communist expansion.[46]

What aroused suspicion among some guild members were not only the ideological measures but the technique used to push some of them through, a technique common to unions with a significant CPUSA contingent. As a meeting would get under way, certain members would raise issues that required extensive discussion, then would prolong discussion with a series of motions and questions. After an hour or two, many attendees, growing tired of the tedious proceedings, would start to walk out. Ultimately those remaining would be dominated by a determined and exceedingly patient Communist faction—the "iron buttocks brigade," as Hollywood Communist Paul Jarrico once called it—which would then find itself with a majority and the ability to pass its pet resolutions.[47]

Taken together, the Soviet documents, party policies, and firsthand accounts substantiate much of Budenz's allegation and elucidate the CPUSA efforts in broadcasting that had been outlined by party chairman Foster. Still, one important question lingers: Who was the so-called John Howard Lawson of radio, the writer who Budenz claimed was coordinating the Communist initiative within the industry?

Anti-Communists both within and outside broadcasting usually pointed to one man. His name was Peter Lyon.

Little remembered today and rarely mentioned in accounts of the period, Lyon was a respected scripter in the late 1930s and 1940s—"one of radio's ablest writers," according to broadcast historian Erik Barnouw—who was best known for his work on *Cavalcade of America* and the acclaimed sustaining show *The Eternal Light*.[48] He was also active in the Radio Writers Guild, where he served at various times as national president and vice president in charge of the union's eastern council.

Although Budenz in his *American Legion* article might have been coy about the identity of the party's radio steward, he was more forthright when interviewed by the FBI in June 1950. He described Lyon as a "concealed Communist," and recalled that the writer "sat in on at least one hasty meeting with [Abraham] Heller and myself and some others on the possibilities of infiltrating radio."[49] Once again, even if we assume Budenz was essentially reliable, his statement requires some form of corroboration.

One sympathetic account of Lyon's career describes him as a liberal New Dealer; an acquaintance in the guild characterized him vaguely as some sort of radical leftist, perhaps a socialist.[50] A trail of evidence, some circumstantial and some anecdotal, provides a more complete picture and makes Budenz's statement appear plausible.

Part of the evidence concerns Lyon's World War II service in the OWI, where he worked as labor editor in the International Press and Radio Division. When the Labor Short Wave Bureau lodged its complaint that its stories were receiving a pro-Communist slant, the news service was basing its allegations on a digest it had compiled of reports featured on OWI's labor show, written by Lyon. Faced with this analysis, OWI head Elmer Davis, who was hardly a Red-baiter, decided to transfer Lyon from the labor desk and reportedly said at the time that the digest of Lyon's work was "prima facie evidence of Communist infiltration."[51]

Other information connects Lyon, directly or indirectly, with Communist party activities. On March 9, 1941, a fund-raising performance of the *Songs for John Doe* album was held at Lyon's apartment at 57 West Twelfth Street in Manhattan. Although this event qualifies, strictly speaking, as a front activity rather than an official CPUSA function, it is difficult to explain away someone's involvement in an enterprise that so transparently followed such a wrongheaded, party-inspired policy. Another meeting at Lyon's home, tracked by the FBI, places him somewhat deeper within the CPUSA orbit. On the night of December 30, 1943, Lyon hosted a meeting concerning the Communist-backed Jefferson School of Social Sciences, attended by party stalwart Alexander Trachtenberg.[52]

The FBI began keeping tabs on Lyon during World War II, perhaps as part of their investigation of the OWI. At least one of the Bureau's informants identified Lyon as a CPUSA member, but the agents handling the case could not vouch for their sources' reliability, and the Bureau's survey of Lyon's involvement in front groups like the People's Radio Foundation also failed to establish a clear link to the party. Two statements later delivered under oath, however, corroborate the essence of the informant allegations. In his appearance before HUAC in 1953, actor Lee J. Cobb testified that he and Lyon had belonged to the same Communist party group. The same year a writer and former Communist named Pauline Swanson Townsend told HUAC the story of her moving from Los Angeles to New York City, a move that had required her to present a CPUSA transfer slip to a representative of the New York branch of the party who had been notified to contact her. The person who contacted her was Peter Lyon.[53]

As for the other question left open in the *American Legion* article—the identity of "Peter Ivy," the mystery *Daily Worker* columnist—Budenz, in his FBI interview, pointed once again to Lyon, though not definitively, framing his statement as a qualified recollection. To add another element of doubt, Lyon's widow in later years categorically denied that her husband had written under the Ivy pseudonym. Whoever Peter Ivy might have been, the columns he wrote clearly served the purpose outlined by Budenz: to promote the career of acclaimed Popular Front auteur Norman Corwin and, specifically, to encourage a letter-writing campaign to keep his latest series, *Passport for Adams*, on the air. Predictably, Ivy lavished his highest praise—"undoubtedly the best of this wonderful series"—upon the episode that characterized the Soviet Union as a "young and powerful and amazing country," known especially for its humane treatment of prisoners of war. The show's pending cancellation, Ivy warned, would be a "cultural tragedy."[54]

For anti-Communists within the Radio Writers Guild, the details about Lyon might have been difficult to pin down—and remain a bit hazy today—but they continued to regard his union leadership with growing suspicion and harbored doubts as well about the guild's parent organization, the Authors League of America. Some even suspected that Lyon and his allies were placing ideological interests ahead of successful contract negotiations. Although convinced of the pro-Communist nature of Lyon's faction, anti-Communists were frustrated by their inability to expose their opponents' agenda in any definitive way, no matter how many times they tried to smoke them out.

In one early attempt, in January 1947, an eastern region council member issued a challenge to his fellow guild officers. "If we are a Communist front organization, let's admit it," he said, "but if we are not, let's be able to prove that we are not." According to an FBI informant, Lyon "scoffed" at this proposal, dismissed it as "nonsense," and refused to discuss the issue. At the close of 1949, after several other failed attempts to provoke a revealing response, a writer stood up at a membership meeting and came right out and accused Lyon of being pro-Communist and demanded that he declare whether this was true or not. Despite being cornered, Lyon managed to craft an answer that managed neither to "affirm or deny a belief in communism," leaving his opponents even more exasperated.[55]

The issue finally came to a head several months later, after the invasion of South Korea brought the cold war to a boil. At the July 25 meeting of the eastern region council, Welbourn Kelley proposed a resolution that he and his allies thought would both serve an honorable purpose and force their adversaries out into the open:

> Recognizing that writers in all media are of the utmost importance in the dissemination of vital information during a time of national crisis, now therefore be it resolved that the Eastern Region of the Radio Writers Guild urges the Authors League of America to offer to the proper United States Government officials the League's fullest cooperation in any non-political or educational capacity in which the League or its Guilds may be of service.[56]

James Hart, an alleged Lyon ally, responded to the resolution by saying that America "had no business in Korea," while another council member, Jack Bentkover, sounding like a *Daily Worker* editorial, declared that America's only purpose in the war was "to smash Korean labor unions." Lyon himself moved to table the resolution, and the council carried the motion by a vote of four to three. But Kelley was not quite done. He pressed on with a second resolution. Acknowledging that the council had refused to vote for or against cooperation with the government at a time when American troops were fighting Communist forces, the new resolution stipulated that it was the council's position not to work with the U.S. government if "such cooperation places the Guild or its members in opposition to Communism."[57]

This baiting tactic got its response. Chairman Sheldon Stark immediately ruled that the resolution was out of order, and the council upheld the ruling on the grounds that the issue "involved discussion of a political matter." In an attempt to underscore the supposedly nonpolitical stance of the majority, Bentkover then proposed a motion stating that the council's refusal to consider Kelley's resolution "did not involve any expression of sentiment on the issue of cooperation or noncooperation with the United States government." After the council passed Bentkover's motion, Kelley resigned in protest.[58]

Still determined to clarify the issue, Henry Denker, Ruth Adams Knight, and other anti-Communists proposed a resolution at a September membership meeting that demanded the guild "denounce Communism, the Communist Party, fascism, and totalitarianism in all forms." Once more the council took the most slippery course available, deciding to let the Authors League decide, while adding its own resolution that forbade the guild to take any political position whatsoever.[59]

From the anti-Communists' perspective, the council's actions revealed its extreme ideological bent, no matter what the camouflage. Certainly, from any perspective, the confrontations exposed the Lyon faction's rationalizations. The leadership's claim that they could not take any political stand was demonstrably false. Just two years before the Korean War resolution, they had endorsed a condemnation of the aggressively anti-Red Mundt-Nixon Bill. Their apolitical principles arose, apparently, only when the political gesture threatened to oppose communism. Even among those who accepted the nonpolitical policy at face value, the argument was debatable. Morton Wishengrad maintained that, as a trade union, the Radio Writers Guild was "not exempt from acting in concert with the overwhelming majority of American trade unions in denouncing an act of Communist aggression and in defending democracy," and that other unions had passed such a resolution "without in any way diminishing their economic effectiveness."[60]

By the time of these guild battles, *Counterattack* had already raised suspicions about Lyon, the Radio Writers Guild, and other broadcast unions. Old evidence available at the time, augmented by new revelations from recent years, may not add up to the dire, imminent crisis that the *Counterattack* publishers had outlined when *Red Channels* was released, but the combined information does lend credence to their concerns and establishes, at the least, that the CPUSA was attempting to influence the broadcast business. The apt question is not so much whether there was a Communist campaign in this field but what should have been done about it. Was the situation truly serious enough to warrant raising an alarm about people like Jean Muir? She was hardly the best example that Keenan, Kirkpatrick, and Bierly could cite to make their case.

Was there any reason to believe that Muir played a significant role in CPUSA activities? On one side of the ledger were her denials of and explanations for her various front associations, which fit the pattern of an idealistic liberal who had not bothered to analyze every detail of the organizations she might have aligned herself with. On the other side, as *Counterattack* was eager to point out, was the 1940 testimony of John L. Leech, who claimed that Muir once belonged to a Communist study group in Hollywood. But here the newsletter stood on shaky ground. This was the same John Leech who had identified Fredric March as a Communist and whose credibility was described in a *Counterattack* memo as "extremely doubtful." Perhaps more revealing was a news clip in the *Counterattack* files dating back to 1936. Written by future Pulitzer Prize–winner Ernie Pyle, the article was a celebrity profile of Muir that described her as someone who "doesn't make small talk," someone who "has a social conscience. In fact, she is a worker in the 'cause.' She is Hollywood's radical."[61] Not meant to smear her, the article merely acknowledged that Muir was part of the movie industry's dedicated leftist crowd. The picture that emerges from the piece is that Muir might have dabbled in the Communist politics that had become fashionable in Hollywood during those early Popular Front years. Even so, this sort of political background did not qualify her as a potent Soviet agent of influence.

Regardless of her actual place in the larger scheme of things, the upshot of Muir's case would hinge primarily on perception rather than fact. This was understood very well by radio writer Erik Barnouw, a liberal and a critic of *Red Channels*, who resigned his position on the eastern region council of the Radio Writers Guild after the scuttling of the Korean War resolution. In his letter explaining the reasons for his decision, he discussed the rumors that a Communist faction was "trying to dominate" the guild and, more to the point, focused on the council's response to the accusations. Those council officers who dismissed the allegations as "politics," Barnouw maintained, "are living in a cloud." For the rest of the country, the idea of Communist infiltration at a time of war against Communist forces was not something to be belittled. Both the public and rank-and-file guild members were "entitled to reassurance," something that could be achieved by a new election of council officers and the simple democratic principle of candidates who are willing to "state what they stand for."[62]

Fanning the flames of conspiracy thinking were, of course, vehement right-wingers who for many years had been agitating against Communists. In one sense, some of these conservatives, who had supported the America First isolationist movement before America's entry into World War II, should have been more forgiving of those who allowed themselves to associate with totalitarians. Columnist George Sokolsky, for instance, a fierce critic of Communist-front activity, had once defended the indefensible Merwin K. Hart, of the New York State Economic Council, and the

Reverend Gerald L. K. Smith, which qualified him, by the standards that he himself set, as at the very least a fascist dupe.[63]

The perception that the country faced a threat was underscored on the broader national scene on September 23, less than a month after the Muir story broke, when an overwhelming majority in Congress voted to override Truman's veto and authorize the McCarran Internal Security Act. Originally called the Mundt-Nixon bill, this sweeping anti-subversive law not only required the registration of Communist-front organizations but also authorized the detention of suspected disloyal citizens in time of war or national emergency.

As long as leaders of broadcast organizations would not, or could not, provide forthright reassurances, the perception of conspiracy would continue to hover above the industry. In such an atmosphere the front records of people like Jean Muir assumed far greater importance than they deserved. At one end of the political spectrum, Communists had succeeded in blurring the line between themselves and liberals, and many liberals, in turn, had failed to distance themselves from extremists. On the other side, right-wing zealots were all too quick to conclude the worst from inconclusive evidence. These forces combined into a formidable array of confusion and alarm that was sure to produce a purge mentality.

As for actual Communist activity within the broadcast industry, it was reasonable to monitor the phenomenon in a time of war, and to take measures that would contain potential problems. But in order to guard against anti-civil-libertarian excesses, those in charge needed to exercise level-headed analysis and maintain a sense of proportion. Neither of these qualities, unfortunately, was to be found in large supply among broadcast sponsors and network executives, who would ultimately make the crucial decisions. What they did possess, and in spades, was a clammy fear, not of totalitarianism but of the prospect of lost short-term profits.

FOUR

Comrades of the Comrades

Counterattack had been keeping a watchful eye on CBS for some time. Not that the newsletter's publishers ignored the other broadcast outlets, but the so-called Tiffany Network incensed them most of all. This preoccupation was nothing unusual in certain political quarters.

The network's liberal news correspondents, led by Edward R. Murrow, and its Popular Front dramatists, exemplified by Norman Corwin, had long made the Columbia Broadcasting System the bane of right-wingers everywhere. According to the author Robert Metz, J. Edgar Hoover had once told CBS head William S. Paley that the network might best be called the Communist Broadcasting System. In the eyes of Hoover's protégés—Keenan, Kirkpatrick, and Bierly—CBS was riddled with writers, performers, and reporters who hewed altogether too close to the party line. The network's executives were not pro-Communist, but they had a habit, *Counterattack* claimed, of employing people who "at the very least are comrades of the comrades."[1]

Occupying such a vulnerable position as the most left-leaning network, CBS explored ways of fending off further attacks well before *Red Channels* appeared. As early as July 1949, after *Counterattack* published a scathing article on the network, CBS attorney Joseph H. Ream arranged the first of several meetings with Kirkpatrick to solicit his advice on how best to identify and purge Communists at the network. News executive

71

Sid Mickelson noticed some results from this effort a few months later. In January 1950, CBS president Frank Stanton presented him with a list of alleged Red sympathizers who were not to be employed by the network. Most likely this was one of the undocumented lists of so-called undesirables that had come to *Counterattack's* attention and had prompted its publishers to assemble a list of their own. CBS tried to inoculate itself further by subscribing to *Counterattack* and distributing the newsletter to its executives as a guide to future hiring choices. In April, though, more unwanted attention came the network's way. That was when one of its radio directors, Betty Todd, was implicated in the case of suspected Soviet agent William Remington. Called before HUAC, she invoked the Fifth Amendment and refused to answer questions regarding either Remington or the Communist party. When she returned from the hearings, CBS fired her.[2] Still, the company's upper management did not believe they had done enough. After the publication of *Red Channels* and the controversy triggered by the Jean Muir incident, the backpedaling quickened.

The job of protecting the network from further "Red network" allegations went to attorney Ream, who also served as executive vice president. A combination of homespun Americana and Ivy League sophistication, Ream polished his Kansas-bred perspectives while attending Yale Law School before starting his career as a Wall Street attorney. There he put his shrewd country-lawyer acumen to use in the cosmopolitan world of financial and corporate affairs. He came to CBS in 1934 as the network's general counsel and over the years acquired a reputation for being both incisive and scrupulous. Late in 1950 he confronted the challenge of devising some way, as he later put it, to "reassure the advertisers we weren't a nest of Commies." His solution was a questionnaire that became known as the CBS loyalty oath.[3]

What inspired Ream was the loyalty program instituted three years earlier by the Truman administration, which sought to deflect charges that it was soft on communism by requiring government employees to sign a statement disavowing any connection to subversive organizations. Another factor in Ream's calculations might have been a precedent set in the radio and TV industry the previous June, when KFI, a local Los Angeles broadcaster, had required its employees to sign an anti-Communist pledge. Ream's version posed three questions for CBS employees: Are you or have you ever been a member of the Communist party? Are you or have you ever been a member of a fascist organization? Are you or have you ever been a member of an organization advocating the overthrow of the American government? To clarify which groups were included in the third question, Ream provided on the back of the statement the attorney general's list of totalitarian and subversive organizations, though the company would show leniency toward front activities that dated back to the U.S.-Soviet alliance of World War II.

Although it was commonly called a loyalty oath, the term was a misnomer in the strict legal sense because signers did not have to swear to the truth of the statement before a notary public. Still, the requirement was rigorously enforced: all full-time CBS employees, numbering approximately 2,500, would be expected to sign. The only exception, the *New York Times* reported, were those who worked on programs aired by CBS but produced outside the network.[4]

Ream knew that his plan would be pointless unless it placated the watchdogs that were nipping at the network's heels, so he contacted Kirkpatrick early on in the process and made sure he had *Counterattack*'s approval. Ream also needed to know that the questionnaire would meet with as little resistance as possible within the network. To test the waters, he met with Murrow, not only the head of CBS news but also a member of the network's board of directors and, perhaps more important, the epitome of liberal-minded integrity who commanded the respect of both the network's journalists and creative personnel. Murrow opposed the influence of *Red Channels*, but he was also as pragmatic a man as he was principled. After Ream explained the practical necessity of the oath, the newsman reluctantly gave his approval. Armed with his backing from both conservative and liberal perspectives, Ream now brought his proposal to president Frank Stanton, who, as Ream later told author Sally Bedell Smith, approved the program "right quick."[5]

Over the course of his distinguished career, Stanton represented for many of his colleagues the highest principles of broadcasting, especially so in 1971 when he became a First Amendment hero for his refusal to cooperate with an intrusive congressional probe of a CBS exposé of the Pentagon. In a typical assessment, a former associate remembered him as "the most moral man I ever met in this industry."[6] But Stanton's decision to approve the loyalty oath had less to do with absolute morality than with relative values and a sense of expediency.

In addition to the fear that advertisers might withdraw from a politi-cally suspect network, Stanton believed that affiliate stations would stop carrying CBS programming if the network didn't act decisively. More than that, according to former CBS executive Alan Wagner, Stanton feared that the licenses of the network's stations were in peril. "I think he felt if he didn't do this, the FCC was going to come down or Congress was go-ing to come down and clobber us in a way that would be ultimately dev-astating." Reviewing his actions from the vantage point of the late 1990s, Stanton would say that he could not "look back on that period and be proud of it."[7] At the time, though, he believed he had no choice but to act as he did.

Was the situation truly as dire as he thought? The FCC did indeed have the authority to pressure broadcasters and theoretically could have crippled a network by refusing to renew licenses for its affiliate stations. Whether the commission was actually inclined to do so is another matter. As FCC scholar Susan L. Brinson has pointed out, the commission scru-tinized alleged Communist influence at two broadcast companies in the late 1940s but did not deny licenses to either of them. Neither did the FCC during this period show any inclination to interfere in broadcasters' programming decisions. In Brinson's opinion, the commission "was un-likely to punish CBS by causing licensing review problems." True, CBS did not have the benefit of scholarly hindsight at the time, but neither did its executives have the resolve to put the issue to the test. Even Paley, the most powerful person at the network, seemed to regard himself as power-less in this situation, or at least characterized his situation in that way. Once, in discussing *Counterattack* with Stanton, he reportedly said, "If I didn't have stockholders, I would fight these guys."[8] Ultimately CBS would be alone among the networks in imposing a loyalty oath for its en-tire staff (NBC required a similar statement from new employees)—and those networks that did not take this step were never penalized by the FCC.

One broadcaster in particular had recently demonstrated that it was possible to stand up to pressures from the anti-Red watchdogs. In mid-September, Edward Clamage of the Illinois American Legion had sent a telegram of protest to Robert Kintner, president of ABC, concerning the upcoming premiere of *What Makes You Tick?*, a radio quiz show to be hosted by Gypsy Rose Lee. The stripper turned writer-actress was listed in

At CBS, network president Frank Stanton (left) authorized the loyalty oath to appease the blacklisters while newsman Edward R. Murrow went along with the process as he waited for the opportunity to take a public stand on other cold war issues. *(CBS Photo Archive/Getty Images)*

Red Channels, and Clamage regarded her as "a dear and close associate of the traitors of our country," someone who most definitely did not belong on the American airwaves. After Lee denied the pro-Communist charges, Kintner wired back a demand that the American Legion prove the allegations. Clamage, forced into the position of having to supply something other than demagoguery, could do nothing more than pass the buck, responding, quite lamely, that "the answer should come from the publishers of *Red Channels*." The *Counterattack* partners, in turn, also dodged responsibility. They would offer no further information than had already appeared in the booklet's citations based on public records, Kirkpatrick told the press, because ultimately it was up to the reader to judge the significance of the allegations.[9] A more likely rationale for the company's decision was that the publishers knew themselves that the Lee citations were insignificant.

By issuing its commonsense challenge to the American Legion, ABC succeeded in keeping Lee on the air without suffering any important hardship. Not only that, seven months later the network received a special Peabody Award honoring its refusal to cave in to "organized pressure." As for Clamage and the Illinois American Legion, their actions invited public ridicule, especially from the *New York Post*. Referring to Lee's original profession, the newspaper quipped, "Perhaps Clamage has mixed his metaphors: he may associate Miss Lee with what he thinks is the modern Communist battle-cry: 'Take it off, you have nothing to lose but your chains!'"[10]

Some might have been inspired to emulate ABC's defiance, but not the executives at CBS. Instead they chose to move in the opposite direction by announcing plans to institute their loyalty oath on December 20, 1950. At the same time, the *New York Times* reported, the network announced it would tighten security by hiring armed guards to prevent a takeover of transmitters or control rooms in a time of emergency. If there was, in fact, a need for CBS to reassure the public—as Erik Barnouw had demanded of the Radio Writers Guild three months earlier—the new security precautions to protect its facilities might have been sufficient. As for the loyalty oath, it might have produced, if anything, the very opposite effect.

By demanding a signed statement from all its employees rather than concentrating on just those with access to its most sensitive broadcast operations, the network was implying that the problem was potentially more widespread than the public might have otherwise assumed. If secretaries and pages were under suspicion, the public was more likely to believe that the entire network was operating under a cloud of conspiracy.

Counterattack praised the CBS move, going so far as to suggest that its readers write congratulatory letters to Ream. But others in the broadcast unions and the mainstream media decried the loyalty statement. Once again Jack Gould of the *New York Times* offered a well-reasoned critique. Not only did the new CBS policy contribute to a gathering alarmism that blurred the issues, Gould wrote, but "never in a thousand years will it turn up the avowed and active Communist" who would have no compunction about lying to cover up his or her true beliefs and intentions. A far more effective measure, Gould concluded, would have been a concerted effort to air "hard-hitting and factual programs which make plain the imminence of the Communist danger" and "emphasize positively the advantages of democracy."[11]

Opposition could also be found within the ranks of CBS. According to Murrow biographer Joseph Persico, a potential mutiny began brewing in the news department when Bill Downs, Eric Sevareid, Charles Collingwood, Alexander Kendrick, Don Hollenbeck, and David Schoenbrun all resisted the idea of signing the statement. But the uprising didn't last long. Murrow, living up to his agreement with Ream, convinced his disgruntled subordinates that their refusal would serve no practical purpose. The news chief fended off outside pressure as well, Persico wrote, when Morris Ernst of the ACLU told him he should refuse to sign, reasoning that Murrow was the one executive at CBS with both the integrity and the prestige to be able to defy the new policy successfully and set an example for others. Murrow declined, relying on a pragmatic argument once again. "I have too many fights on my hands," he explained, "and I'll weaken my position on them if I fail to sign." Efforts within the unions were just as ineffectual. The Radio Writers Guild succeeded in gaining a delay for its members in complying with the new procedure, in the hope it might negotiate a less objectionable statement to sign, but within a month most writers at the network had already met the new requirement. For anyone wondering what would be the consequence of not signing, the question was answered in no uncertain terms by late January. A female office worker told Ream that she was not a member of any of the suspect groups listed on the statement, but still, as "a point of principle," she would not sign. She was promptly fired.[12]

Those who believed the loyalty program would encourage a purgelike atmosphere would not have to wait long to see their predictions become reality, and not only at CBS. The new attitude became most visible in the case of Philip Loeb.

A veteran character actor, Loeb had given his first Broadway performance in 1916 and had appeared since in some thirty plays, the most recent of which was *Me and Molly*, a stage adaptation of the popular radio series *The Goldbergs*, featuring Loeb as the father of the titular family. He went on to reprise the role in the TV version that premiered on CBS in January 1949, sponsored by General Foods. *Counterattack* quickly registered a protest. At a meeting in February, Kirkpatrick warned a General Foods executive that Loeb was a Communist party member, though at the time the sponsor saw no need to act. The appearance in *Red Channels* of Loeb's name along with seventeen front associations also produced no immediate effect, but letters of protest arrived at the offices of the network and the sponsor—four letters, to be exact.[13] Still, in the closing months of 1950, even the smallest ripple of a protest could put broadcast executives on edge.

For now, General Foods wavered, unsure which of its critics it should reassure. The company was embarrassed by the indignant response to its decision to remove Muir from *The Aldrich Family*, and it tried appeasing its critics in late September by declaring that it would fire no other performers in such a rash manner. For now, at least, this meant that Loeb would appear in the new season of *The Goldbergs* despite his listing in *Red Channels*.[14] For all the public posturing about resisting outside pressure— pressure exerted, at least at first, by four letters—General Foods was already hedging its bets behind the scenes. The sponsor began talking to Gertrude Berg, the show's star, writer, and owner, about the possibility of replacing Loeb with another actor.

The targeting of Loeb was not entirely arbitrary. A politically active member of Actors Equity, he had attracted controversy more than once before, most noticeably in 1940 when U.S. congressman William Lambertson accused him and six other Equity officials of being Communists. Nothing came of the accusation, and no public evidence ever indicated that Loeb was a CPUSA member. Secret investigations by the FBI corroborated this assessment. Although the Bureau considered Loeb "at least a Communist sympathizer," it concluded in 1949 that he was not a party member and saw no reason to monitor him further. But Loeb tended to add fuel to controversy's fire by aligning himself with inflammatory causes before exercising a healthy dose of skepticism. Among his front associations was his service as an officer in the Theatre Arts Committee, the Broadway group that revealed a distinct Soviet bent during the years of the nonaggression pact. Even though Loeb himself had sided with those seeking to aid Finnish victims of Soviet aggression, his involvement with TAC was a black mark against his name in the eyes of anti-Communists. More distressing was his earlier willingness, in 1938, to sign a statement in support of the Moscow purge trials. Even more recently, he still failed on occasion to discriminate between progressive unionism and CPUSA machinations. As late as May 1950 he sent a written tribute to the funeral of Bob Reed in honor of the man's contributions to Actors Equity, as if completely unaware that Reed had been the party's principal organizer in the union. Assuming Loeb did not know of Reed's place in the Communist party hierarchy—and perhaps he was that naive—he still might have thought twice about placing himself in the company of such other eulogists as V. J. Jerome and Samuel Sillen, both high-ranking CPUSA functionaries, who praised "Comrade Robert Reed" as a tireless fighter "in the cause of the Party."[15]

Loeb's political life provides an instructive example of how the Communist movement could make a careless ally out of a non-Communist leftist. His endorsement of the Moscow trials, in particular, provides an especially egregious instance of how a non-Stalinist could allow himself to defend totalitarian repression at its most indefensible. None of this, though, made Loeb any more of a CPUSA functionary than Jean Muir had been. American Business Consultants, though they listed Loeb in *Red Channels*, gave him only the most cursory attention in the pages of *Counterattack* while devoting much space to other broadcast performers whom the firm apparently considered more important. Even from a hard-line anti-Red perspective, the purge of broadcasting was once again fastening its attention on an unlikely target.

Counterattack might not have marshaled a drumbeat against Loeb, but during the 1950–1951 television season General Foods received more letters objecting to Loeb's prominent place in *The Goldbergs* cast. The company continued to pressure Gertrude Berg to fire him. She wavered at one point—offering to buy out Loeb's contract for $85,000, which he refused—then resisted mightily. She later insisted that Loeb had told her that "he is not and never has been a Communist. I believe him."[16] She did not address the question of whether Loeb would have been entitled to keep his job even if he were a Communist. Typical of many in broadcasting, and of most of the country at a time of war, she was postponing, if not completely ignoring, the central civil liberties issue. Still, even Berg's more conservative, more easily defended position was not enough to dispel the sponsor's growing panic as the number of the protest letters reached one thousand. Seeing that it could not persuade Berg to abandon Loeb, General Foods withdrew from the program when the season ended in the spring of 1951.

Berg tried to conjure up a way to keep both the show on the air and Loeb in the cast. In August, after CBS failed to support her efforts, she took the program to NBC and began the search for a new sponsor. A month went by and the new fall 1951 season began, and still she had no success. Some companies were willing to back the program but not as long as Loeb was part of the package. Once more Berg attempted to stand by her co-star, yet by the beginning of 1952, after some twenty sponsors had turned her down, she realized her efforts were futile, and she decided to salvage what she could from the situation. She cast Harold Stone in the role of Papa Goldberg, secured three sponsors, and agreed to pay Loeb for the remaining two years on his contract.[17] *The Goldbergs* returned to air, without Loeb, on February 4, 1952.

While this controversy unfolded, others listed in *Red Channels* also faced difficulties.

Ireene Wicker was a children's programming personality, known as "The Singing Lady," who presented fairy tales by enacting all the voices of the stories' characters. A staple on radio since 1931, she had recently made the transition to TV in an ABC show sponsored by Kellogg when *Red Channels* listed her name. She had originally come under suspicion because she was married to Victor Hammer, son of one the founders of the American Communist party and brother of the famed industrialist Armand Hammer, who, according to recently uncovered documents, had laundered money for the Soviet Union. Wicker's husband Victor, however, was never implicated in his brother's schemes. The children's show host's one citation in *Red Channels* was a *Daily Worker* article that had listed her as a sponsor of the reelection committee for Communist New York City councilman Benjamin J. Davis. On August 6, Kellogg canceled her show despite its high audience rating. Setting a pattern for corporate evasiveness, the sponsor explained that the decision was "simply a matter of business."[18]

Wicker had some success in refuting the booklet's allegations—as opposed to those who knew they could not disprove them because they were more deeply involved in CPUSA activities than their allegations suggested. Her lawyer obtained Davis's nominating petitions, none of which, it turned out, included the performer's name. In the face of this evidence, and in accordance with its stated policy of allowing its targets to present their side of the story, *Counterattack* published Wicker's denial in its October 27 issue. The lawyer's discovery was dramatic and, in some people's eyes, convincing, but it failed to address the actual allegation. *Red Channels* had never said that Wicker signed a nominating petition, only that she was a member of Davis's reelection committee. This might be the reason Wicker's career did not immediately rebound, but neither did her career suffer the catastrophic reversal that some writers have claimed. While fighting the lingering suspicions in the broadcast industry about her loyalty, she performed a series of children's plays at New York City's Barbizon Plaza Hotel, then found a new entrée into radio on a local station in North Adams, Massachusetts. In 1952 she returned to New York City broadcasting with her own television series on WABD and the following year moved on to another show for ABC-TV.[19]

Others who denied or explained their *Red Channels* listings in the pages of *Counterattack* included scriptwriter Samson Raphaelson, folksinger Josh White, and actors Meg Mundy and Burgess Meredith. Despite their efforts to exonerate themselves, their careers all suffered.

Sometimes the effect of *Red Channels* could be less direct. Pert Kelton, who had two citations in the booklet, was a successful comedic character actress, known for her tart-tongued delivery of murderous one-liners. She made the transition from radio to TV by becoming a regular on Jackie Gleason's *Cavalcade of Stars* for the DuMont Network, where she created the character of Alice Kramden on the original "Honeymooners" sketches and, with Gleason's backing, continued on the show through the 1951–1952 season, well after *Red Channels*'s publication. When Gleason prepared to take his show to CBS the next year, he promised to keep her in his troupe. That summer they went on a promotional tour to perform the "Honeymooners" routines at movie houses in five cities. In Chicago, Kelton became ill but insisted on doing the four shows scheduled that day. Perhaps she felt that, with a cloud over her head, she couldn't afford to miss a performance, even for one day. Whatever the motive, the consequences of the decision were devastating. She ended up hospitalized with a heart attack. Gleason wanted to include her in his CBS show's premiere that September, but she could not recuperate in time, and Audrey Meadows took her place.[20]

As for those with clear ties to the Communist party, the prospects were even grimmer. Pete Seeger, formerly of the party-line Almanac Singers, had been a follower in the Communist cause since the early 1940s. He was now part of a new folk group, the Weavers, and his prolific songwriting and charismatic performing were instrumental in elevating the quartet from the relative obscurity of progressive fund-raisers and trade-union musicales to elegant nightclub gigs and best-selling records. While with the Weavers in 1950 and 1951, Seeger was no longer singing anything quite as incendiary as his hands-off-Hitler tunes from the nonaggression pact days—at least not when performing in mainstream venues—and in fact he and his new group had been criticized by their more radical associates for becoming too commercial. Even so, the CPUSA still regarded the Weavers as valuable cultural workers.[21] This view that the singers were close to the party was shared by American Business Consultants. The combination of Seeger's listing in *Red Channels* and a *Counterattack*-instigated letter-writing campaign led to the cancellation of a Weavers appearance on the *Garroway at Large* TV show in June 1951. Before long Seeger was banned from the major broadcast outlets altogether and would not return to network TV until 1967.

The media disappearance of Communist activist Dashiell Hammett was just as sudden and complete. At the time his name appeared in *Red Channels*, much of the mystery author's income was generated by three radio series based on his stories—*The Adventures of the Thin Man*, *The Adventures of Sam Spade, Detective*, and *The Fat Man*. By the end of 1951 all were canceled. Not another show based on Hammett's work would appear on the airwaves until 1957, just four years before his death.

When they founded *Counterattack* in 1947, Keenan, Kirkpatrick, and Bierly had sought to exert an influence upon the domestic struggle against communism. Now, in the field of broadcasting, they had succeeded perhaps more than they had ever anticipated. At times it seemed they were not quite sure they wanted to take credit for their newfound stature and the impact they had on people's lives.

Counterattack's September 13, 1950, issue announced their official position on the broadcast purge, which might charitably be called nuanced but perhaps more accurately would be described as confused. The newsletter categorically declared that *Red Channels* "was not meant to be used as a 'blacklist' in the industry," yet a few paragraphs later it underscored the need for a blacklist by saying that "no sponsor of any radio or TV program should have a totalitarian of any kind on the air." In response to the accusation that the company had set itself up as a Star Chamber, the newsletter reiterated what Kirkpatrick had recently been telling the press: "no individual should have the right to 'absolve' or convict anyone, in or out of radio, of pro-Communist leanings." The newsletter continued, "When all the facts are brought out . . . as they should be . . . the public will decide such issues." Despite this claim that they were above the fray, the publishers consistently prodded the public by urging protests against the employment of certain actors, writers, and directors. The firm's internal communications revealed a similar activist sentiment. In a report on the release of an anti-atom-bomb song, *Counterattack*'s West Coast researcher warned that something "should happen damn quick or else 'Old Man Atom' will be a radio hit."[22]

The contradictory stances reflected some difference of opinion among the principals. Although Bierly had once articulated the third-violinist theory, he could also at other times advocate a more cautious approach. In the case, for instance, of news commentators and talk-show guests with front affiliations, he did not think they should necessarily be barred from the air. Rather, he wanted their backgrounds brought into the open to counteract what he considered "a fraud on the public." Keenan, in contrast, pulled no punches, believing unequivocally that the firm must strive to "get rid of the Commie." Going even further, he had no sympathy for those even loosely associated with the Communist movement. "Performers who've been duped by the Commie front groups," he said, "should suffer for their sins." Somewhere in between hovered Kirkpatrick, who maintained that broadcast personnel should be taken off the air, but only if they had a "significant and continuing record."[23]

Despite this mixed message, the partners attracted their share of staunch supporters, especially among fiercely anti-Communist newspaper columnists such as George Sokolsky and Victor Riesel. *Counterattack*'s growing prominence also stirred an equally fierce opposition. Networks and sponsors might have been cowed by the newsletter's attacks, but many others felt free to denounce what they considered a trend toward repression.

Through the fall of 1950 and into the spring of 1951, public rallies protested the influence of *Red Channels*, one of them adopting the especially provocative slogan "Crack the Back of Counterattack." Several of these events were organized by the National Council of the Arts, Sciences and Professions, a fact that *Counterattack* seized upon in discrediting these meetings. A front organization, the NCASP had been the principal sponsor of the notorious Waldorf Peace Conference, a thinly veiled pro-Soviet event. *Counterattack*'s accusations aside, the NCASP's own actions had already undermined its claim to be a champion of unfettered cultural freedom. Just months before, in April 1950, the group had organized pickets to protest the concert appearance of operatic soprano Kirsten Flagstad, who had been under a cloud since 1941 for returning to her native Norway to be with her husband, an alleged Nazi collaborator. For the leaders of the NCASP, apparently, attacking the livelihood of artists for alleged associations with totalitarianism was only wrong when it involved those people on their side of the political spectrum.[24]

Not as easy for *Counterattack* to dismiss were the outraged columns of reputable liberals, not only Gould of the *Times* but also Rex Lardner of the *New York Post* and John Crosby of the *New York Herald Tribune*. Crosby, in particular, brought up an especially persistent issue among *Counterattack* critics when he wrote that the motives of Keenan, Kirkpatrick, and Bierly were "open to question, if not downright sinister."[25]

Many were ready to pose this question, and some had already supplied an answer: the motivation for the *Counterattack* publishers was pure, unmitigated greed, and the method for satisfying that greed was no different from those tactics used by any other protection racket. By the end of 1950 the charge of racketeering was already circulating among *Red Channels* opponents. Over the years the allegation would gather momentum, and recent histories of the period have repeated it as established fact.

What is the source of this charge? The first publication to accuse *Counterattack* of extortion-style tactics might have been an obscure journal put out by a leftist CIO union, but the exposé that is most often cited appeared in the July 17, 1950, issue of a weekly newsletter called *In Fact*. Edited and written by George Seldes, the newsletter asserted that Keenan, Kirkpatrick, and Bierly originally formed American Business Consultants as a way "to cash in on the cold war." The article then provided a specific example of *Counterattack*'s shakedown tactics within the broadcast industry by relating an incident involving Thomas Brady, one of *Counterattack*'s representatives, and the Hutchins Agency, an advertising firm that supervised the broadcasting account of the Philco appliance company. In February 1950, according to Seldes, Brady met with Hutchins executives at their offices and told them they were using an actress who was a "commie" on Philco's show—a serious problem, Brady stressed, but not a problem that could not be solved. For a fee of one thousand dollars, American Business Consultants could provide all the information the agency needed to make sure this sort of mistake never happened again. When the agency failed to take Brady up on his offer, *Counterattack* proceeded to punish the firm by publishing an article that condemned Philco for using the suspect actress and "urged its readers to protest."[26]

As was to be expected, the *Counterattack* partners offered another version of this incident. They conceded that the company had sent Brady (Keenan's brother-in-law) to solicit business from advertising agencies as part of the research services the firm offered apart from its publishing operations, but Keenan characterized the Hutchins affair as a misunderstanding. Brady had met an executive who "talked like one of those fellow travelers," Keenan said, and the two naturally began to argue. Keenan suggested that in the heat of the moment Brady might have said some things that exacerbated the situation. Within two months *Counterattack* did indeed publish a story on Philco Television Playhouse, focusing on the appearance of actress Adelaide Klein and describing her as a Communist fronter. Kirkpatrick claimed, however, that Sam Horn, who wrote the piece, was not aware of the Hutchins incident.[27]

Going beyond the conflicting versions of the event, there are reasons to take issue with Seldes' conclusion. Although the Hutchins episode is the only example he mentioned of *Counterattack* strong-arming, he considered this sufficient to intimate that the newsletter was waging a systematic campaign of extortion throughout the broadcast industry. His attempt to generalize from this incident was weak. After reporting that the Hutchins Agency rebuffed Brady, he wrote, "No one knows, however, how many sponsors, stations, and advertising agencies have subscribed to Counterattack's special services, considering $1,000 a cheap price for protection from annoyances like those experienced by Philco."[28] While straining to imply that *Counterattack* routinely used high-pressure tactics, Seldes revealed that he had no information to back up the claim.

Seldes' reasons for tugging the largest conclusion out of the smallest amount of information should not be mysterious. Although he has been lionized in recent years as a fiercely independent journalist, he wasn't particularly independent when it came to challenging party-line appraisals of current events. An early critic of the Soviet Union, he changed his tune in the mid-1930s and from then on stayed close behind the party's lead by rationalizing the Moscow purge trials and the nonaggression pact, and condemning U.S. policies after World War II as an inexorable march toward fascism.[29]

If Seldes' slanted reporting were the only basis for the charges against *Counterattack*, there would be reason to doubt the allegations. But over the years other information emerged to buttress Seldes' claim. Late in 1950 an advertising executive at Young & Rubicam named David Jacobson recalled that Kirkpatrick once gave him a call after *Counterattack* had published an article about an actor in one of the agency's shows. Previously Kirkpatrick had suggested that Jacobson's agency should hire *Counterattack*'s research service. "It's kind of funny," Kirkpatrick now broadly hinted, "but some agencies always seem to have this kind of trouble, and some never do." A similar incident was revealed in an FBI report concerning Kirkpatrick's 1949 visit to General Foods about their use of Philip Loeb in *The Goldbergs*. When Kirkpatrick proposed that the sponsor subscribe to *Counterattack*, the General Foods executive regarded this as "a mild threat" that the newsletter might feature a story on Loeb if the sponsor did not subscribe.[30]

Other writers have leveled another charge of virtual extortion against the *Counterattack* partners, one that is much less convincing: they assert that blacklistees would have to pay the newsletter a fee in order to obtain clearance and resume working. But writers such as Walter Bernstein and Mona Z. Smith who have made this charge cite no examples. Contradicting them is John Cogley, a researcher for a liberal think tank, who concluded in the mid-1950s that there was no evidence that American Business Consultants charged clearance fees. More recent accounts of those who approached *Counterattack* in order to clear themselves also suggest that no fee was paid. A recent biography of Josh White, for instance, details the folksinger's experience as he met with the *Counterattack* editors to explain his front associations listed in *Red Channels*. Eventually the newsletter reported his act of contrition. Nowhere in the book's account is there any mention of money exchanging hands, though the author clearly has contempt for American Business Consultants and has no reason to withhold this sort of information.[31]

Still another, somewhat less noxious charge concerned the way the *Counterattack* publishers presented their FBI background to potential customers. Here the allegation was clearly true, but the three ex-agents were willing to rectify the situation. In the summer of 1949 the newsletter's subscription salesmen were approaching business owners with a credentials card that read: "The Undersigned, Former Special Agents of the Federal Bureau of Investigation, have commissioned the bearer, ————, to discuss with you a matter of the utmost importance." Beneath this were the names of Keenan, Kirkpatrick, and Bierly. Based upon a quick glance at the card, some potential customers got the impression that the newsletter was connected to the FBI. When confronted by a special agent from the Bureau about this matter, Kirkpatrick seemed genuinely concerned about the implications of the credentials and agreed to discontinue their use.[32]

Of all the charges, the one originated by Seldes alleging strong-arm tactics remains the most substantial. What Keenan, Kirkpatrick, and Bierly failed to understand or, more likely, willfully ignored was the unethical conflict of interest posed by selling research services to companies they reported on in their newsletter. Even so, equating their methods with criminal protection rackets is a stretch. To take the Jacobson story, for instance, it should be pointed out that when Kirkpatrick tried to sell research services to Young & Rubicam, Jacobson turned him down flat. And then, for good measure, he challenged Kirkpatrick by saying, "If you've got any charges to make against this agency, let's hear them." At this point,

according to Jacobson, Kirkpatrick backed down (not surprising considering that he had once been described as "not tough enough in finance collections").[33] The story makes it clear that Jacobson was not intimidated by
the *Counterattack* executive and had no trouble spurning him—hardly
the way a protection racket is supposed to work.

Another, larger factor to consider: if the *Counterattack* partners were
as ruthlessly exploitive as some of their critics claimed, it would be reasonable to assume that the firm was a thriving enterprise. The company
did, in fact, expand—in March 1950 the firm had moved to a larger suite
of seven offices at 55 West Forty-second Street and by the fall was employing fourteen people—but this did not necessarily mean it was awash
in profits. *Counterattack* brought in a little more than five thousand subscriptions at $24 each per year, for an annual total of more than $100,000.
Costs and debits, though, had their effect. In 1951, according to a
Newsweek report, the special research projects, which had so often been
condemned as an extortionary practice, suffered a loss of approximately
$24,000. After figuring in salaries and other expenses, profits to stockhold-
ing members of the staff that year amounted to only $666. As for salaries
for the principals, Kirkpatrick and Bierly each received $6,000 a year
while Keenan received no salary at all, relying instead on his work at the
law firm of Alexander & Keenan for his income.[34]

If the *Counterattack* partners had, in 1947, been looking for something
to "cash in on," as Seldes claimed, they could have found more lucrative
ventures to pursue. Keenan and Bierly, in particular, with both law degrees and FBI experience, could have easily made a comfortable living.
Instead all three chose a more uncertain route. The more likely explanation for the partners' choice was the one they themselves offered: a deeply
felt commitment to their cause. The troubling excesses of the company
probably had less to do with avarice than with pushing their crusade to an
extreme. For them the questionable coupling of consulting and journalism was a means to an end. Any research projects they performed would
advance the cause they believed in, and the income from these ventures
would help them continue in their work.

Perhaps more disturbing than the racketeering allegations was the
partners' high-handed manner in dealing with those people who sought to
clear their names. As a *New York Post* story reported at the time, Ireene
Wicker went to the *Counterattack* offices to meet with Kirkpatrick after

her show had been canceled, and explained that she had had nothing to do with the Benjamin Davis campaign as had been alleged in *Red Channels*. Not only was Kirkpatrick skeptical about her denial, he insisted she prove that she was more than merely non-Communist. Prepared to document her pro-Americanism, Wicker presented copies of scripted patriotic material performed on her show, but this made little impression. Neither did she help herself by telling him that "much of my work was deeply religious." "Just being religious is negative," Kirkpatrick interjected, "what have you done positive against Communism?"[35]

Kirkpatrick, usually the one to handle these negotiations, was convinced he was helping those who came to discuss their political record, shepherding them back into the fold of responsible citizenship. Consumed with political righteousness, he could get prickly when one of his reclamation projects failed to heed his guidance, as folksinger Oscar Brand discovered in the latter half of 1949. After *Counterattack* denounced him for his Communist-front affiliations, Brand contacted Kirkpatrick to explain that he had appeared at front events purely as a paid entertainer, not as an ideological supporter, and apparently assured Kirkpatrick that he would refrain from similar engagements in the future. When Kirkpatrick learned that the folksinger subsequently appeared at an event sponsored by the front group People's Artists, he called Brand demanding to know how he could have done such a thing after their discussion. He maintained that Brand's recent appearance was no better than if the *Counterattack* publishers had attended an event staged by the fascist Gerald L. K. Smith.[36] Kirkpatrick and his partners were so convinced of the need to regulate other people's associations that they viewed any backsliding on that score to be a personal affront.

Brand's attitude also reveals how difficult it could be for some entertainers to separate themselves from the front movement, either because of their naiveté or professional inconvenience. In a letter to *Counterattack*, Brand mentioned that he had recently performed for a front event, but he saw no problem "so long as they pay and don't try to use me as a lure or a dupe"—even though, as Kirkpatrick undoubtedly pointed out, his very appearance helped legitimize the event. When Kirkpatrick confronted him about his latest association with People's Artists, Brand replied that he understood the significance of the group's political intentions but added that it "has such a monopoly on arranging engagements for folksingers." This was no small matter for Brand. *Counterattack*'s article about him had made it difficult to find work with other groups.[37]

Cooperating and suffering in silence were common routes followed by those listed in *Red Channels*, but not everyone was willing to confine themselves to these alternatives. In the fall of 1950 those interested in taking a more aggressive approach were invited by ACLU attorney Arthur Garfield Hays to attend a meeting to consider legal action.

An eminent civil-liberties advocate of long standing, Hays had accumulated enough wealth from his lucrative corporate practice that he could afford to champion such causes over the years as the Scopes trial and the Sacco-Vanzetti case. Challenging the broadcast blacklist was his latest crusade. Actor Joseph Julian, one of the *Red Channels* listees who gathered in Hays's office, recalled that the lawyer "offered to represent everyone individually on a contingency basis," but only if "they could convince him that they had in fact been libeled." Not everyone there welcomed the proposal. Some preferred a single legal action that would include all of those present, but Hays dismissed the idea. As Julian recalled, Hays suspected that these people wanted to pursue "the group action in order to use us to mask their membership or former membership in the Communist Party."[38] Four actors at the meeting, confident they could prove their listings were false or misleading, agreed to take Hays up on his offer. Julian, Selena Royle, Ralph Bell, and Pert Kelton would each demand more than $100,000 in damages.

By early 1951 the opposition to *Red Channels* was digging in its heels, prepared to fight what seemed to be a formidable enemy. But what they didn't know was that fissures were already beginning to crack the *Counterattack* foundation, exposing widening differences among the company's partners. Kenneth Bierly, who had already expressed a preference for a more measured approach to the issue of communism in broadcasting, began to reconsider his role in American Business Consultants. In April he decided to leave the company.

To a certain extent the problem might have been personal. Bierly and Keenan embodied strikingly different approaches to the company's work, one cautious, methodical, and the other more daring, sometimes brusque. Fellow FBI agent Charles Blaisdell was a friend and admirer of Keenan, but he was also aware that his friend could sometimes be difficult, even with those on his side. "Jack was a guy who felt he was right," Blaisdell recalled, "and if you agreed with him then it was fine, but if you disagreed with Jack he wouldn't take disagreement or difference lightly. He took it unto himself, he personalized differences. That was his temperament."[39] Another observer was not as charitable. As a young man, Herbert Romerstein worked in the *Counterattack* research department, primarily with Bierly, and left the company at about the same time he did. Romerstein regarded Bierly as his mentor, who taught him "don't say more than you know, don't conclude more than the evidence shows." As for Keenan, "I didn't have much contact with him," Romerstein said, "but when questions would come up of what the Party position was or things like that, Keenan was not the guy you went to. You went to Ken Bierly, who understood the Party and how it functioned." Romerstein was not privy to Bierly's opinion of Keenan, but he offered his own, describing Keenan as "a pompous ass."[40]

Whatever his private feelings, Bierly made public his political and business reasons for leaving. His first dispute with the company concerned mistakes in the way *Red Channels* had been prepared. "One, no genuine investigation was made of the people listed," he told a reporter at the time. "Second, the book didn't attempt to categorize whether the performers were innocent, dupes, or Reds. It just listed all these people, as reported by public records, under one cover." He also took issue with the course being followed by *Counterattack*, maintaining that the newsletter had "changed into an opinion and editorial sheet—short on facts and long on opinion." Bierly encouraged the publishers to "re-examine their policy of urging readers to protest to sponsors about alleged Reds being hired on shows," protests based occasionally on no more than a single allegation. The net result of all these policies, he said, was "lots of people getting kicked around."[41]

Bierly never specified what cases had convinced him that injustices had been done, but the plight of one actor in particular comes to mind as a likely candidate. Joseph Julian, one of the performers who had decided to sue American Business Consultants, had once been one of the busiest character actors in radio, so busy that he was "frequently turning jobs down for lack of time."[42] After his listing in *Red Channels*—for associating with a World War II organization called Artists' Front to Win the War and for attending a meeting that called for the disbanding of HUAC— his workload and earnings fell dramatically. If ever there was an example of a liberal being penalized for brief front affiliations, this was it. In 1948, as Bierly must have known, Julian played the lead role in the controversial exposé "Communism—U.S. Brand." It is impossible to imagine a Communist participating in such a program, yet Julian was treated as if he were. For someone like Bierly, who was concerned with accuracy, this must have demonstrated exactly how *Red Channels* was being misused.

Bierly's new enterprise, Kenby Associates, was located just two blocks away from *Counterattack* headquarters, at 8 West Fortieth Street, and its operations, in some people's opinion, were similar to his previous work. But to Bierly's mind the difference was significant. Although he still believed that *Counterattack* had directed the public's attention to an urgent problem, and he still supported the practice of keeping Communists off the air, he felt there was now a need to clarify those distinctions that the newsletter and *Red Channels* had made so indistinct. His new outfit would help companies clear those employees that *Red Channels* and other publications had unjustly accused. Among his clients was Columbia Pictures, which hired him to help clear actress Judy Holliday, a *Red Channels* listee.

Although Bierly's resignation marked the beginning of changes that would eventually lead to *Counterattack*'s decline, the anti-blacklist forces could not foresee those developments in April 1951 and detected no signals in the broadcast scene to make them particularly optimistic. The blacklist showed no signs of waning. If anything, it was gathering momentum.

Confronting an Institution

WHILE SOME in broadcasting protested out loud and some took legal action, others simply bridled out of public view, privately nursing a bitter resentment at the new requirements imposed by the cold war. Among those who found the industry purge especially distasteful—even if he shared his opinions only with close friends—was a promising new radio personality at CBS. He submitted to the loyalty oath process only with the greatest reluctance and regarded the politically inspired firings and frantic explanations of past affiliations as an ominous development, at odds with the American experience as he understood it.

Listeners to his humorous, lighthearted program would have been surprised to learn about this serious, impassioned side of him, but John Henry Faulk's political perspectives were bred deeply in him, cultivated years earlier in his boyhood and early manhood. Those beliefs, formed in a place far from the blacklist battleground of New York City, also determined the path he would take in years to come.

Certain places just naturally conjure up images of progressive activism—New York City, for one, or Boston, or any town centered on a liberal-minded university. The Texas farm country, imbued as it has been with Dixiecrat culture and Bible-belt values, would hardly be a likely candidate for this list, but it was here that John Henry Faulk absorbed the left-wing perspective that would play such an important role in his life.

Faulk, born in 1913, had been raised in this part of the country from the age of three. He grew up on the rural outskirts of Austin, Texas, in a Victorian house erected on a broad expanse of open land, where the only route leading to more citified enclaves began with an unpaved road. His parents were churchgoing Methodists, like so many of their neighbors, and pursued their faith so far as to teach Sunday school as well. Yet as Faulk biographer Michael C. Burton has pointed out, they pushed against the prevailing currents of their time and place. They advocated racial equality in the heart of the segregated South and did all they could to help the poor Hispanics and African Americans in their area. Faulk's father, especially, projected a clear progressive voice. An attorney and, for a short time, a newspaper publisher, Henry Faulk believed in the democratic socialist ideas of Eugene V. Debs and acted upon those principles on the Texas scene by litigating against oil monopolies, speaking out against the Ku Klux Klan, opposing American involvement in World War I, and championing women's suffrage. He loomed large in John Henry's life but at an emotional distance. "The recognition that he yearned for from his father," wrote Burton, "was never really attained."[1]

Faulk's escapades as a small boy did not help matters. He seemed determined to sabotage any chance of winning his father's approval by becoming—depending on one's point of view—either a troubled delinquent or a latter-day Huck Finn. Running with a disreputable crowd, he pilfered from neighbors, lied to cover up his misdeeds, and intentionally missed school—or, as those inclined to sympathize with country rascals might put it, he borrowed others' property, told some stretchers, and played hooky. Faulk, predictably, took the more Twainesque view. In his rebellion, he later wrote, "against what I considered the cruelty and hypocrisy of smug South Austin society as a little boy, I did indulge in some pretty raw cussin and carrying on, that was anti-social to the nth degree." Through it all, he did manage to latch on to something that paralleled his father's high ideals: while spending much of his time with Hispanic and black children, he came to develop an affinity for minorities and the underclasses.[2]

By the time he reached high school, John Henry had settled down considerably. He turned himself into a respectable student and developed a verbal talent that was likely passed down from his father, a man who was known as someone who could hold forth in the courtroom with a folksy common touch while dealing with sophisticated ideas. Although John Henry tried putting this skill to use in the similar venue of the school debating club, he was more inclined to explore an altogether different kind of speechifying. He became known for his yarn-spinning and his imitation of local dialects, and for his droll wit.[3] Although he might not have realized it at the time, he was already headed toward a career as an entertainer.

When he entered the University of Texas at Austin in 1932, Faulk intended to fulfill his family's expectations by studying the law as his father had done. Before long, however, he was well on his way along another path. He saw himself as a writer, not a litigator, an aficionado of local folklore, not a reader of Blackstone's Commentaries. After earning his degree in English, he completed a master's thesis on the sermons of black preachers as a folk art form. During these years, as he applied himself to an academic career, he continued to develop his knack for impersonation and earthy, humorous storytelling. This dual pursuit—a balancing act between scholarly endeavor in the spirit of his serious-minded father and folksy entertainment that would become his show-business trademark— would characterize his personality for the rest of his life. As Louis Nizer, Faulk's future attorney, would later observe, "his airy and amiable manner did not mean that Faulk wasn't a man of deep conviction and feeling."[4]

In 1940, Faulk began teaching English at the university and in the same year met his first wife, Hally Wood, a music major and a student in one of his classes. They married in November. Her passion for folksinging and his interest in folklore must have formed part of the common ground between them. Just as important must have been their political activism. While an undergraduate, Faulk had joined the League for Industrial Democracy, a socialist organization that his father would undoubtedly have approved of, and as a teacher he pursued his commitment to civil rights by joining the NAACP and supporting the Southern Conference for Human Welfare. Hally shared his political concerns, though she soon became more overtly radical. In 1942 she joined the Young Communist League for several months and also subscribed to the *Daily Worker*.[5]

In November that year, the FBI began to take notice of Faulk.

An informant told the FBI's Houston office that Faulk had been recruited into the Texas branch of the Communist party. Unable to draw a definitive conclusion on this score, the Bureau report mentioned another source who described Faulk as "patriotic but liberal" and went on to indicate that agents would continue to investigate. Subsequent reports suggested that the Bureau was more interested in Hally, who was described as a possible party recruiter and delegate to the party's state committee. Still, in April 1944 the FBI was sufficiently suspicious of Faulk to enter his name on a security index card, which meant that he could be detained during certain types of national emergencies.[6] The FBI would continue to monitor and reevaluate his activities for several years.

During this period when his politics first came under suspicion—without his knowledge—Faulk devised a way to join the war effort and the fight against fascism. While a teenager, he had lost most of the sight in his right eye due to a severe infection and as a result could not now pass an army physical. Determined to do his part despite his handicap, he joined the Merchant Marines in 1942. He served on a tanker bringing supplies to the British, then did a stint overseas in the American Red Cross before finally, in 1944, gaining entrance into the army in a noncombat role. Stationed in his home state, he continued to participate in local political causes and once again came under FBI scrutiny when an informant claimed Faulk had become involved with a group called the People's Educational and Press Association, which the Bureau regarded as a Communist organization.[7] As before, he remained unaware that he was the subject of federal surveillance.

By the time Faulk left the army, the aspirations of the entertainer that resided within him were getting the better of the inclination to return to the stable but less exciting prospects that awaited him at the University of Texas. He began tinkering with an idea for a radio show to be broadcast on a local Austin station, but other options presented a more auspicious opportunity when he traveled to New York at the end of 1945 to visit an old and now prominent friend. Faulk had met Alan Lomax, the great folksong musicologist and promoter, while they were both at the University of Texas. At the time Faulk looked him up in New York, Lomax was producing shows for CBS radio and was in a position to introduce Faulk to the right people. One of those people was a CBS programming executive named Davidson Taylor, who shared Lomax's belief that radio would be a good medium for Faulk's storytelling. The following April, Taylor launched Faulk's first radio program, a weekly show broadcast over the CBS network called *Johnny's Front Porch*. Very quickly, Faulk had graduated from vague show-business ambitions to big-time broadcasting, but it would prove to be a false start. The show never attracted much of an audience—or, as *Variety* put it, the show "came a cropper"—and was off the air within a year, forcing Faulk to start once again on a smaller scale and build a reputation before gaining another chance with a major network.[8]

He began to pay his dues by hosting shows on New York City–area stations, none of which was terribly gratifying. They required that he project a cornpone version of his earthy Texas style without, as his biographer explained, "opportunity to inject some of his own social and humorous commentary." To satisfy his passions for folklore and politics, meanwhile, he had to explore avenues outside of work.

He found he could embrace both interests when he and his wife became involved in the politically charged folk music scene that had taken hold in New York City during this time. Hally furthered her own career by teaming up with Pete Seeger and other People's Songs performers in a series of concerts and recordings. Along with pure traditional folk tunes, they specialized in activist songs such as "Voting Union," "Oh What Congress Done to Me," and "No No No Discrimination," and performed at political events like the American-Soviet Music Society, an attempt to emphasize what the United States had in common with Stalinist Russia. Through Hally, Faulk became tangentially involved himself with the folk movement, both personally and professionally. For Alan Lomax he hosted a CBS radio special featuring both Seeger and Woody Guthrie, and for People's Songs he had the chance to take a stand on an issue that concerned him by acting as master of ceremonies for an anti-HUAC hootenanny entitled "Sing Out Against the Witch Hunters."[9]

These shared interests were not enough to keep Hally and him together. Their marriage had always been troubled, and in 1947 it came to an end. Within a year, politics again helped Faulk forge a bond with another woman. After meeting at a fund-raiser for presidential candidate Henry Wallace, Faulk and a young woman named Lynne Smith became romantically involved and married in June 1948. Eventually this marriage too would be relatively short-lived, but Faulk's attachment to the issues of the 1948 campaign would prove to be a far more long-lasting affair.

By this time Faulk had concluded that Truman's policy of containment of communism was a disastrous idea. He ridiculed Truman's campaign to aid the Greek government against Communist guerrillas, characterizing the Communists as nothing more than a ragtag, ineffectual outfit unable to break out of the Greek hinterlands. He castigated American efforts to prevent the local Communist party from controlling the government in Italy. And he believed Stalin posed no threat because his country had already suffered too greatly from the last war. Lurking behind all of Truman's foreign-policy actions he saw the sinister machinations of "our War Minded Militarists and Wall Street crowd."[10] For Faulk, Wallace, FDR's former vice president and a prominent New Dealer, presented the only promising alternative in the 1948 presidential election.

Faulk took part in rallies for Wallace in both Texas and New York. By backing him, he was aligning himself with a political movement that placed most of the blame for the cold war on the United States.

Wallace's detractors claimed that the candidate's organization, the Progressive party, was influenced, if not dominated, by Communists. It is true that Communists supported Wallace, as the CPUSA publication *Political Affairs* made clear: "The new Progressive Party is an inescapable historic necessity for millions who want a real choice between peace and war, democracy and fascism, security and poverty."[11] It is also true that Communists accounted for a substantial portion of the Progressive party's workers. But they comprised only a minority, and Wallace himself was certainly no Communist. Still, his ideas on foreign policy could not have been much friendlier to the Soviet view of the world. He opposed the Marshall Plan, rationalized the Soviet takeover of Czechoslovakia in 1948, was ready to abandon West Berlin during that city's crisis the same year, and endorsed a party plank that condemned totalitarianism only in its fascist form. What's more, he had proven his gullibility in the face of Soviet propaganda several years earlier during a wartime visit to Russia. Completely bamboozled by a heavily stage-managed tour, he came back praising the Soviet Gulag as a healthy workplace.[12]

Faulk himself could also fail to grasp the true nature of Stalin and his allies. When he belittled the importance of the Greek guerrillas, he was choosing to disbelieve reports of their abductions and deportations of thousands of Greek children. When he saw no danger in Communists gaining a foothold in the Italian government, he was ignoring the repression recently imposed by Soviet-backed parties in Eastern Europe. And when he believed Stalin was incapable of military adventures because of his country's World War II suffering, he was assuming that Stalin, the mass murderer, would refrain from imposing hardships upon his people.

Faulk's political ventures during the 1948 campaign did not escape the attention of the Texas-based FBI agents who still kept tabs on him. A report dated August 5, 1948, noted that Faulk was "very interested in the Wallace for President movement" but acknowledged that no recent information indicated he was "active in connection with Communist Party activities." With this in mind, the Bureau cancelled his security index card in January.[13]

As election day neared, Faulk broke with the Wallace campaign, but not because of the candidate's inability to recognize Stalin's aggression and atrocities. Rather, Faulk's decision was purely pragmatic. He realized that Wallace had no chance of winning, and he was unwilling to throw away his vote. In the end he voted for Truman in order to help defeat the Republican candidate, Thomas E. Dewey. When the results were in, Faulk was happy that Wallace had not split the Democratic vote and allowed Dewey to win, but he could not exult in the Truman victory. He had little faith in the incumbent, and he minced no words on the subject. As he explained in a letter to a friend, "Truman has about the same chance of effecting any real peace in the world or any of the domestic reforms he talks about as a sick whore has of graduating from Harvard Law School, as long as he maintains that stable of militarist–Wall Street bulls he uses for advisors."[14]

Although the election did little to please him, Faulk found satisfaction in his personal life. Working now at WPAT in Paterson, New Jersey, he appeared on the air under the moniker of Pat the Rancher. He was still restricted to a type of material that could best be described as cowboy corn, but a lecture tour at the same time allowed him to cultivate his true persona while keeping him "busier than all get-out." By the close of 1949 his radio format improved too as he began to host a new program that was more in keeping with his lecture-tour material. Now he could tell stories closer to his own experience, regaling listeners with stories about such back-home characters as Uncle Lee, Granma Beckett, and Congressman Guffaw, and could find ways to offer a more thoughtful point of view. The new format put his talents to better use, and powerful broadcast executives began to take notice. In 1950 the national networks again came calling. This time they tried him on TV panel shows such as NBC's *Leave It to the Girls* and CBS's *We Take Your Word*, which put Faulk's talent for ad-libbing to the test and demonstrated how pleasingly videogenic his friendly, round-faced features could be, projecting, as one reviewer put it, a "relaxed, natural" presence and "so warm a personality." By December 1951 he had earned another shot on CBS radio.[15]

The *John Henry Faulk Show* aired over the network's flagship station, WCBS in New York City, on weekdays between five and six in the afternoon, a "radio series of stories and recorded music," according to an advance *New York Times* announcement. Capitalizing on his authentic drawl and colorful Western anecdotes, WCBS promoted its new on-air personality as a professional Texan, a label Faulk did not care for, though it was preferable to Pat the Rancher. More important, he was free to tell his personal South Austin anecdotes as well as stories concerning his current passion of bird-watching, while also weaving some gentle, wry commentary into his folksy observations.[16] Moving with his family to the Upper West Side of Manhattan, he was now back in the center of American broadcasting. This time his prospects were more promising.

Unlike his first CBS show, his new afternoon program struck a responsive chord with both the public and the critics. A *Variety* reviewer noted that Faulk had "made considerable strides" since his first program, though the writer still reserved judgment on how well the new series would fare. Less circumspect was the *Billboard* critic who informed his readers that Faulk "can tell a story with the best of the tale-spinners and his opinions are worth hearing," and predicted that New York City "will find John's manner to its liking." Adding to his value to the station, Faulk became, over time, an engaging pitchman for products advertised on the show, both on the air and out in the field where he would visit local supermarkets to promote his program and its sponsors.[17]

Faulk's new work at CBS led not only to an enhanced livelihood but also to a new friendship that would play an important role in his life. He had made the acquaintance of CBS executive Edward R. Murrow when he first became associated with the network in 1946, and by the time he began his afternoon WCBS show five years later he had become one of the newsman's drinking companions. According to Faulk's biographer, they

Radio personality John Henry Faulk projected an easygoing, homespun persona over the airwaves, but in private he nurtured a seething resentment against the blacklist and U.S. cold war policies. *(Center for American History, University of Texas)*

spent much of their time discussing politics, particularly McCarthyism and anti-Red hysteria.[18]

Faulk's opposition to the cold war politics of the time was reinforced to a great extent by his views on the Korean War. Unlike *Daily Worker* pundits and their like, he conceded that the Soviets were behind the North Korean invasion, but he had no use for Truman's military response, which he believed was accomplishing nothing except "rendering Korea a stinking desert." In a letter to a Texas friend in mid-1951 he outlined his theory on the origins of the war. "There is ample evidence on hand," he wrote, "that the entire Korean affair was deliberately planned by Dulles, MacArthur, and Chiang, aided and abetted by the Pro-Chiang lobby of Knowlands and McCarthys here, who had to resort to something desperate last year after Truman and the State Dept. both announced that the U.S. was writing Chiang's Nationalists off the books." Faulk also detected, once again, the insidious specter of Wall Street, which "stays in a constant state of jitters for fear that Russia will come up with a peace proposal that we can't afford to turn down and leave our flourishing War Business dangling." The only thing preventing an all-out global conflict was the fact that the "Russians don't want war," and American warmongers were unable to "trap old Stalin into one."[19] Here, like his onetime candidate of choice Wallace, Faulk steered clear of the party line when it came to supporting the Soviet Union, but his outrage was directed almost exclusively against the United States.

On the home front Faulk believed the country was headed toward militarization and suppression of free speech. In formulating his ideas, he especially admired the writings he found in the *Monthly Review*. This cerebral journal promoted ideas similar to Faulk's about a coming American fascism and in August 1951 also mirrored the essence of his theories, advanced earlier, about a secret Korean War conspiracy involving MacArthur, Dulles, and Chiang.[20] He might well have believed that the publication lived up to its subtitle, "An Independent Socialist Magazine," but the *Monthly Review* consistently provided tortuously intellectual rationalizations for Soviet-style totalitarianism.

Closer to home, Faulk saw the seeds of American repression germinating within his own industry and entangling his friends. His mentor Alan Lomax was listed in *Red Channels* and soon found his livelihood so badly impaired that he left for Europe to find work. Faulk was convinced that the Red hunters "will get around to everybody that ever had a thought of his own before long." As usual, he perceived manipulative forces at work behind the scenes, out of the public eye. In this case, one of those forces, he believed, was the Catholic church.[21]

In discussing issues of the day with Faulk, Murrow might not have gone along with all of his friend's conspiracy theories, but he certainly agreed that the country was besieged by alarmist, repressive trends, within broadcasting and throughout the professions. The two men differed, according to Faulk's biographer, not in their opposition to these forces but in how to deal with them. Faulk favored a combative approach. The media should "take the issues and personalities head-on," he argued, attacking McCarthy and his allies bluntly and unequivocally. Murrow felt just as strongly on the issue, perhaps even more so—in 1948 a friend of his, former State Department official Laurence Duggan, had jumped out of a six-teenth-story window to his death after being implicated in the Alger Hiss spy case. Nonetheless Murrow still advocated his usual cautious, prag-matic tack. Faulk's biographer suggests that, for the time being, Faulk was dissatisfied and impatient with this thinking, yet he was in no position to launch the kind of media assault he had in mind. If he tried to transform his easygoing, mildly humorous program into a political diatribe, his sta-tion and sponsors would withdraw their support and he would be off the air. Whether he believed in it or not, he would have to exercise a Murrow-like patience. And, indeed, he followed Murrow's example in April 1952 when he agreed to sign CBS's loyalty oath. As he explained to one of his Texas friends, he made a habit of concealing his political convictions to most people in New York, maintaining instead "a naive, simple pose." He confessed he had "very little to be proud of as far as acting on my true feel-ings are concerned at this time of agony in my fair country."[22]

For now he would watch developments from the sidelines and do nothing to try to influence events, no matter how much they made him seethe.

📺 What Faulk was witnessing was a blacklist taking hold throughout the broadcast industry. To some extent the phenomenon was fueled by the HUAC probes into Communist influence in the entertainment business. While focused chiefly on the movie industry, the hearings also touched upon broadcasting, and in February 1952 the committee warned that tele-vision in particular must guard against Red infiltration. Still, congres-sional committees were several steps behind *Counterattack* and other private groups like the American Legion in pressuring the industry. By the end of 1951, a year and a half into the Korean War, as the American pub-lic braced itself for what was becoming a prolonged, bloody conflict, the anti-Red warnings were producing an effect that went beyond individual blacklisting cases and prodded broadcasters into installing a system for clearing talent.

At Faulk's network, Joseph Ream built upon his loyalty-oath program by hiring an ex-FBI agent named Alfred Berry to help organize a thorough investigation of CBS employees. From now on, producers would have to check with Ream's department before hiring anyone for their programs.

In this way the network avoided a public relations problem. By excluding certain people before they could be employed, CBS would not be pressured into firing them later and could sidestep the embarrassment of a Muir-like incident. Ream himself would not supervise the system for very long. Never quite comfortable with his new duties, he left CBS in 1952 and was succeeded by another Ivy League attorney named Daniel T. O'Shea, who became more closely associated with the talent-screening process.[23] For three years O'Shea served as the network's security chief and played a key role in establishing CBS, once the heart of broadcast liberalism, as the harshest of the networks in enforcing the blacklist.

To some O'Shea was a severe, unyielding obstacle to employment. To others he could be a kindly advocate—provided, that is, the accused was willing to come clean about past controversial activities.[24] For many who had nothing to hide but were reluctant to play the game, O'Shea could use an ingratiating manner to win cooperation. Liberal, non-Communist director Sidney Lumet remembered going to see O'Shea about the requirement to sign the loyalty oath. Although ready to resist, he found he was quickly disarmed by O'Shea's manner.

"First words out of his mouth were, 'Don't come in with your hands up,'" Lumet recalled. They calmly discussed the issue, and O'Shea gave Lumet the opportunity to express his objections to the oath while at the same time easing him into complying with the requirement. "I said that I thought that the whole idea of loyalty oaths was un-American," Lumet said. "He was all sympathy. He didn't argue for it, he was talking about it as one of the sad things that this time was demanding. It was summed up really in his remark to me as I was leaving his office. I said to him, 'Dan'—we were on a first-name basis by then—'Dan, how can you do this job?' And he said to me—great, great remark—he said, 'Better one of us than one of them.' Of course, the wild irony of that, in essence he was really doing their work for them, but still in his own mind had rationalized it to the fact that he was on our side."[25]

Just as important were the new clearance departments at the advertising agencies. At that time, sponsors often owned programs, and the agency representing the sponsor served as the production company in charge of hiring the show's personnel. In some cases the screening process was handled by the agency's legal department, but in other cases the agency might hire someone specifically to handle the task. The most influential of these agency troubleshooters, sometimes called security officers, was an old ally of Keenan, Kirkpatrick, and Bierly—the former FBI informant Jack Wren.

After leaving the *Plain Talk* research unit in the late 1940s, Wren joined the prestigious advertising firm of Batten, Barton, Durstine & Osborn. He had worked in advertising before, but his qualifications for his new job had more to do with his association with the FBI and his experience as a researcher of CPUSA politics than with a typical ad-game background. While with BBD&O, Wren maintained contact with his old employers, sometimes forwarding information on Communist fronters to the *Counterattack* publishers, at other times tipping them off to anti–*Red Channels* protests. It might have been this connection to *Counterattack*, the perception that he had insider access to special information, that accounted in part for the influence he wielded on Madison Avenue. Within his own agency he projected a counterintelligence aura that belied his diminutive, balding appearance. One fellow BBD&O employee recalled an impression within the agency that Wren was an ex-FBI agent, which was nearly but not quite the truth.[26]

Providing a glimpse into Wren's work was his handling of the case of Abe Burrows, the comedian and playwright who was Faulk's co-star on *We Take Your Word* and a featured performer on other panel shows as well. After Burrows's name appeared in *Red Channels*, the sponsor of one of his programs claimed to receive some six thousand letters of protest a week. Burrows did little to help his now precarious position in the industry when he first denied any Communist party affiliation in a letter to Joseph Ream at CBS in November 1950, then retreated a bit the following March by telling an executive session of HUAC that he had participated in groups that might have been associated with the party. His hedging stirred up the suspicions of some anti-Communist groups, especially the Catholic War Veterans.[27]

One thing this case makes clear: Wren's job description did not include standing up to pressure groups that claimed veto power over broadcast hiring practices. When the Catholic War Veterans lodged a complaint about Burrows, Wren accompanied one of the group's officials on a trip to the Capitol in Washington, where they spoke to HUAC investigators about Burrows's testimony. Deciding that the entertainer had not been sufficiently forthcoming and contrite, Wren then insisted that Burrows supplement his testimony with a full written statement on his political past in order to convince the Catholic War Veterans that he had nothing further to conceal. Burrows and his attorney resisted this demand. They believed broadcasters should not kowtow to self-appointed watchdogs, but when Ream explained that Burrows's refusal could force CBS to fire him, their resistance soon crumbled. Even after securing this concession, Wren continued to supervise the process. Burrows's attorney duly forwarded a copy of the statement to Wren, and the BBD&O security officer pored over it and insisted that Burrows make revisions before the Catholic War Veterans finally decided that the statement was "very acceptable."[28]

Wren's interventions could help get people's careers back on track, provided the entertainers were willing to do as they were told. This could be a painful process. Wren did not necessarily confine himself to requiring written statements. The comedian and *Red Channels* listee Henry Morgan followed the security officer's instructions through a succession of acts to clear himself: he attended an anti-Communist social gathering; he publicly criticized Philip Loeb at an actors union meeting; and then, finally, and once again at Wren's behest, he wrote a letter to the security officer commending him for the fairness of his efforts. Years later Morgan still harbored resentment over this experience. To his mind, Wren was the "worst part" of the blacklist phenomenon.[29]

While observing developments through this period, Faulk must have also become uneasy about activities within his own union. The American Federation of Radio Artists began to address the issue of the blacklist as early as August 1949 when its officials participated in an industry-wide effort to determine if broadcasters were firing entertainers on the basis of their political beliefs. After the publication of *Red Channels*, the union continued to grapple with this problem but also simultaneously moved in another direction. At its national convention in August 1950, when AFRA members passed a resolution condemning the blacklist, they also passed three anti-Communist resolutions, two of them denouncing communism in principle, the third proposing that anyone identified as a Communist by a government agency be expelled from the union. A year later AFRA members went a step further by voting 2,118 to 457 to turn this measure into an amendment of the union's constitution.[30]

Although broadcasting's anti-Red purge was clearly taking root, and even though progressive entertainers like Faulk might perceive the trend as evidence of incipient fascism, the blacklist had not become an airtight ban against leftist talent. Some individuals, to be sure, were locked out of the broadcast business, or came uncomfortably close to it. Philip Loeb no longer worked in radio and TV. By 1952, Larry Adler, the litigant who had sued Hester McCullough for libel, had decided to move to Europe to find work. And poet Louis Untermeyer, once a staple on panel shows, saw a decline not only in broadcast jobs but in lecture bookings as well. As for Peter Lyon, the alleged leader of the Radio Writers Guild's pro-Communist faction, he was dropped by the program *Big Town* after the publication of *Red Channels*, and was reduced to scraping by on occasional scripts for *The Eternal Light*. His income during this time fell from $20,000 a year to $2,500. But others in the broadcast industry saw no noticeable effect at all from their *Red Channels* listings. Among them were producer Himan Brown, writer Marc Connolly, and news correspondents Alexander Kendrick and Howard K. Smith. The actress Uta Hagen, cited for nineteen alleged front activities, continued to work on Broadway, where the blacklist had little or no effect. Even Norman Corwin, the great standard-bearer for Popular Front radio, might have found some job negotiations more difficult, but, according to his biographer R. LeRoy Bannerman, he "was never denied gainful employment" despite his eleven *Red Channels* citations.[31] True, he was no longer a fixture in commercial network radio, but other developments accounted for this change in his career, primarily the networks' waning interest in the sort of serious-minded sustaining shows that had won Corwin so much praise during World War II. Determined to pursue this kind of programming, he left network broadcasting and found an outlet for his talents with United Nations Radio while also writing occasional film scripts for the Hollywood studios, where the blacklist did not prevent him from working.

Other entertainers fell somewhere between these two groups. Their earnings declined, but they still made a living. Following his listing in *Red Channels*, character actor Ralph Bell had difficulty getting work on programs that were produced by BBD&O (Wren's agency); but another advertising firm, Young & Rubicam, still employed him, as did certain producers and directors. Bell's wife, comedic actress Pert Kelton, was also listed in *Red Channels* but continued to play a prominent role on the radio series *The Magnificent Montague* until its cancellation in October 1951. She also co-starred with Jackie Gleason on his TV variety show, where she created the role of Alice Kramden in the original "Honeymooners." If not for her heart attack in the summer of 1952, she might have continued with Gleason. As researcher John Cogley would later point out, most people affected in these years qualified not as blacklisted but as greylisted, meaning they were barred from some shows but not all. "Few persons," he wrote, "are thoroughly blacklisted in this sense."[32]

Not everyone in the industry was committed to the purge of suspected performers. CBS might have enforced the blacklist consistently, but the other major network at the time, NBC, was less stringent. Years later NBC executive Pat Weaver claimed there was no blacklist at the network in the early 1950s. The facts belie this statement, as in the case of comedian Jack Gilford, who found himself suddenly shut out of the NBC variety shows that had been employing him in TV's early years. Even so, the blacklist at NBC could be quite porous. The comedy series *The Magnificent Montague*, for instance, ran on NBC radio for two years, not only with Pert Kelton in the cast but with *Red Channels* listee Nat Hiken as producer, writer, and director. Writer Ernest Kinoy also found that NBC could resist the usual pressures. In June 1951 he was named a pro-Communist before a congressional committee but suffered no consequences. NBC executives, he said, "just simply ignored it, which at the time I thought was an interesting phenomenon."[33] The reputation of NBC head David Sarnoff as a conservative anti-Communist might have allowed the network occasionally to ignore the demands of anti-Red watchdogs. Unlike CBS, Sarnoff's network did not have to defend itself against charges of being soft on communism.

Individuals could also buck the tide. At a time when the rules of doing business in the new medium of television were still uncertain, strong-willed producers could exert themselves, whether that meant insisting on aesthetic quality or demanding control over whom they could hire. Pioneering drama producers like David Susskind and Herbert Brodkin would sometimes be able to defy the blacklist or at least find some way to circumvent it.[34] One of the most effective resisters was Mark Goodson, one of Faulk's employers during this time.

With his partner Bill Todman, Goodson dominated the field of TV game shows throughout the 1950s. He encountered the blacklist early on when, in 1950, letters protested the appearance of Louis Untermeyer as a panelist on *What's My Line*, and lawyers from CBS pressured Goodson to drop him. This time, Goodson felt he had to play along. Soon, though, as the blacklist became more entrenched, he decided to dig in his heels. In 1952 the William Esty Agency, acting on behalf of the sponsor, the Reynolds Tobacco Company, demanded that Goodson dismiss Henry Morgan from *I've Got a Secret*; but the producer announced that either the next show included Morgan or he would not deliver the program. Faced with this ultimatum, the agency and advertiser backed down. Goodson was able to get his way again when similar protests surrounded another panelist, Faye Emerson. As Goodson later recalled, "I began to find out that in my business if you fought back you could win."[35] An intriguing question to consider: how widespread would the blacklist have been if more producers, and the networks themselves, had taken a similar stand?

Although the blacklist might not have been complete and irrevocable, opponents of the practice saw little reason to take comfort, particularly so at the end of 1951 when the broadcast purge seemed to inflict its first mortal casualties. On October 28 actress Mady Christians died of a cerebral hemorrhage. The Austrian-born actress had appeared in movies and on radio but was best known for her work on stage, where she had originated the role of the immigrant matriarch in *I Remember Mama*. Many at the time believed that her death at the age of fifty-one was brought on by the emotional stress caused by her listing in *Red Channels* sixteen months earlier. It is difficult either to confirm or to refute this conclusion. The *Red Channels* allegations had an impact on Christians's career, but they did not keep her from working altogether. Although she might have encountered difficulties in broadcasting, one writer's suggestion that *Red Channels* prevented her from reprising her most famous role in the TV version of *I Remember Mama* was clearly false: the program aired a year before the booklet appeared. As for the stage, her primary outlet, Christians continued to work in touring companies throughout the summer of 1951, and in fact she first became seriously ill while appearing in the play *Black Chiffon*. Still, the experience of being targeted by Red hunters could have easily taken its toll and quickened the onset of high blood pressure that preceded her death. However ambiguous the bare facts might have been, her friends held no doubts. As playwright Elmer Rice put it in a letter to the *New York Times*, "No one who knew her or who saw her during the last tortured months of her life can doubt that her death was hastened, if not actually caused, by the small-souled witch-hunters who make a fine art of character assassination."[36]

Outrage also surrounded the death on December 6 of character actor J. Edward Bromberg. Here was someone whose career clearly suffered after the release of *Red Channels* and whose background surely came under damaging scrutiny. Bromberg had been identified as a Communist by both director Frank Tuttle and actor Marc Lawrence—and would later be named as a member of a Communist theater group by Elia Kazan—and, while testifying before HUAC, had also been confronted with information about his CPUSA membership card. Already on shaky ground, Bromberg then failed to help his case when a committee member asked if he would be willing to fight in a war against a Communist country. "I can't answer yes or no," Bromberg replied.[37] By 1951 his job offers had dwindled, prompting him to leave for England, where he was appearing in a play at the time he died at the age of forty-seven.

Counterattack played a role in dogging Bromberg in the months before his death in what might have been the newsletter's worst exhibition of callousness. The May 25, 1951, issue noted that Bromberg would appear in a regional-theater production of *The Royal Family*, then jeered at the actor's request that he be excused from testifying before HUAC because of a heart condition. "Yet Bromberg's 'heart,' which won't support him while he sits in a witness chair in Washington," *Counterattack* asserted, "is scheduled to pump him through five successive days of acting in 'The Royal Family.'" When the actor finally did testify, the newsletter's headline crowed, "J. Edward Bromberg Sweated, But His Heart Did Not Fail." Less than six months later, Bromberg died of a heart attack. Still not done, the *Counterattack* publishers went on to attack Bromberg's funeral as a Communist propaganda event. This it might well have been, but a more restrained publication would have been reluctant to dance on someone's grave, especially when it had so recently sneered at the ailment that had caused the person's death.[38]

Throughout 1951 and even before the deaths of Christians and Bromberg, sectors of the media continued to take *Counterattack* to task. In June, Random House published *The Troubled Air*, a novel by Irwin

Shaw that featured a thinly fictionalized version of *Counterattack* entitled *Blueprint*. Although Shaw had distanced himself from Communist front groups after the outbreak of the Korean War, he was eager to demonize the *Counterattack* publishers by tapping into rumors that they were backed by a secret, sinister combine. In his novel the powers behind *Blueprint* consist of three powerful backers, two of whom are kept nameless and mysterious while the third is identified as a reptilian, diabolical ad agency president with contacts in high places (though they too remain anonymous). In case his evil intent is not quite clear, the character tells a suspected Communist sympathizer that the *Blueprint* cabal will "hound you and defame you and we won't stop until you're all behind bars or swinging from trees, as you ought to be."[39]

A more sober, comprehensive critique was launched four months later by a broadcast trade publication. Beginning in October, *Sponsor* magazine began a three-part exposé of *Red Channels*, which it characterized as both an industry Star Chamber and a kangaroo court. The first installment reprised the professional ordeals of Muir, Loeb, and others listed in the American Business Consultants booklet; the second revolved around an unflattering interview with Keenan and Kirkpatrick; and the third urged broadcasters to find a way to monitor possible subversives without succumbing to the pressures of *Counterattack* and its allies. The *Sponsor* series was strong enough to provoke an irate response from *Counterattack*, which described it as a smear, "largely a rehash of material that had previously appeared in Communist-line publications."[40] But a far more extensive rebuttal to *Red Channels* appeared several months later in the Merle Miller book *The Judges and the Judged*.

The book had its origins in September 1950, at the time of the Muir incident, when the American Civil Liberties Union commissioned the journalist and novelist Miller to investigate the charge that a blacklist was emerging in radio and TV. After conducting an extensive series of interviews—with the *Counterattack* partners as well as broadcast professionals and columnists covering the industry—Miller wrote a report that was originally supposed to fill nothing larger than a pamphlet but quickly expanded to book-length proportions. It was published by Doubleday in April 1952. *The Judges and the Judged* concluded that a small group of alarmists, spearheaded by American Business Consultants, was spreading panic throughout broadcasting and was ruining the careers of many people. If there actually was a problem of subversive activity within the industry, Miller wrote, "it is difficult to see how the services of the former FBI agents who publish *Counterattack* can be or have ever been of the slightest value in this area."[41]

Not merely a publishing event, the book also led directly to a legal action that raised an intriguing question about the government's possible role in the blacklist situation. Unlike executives at CBS, who feared that the FCC was authorized to punish broadcasters for failing to ban suspected Communists, the ACLU believed the agency was compelled to punish broadcasters for the exact opposite reason: for excluding talent on the basis of political associations. Based on the findings of *The Judges and the Judged*, the ACLU filed a complaint with the FCC on the day the book was published. The petition singled out the four major networks (CBS, NBC, ABC, and the soon to be defunct DuMont) as well as two local stations, and insisted that the agency deny licenses to all six until they halted their blacklisting practices. Although the petition might have raised hopes among blacklist opponents, it ultimately did nothing to change the situation. In June the FCC refused to take action.[42]

Miller's book itself stirred an agitated response within the media. Although written by a journalist and novelist, *The Judges and the Judged* offered little journalistic clarity or novelistic narrative—or, for that matter, any cohesive organization. But more important and far more controversial than stylistic issues were questions of fairness and accuracy. To no one's surprise, *Counterattack* blasted the ACLU book on both counts, calling it "the biggest gun" fired in the campaign to whitewash Communists in broadcasting.[43] Some of the broadsides against the book, however, originated from the other side of the political spectrum as well. One was a scathing review by Murray Kempton, the liberal columnist for the then-progressive *New York Post*. Another came from within the ranks of the ACLU itself.

Melvin S. Pitzele, a member of the ACLU board of directors, pondered his organization's book for a month before airing his complaints in the pages of the *New Leader*. On the question of accuracy, he challenged Miller's characterization of the *Red Channels* citations. The booklet's publishers, Miller had asserted, placed an inordinate emphasis on people's activities that had predated the current cold war, including those years when the United States and the Soviet Union were World War II allies. Many of those listed in *Red Channels*, he wrote, "had no listing after 1941; a sizable minority, none after 1945." Pitzele countered that the "'many' with no listing after 1941 amount to exactly three. The 'sizable minority' with none after 1945 amount to just two more." (My count came to two with no listing after 1941, and three with no listing after 1945.) But erroneous figures, even when slanted to suit a political purpose, were only a small part of the problem, Pitzele argued. A more pervasive and disturbing flaw was Miller's reliance on anonymous quotes. In his introduction, Miller explained that he had left most of his sources unnamed in order to protect them from possible repercussions. Not only did this decision deprive the reader of a means of verifying the many charges leveled at the *Red Channels* publishers, it also, wrote Pitzele, violated one of the ACLU's most cherished principles: "If the ACLU has not been the first, it has certainly been the most articulate foe of anonymous accusations and testimony."[44]

Research into the ACLU archives, which contain the identities of the unnamed sources, raises another question: why did some of these people need to resort to anonymity? One of the interviewees masked by the author was Arthur Miller, who was no longer writing for radio and was now a critically acclaimed playwright, winner of a Pulitzer Prize and two Tony awards, and a leading figure on Broadway, where the anti-Red purge was virtually nonexistent. What did he have to fear from broadcast blacklisters? Not only that, Miller was just months away from the opening of his latest play, *The Crucible*, an overt parable about the evils of McCarthyism. Why would he feel the need to disguise his views on the same subject in *The Judges and the Judged*? Just as difficult to understand were the unnamed quotes of actors Joseph Julian and Ralph Bell, both of whom were in the process of suing American Business Consultants. Their animosity toward the *Counterattack* publishers was already a matter of public record and hardly a secret. And perhaps most puzzling of all was the anonymity granted William S. Paley, chairman of the board of CBS and perhaps the most powerful man in broadcasting. Making Miller's decision here especially bewildering is the utterly innocuous nature of Paley's comments. In one case, Paley merely noted that "it is impossible to say that one job in radio or television is more 'sensitive' than another."[45] In some of his choices, Miller appeared to promote timidity when the time demanded forthright discussion and verifiable documentation.

The ACLU's archives also shed light on another controversy surrounding Miller's book, namely the competing claims of victimhood: who was more discriminated against, left-wingers or right-wingers? Contrary to what some critics alleged, Miller and his researchers did attempt to investigate the claim that anti-Communists too had been blacklisted, but internal reports clearly indicated whom the researchers were inclined to believe. One report commented that right-wingers seemed "to make out the flimsiest of cases" that lack "concrete signs of proof," even though similar claims by left-wingers also tended to be vague. A more fair-minded approach would have acknowledged that any charges of blacklisting were likely to lack conclusive proof due to the shadowy nature of the practice.[46]

The larger point that troubled Pitzele, and Kempton as well, was the book's distortion of liberal values, its reluctance to take a hard look at the crushingly illiberal totalitarianism of Communists. Miller's book implied, according to Kempton, "that a man who signed a letter praising the Soviet Union after the Moscow trials has no reason to apologize." He also detected a sentiment that would later become common in revisionist accounts: not content to make the point that *Red Channels* listees were unjustly barred from employment, Miller implied that they were "the flower of humanity and radio artistry."

Pitzele, for his part, focused on the tendency to sanitize suspected Communists by portraying them as "independent thinkers." He argued that liberals, particularly those in the ACLU, should return to their original beliefs, "those civil-libertarian principles which did not defend Fascists on the sleazy ground that they were not really Fascists, but defended them because Fascists, too, have rights."[47]

As Pitzele suggested, a new polarization was beginning to dominate the debate. Egged on by McCarthyite excesses, many liberals were retreating to the position that anti-Communist zealotry alone was the problem. This perspective could be seen in the conspiracy theories and cries of fascism coming from progressives like Faulk, or in the work of columnists like Rex Lardner, whose positive review of *The Judges and the Judged* concluded that Keenan and Kirkpatrick were "two very evil gentlemen."[48] But it was more commonly found in the phenomenon of anti-anti-communism. A clumsy term, to be sure, but still one that accurately characterized a growing sentiment, it was championed by Henry Wallace in the 1948 campaign and adopted by some in the anti–*Red Channels* camp who, like Miller, showed little interest in examining how Communists could mold organizations and the media to their own purposes. Communists may have had no chance of transforming network programming into overt Soviet propaganda, but the potential nonetheless existed for promoting destructive mischief in a time of war. The most obvious example of this was the 1952 effort to smear the American military.

The Soviet Union and China charged at the time that American troops were using germ warfare to annihilate civilians not only in North Korea but in Manchuria and China as well. Soviet documents uncovered in the 1990s would later establish that this charge was a fabrication, but during the last two years of the Korean War it became the basis for a worldwide misinformation campaign that succeeded in creating a false issue at the United Nations and in poisoning the truce negotiations in Korea. To back up the accusation, the Communists coerced confessions from American POWs and enlisted public defenses of the charge from seemingly respectable scientists, attorneys, clerics, and scholars. Among those trafficking in this cynical lie was Dr. Gene Weltfish, an anthropology instructor at Columbia University, who had also been a recurring target of *Counterattack* since 1947.[49] In this case *Counterattack* had been right in raising suspicions, but critics were unwilling to concede that the newsletter could be correct on any score.

If *The Judges and the Judged* accomplished anything, it kept the debate about the blacklist alive and provided a rallying point for those concerned about the current state of civil liberties, even if some took exception to the way Miller presented his argument. While the debate about the book raged, one especially serious deficiency went unnoticed: *The Judges and the Judged* was already out of date. When Miller finished his research in the fall of 1951, he was unaware of a new figure entering the conflict and a new force gathering momentum in an unlikely place well outside broadcasting's headquarters in New York City. Within months the industry would see the full impact of this development as it introduced a new economic pressure to cleanse the airwaves.

SIX

The Boys from Syracuse

POLITICAL PASSION often springs from youthful exuberance, but Laurence A. Johnson was no young Turk in 1951 when he joined the fight against American communism. He was already sixty-two, an age when most men would be looking ahead to a quiet retirement after a lifetime of hard work. And Johnson's life until then had certainly qualified as industrious and diligent, the epitome of self-made prosperity that had produced for him both economic stature and social respect in his hometown of Syracuse in the heart of central New York. His decision at such an advanced age to launch a crusade against domestic subversion was surprising, if not inexplicable, to many people. But in one sense it was perfectly logical. His life had always been dominated in one form or another by a devotion to Americanism.

Johnson's family traced its beginnings in America back to the eighteenth century, to a man named Edmund Johnson, a native of Rhode Island, who proved his patriotism on the battlefield, first in the French and Indian Wars, then in the Revolution. Along with setting a standard for dedication to the country's interests among succeeding generations, Captain Johnson also initiated a new phase in the family's history by planting the clan's roots in New York State. In Saratoga County, just south of the Adirondack Mountains, he built a home on land granted to him by the government, a family history tells us, as payment for his military service.

By the mid-nineteenth century one branch of the family had migrated westward, settling between the Finger Lakes and Lake Ontario outside a village called Savannah. It was on a farm there in 1889 that Laurence Ayres Johnson was born.[1]

Johnson's father, who bore the name of the Revolutionary War hero Francis Marion, spent the warm months working the farm and occupied himself during the winter by teaching school in South Butler, just a few miles to the north. Johnson never had the chance to get to know his father very well. He died when Laurence was only two, succumbing to the perils of a laborious life that were common in those parts. According to a family genealogy, Francis Marion Johnson "caught a cold in his hips while sitting on the ground topping onions in the spring which was said to have brought on an abscess." This crippling condition seems to have led to his death "after much suffering."[2]

Johnson's mother remarried, and the family moved to North Carolina but returned soon to Savannah where Johnson spent the rest of his childhood growing up on the family farm. Later news reports suggest that he inherited his lifelong interest in history from his mother, an interest fed at first by both nonfiction books and *The Leatherstocking Tales* of James Fenimore Cooper.[3] The Cooper novels in particular must have cultivated his fascination with both local lore and his own family legacy; most of the stories were set in upstate New York, and two of them concerned the French and Indian Wars, the scene of Captain Johnson's early exploits.

Another of Laurence's interests developed during boyhood visits to the hamlet of South Butler. The boy who would much later be identified as "the grocer from Syracuse" spent a good deal of his time there browsing through a traditional crossroads general store. At first he was attracted, as any child would be, by the enticing display of chocolates and multi-colored hard-candy balls, but he was also drawn to the place's social atmosphere, a congenial meeting ground where, as he later remembered it, he listened to "the old boys lying about their experiences in the Civil War." Here was an experience of pure Americana, a fixture of small-town life going back a hundred years that was bound to intrigue a boy absorbed in local history. And the storekeeper himself was clearly, to young Johnson's eyes, a prominent figure in the community, and not only as a provider of essential goods. Johnson noticed the larger qualities associated with the proprietor when the store became a venue for political discussion. In a book he would later write on the American country store, Johnson described the storekeeper as "a man of consequence, his opinions respected, if not always agreed with."[4] At an early age, Johnson decided he wanted to pursue this line of work and hold that position within his community.

In taking this path he would be following in the footsteps of others on his mother's side of the family, but circumstances forced him to put off not only his mercantile ambitions but his formal education. While he was in high school, his mother became ill, and he was required to remain home to help with the farm. Eventually he returned to school in the nearby town of Clyde. More significant in terms of his future occupation, he took a job there at a grocery, but once more a family emergency reeled him back to the Savannah homestead. He stayed put for the time being, running his own fruit farm, marrying a woman named Hermione Cartner, and starting a family of his own. He passed through his twenties in this way, but he was not ready to forget his earlier ambitions. In 1918, at the age of twenty-nine, he left the farm behind and moved to Solvay, just east of Syracuse, and took a job in another store while at the same time devising a way to go into business on his own. A year later, with the help of a two-hundred-dollar loan, he opened a grocery on Lemoyne Avenue in Syracuse, the start of a career that would combine a fondness for what he regarded as a golden American past with a shrewd ability to sense opportunities in the forward-looking American business scene.[5]

Although it was an affection for the traditional country store that originally led him to the merchant's trade, Johnson was one of the first to grasp the need for a new way to serve the modern shopper. In the early twentieth century, people still bought their groceries in serial fashion—going from butcher to produce shop to baker to fish market—and they still relied on clerks to measure and package the goods they wanted to buy. This began to change—and Johnson monitored the development with keen interest—when in 1930 a man named Michael J. Cullen opened a store that featured all types of food in one place, most of them already packaged, and selling for economical prices. The King Kullen outlet, located in the New York City borough of Queens, was the country's first supermarket. In 1931, when he was forty-two years old, Johnson formed a partnership with two other Syracuse retailers and founded Associated Foods to bring this new concept to central New York. Johnson's involvement with the company, however, did not last long. It seems reasonable to assume, based upon his later management style, that he was not fond of sharing control of the enterprise. In 1932, setting out on his own, he opened Johnson's Supermarket on South Salina Street in downtown Syracuse, and within ten years added two more supermarkets in Syracuse and another two north of the city in Fulton and Oswego, making him one of the first supermarket-chain operators east of the Mississippi.[6]

While pioneering a new era in food retailing, Johnson also satisfied his other great interest by scouring the central New York region for relics of the past. He collected country-store paraphernalia and nineteenth-century toys as well as artifacts of early American political campaigns. In February 1941 he combined his business interests and his collecting hobby by transforming a corner of his flagship supermarket on Salina Street into a replica of a vintage country store. Here he recreated the general stores of his youth, replete with potbellied stove, cracker barrels and checkerboard, and an assortment of such archaic merchandise as buggy whips, tobacco plugs, derbies, and paper collars. A year later Johnson added the detailed interior of a frontier log cabin. "Syracuse of a Century Ago Still Lives!" a Johnson's Supermarket ad proclaimed. "Yes, romantic old Syracuse still lives . . . actually and truly LIVES. You may see it . . . touch it . . . thrill to the color and drama of personal contact with pioneer times."[7]

To add educational value, Johnson hired a seventy-seven-year-old clerk, who had himself once worked in an old-fashioned country store, to act as docent for visitors to the Americana exhibits. Although sincerely concerned about promoting an understanding of the old days, the pragmatic Johnson also found a way to profit from his historical displays. Not only did the exhibits draw customers but the country-store replica in particular spurred sales by underscoring how far marketing had come over the years, effectively accentuating the advantages to be found in Johnson's otherwise modern and streamlined supermarket—"an outstanding example of merchandising by contrast," as *Modern Packaging* magazine noted at the time. This recognition of his efforts no doubt enhanced Johnson's position in the larger retail grocery industry, and within a few years he was appointed secretary of the Super-Market Institute, a national trade association.[8] The exact extent of his influence among his colleagues at this time is unclear, but one thing is certain: it would become a critical question years later when he wielded his purported prominence as an economic weapon.

Through the 1930s and 1940s Johnson's stores flourished. For someone so enamored of the American experience, his own success story must have redoubled his belief in the greatness of his country, for he was living proof that the American Dream worked, that a man of limited means could pull himself up by the bootstraps by dint of ingenuity and hard work. And not only did his resourcefulness bring him material comfort but—as he had surmised it would in his youth—it also brought him social respectability. Physically he was perfectly cast for the role. As he entered his fifties, with his white hair, square features, and wire-rimmed spectacles, he looked every inch the solid citizen, the epitome of the forthright Middle American businessman.

Within the Johnson stores his employees might not have viewed him as an idealized Norman Rockwell icon, but generally they regarded him with varying degrees of respect. He was known as a stickler, a highly opinionated man who showed no patience when workers failed to do as he expected. If a display of products displeased him, one employee recalled, he wouldn't bother to offer constructive criticism. He would kick the display down. Despite this explosive temper, other employees took a more charitable view of him, considering him demanding but fair. "He'd let you do your work," Stephen Mayka recalled, "and as long as you were doing it he'd let you alone."[9]

To those outside his business, Johnson was perceived as an indefatigable participant in a wide range of civic and social organizations. He was a member of the Free Masons, the Independent Order of Odd Fellows, and the Kiwanis Club; he belonged to both golf and yacht clubs as well as the Syracuse Advertising Club, the New York State Historical Association, the local chamber of commerce, and, perhaps most significant to him, the Sons of the American Revolution. During World War II, when the United States waged its first major fight against totalitarianism, he was in his mid-fifties, too old to serve in the armed forces but still able to put his contacts in the community and his merchandising skills to use by helping to sell U.S. war bond stamps and, through the United War fund, raising money for soldiers serving in both Europe and the Pacific.[10]

After the war his life settled back to its normal routine. He continued to promote his supermarket chain—now comprised of six stores—and worked on his collecting hobby at home, a ranch-style house near the eastern edge of the city where he immersed himself in Americana. He and his wife, Hermione, furnished their home in Early American decor, decorated the walls of their garage with nostalgic Currier and Ives prints, and converted their basement into a private museum that included a wall display of nineteenth-century dolls (assembled by his wife) and a fully provisioned old-time apothecary that he had acquired intact from the nearby town of Turin. This period, however, also marked the beginning of medical problems for Johnson that would soon evolve into a spastic esophagus, which could make it difficult for him to swallow and could sometimes make it seem like he was experiencing a heart attack.[11] Some believe that emotional stress can aggravate the condition, and in the case of Johnson, a man known for sudden flashes of temper, this certainly could have been a factor. The ailment would plague him for years.

As he continued to build his collection of American artifacts, Johnson's reputation as an amateur local historian grew, and on occasion he appeared on Syracuse radio shows to discuss his latest discoveries. This and his purchase of local airtime to advertise his stores constituted, for now, the full extent of his involvement in broadcasting. That would soon change.

As late as May 1950, Johnson's public concerns were largely confined to his profession. At a Supermarket Institute convention that month, he spoke on the three chief complaints currently faced by grocers: "poor packing at the checkout counters," "slow service at meat counters," and "absence of delivery service."[12] A turning point for Johnson came one month later with the outbreak of the Korean War. He had already shown during World War II that he was prepared to take action when his country battled tyrannical aggressors—the antithesis of the idealized Americanism that he held so dear—but this time much of the impetus came from the youngest of his three daughters.

By the time Eleanor Johnson married in September 1947, her groom, John A. Buchanan, had already served in the Marines during World War II. She had every right to expect that his military obligations had been fulfilled, and that their orderly life as a married couple would not be disrupted. After the war, John had finished college with a degree in forestry and was settling in to civilian life as an assistant manager for the A. C. Dutton Wholesale Lumber Corporation in Poughkeepsie, New York. Eleanor, meanwhile, began teaching geology at nearby Vassar College. Then, just three years into their marriage, the Korean War created a new national emergency. The Marines called John back to duty and shipped him to the front lines where he fought as a first lieutenant in a mortar company.[13]

Moving back to live with her parents in Syracuse, Eleanor kept track of the war in the newspapers and read about the hardships her husband suffered in the letters he wrote home. By the end of 1950, as the war taking place thousands of miles away turned increasingly brutal and indecisive, there were things close at hand that increasingly infuriated her, specifically things she heard on radio and saw on TV. Entertainers associated with Communist fronts were appearing on the airwaves, helping to promote sponsors' products that she herself was buying. She was incensed by the connection she saw between Communist fronts at home—for which some entertainers were able to raise money because of their broadcast celebrity—and the Communist aggression that her husband was fighting overseas. As she would later put it in one of her many letters to broadcasters, "My husband is now in Korea facing the bullets bought by Communist money."[14]

To learn more on the subject, she bought a copy of *Red Channels* and consulted the pages of *Counterattack*. In early 1951 she decided she had to take her case to the public. She spoke before local meetings of the Kiwanis Club, the Rotary Club, and the American Legion. A special focus of her speeches was the rising popularity of the Weavers, and she was known to bring a portable phonograph with her so that she could back up her comments by playing the folksinging group's records. One song in particular she wanted her audiences to hear. Along with traditional, innocuous folk songs, the group had recently recorded a tune called "The Banks of Marble," a throwback to the more overtly radical Almanac Singers days, a song that promoted class conflict if not outright class warfare. The verses cataloged the economic desperation of people all across the country—as if the United States were still mired in the Great Depression rather than enjoying the opportunities of a postwar prosperity—while the chorus's refrain reminded the listener of those heartless, fortresslike banks hoarding loot earned at the expense of the working class. The song concluded by urging the workers to rise up:

> Then we'd own those banks of marble
> With a guard at every door
> And we'd share those vaults of silver
> That we have sweated for!

Few people at the time were likely to make as strong an impression on conservative groups as the young, worried wife of a combat Marine fighting the good fight against godless, anti-free-enterprise Reds. Eleanor Buchanan seems to have made the most of that advantage with speeches that were, according to one observer, "straight from the heart." She used a similar approach in her correspondence. A circular to fellow housewives began, "Will you join me? No money—No pledge signing—Nor club membership involved." After identifying herself as the wife of a Marine in Korea, she asked the recipient of the letter, "Are you aware that some of YOUR money is being paid to Communist supporters operating behind his lines?" Within a few months her reputation within anti-Communist circles grew to such an extent that the American Legion dubbed her "The Joan of Arc of Syracuse."[15] Just as impressed, and for obvious personal reasons, was her father, who adopted her crusade and shared her outrage. His son-in-law John was not his only relative drawn into the military buildup for the Korean War; two of his nephews were also in the armed forces.[16] Johnson began to consider how he too could play a part in his daughter's fight to rid the airwaves of those people he regarded as either America's enemies or their unwitting tools.

When his daughter spoke of the goods on the market that were tainted by their association with Communist-front entertainers, Johnson saw a natural role for him to play. A great many of the products advertised over the air were, after all, displayed on his supermarket shelves. He decided he would remind broadcast sponsors in no uncertain terms of the important link between advertisers and the customers that he and other grocers supplied.

To help him launch his new campaign, he organized the veterans who worked in his stores into a group that first went under the ad hoc name of Veterans of World War II of Johnson's Organization. Later it became known as the Veterans Action Committee of Syracuse Super Markets. The group underscored its economic leverage by circulating a flyer bearing a drawing of a supermarket operated by freshly scrubbed, white-coated clerks; on one wall is a sign that reads, "Eternal Vigilance is the Price of Liberty!" while under the cash register is another sign: "Freedom Rings Here." Beneath it all in large, bold lettering is the line, "We love to Push the Products of Patriotic Suppliers!"[17]

Of the twenty employees listed on the organization's letterhead, some were actively involved, others merely lent their names.[18] The primary participant was Francis Neuser, Johnson's food and vegetable buyer. Neuser does not seem to have acted out of ideological fervor—his widow, Margaret Neuser, maintained that he had no previous interest in anticommunism—but, instead, spearheaded the veterans group out of personal loyalty.

Neuser was one of those Johnson employees who held their boss in high regard. Johnson not only reciprocated the feeling but had probably initiated it through his considerate treatment of Neuser, contrary to Johnson's occasional habit of being "a mean son of a gun," as Margaret Neuser put it. She believed that the two men formed a surrogate father-son relationship. Johnson never had a son and may have come to regard his hardworking buyer as a substitute. Neuser's experience with his own father had been difficult, and he responded with great affection to his older and, in this case, kindly boss. Unlike his often stern manner with other employees, Johnson lavished this treatment not only upon Neuser but upon his wife as well. If, for instance, he needed to send Neuser on a business trip, he would phone Margaret to make sure the trip would not inconvenience her.[19]

When Johnson needed someone to handle the correspondence for his new veterans group, Neuser eagerly took on the responsibility.

From the beginning he displayed a flair for capturing his readers' attention. In one of the Syracuse veterans group's first initiatives, in September 1951, Neuser worked with Johnson to persuade CBS to stop using "a subversive like Jack Gilford" on any of its programs. A telegram to network sponsors began with the line: "Why are you helping to kill our friends in Korea?"

In this early effort to get Gilford off the airwaves, Johnson and his associates established their method of persuasion—or intimidation, depending on one's point of view. In its initial response the network neither

Many sponsors and broadcast executives were willing to curry favor with Laurence Johnson, "the grocer from Syracuse," and his campaign for Americanism. *(Center for American History, University of Texas)*

defied nor capitulated but instead chose to explain away Gilford's appearance on an episode of *Arthur Godfrey and Friends* by saying that the show's usual producer-director was away when the decision to hire the comedian was made. Johnson's veterans were not satisfied. They informed the sponsors that if Gilford and his like continued to appear on the Godfrey show, they would make a point of not selling the advertisers' products "when part of the money from the sale of such products help the Communists kill, wound and cripple for life our friends in their death fight in Korea." They then told CBS that they intended to poll their customers to determine consumers' thoughts on buying products that bore a connection, the Syracuse group insisted, to the Communist cause.[20]

Joining the campaign at this early stage was another Syracuse contingent, Post 41 of the American Legion, one of the hosts of Eleanor Buchanan's early speeches. Leading the fight, and heading the post's un-American activities committee, was a man named John Dungey, who was nothing if not a true believer. The Syracuse native had fought Nazism in Europe during World War II and brought a combative attitude home with him, an attitude that surfaced a few years later when he was confronted with another absolutist ideology. He was working at the time in the sales department of the O. M. Edward Company, a manufacturer of windows and doors for trains and telephone booths, located on Plum Street in downtown Syracuse. Just a few blocks away on North Franklin was the Onondaga County headquarters of the Communist party. One day, when Dungey saw that the CP office had an American flag on display, he took offense at what he regarded as a mockery of the nation's symbol. He grabbed the flag, brought it home, and wrote an inscription on a piece of masking tape that he affixed to the flagpole, as if identifying a spoil of war:

Taken from Communist Headquarters
N. Franklin
Syracuse, NY
Sept. 12, 1950[21]

There was a personal connection between Dungey and Johnson— Dungey's wife had known the grocer's daughters while growing up—but the Legionnaire would no doubt have embraced Johnson's cause under any circumstances. From the basement of his home on Bellevue Avenue, Dungey began writing and editing a monthly anti-Communist newsletter, entitled *Spotlight*, which often attacked the same entertainers that Johnson was singling out. He also took part in Johnson's letter-writing campaigns directed at sponsors and networks. A particularly notorious feature of Dungey's newsletter was the "Monthly Box Score," which gloated over the Syracuse group's successes ("Jack Gilford—Still Out," "Philip Loeb— The End") and gnashed its teeth over its continuing frustrations ("Charlie Chaplin—an alien Fronter better off in England").[22]

Taken together the Syracuse anti-Communists—Johnson, Neuser, the Veterans Action Committee, Dungey, American Legion Post 41—soon became known in the broadcast industry as "the upstate group." But clearly the most important of them was Johnson. By the summer of 1952, Alfred Kohlberg's American Jewish League Against Communism was praising the grocer for coming up with "a unique method" for driving pro-

Communists off the air, a sensible, down-to-earth approach of speaking to sponsors "as one businessman to another" that made his technique "one of the most constructive examples at the present time."[23] Also applauding Johnson's efforts were the publishers of *Counterattack*, who soon became his allies. Johnson's method—aimed at banning such talent as Abe Burrows, Martin Ritt, John Randolph, and José Ferrer—began to have its effect as his rhetoric intensified, making the pages of *Counterattack* seem relatively restrained.

In a circular to supermarket owners, the Veterans Action Committee complained about an alleged fronter directing a CBS soap opera and posed the question to its grocery-store colleagues: "How can you help in this matter of keeping Stalin's little creatures from crawling over our super-market shelves?" Following up on this theme, Johnson pressured sponsors by threatening to subject their products to distinctly unflattering displays within his stores that would inform his customers that the company used Stalin's little creatures on their programs.[24]

Not content with using the U.S. mails, Johnson occasionally drove his Cadillac down to New York City, checked into a midtown hotel like the Park Sheraton or the Hampshire House, and applied the personal touch as he made the rounds of ad agencies on Madison Avenue. His economic warnings had their effect. Sponsors and broadcasters could not appease him fast enough, some of them rushing to Syracuse rather than waiting for Johnson's next Manhattan visit.

One of those firms eager to placate Johnson was the Borden Company. In July 1952 the Veterans Action Committee fired off a scathing letter to the firm, deploring its use of "Stalin's Little Creatures" on the TV series *Treasury Men in Action*. While making an obligatory concession that the company was free to hire whomever it wanted, the committee then turned the screws. The letter pointedly reminded Borden that its stores carried the company's products and went on to ask how the company's stockholders "would feel about the employment of Communist fronters. Could you send us a list of the Borden stockholders?" the letter asked as a final parting shot. Stuart Peabody, a Borden vice president, immediately phoned Johnson and Neuser and scrambled to explain his company's actions. Borden had done everything possible, Peabody maintained in a follow-up letter, to keep subversives off its programs. Not only had it "checked all names against *Counterattack* and *Red Channels*," it had hired American Business Consultants' research service to identify suspect entertainers it might have somehow missed. Even so, Peabody acknowledged, more had to be done. He flew to Syracuse the next week to meet with Johnson in his office. A subsequent note thanked the grocer effusively for instructing him on the full scope of the problem.[25]

Among the other corporate executives who made the Syracuse pilgrimage was John M. Fox, no less than the president of Minute Maid, who visited Johnson that fall to discuss the appearance of leftist lithographer Adolph Dehn as a guest on the *Kate Smith Show*. As soon as he returned to New York, he sent off a note to Johnson describing the visit as "the most revealing and informative day that I have experienced in a long time," and extended a "thousand thanks for waking me up."[26]

Looking back at incidents like these from the perspective of a later time, it is difficult to understand the executives' actions. Why would powerful officers in major manufacturing corporations feel they had to curry favor with a grocer from Syracuse? True, the Johnson strategy was aimed at the corporations' most vital organ—their profit margin—but was there really any reason to believe that Johnson could make a serious dent in the companies' sales? Johnson was fond of suggesting that he had influence among retailers in the greater central New York region and even implied that his prominence extended to the national scene through his involvement in trade associations. What, however, was the evidence that he commanded such respect?

Assuming that advertisers bothered to scrutinize this situation, they would have been hard pressed to discover any such evidence. Johnson's surviving correspondence certainly does not indicate that he was a man of dominating influence in his field. A letter he wrote to a Michigan American Legionnaire, for instance, reveals that he knew the owners of only one supermarket in Detroit in mid-1952, near the beginning of his anti-Red campaign. In another instance, in 1954, Senator Karl Mundt wrote Johnson to praise his "formula" for combating communism, "which— if followed by even five hundred similar entrepreneurs—would bring to a grinding halt the use of Communists and fellow-travelers in the advertising business of this country." In other words, even one of Johnson's staunchest supporters did not believe that the grocer commanded a widespread following—and this after Johnson had been marshaling his forces for two years.[27] Broadcast sponsors did not, obviously, have access to these letters, but they surely must have noticed that, despite his implications that he represented some sort of supermarket consortium, Johnson and his Syracuse cohorts were the only merchants who made a habit of pressuring radio and TV advertisers.

One of Johnson's favorite techniques brings up another question. If a sponsor continued to use talent on its show that the grocer found suspicious, he would notify the company that he was terminating the merchandising agreement that was designed to promote the sponsor's products in his stores.[28] This action was based on Johnson's assumption — or, perhaps better put, his *presumption* — that major manufacturers needed him more than he needed them. Merchandising agreements were supposed to benefit both the store and the manufacturer. How did the cancellation of this agreement become a weapon in Johnson's arsenal? If a sponsor chose to cancel such an agreement, wouldn't that have punished the grocer just as much, if not more?

Perhaps companies like Borden and Minute Maid were not sure of Johnson's clout, but the real point is that they never chose to test the Syracuse group's claims, they never called Johnson's bluff. Why were they so willing to relinquish control over their own companies' hiring decisions? The fact that the country was at war provides part of the explanation. In earlier conflicts, citizens had gone along with extreme tactics against perceived fifth columnists, but in the case of the two world wars, for instance, measures like the Espionage and Sedition Acts or the internment of Japanese Americans were enforced by the power of the federal government. Here the whip hand was held by someone with six stores in central New York. Ultimately the abject behavior of some companies can only be explained by the stampede instinct. After *Red Channels* had succeeded in rattling nerves in the broadcasting industry for more than a year, even the suggestion that profits might decline or stockholders might revolt was enough to spook some executives into a headlong panic, regardless of who might get trampled underfoot. But, contrary to the impression that some accounts have created, not everyone reacted that way.

Certain descriptions of the period make it seem that Johnson and his allies had a stranglehold over the entire broadcast industry. Some in the media, though, were not particularly impressed with the upstate group.

Some resisted outright while others were at least willing to parry with the grocer from Syracuse. Together they underscored the point that Johnson enjoyed only as much power as others were willing to give him.

Johnson and his allies were occasionally frustrated in their efforts, sometimes by a network like NBC that enforced the blacklist but inconsistently, other times by a major advertising agency like Young & Rubicam, which never, Johnson claimed, "gained a reputation of ever being tough on Communist Fronters or Communist helpers," despite its firing of Jean Muir in the blacklist's earliest days. Others simply failed to be sufficiently obsequious. Many might have sweated bullets whenever they received a phone call that began with the words, "This is Larry Johnson from Syracuse," but Samuel Dalsimer of Grey Advertising was unflustered. Johnson once called Dalsimer to notify him that his company's hiring practices were liable to place it on a list of uncooperative agencies. When Dalsimer heard what other firms had already made this list, he had the effrontery to reply, "I would be pleased to be in their company." Galling as this was to the temperamental Johnson, it paled in comparison to the experience he had with *Life* magazine after the Veterans Action Committee had scolded the publication for running feature articles on José Ferrer and Charlie Chaplin. Richard L. Williams, a *Life* staff writer, responded, "Your story moves me deeply but not to sympathy. Your literature is returned herewith."[29] The upstate group fumed, and Dungey's *Spotlight* in particular blasted the magazine in its March 1952 issue, ending its article with an appeal to its readers to write HUAC demanding an investigation of Communist influence in magazine publishing. But the Syracuse group had no real leverage to exert in this instance and produced no results.

Perhaps most troubling to Johnson was his ongoing feud with Procter & Gamble. The Veterans Action Committee began harrying the manufacturer as early as March 1952 when it castigated the company for using *Red Channels* listee Charles Irving as a director on the soap opera *Search for Tomorrow*. Within two months Johnson escalated his efforts by canceling his promotion agreement with the manufacturer. At first Procter & Gamble acted no differently from other firms that had succeeded in convincing themselves that Johnson was a force to be reckoned with. Howard Morgens, a Procter & Gamble vice president, made the trip from corporate headquarters in Cincinnati to Johnson's Salina Street supermarket in

Syracuse for a meeting that he later described to the grocer as "both pleasant and instructive." Eager to feed Johnson's sense of importance, he added, "If you have any further suggestions to make about our radio and TV talent, I'd consider it a personal favor to hear from you directly." Still not done, Morgens later promised to follow up on one of Johnson's suggestions by hiring a troubleshooter to monitor future hirings. Johnson, however, was not appeased. A small-city operator he might have been, but he was not so easily bamboozled by big-corporate flattery. Even as Procter & Gamble appeared to be fawning over him, he could see that the firm was also quietly defying him: after keeping Charles Irving off the air for a brief hiatus, the company reemployed him and then infuriated the combustible Johnson further by endorsing an anti-blacklist statement produced by the left-oriented Radio Writers Guild. At times Johnson became so incensed that he would stomp down the aisles of his stores pulling Procter & Gamble products from the shelves.[30]

The tentative gestures of companies like Procter & Gamble revealed weaknesses in Johnson's methods and might have even slowed him down, but they never came close to halting his campaign of intimidation. The resistance was far too limited to accomplish that. But one group of broadcasters demonstrated exactly how hollow Johnson's threats really were. This group of radio and TV executives knew Johnson very well, far better than national sponsors and advertising agencies did.

Local Syracuse broadcasters were pressured by Johnson in the same way their national counterparts were. Most often the grocer focused on the records that local radio stations played, demanding that they stop airing the songs of the Weavers, the musical bête noire of the anti-Communist camp, as well as bandleader Artie Shaw, who had fourteen citations in *Red Channels*. The station WOLF, whose programming was dominated by recorded popular music, received the brunt of Johnson's attentions. Also feeling the heat was the Syracuse University station WAER for featuring the on-air comments of a professor who had defended a student arrested at an American Labor party rally. This last Johnson protest might have been decisive, but not in the way the grocer had hoped. Don Lyon, an instructor in the university's radio department and a supervisor at WAER, was angered by Johnson's attempt to dictate programming choices and concerned about the grocer's larger campaign. Contacting the other broadcasters in the city, he arranged a meeting to discuss how best to deal with the issue.[31]

With Lyon acting as chairman of the gathering, executives from Syracuse's five commercial broadcasters met with a representative of WAER at the university's Carnegie Library. For them the issue was not communism versus anti-communism but the proper response to outside pressure. And the pressure in this case involved direct economic consequences. When dealing with national firms, Johnson might have implied that the sales of their products would suffer if they didn't comply with his demands, but this was an indirect threat at best, one that was never truly substantiated. Here in Syracuse, however, he bought airtime to advertise his stores and warned that he would pull his commercials if not satisfied with broadcasters' decisions—an action that would clearly cut into commercial stations' revenues. Still, the Syracuse broadcasters were unfazed. Their decision was unanimous: they would not give in to Johnson's demands.[32]

The decision does not seem to have been based on personal politics. WSYR executive E. R. Vadeboncoeur, for instance, had been a Roosevelt Democrat during the 1930s but was now an Eisenhower Republican. "That to him didn't have any bearing over this situation," said his daughter Joan Vadeboncoeur. "It was what was right and what was wrong. I remember him saying that Johnson was wrong in what he did and how he was trying to exert pressure. It's interesting because this is a conservative community and always has been. But certainly the broadcasters weren't going to knuckle under."[33]

Lawrence Myers, who represented the university station at the meeting, believed that the rules governing the stations' licenses required that the broadcasters decide as they did. "It was a general feeling," he recalled, "that a person outside any station organization should not have any direct say in the programming of that station. That was strictly the responsibility of those in charge of the station as noted by the Federal Communications Commission." Some might dispute whether FCC regulations should be interpreted in that way, but there was little dispute about the effect of the Syracuse broadcasters' decision. Johnson, confronted with strong resistance, gave up on his local campaign to regulate the airwaves.[34] Small-city radio stations, under the direct threat of reduced revenues, had succeeded in doing what major corporations were unwilling even to attempt.

Aiding the Syracuse broadcasters was a sense of solidarity. Throughout this period, radio and TV executives in the city periodically met to discuss ways they could fulfill their obligations to serve the community, whether

it was promoting a worthy nonprofit organization or, as in the Johnson affair, maintaining their responsibility to control programming in the face
of outside economic pressure. In a city the size of Syracuse this was obviously easier than it would be in a metropolis like New York City or among
sponsors with headquarters scattered throughout the country. But policy
meetings among major media players were not impossible or unheard of.
In 1947 as many as fifty representatives of the Hollywood film industry met
in New York's Waldorf-Astoria Hotel and agreed to institute a blacklist. If
media executives could reach a consensus on one side of the issue, they
could also have chosen to congregate and take a stand on the other side,
finding a way to resist outside protests designed to supersede their own hiring practices. Instead sponsors, advertising agencies, and broadcast networks chose to remain unorganized and often to appease the Johnson
group. For one Syracuse broadcaster, this attitude was mystifying. "I don't
know what's the matter with those people in New York," he said. "Maybe
they're so big they have to be stupid."[35]

Johnson's power might have been little more than a mirage, but some
continued to assume illusion was reality, and executives and entertainers
continued to obey the upstate group's commands. Among those who submitted to the group's alleged authority were actor Joseph Cotten and the
producers of his radio show *The Private Files of Matthew Bell*. In the fall
of 1952, Johnson sent a letter to the show's sponsor, Seabrook Farms, to
complain about Cotten's political affiliations. Responding in now stereo-
typical fashion, Seabrook sent its company plane to Syracuse, taking not
only C. F. Seabrook, president of the firm, but also the company's lawyer,
an executive from the sponsor's advertising agency, and Cotten himself.
They met in Johnson's supermarket office, then in a nearby restaurant
where Cotten denied the charges made against him. Johnson responded
by saying that he could only go by the record "as to who was American
and who was not American." Johnson eventually decided that Cotten
could continue on the show after Seabrook agreed to produce a pro-Amer-
ican public service announcement to be aired with each episode. But the
grocer, emboldened by his newfound power, did not leave the matter
there. He went on to request that the actor stop by his supermarket to sign
autographs for customers. Unwilling to test the upstate arbiter of broadcast
practices, Cotten agreed to go along with the publicity stunt that would
boost the business of the man who had just tried to run him out of radio.[36]

Cotten was not the only entertainer who made a point of traveling to Syracuse. And not all of them were reluctant. Some were inspired by Johnson's crusade and enthusiastic about making the trip. The most prominent among them was the anti-Communist actor Adolphe Menjou, who was quite willing to appear at Johnson's stores and helped bolster the grocer's prestige. Support for the upstate group also came from politicians, including the era's definitive anti-Communist icon, Joseph McCarthy, who once met with John Dungey at the Syracuse airport for a photo opportunity.

As for broadcast executives who continued to inflate Johnson's importance, the grocer was known to show them his volatile temper when he failed to receive the deference he expected, as if he now felt he could treat radio and TV professionals as his own employees. Once while phoning a network executive, the *New York Post* reported, Johnson took umbrage when the broadcaster attempted to present his side of the issue. Johnson cut him short: "This is my call. If you have anything to say, make your own call."[37]

Johnson now possessed a stature that transcended his original ambition to become a local man of respect. Some, like Veterans Action Committee leader Neuser, helped him attain this stature out of personal loyalty. Others, like Dungey and Menjou, assisted him because of their commitment to the cause. One other ally came on board simply to go along for the ride.

By the time Harvey Matusow met Laurence Johnson he had already made something of a name for himself within anti-Communist circles as a witness before congressional investigating committees. Within just a few years the validity of all his testimony would come into question, but for now, in 1952, he was a young man on the rise.

A stark ethnic contrast to the WASPish central New York grocer who would become his mentor, Matusow was a child of the New York City melting pot, born and raised near the Grand Concourse in the Bronx, the son of Russian-Jewish immigrants. He spent much of his early years in a whirl of social striving, desperate to measure up to his athletic, talented brother, eager to acquire the status enjoyed by more quick-witted, more popular schoolmates. "I tried too hard," he later wrote, "and I pushed, bluffing my way through, being loud and glib, pretending that I could do but not proving it." He clamored for recognition in scholastics, in sports,

in the give-and-take of street-corner banter, and in his hobby of pup-
peteering, one of his earliest attempts at show business.[38]

If Matusow had one thing in common with Johnson, it was an early
experience in shopkeeping. To help his family make ends meet during the
depression, he worked in his father's combination cigar store and lunch-
eonette in midtown Manhattan. The business needed a steady supply of
coins to feed its pinball machines, and he would go to the theater next
door to exchange bills for rolls of nickels, a task that earned him the
moniker Kid Nickels. The Runyonesque aura of this nickname turned out
to be fitting. When not helping at the family store, Matusow was running
errands for a neighborhood gambler known as Phil the Bookie.[39] From an
early age he began to develop a penchant for hustling.

Matusow found a club that would have him as a member when he enlisted in the army, and found another after returning home when he
joined a front organization called American Youth for Democracy. There
he followed some of the group's members into the Communist party. He
might have thought he had found a place for himself working his way up
the CPUSA's bureaucratic ladder—from Communist bookstore clerk to
state literature director for the Labor Youth League—but he soon learned
how treacherous his new path could be as revealed by his biographers
Robert M. Lichtman and Ronald D. Cohen. In 1950, after he went to
work as a debt collector in Harlem, his party superiors pronounced him
guilty of "white chauvinism," part of a larger CPUSA purge that lasted from
1949 to 1953 and affected several thousand members. To punish Matusow
for his political incorrectness, the party took away his Labor Youth League
title.

This encounter with high-handed party discipline must have angered
him and contributed to his eventual disillusionment with the CPUSA, but
other considerations might have played a role. Public opinion at the time
was clearly turning against the Soviet Union. As is suggested by his biographers, the opportunistic Matusow was probably eager to ride the country's gathering wave of anti-communism. Whatever his motives, by March
1950 he had switched sides. He arranged a meeting at FBI headquarters in
downtown Manhattan, where he offered to provide the Bureau with information on the Communist party.[40]

For ten months Matusow worked as a paid undercover informant, until the party became suspicious enough to expel him and the FBI had no

further use for him. Adrift once more, Matusow tried anchoring himself by joining the air force, where he could at least enjoy the status that came with a military uniform. What he would not find, however, was peace of mind. After coming under suspicion within the air force because of his Communist past, he suffered a nervous breakdown.[41] Soon, though, he would find yet another calling that would not only rescue him from emotional despair but win him the attention and recognition he craved.

Living near his Ohio air force base was a couple who had testified before HUAC about local Communist party activities. After learning that Matusow was interested in telling the public about his CPUSA experiences, they befriended him and helped arrange for him to appear before HUAC as a witness. Matusow's congressional committee debut came in late November 1951. He had arrived on the national stage but not as he hoped he would—his appearance was confined to a secret executive session not covered by the media. But that would change three months later, after he left the air force, when he made his first public HUAC testimony. His appearance, focusing on Communist youth groups, garnered attention in newspapers across the country. Matusow was not satisfied. He complained that King George VI of England had hogged the front-page headlines after having the nerve to die in the middle of Matusow's HUAC testimony. His grousing, though, was unwarranted. His career as an anti-Communist witness was taking off. Within a week of his HUAC testimony, he appeared before the Senate Internal Security Subcommittee, chaired by the prominent Red hunter Senator Pat McCarran, and in July he testified at a Smith Act trial of CPUSA leaders accused of advocating the violent overthrow of the U.S. government.[42]

Matusow and Laurence Johnson met during this period through their mutual association with *Counterattack*. Matusow's connection to both the grocer and the newsletter had special significance for him.

Ever since putting on puppet shows while growing up, Matusow had been fascinated by the field of entertainment. More recently he viewed his committee appearances and trial testimonies as a form of theater. He was eager to gain an entrée into *Counterattack*, the monitor of broadcasting, because it would provide "the opportunity to get into the glamorous limelight of show business."[43]

After first relegating Matusow to selling *Counterattack* subscriptions, Theodore Kirkpatrick saw something more substantial in him. In February 1952 he sent Matusow a letter praising his HUAC testimony, and in the spring he and Keenan decided to hire the congressional witness as an assistant editor.[44]

At *Counterattack* Matusow began to insinuate himself into the showbiz world in his own peculiar way. When he learned in June that New York Yankees catcher Yogi Berra would appear on NBC's *All-Star Revue* alongside Jack Gilford, he made a series of calls to the Yankees front office. Using his puppeteer's skill for manufacturing an array of voices, he took on a different persona with each call as he simulated a groundswell of irate fans who were shocked that a Yankee star would share a TV soundstage with a Communist fronter. His deception worked. A Yankees public relations executive told NBC that Berra would not appear on the same show as the suspect comedian, and the network took Gilford off the program.[45]

As amused as he might have been by this prank, Matusow was interested in playing a more substantial role in the entertainment field. He got his opportunity when he struck up a friendship with *Counterattack* ally Johnson. As he had done with Francis Neuser, Johnson took a paternal interest in the pudgy young man with dark curly hair, and for his part Matusow was infatuated with the power that the grocer seemed to wield. Here was someone who, as Matusow later explained, could waltz into a prestigious Madison Avenue advertising agency and be "immediately ushered into the meticulous, luxurious office of one of the agency's vice presidents."[46] Attaching himself to such a figure could obviously reap advantages for a young man who wanted to exert real influence in the business of radio and TV.

His paternal interests aside, Johnson must have also seen some practical value in his friendship with Matusow. Being headquartered in Syracuse might not have prevented the grocer from having his say in New York City broadcasting, but it did deprive him of the ability to keep a close eye on the situation. Matusow, the streetwise New York City kid, could be his forward observer, ready to provide inside information on entertainers unavailable in HUAC transcripts or the latest issue of *Counterattack*. He could also act as an enforcer, on hand to make sure broadcasters fulfilled their patriotic duties as defined by upstate pro-Americans.[47]

The friendship between the two men grew late in the summer during a visit Matusow made to Syracuse. On his next trip to Manhattan,

Johnson began to take Matusow with him to important meetings with advertisers. After checking into the Hampshire House on Central Park West, the grocer set up an appointment to deal with his latest TV concern, the *Schlitz Playhouse of the Stars*, a drama anthology on CBS, which Johnson believed had become a safe haven for Communists. He brought Matusow with him to his hotel's restaurant for a meeting with Francis Barton, an executive with Lennen & Mitchell, Schlitz's advertising agency. After the grocer delivered a lecture on the importance of vigilance on the airwaves, Barton raised his own concern that the agency might be barring performers without enough information, at which point Johnson flew into one of his fits of temper. As Barton recalled, Johnson "got thoroughly angry with me and started to pound the table and raise his voice sufficiently to attract attention around the dining room." Once under control again, Johnson came up with a solution: Barton's agency could acquire all the information they needed by hiring Matusow as a consultant.[48]

This was not the only time Johnson promoted his protégé within the broadcast industry. He also pressured producer Himan Brown to report on his hiring choices to Matusow and tried unsuccessfully to persuade the agency of Hilton & Riggio to hire Matusow as a writer. In the case of his relationship with Brown, Matusow's actions revealed that, no matter how much new prestige he enjoyed, he never strayed too far from his street-corner-hustler ways. Still essentially a *shnorrer*, as they would have called him in his old Bronx neighborhood, he managed to wangle free lunches out of his meetings with Brown and then, for good measure, would sponge a couple of dollars off the producer for his carfare home.[49]

With Johnson as his mentor, Matusow expanded his contacts in the New York media. He began to work with BBD&O's Jack Wren, another former FBI informant, in assessing the ideological credentials of suspect entertainers, and developed relationships with such anti-Communist columnists as George Sokolsky and Victor Riesel, who also played an important role in the blacklisting process. Each contact he made helped him manage Johnson's crusade on the New York scene. Among his escapades, he took part in one of the grocer's most protracted battles, waged against the CBS-TV series *Danger*.

A memorable if now forgotten show, *Danger* was a product of those early years of television when producers were still formulating the rules of the medium with relatively few restrictions on content. The program fit into the crime melodrama genre, but it ventured beyond those confines by emphasizing stories based on character, offbeat situations, and downbeat endings, served up with a theatrical-style immediacy made possible by a live broadcast. Shaping the series was an illustrious collection of talent. Its first director was Yul Brynner, just before taking his career-making Broadway role in *The King and I*, to be followed by Sidney Lumet, the future filmmaker with such credits as *The Pawnbroker* and *Serpico*, succeeded by John Frankenheimer, who would later go on to make such films as *The Birdman of Alcatraz* and *The Manchurian Candidate*.

For Johnson and his associates, though, it was not the quality of the show that mattered as much as the political affiliations of the people who worked on the series, especially such actors as John Randolph, Salem Ludwig, Martin Ritt, and Lee Grant. Johnson was convinced that *Danger's* sponsor and producer were not diligent about enforcing the blacklist. He was right.

Charles Russell was a former actor who now, as producer of *Danger*, filled the role of a dapper and dignified executive. Left-wingers who contributed to the show later described him as a man without political interests, someone who would not oppose the activities of Laurence Johnson out of ideological conviction. Instead he instinctively resisted the idea of barring talented contributors to the program on the basis of outside protests. Not only did he occasionally use actors after they had been named as subversives, he was also willing to resort to subterfuge to undermine the blacklist system. Often he hired the Communist writers Walter Bernstein, Arnold Manoff, and Abraham Polonsky through the use of fronts, people who were willing to assign their names to blacklisted writers' scripts.[50] (Bernstein later dramatized this experience in the 1976 comedy *The Front*, directed by fellow *Danger* alumnus Martin Ritt.)

Melvin Block, president of the Block Drug Company which sponsored the program, might not have been aware of Russell's undercover operation, but he was willing to run interference for those named by the upstate group. He tried to put off Johnson and his allies by claiming that CBS, not his company, was responsible for casting decisions, and he would assure them that Block Drug was doing everything possible to make sure the network kept the show "as clean as a whistle." When the Veterans Action Committee seized upon the political record of Lumet, Block wired Neuser to state unequivocally that the show's director was "neither a commie or a commie sympathizer," which was true. Although clearly left wing in orientation, Lumet had steered away from communism when he was a teenager, after a Young Communist League meeting had demonstrated to him the oppressively dogmatic nature of the party. But in this case the plain truth proved to be an insufficient defense. The pressure continued. In New York City, Matusow, assisted by columnist Riesel, confronted Block with a photo from the *American Legion Magazine* that purportedly showed Lumet attending a Communist meeting. From Syracuse, Johnson wrote Block to propose his pet display scheme for one of the manufacturer's products, Ammident toothpaste. The grocer would display a competing toothpaste with a sign that would explain that this company tried "not to use any of 'Stalin's Little Creatures' in their advertising." Then a second display for Ammident would feature a sign of the manufacturer's making that would give the company "an opportunity to test out your beliefs on the reasons why you have consented to Communist Fronters advertising Ammident." Believing he could not appease the grocer any longer, Block asked that Lumet meet with Matusow and Riesel in the hope he might convince them to back off.[51]

As he walked to the meeting at Block's Park Avenue apartment, Lumet was still unsure how he would act when confronted by his accusers. As he later recalled, he entered the apartment and was introduced to Riesel and Matusow—"Harvey was sitting there, just a big fat dumpling"—and then, without "even knowing how or why I was doing it, I just started cursing at the two of them, calling them every name in the book. Harvey stood up and said, 'Calm down, don't get your balls in an uproar—you're not the one.'" Now that Lumet stood before them, Riesel and Matusow could plainly see that the suspect person in the photo was not him after all. An awkward silence descended upon the room, followed by some equally awkward small talk before Lumet announced he was leaving. Matusow walked out with him and accompanied him into the elevator down to the first floor. Exuding bonhomie, as if they had just shared a drink together, he offered to give Lumet a ride home.[52] The director managed to turn him down politely. If nothing else, the incident revealed that Matusow was willing to admit when he was wrong. It also revealed that he was incapable of understanding that others did not regard his activities as little more than a game.

For Matusow, though, the game was yielding personal victories. At the same time his association with Johnson was moving him toward the heart of New York broadcasting and journalism, he began campaigning for Joe McCarthy's 1952 reelection, allowing him to enter the demagogic senator's inner circle. At the end of the year he received a special assignment. He was to accompany Arvilla Bentley, a wealthy divorcee and McCarthy supporter, to the Bahamas so that she could avoid a congressional subpoena concerning the senator's alleged misuse of money she had contributed to his campaign. The experience of escorting Bentley out of the country in secret must have appealed to Matusow's sense of drama. Even more appealing was the romance he struck up with his glamorous companion. He married her the following March.[53] Two months later Matusow ascended another step in his climb toward reflected power and notoriety: he became a consultant to McCarthy's newly formed subcommittee that would become the vehicle for his most controversial Red-hunting investigations. Matusow had truly arrived. With the help of Johnson's sponsorship, he had risen from the ranks of informers and black-listers to the upper echelons of congressional investigators.

Among the various sectors of the anti-Red crusade, the House and Senate committees generated the biggest headlines and did the most to shape the public's attitudes on the issues. Matusow's new appointment would, for the most part, take him out of the issue of communism in entertainment—McCarthy never paid much attention to that part of the subversion controversy. But other committees made it their special concern and were eager to stir up public outcry over this special breed of Red infiltration.

Congressional Oversight

FROM THE START, both Laurence Johnson and the *Counterattack* group argued that the scope of their cause reached far and wide. The implications of guarding the airwaves, they insisted, were not confined to a single industry but extended across the country and were worthy of some sort of federal intervention. Yet for two years after the release of *Red Channels*, private activism continued to sprint ahead of congressional probes. While HUAC might have triggered the movie industry purge with its grilling of the Hollywood Ten, the committee was slow to focus on radio and TV.

The first shift in emphasis, however slight, came in April 1951 when HUAC questioned former Radio Writers Guild president Sam Moore. Over the next year and a half the committee went on to subpoena such other radio scripters as Reuben Ship, Anne Ray, and Abe Burrows. Still, broadcast professionals constituted a small percentage of entertainment figures brought before the committee, which continued to group its hearings on the subject under the title of "Communism in the Motion Picture Industry," as if committee members were unable to shake off their starstruck fascination with Hollywood long enough to look at the somewhat less glamorous industry of broadcasting. In February 1952 the *New York Times* reported that HUAC "warned the television industry against widespread Red infiltration," a hint that it might yet launch a full-scale investigation into that field.[1] If it hoped, however, to produce a new set of headlines by taking this direction, another congressional committee beat it to the punch.

Senator Pat McCarran loomed large among congressional Red hunters. A flamboyant Democratic party maverick, he had opposed both the New Deal and America's entry into World War II, and more recently had taken up the anti-Communist crusade before the Republican McCarthy had even discovered the issue. He is perhaps best known today as the sponsor of the notorious Internal Security Act of 1950, which clamped down on front organizations and empowered the federal government to set up detention camps for subversives. Less frequently remembered is his work as chairman of the Senate Internal Security Subcommittee. One series of hearings, conducted between April 1951 and May 1952, was entitled "Subversive Infiltration of Radio, Television and the Entertainment Industry."

Released to the public in August 1952, the first half of the McCarran Committee testimony dealt with the ideological battles within the Radio Writers Guild. Two years earlier *Counterattack* had first alleged that pro-Communists dominated the union. Now the issue found its place in newspapers across the country.

Charges against the Radio Writers Guild leadership were based for the most part on the testimony of three anti-Communist union members. Ruth Adams Knight and Welbourn Kelley talked about the changes in the guild that had convinced them during the 1940s that a pro-Communist group had taken control. Corroborating their comments was Paul Milton, who had organized an anti-Communist faction within the union in October 1950, under the name of "We the Undersigned." All three placed particular importance on the guild leadership's opposition to the resolution pledging support to the U.S. government during the Korean War.[2] From the other side of the union's political divide, the committee subpoenaed Peter Lyon, the alleged leader of the pro-Communist faction. Supplying the basis for the aggressive questioning of Lyon were confidential reports furnished by the FBI.[3]

Also subpoenaed was Millard Lampell, the former member of the Almanac Singers and currently a radio writer best known for "The Lonesome Train," a folk cantata written in collaboration with Earl Robinson and produced on radio by Norman Corwin. Although the mainstream press had not paid much attention to him, *Counterattack* had been scrutinizing Lampell's front associations since mid-1947. As always, allegations of this kind were regarded as proof of subversive activity by fervent anti-Reds and as an illustration of Red-baiting hysteria by their opponents. Other information that has emerged in the years since has helped create a more complete picture.

According to an interview he gave in the 1990s, Lampell joined the Communist party while a member of the Almanac Singers in the early 1940s but then left it when he went into the army during World War II. His connection to the party after that is more difficult to define. Lampell was a prodigious activist in front organizations—nineteen of which were listed in *Red Channels*—but these associations did not by themselves prove involvement in the Communist movement; nor did his registering with the New York branch of the American Labor party, originally a coalition encompassing a variety of left-wing groups that, some people claimed, had come under Communist influence. Other, more intriguing pieces of information come from FBI reports. More than one Bureau informant claimed Lampell was a dedicated Communist in California in the late 1940s. A HUAC witness named Sylvia Richards later corroborated this report by placing him during this period in a Hollywood Communist group. The most unequivocal statement came from Louis Budenz, who told the FBI that Lampell was "an active young Communist" and a participant in the party's campaign to infiltrate radio.[4] Like Budenz's allegation against Lyon, this statement has no direct corroboration, so one's belief in it hinges upon the issue of Budenz's reliability as a witness.

Taking its cue from the FBI reports—and, in particular, Budenz's comments—the McCarran Committee approached Lampell as though he were as important a figure as Lyon. The two men responded in the same way. To all questions about Communist affiliations, they refused to answer on the basis of the Fifth Amendment.

The second half of the published hearings, released in September, was less focused than the first, more in line with the desultory nature of HUAC proceedings. Rather than dealing with the specific issue of union infiltration, the committee called four performers, under varying levels of suspicion, who had no connection at all among them. Comedian Sam Levenson, folksinger Burl Ives, and actress Judy Holliday all endured exhaustively and pointlessly detailed interrogation as they explained away their various front associations. Levenson had originally been named by Harvey Matusow in HUAC testimony and had subsequently been exonerated by him in a letter written with the assistance of Jack Wren. Holliday successfully navigated the committee's series of questions and went on to resume her movie career, thanks in part to a dossier compiled for her studio by Kenneth Bierly, now a clearance consultant. Ives too emerged from the hearings able to work again. As for the fourth witness, actor Philip Loeb, he reiterated the position he had taken since his dismissal from *The Goldbergs*: he had indeed been active in left-wing activities—he even conceded that his seventeen *Red Channels* citations had been accurate—but he was not a Communist.[5] It did him no good. He remained unemployable in radio and TV.

For *Counterattack* and the Syracuse contingent, the McCarran hearings vindicated all their efforts and cast a harsh, revealing light on the Communist conspiracy in broadcasting and the dupes who abetted it. For opponents of the blacklist, the proceedings legitimized a witch-hunt, fostered a virtual censorship, and smeared the innocent. The debate over these and other congressional hearings raged through the rest of the decade and continued well after the investigations came to an end. Without doubt, committee members orchestrated the proceedings for the benefit of a sensation-hungry media, but there was more to the hearings' legacy than a lesson in opportunism. In retrospect they could occasionally provide a glimpse into the ideological struggles of the time.

During a period when the country was attempting to contain an aggressive Communist power, the exposure of CPUSA machinations and deceptive front groups had some value, just as there had been good reason to shed light on fascists and their allies during World War II. If the congressional committees had confined themselves to that task, they would probably enjoy a better reputation today. Instead they insisted on bullying witnesses into naming names, a practice that reinforced the blacklist. For this critics have rightly deplored these committees for being vindictive. A more complicated question is whether the committees should have avoided names altogether. Investigations of concealed CPUSA attempts to control unions, for instance, would have meant little without identifying the party functionaries who supervised those activities. But the committees went well beyond that, insisting that their witnesses provide an encyclopedic list of names, no matter how peripheral those associates might have been to the Communist movement. The public had no pressing need to know every person that a former Communist actor might have met in a Marxist study group in 1936. Also undercutting the hearings were strained attempts to divine dangerous subversive messages in programs written by leftists. In her testimony, Ruth Knight declared that there was "no such thing in their scripts as a decent banker and a decent lawyer," while Paul Milton claimed that certain writers could disseminate Communist ideas "by holding up to ridicule the various American ideals of free enterprise, of democracy, of capitalism as we understand it." The only specific example offered of leftist-slanted writing was an episode of *Cavalcade of America* in which scripter Peter Lyon likened Communist partisans in Yugoslavia to the American Revolutionary war hero Francis Marion. If Lyon's script did in fact include this comparison, however, it was deleted before the show's broadcast.[6]

Looking beyond the vague theorizing and the naming-names ritual, some testimonies rise above the hearings' usual fare of ham-fisted political theater. From a historical perspective, the most interesting participants tend to be those who have attracted the most criticism over the years—the ex-Communists who became so-called friendly witnesses. Many, to be sure, testified solely to save their careers. Some were driven by the sincere intention to expose an ideology they had come to mistrust, if not despise. Others were driven by a mixture of both motives. Whatever the underlying reason—and whatever the intentions of their headline-grasping interrogators—their testimonies offer a useful oral history of the American Communist experience and its role in the broadcast field, especially when combined with other sources.

As for the veracity of these witnesses, it should be noted that they testified under oath and would have been subject to perjury charges if they had lied. Taking an oath obviously does not guarantee the truth, but it should also be pointed out that unfriendly witnesses, who repeatedly denounced cooperative witnesses as informers and stool pigeons, were typically reluctant to say, under oath, that these people were lying. In a revealing HUAC exchange, Communist screenwriter Paul Jarrico railed against fellow writer Richard Collins for cooperating with the committee, going further than most by saying that Collins was "perjuring himself." When a committee member asked if Collins had perjured himself when he had said Jarrico was a Communist party member, Jarrico replied, "I refuse to answer that question on the grounds that it may tend to incriminate me."[7]

Generally the cooperative ex-Communists had never been fierce ideologues. They were not the sort of people who would have been fired with a messianic sense of purpose by William Z. Foster's *Toward a Soviet America*, the CPUSA official's 1932 clarion call that had predicted an American dictatorship of the proletariat that would abolish all non-Communist political parties. Rather, they joined the Communist movement either at the start of the Popular Front or in the early days of World War II when the party was at its most eager to promote a reasonable, reformist image. As radio script supervisor Judith Raymond put it, she became a Communist because she thought the party was all about "winning the war and civil rights." Other Popular Front causes that attracted people could be trade unionism, Spanish Civil War relief, or the plight of migrant workers. Communist recruiters emphasized the party's mainstream intent, or as one party member explained it to radio writer Stanley Rubin, communism "was the answer for any man of liberal views."[8]

Once in the CPUSA—or the Communist Political Association, as it was called between 1944 and 1945—entertainers might be expected to perform at social events designed to raise money for party activities, but broadcast recruits might also be dragooned into far more menial tasks. Some might have to hawk copies of the *Daily Worker* on street corners, which was not necessarily the best way to win the allegiance of those who prided themselves on their creative accomplishments. The party would then strain the patience of its recruits still more by subjecting them to ponderous, barely decipherable lectures on the Marxist interpretation of history or the Marxist approach to show business. Delivering some of these talks to Hollywood radio people at this time was Bruce Minton, later identified as a contact of Soviet spy Jacob Golos.[9]

Although party officials sought out entertainers, they weren't always terribly pleased with the mentality of show-business people, especially those who made a living out of comedic irreverence. During World War II, *New Masses* editor Joseph North had approached Abe Burrows, then the head writer for radio's comedy hit *Duffy's Tavern*. North asked him if he would write a humor column for his magazine, but Burrows turned him down, perhaps sensing the difficulty that his talents would have of surviving in the journal's arid ideological environment. He soon saw firsthand how humorless the comrades could be when a sacred cow of theirs was threatened. At one of the leftist Hollywood parties where he entertained, Burrows once lampooned the sort of radio documentary popularized by Norman Corwin and other Popular Front writers during the war, "very pontifical radio programs," as he later described it, "with everybody talking very loud and introducing Thomas Jefferson and Abraham Lincoln at every opportunity." Burrows's routine normally went over very well with some groups, but here with this crowd his performance was greeted with nothing but silence. One of the attendees took Burrows aside and told him, "I think that is a very bad thing for you to do, Abe, you know." When Burrows asked why, the only response he got was, "Because I think it is wrong."[10]

Like others who joined, some broadcast writers, actors, and directors were willing to endure the minor indignities of party life because they believed they were part of a movement that would help win the war and promote FDR's New Deal. Those who stayed on would be introduced to a worldview in which a person's essential worth could be judged solely on the basis of his or her ideological bent. Former Communist Allen Sloane recalled that his fellow broadcast writers in the movement conveyed this attitude in everyday conversation through "Aesopian language":

> When a Communist introduces somebody to you as a terrific guy it means you are being introduced to somebody who is a fellow Communist. When he is called a good guy it means you are being introduced to somebody who is known to be a fellow traveler, or not unsympathetic to your being a Communist. When you refer to somebody or ask about him and are told he is a bastard that does not mean he is of illegitimate parentage but an active anti-Communist and to watch your step.[11]

During the 1940s many had charged that this attitude among broadcast leftists translated into a blacklist against anti-Communists. HUAC testimony, particularly that of radio director Owen Vinson, indicates that there was indeed an inclination among Communists to hire fellow comrades, but it did not constitute an industry-wide conspiracy. "I suppose," Vinson said, "I gave preference to those people who were members of the Communist Party, all other things being equal, just as one would a fellow Elk."[12]

Doubts about the CPUSA might have emerged for some Popular Front Communists when they noticed inconsistencies and peculiarities in party stances on New Deal issues that were so important to the liberal agenda. Prominent among these issues during the war years was what the party called the Negro question. Over the years the CPUSA had identified itself as a civil rights champion through its active support of such causes as the Scottsboro Boys case. In broadcasting a similar attitude could be seen on the show *Danger*, created largely by Communists and Popular Front liberals, which often featured black actors in brief but nonstereotypical roles, something that was still a rarity in those days. But the party also had estranged some potential liberal allies with its ultimate solution to the country's racial divide: a separatist African-American republic in the South's so-called Black Belt. Making the party's position even more suspect were its violent policy shifts, depending on whatever happened to be the Soviet-dictated line at the time. Communists insisted on Black Belt self-determination during the early 1930s, then played down the demand after 1935 when the Comintern dictated a more accommodating Popular Front approach, then brought the issue to the fore once again after the Soviet Union signed the nonaggression pact with the Nazis.[13]

By the time Communists were supporting both FDR and the war effort in the early 1940s, self-determination had receded once more—as had nearly all civil rights initiatives. Recent recruits might have wondered why the CPUSA was denouncing A. Philip Randolph's 1943 plan for a "March on Washington" to protest racial discrimination. Randolph, the party said, was "an enemy of the war effort." In another incident two years later, Communists attacked four African-American WACs for protesting the inadequate medical treatment given wounded black soldiers at a Massachusetts army base. The WACs had "made a serious mistake," wrote Benjamin J. Davis in the *Daily Worker*; by inflaming racial issues in a time of war, their "undisciplined methods play into the hands of provocateurs." Those, like the NAACP, who took a hard look at the party's handling of civil rights issues could see a clear pattern: when the Soviet Union was under attack, the African-American struggle for equality was, at best, a secondary concern. One ex-Communist witness, actor George Hall, found that he had reflected this high-handed, patronizing approach by taking on a "very pompous and a big brother attitude toward certain racial minorities who needed my help like they need a hole in the head."[14]

The party hierarchy's tendency to follow the Soviet line might have seemed remote to some rank-and-file members, but Communists in the broadcast field began to see evidence close at hand of the movement's overbearing style when the war ended and the CPUSA reverted to an overt revolutionary stance. Patriotic progressives who thought they had signed on for "Twentieth Century Americanism" now encountered a very different portrayal of their country at party meetings. "As far as the United States was concerned, there was nothing that ever happened here that was of any value at all," said actor Paul Marion. More than abstract discussions, the party's policies impinged directly on members' lives. Even before the postwar shift, party leaders would tell members to stop associating with certain types of people, either professionally or socially, whether they were right-wingers or, worse, Trotskyites, the bane of the Communists' existence. Directives extended to books that members should avoid, especially those of Communist apostate Arthur Koestler who had outraged his former comrades in 1941 when he had written *Darkness at Noon*, his devastating fictional account of Soviet-style repression.[15] For writers in particular, CPUSA policies after 1946 imposed upon the way they approached their work.

Early that year, screenwriter Albert Maltz wrote his controversial article in *New Masses* that proposed a greater creative freedom for writers, transcending strict ideological confines. For this the Hollywood Communists and their CPUSA superiors viciously denounced him. Proving himself to be an obedient party-liner, Maltz submitted to the humiliating process of self-criticism, published a rebuttal to his own article, and became a focal point for discussions among Communist writers in film and broadcasting on the issue of freedom versus political correctness. Not everyone was willing to capitulate to party orthodoxy, at least not at first, anyway. Among those who questioned the official wisdom were writers like Walter Bernstein, but they too would soon stop protesting.[16]

Others, though, lost patience with the new restrictions. Around the time of the Maltz affair, radio writer Sylvia Richards joined forces with Sam Moore to agitate for a less doctrinaire approach to their craft, arguing that "the function of an artist is to reflect the life around him as he sees it, to shape it into a form and to tell the truth with his art." Predictably, their CPUSA branch rejected the idea. Instead their group adopted the ideological strategy pronounced by William Z. Foster in the April 1946 "Art as a Weapon" symposium. Although Richards understood that this debate had little practical effect upon her work within the narrowly defined options of commercial radio, she could not accept this sort of thinking and soon left the party. Writer Pauline Townsend had a similar if more humiliating experience when she proposed that the party steer away from opaque Marxist rhetoric and concentrate on practical progressive issues that the American people could appreciate. At a county party convention, Hollywood commissar John Howard Lawson read aloud excerpts from Townsend's proposal, but only as a pretext for dismissing her work "as infantile and leftist and Trotskyist." Speaking for many of those who left the CPUSA during this period was writer-director Carin Kinzel Burrows, Abe Burrows's wife, who later testified that she felt her party group "had become a real dictatorship. The rank and file of people had nothing to say about making policy and deciding what had to be done."[17]

If these witnesses had chosen to stay with the party much longer, they would have had to come to grips with significantly more oppressive policies. The four-year purge of "white chauvinists" that began in 1949 turned out to be an especially traumatic period that Communists would remember with great dismay for years to come, wrote CPUSA historian Joseph Starobin. "Not a few have asked themselves: if they were capable of such cruelties to each other when they were a small handful of people bound by sacred ideals, what might they have done if they had been in power?" People could be denounced and disciplined for nothing more than using terms like "whitewash" or "black sheep," the charges sometimes leveled out of petty personal animosity. Howard Fast, who was quick to lambast other writers for political indiscretions, was now compelled to denounce himself because, wrote Starobin, "in an old novel of his, one character used racist language and dialect, although this use was quite in keeping with the story."[18]

For many the break from the party came quickly in the postwar period, but for others, like witness Allen Sloane, it was a more gradual process. Sloane was recruited by Millard Lampell into the Communist party in 1943 and left the following year, sensing even during this time—when the party was relatively flexible—that the organization was interfering with his profession. He was, as he later testified, "a little ashamed of myself to realize that here I, a writer, an independent kind of person, was involved in the kind of thing where I had to be told my function as a writer and an artist." Still, he did not dissociate himself completely. Throughout the forties he continued to take part in front activities, often in collaboration with Lampell, acting, as he later put it, as a fellow traveler.[19] This did not change until after a meeting with Lampell following the publication of *Red Channels*.

Sloane's two citations in the booklet led to his losing a radio job, and he contacted his friend to see if *Red Channels* had affected his career as well. Lampell agreed to come to Sloane's apartment to discuss the matter. Sloane extended the invitation even though he had reason to think that his current houseguests might make the visit awkward.

After the war, Sloane and his wife had worked in Europe for the United Nations, and while at a displaced persons camp they had met a young man from Estonia named Reinnarma with an extraordinary story to tell. The young man, Sloane later said, had opposed the Soviet domination of his country and, after the Red Army swept through the Baltics, had been arrested and deported to Russia. Reinnarma, though, had managed to escape and make a harrowing 140-mile trek on foot to return to Estonia. Moved by his story and taking a personal liking to the young man, Sloane and his wife decided to sponsor his entry into the United States. When Lampell came to visit, Sloane testified,

> Reinnarma, his wife Küsu and his baby were sharing our small apartment. I introduced him to Lampell, knowing perhaps that Lampell would not react pleasantly, but feeling that he might see some humanity here. I told him Reinnarma's story, and when Reinnarma left the room Lampell turned to me and said, "How can you bring people like this into your country? What kind of thing is this for you to do? A man like this will take up arms against the Soviet Union!" So I asked him to leave my house and not to come back again.[20]

Confronted with this lack of compassion, a hard-hearted attitude dictated by rigid ideology, Sloane began to make his final break with party-influenced activities.

While friendly witnesses have been pilloried over the years in such books as Victor Navasky's *Naming Names*, unfriendly witnesses who refused to answer committee questions on the basis of the Fifth Amendment have received especially kind treatment. Uncooperative witnesses invoked the Fifth, according to this point of view, as a matter of principled defiance of rogue committees and in defense of civil libertarian ideals. Perhaps the unfriendly witnesses perceived their actions in this way. But a reasonable person who reads the actual testimony transcripts, rather than relying on revisionist accounts of the hearings, is likely to reach another conclusion: some of these witnesses were just as concerned with concealing something as they were with taking a stand.

The Fifth Amendment tactic was at its most suspect when witnesses were confronted with their CPUSA membership documents, or when, as in the case of movie and radio writer Leonardo Bercovici, they were willing to deny current membership in the Communist party but would not say whether they had been members in the past. Witnesses also did not help themselves by trying to have it both ways. Scenic designer Howard Bay, for instance, instructed HUAC interrogators that no inference should be drawn from his refusal to answer, even though just minutes before he had refused to respond on the grounds that the answer might incriminate him. Just as unconvincing were evasive answers to straightforward questions. When asked if he would fight for the United States if it were attacked without provocation by the Soviet Union, screenwriter Waldo Salt would reply only that this was "a highly speculative question."[21]

The uncooperative witnesses might have thought they were obstructing congressional committees by taking the Fifth, but their tactics probably had the opposite effect. By refusing to answer, as the historian William L. O'Neill has pointed out, they helped confirm the impression they were involved in a disciplined, insidious conspiracy, that communism in America was a more potent force than it actually was. All this, in effect, played into the hands of the McCarran and Un-American committees by making it easier for them to justify their continuing investigations.[22]

At the McCarran hearings, in particular, Lyon and Lampell did nothing to dispel suspicions about their activities or about alleged CPUSA efforts to infiltrate broadcasting. After listening to repeated refusals to answer a long series of questions about party and front activities, and after getting no answer to a question about Lampell's involvement with the party's radio commission, Richard Arens, the committee's staff director, tried to frame the implications of these refusals. "So if you have not been active in Communist infiltration in the radio industry," he said, "and have not been active in reporting to the radio commission of the Communist Party, then you would be obliged, would you not, to answer this question which I have put to you by saying, 'No.'" Lampell took the Fifth once again.[23]

Lyon's testimony became especially cagey when questioned about Louis Budenz, whose *American Legion Magazine* article had outlined CPUSA efforts in radio and whose FBI statements had named Lyon as a key figure in those efforts. Not only did Lyon refuse to say whether he knew Budenz, he would not even answer when asked if there existed such a person as Budenz. When asked if he was familiar with the ex-Communist's *American Legion* article, he had to consult with his attorney before replying that he was not sure. An especially curious moment involved the issue surrounding the name Peter Ivy, which, Budenz had claimed, Lyon had used as a pseudonym for a series of radio articles for the *Daily Worker*. Early on during his questioning, Lyon denied ever using the Ivy moniker. A few minutes later, when asked if he had "ever signed the name" to any articles, he took the Fifth.[24]

In the published transcript of the hearings released in August 1952, the introduction accused Lyon and Lampell of being "hard-core Communists." Only now, after this charge was made public, was Lyon willing to say that he was not a Communist.[25] But unlike his testimony, this statement, forwarded by his lawyer to a reporter, was not made under oath.

Another witness also made a statement at this time. Welbourn Kelley, who had testified so forcefully on Communist infiltration of the Radio Writers Guild, now said that the McCarran Committee had distorted a key part of his testimony. The committee had asked him to list those guild members he knew to be part of the pro-Communist faction, and even then Kelley had said, "I am not too keen about it. I don't dislike any of these people personally, and I don't wish them any harm." Just the same, in the published transcript he went on to name twenty-two people, including not only Lyon and Sam Moore, who had been identified by others as Communists, but also such people as Howard Rodman, Philo Higley, and Ernest Kinoy. Now, after the report's release, he claimed in a publicly circulated letter that the committee had pressured him to label all these people as pro-Communists even though he had originally intended to describe them merely as leftists. "I am extremely sorry that I allowed myself to make this mistake," he wrote.[26] Despite his apology, he had already contributed to the growing perception that there was little distinction between Popular Front liberals and Communists.

Counterattack, showing no concern over this controversy, relished the testimony of Kelley, Knight, and Milton on the Radio Writers Guild, which, according to its August 29 issue, "confirmed what *Counterattack* has repeatedly said of Communist control of this strategic union." After listing some of the most pointed questions that Lampell and Lyon would not answer, the newsletter concluded that there was "no excuse now" for any broadcaster to employ the two writers. The *Counterattack* editors need not have worried. The blacklist quickly eliminated both Lampell and Lyon from radio and TV, at least officially. Lyon would have to turn to magazine and book writing to make a living, but Lampell would occasionally manage to land a TV assignment through a front before supporting himself by writing for industrial films.[27]

Now that its perspective was backed up by a congressional report, *Counterattack* might have entered a period of renewed and expanded influence in the broadcast industry, but changes behind the scenes had already disrupted the newsletter's operations. By the time the McCarran report became public, the second of the original three partners had resigned.

In March 1952, Kirkpatrick began looking into the possibility of a political career. A member of the National Republican Club for several years, he now set his sights on a United States representative's seat in a new congressional district in Queens. In April he discussed his plans with Keenan, telling his partner that he planned to continue with *Counterattack* until the time came to announce his candidacy. Keenan did not take the news well. He was not interested in working with a lame-duck partner who had his eye on other pursuits. He told Kirkpatrick he should leave the company at once.[28] Putting the best face on the situation, *Counterattack* announced in its June 20 issue that it had "reluctantly accepted" Kirkpatrick's resignation so that "he may enter other important phases of anti-Communist work."

Kirkpatrick's plans to pursue that work in Congress unraveled by August when, according to an FBI report, two rabbis in his district branded him an anti-Semite, reflecting a recurring sentiment among *Counterattack* critics that both the newsletter and the blacklist it instigated were concentrating to an alarming extent on Jews. Local Republican leaders lost interest in Kirkpatrick after the rabbis informed them that they would rally Jewish voters against him. Kirkpatrick also explored the position of executive director of a Washington, D.C., organization called the All-American Conference to Combat Communism, but ultimately he chose to enter the business world instead. Although reluctant to leave the East Coast, he relocated to the Midwest to take a job in the personnel department at John Deere Harvester Works in East Moline, Illinois.[29]

His rift with Keenan aside, Kirkpatrick does not seem to have had any financial incentive to remain with American Business Consultants, reported *Time* magazine, which said the company "has been barely able to keep its head above water." To try to regain some momentum and generate income, Keenan hoped to publish a new supplement, one that would surpass *Red Channels* by identifying Communist sympathizers in a variety of industries. The booklet, however, never materialized. Keenan still retained one essential employee from the company's *Red Channels* heyday—Frank McNamara as *Counterattack*'s editor—but without the polished Kirkpatrick as its front man, the newsletter lost some of its ability to maintain a public presence, and Keenan might not have been the best choice to take up the slack. Charles Blaisdell, Keenan's friend and former associate in the FBI, noticed a change in the *Counterattack* publisher that had begun following his wife's death in 1949. He began to drink more, and his sometimes brusque manner could become even less tactful.[30]

Regardless of *Counterattack*'s problems, the anti-Communist crusade in broadcasting showed no signs of weakening, driven by events both overseas and at home. The overt fight against communism in Korea still raged as the war degenerated into an agonizing stalemate that consisted of bloody battles for hilltops along the Thirty-eighth parallel. Truce talks had offered some hope of a settlement, but negotiations broke down in October 1952 because the Communists insisted that all Chinese and North Korean prisoners of war be forced to return to their countries. At home, Laurence Johnson and his Syracuse group continued to invoke the sacrifices of American soldiers to shame broadcasters into barring anyone connected to Communist-front causes, and those insisting that broadcasting could be used to create mischief on the home front seized upon an incident that happened to take place just over forty miles south of Johnson's headquarters. Three months before the release of the McCarran documents, a group of twenty-five students at Cornell University took over the campus radio station and, as a prank, announced over the air that the Russians had just bombed London and Marseilles and were sending another fleet of bombers toward American shores. Although it lasted only eight minutes, the broadcast caused panic on the Cornell campus. *Counterat-*

tack quickly picked up on the story and declared, "If a few irresponsible college students could do this, think of what the CP (which has stolen America's top secrets) could do in war time with the industry packed with its trained agents!"[31]

Counterattack might not have been in a position to lead the crusade as it once had, but a former collaborator of the newsletter was now making a name for himself among anti-Communist agitators. With the release of the McCarran report, he made his entrance on the national stage.

Since contributing to *Red Channels* two years earlier, Vincent Hartnett had been writing magazine articles and lecturing before anti-Communist groups, and had more recently appeared as the first witness at the McCarran hearings. He presented himself to the committee as an expert on the subject of Communist infiltration in broadcasting, based upon his experience working in radio and his extensive private research. He then proceeded to support his claim by providing an analytical description of labor and production practices in broadcasting, and by reeling off an encyclopedic list of front activities connected to Lyon and Lampell. About Lampell he made his most incendiary assertion: "Millard Lampell, I respectfully suggest, should be the subject of an intensive investigation by appropriate law-enforcement authorities. He is not only an important figure in Communist infiltration in motion pictures, radio and the publishing world, but he is also a connecting link—and a vital one—between Communists or pro-Communist operatives in all these fields."[32]

Statements like this warranted Hartnett a place in a front-page *New York Times* story on the hearings. Fellow anti-Communist activists, meanwhile, were impressed by his ready command of facts in assessing individuals' political histories. In a short time, Hartnett would eclipse his old *Red Channels* associates as the new champion of the anti-Red purge and as the new bugbear of the anti-blacklist movement.

EIGHT

The Passion

JOSEPH PATRICK HARTNETT was four years old when he came with his family to the United States from Ireland in 1865. He would grow up to fulfill the immigrant parents' dream of success for their offspring in a land of opportunity. After graduating from college in his family's New World home of St. Louis, he set out on his own to find his first job as an adult 350 miles away in Council Bluffs, Iowa, then returned a year later to begin work at the L. M. Rumsey Manufacturing Company, where he began a steady climb through the executive ranks that eventually led to the position of company secretary. He got around to starting a family relatively late in life but was fruitful just the same. He married a woman named Estelle Roche, twenty-one years his junior, from an Irish-French family, and together in the early twentieth century they produced six children. The last of them was Vincent W. Hartnett, born in 1916. For someone who would put so much stock in the virtue of patriotism, Vincent Hartnett's arrival was fortuitously timed: he was born on the Fourth of July.

The family moved a year after Hartnett's birth when his father landed a new position in New York City. He acquired not only a more impressive title but a more elegant profession, as he went from secretary of a company that manufactured plumbing supplies to president of the American division of the French jewelry firm Cartier. For a time the Hartnetts lived in the Irish-American enclave of Rockaway Beach in Queens, then moved above the city to the suburb of New Rochelle, where Vincent Hartnett grew up.[1]

A love of country figured prominently in the lessons of the Hartnett household. Hartnett's father, first-generation immigrant that he was, felt strong emotional ties to the old country, especially to Irish culture and arts, but he made it clear to his children where their ultimate loyalties should lie. While Hartnett was growing up, as he would later remember, "I heard him say earnestly more than once that if—God forbid–there was ever a war between the U.S. and Ireland, we should be loyal to the U.S." A similar devotion came from his mother's side of the family, which had deeper and supposedly historic roots in this country (her family claimed an ancestor "who had been a scout with the Lewis and Clark expedition"). Hartnett remembered his maternal grandmother, in particular, to be "intensely patriotic" and fond of singing "Columbia, the Gem of the Ocean" to express that sentiment.[2]

Just as important in Hartnett's upbringing was the Catholic faith. If, while growing up, Hartnett was looking for an example in translating faith into social activism—the kind he would later weave into his own political causes—he would certainly have found it in his father. Among the organizations the elder Hartnett belonged to were the St. Vincent De Paul Society, known for its charitable works, and the Holy Name Society, whose acts of goodwill encompassed not only providing food and shelter to the needy but such missions of spiritual activism as counseling the wayward.

A diligent and accomplished student, Hartnett spent his first year of college at Fordham University, where he earned a place on the school's highest honor roll. (His time there happened to coincide with John Keenan's senior year at the university, but their paths apparently did not cross.) From there Hartnett moved on to the University of Notre Dame, and here too he excelled, graduating maxima cum laude in 1937 with a B.A. in English, then obtaining his master's two years later, maxima cum laude once again. Pursuing his religious interests, he joined several Catholic societies while at the university and during his graduate years went on to major in apologetics, the defense and philosophy of religion, which involved, to an extent, the intellectually theological tradition of Thomism. Politics also figured into his education. In particular, he began his study of communism, taking such courses as "Russia: Government and Philosophy" and "Communism and Religion," and studying with

Waldemar Gurian, a refugee from Nazi Germany known for his books on totalitarianism of both the right and the left.[3]

When he entered the professional world, Hartnett pursued his literary interests by writing for magazines, sometimes incorporating his spiritual concerns by contributing to such publications as *Catholic World*. America's entry into World War II then focused his attention on more worldly affairs.

He joined the navy three months after the attack on Pearl Harbor and eventually applied the research skills he had developed at Notre Dame to the field of military intelligence in the war against Japan. Near the end of the war he was transferred to a new assignment, covering another part of the world, that would influence the way he viewed future conflicts.

His new duties required that he prepare intelligence reports on the Middle East and the Balkans. Years later, recalling the significance of this period, he would say that it was "harrowing to see the Soviet noose tightening around Czechoslovakia, Hungary and Romania." The takeover of Romania, which proved to be an early template for Soviet domination in the region, had a particularly powerful effect upon him.[4] The disturbing transition from liberation to tyranny began with indecisiveness on the part of the United States and Britain as Romania's weak and divided Communist party was fortified by the presence of the Red Army. The Soviets refused to allow elections, which provided time for the Romanian Communists to form a front with progressive groups and pressure the centrist government sponsored by King Michael to appoint more Communists to key posts. By February 1945 the Communists were ready to take the next step. They instigated a national crisis by staging demonstrations, shutting down newspapers, and brawling in the streets with political adversaries. The government attempted to hold its ground, but, as Red Army tanks gathered in the capital, Soviet foreign minister Andrei Vishinsky arrived in Romania to make it clear to King Michael that he had only one real choice: appoint pro-Communist Petru Groza as prime minister. With no support from the West to combat these moves, the king was forced to do as he was told. Within twenty-one months the Communists completed their seizure of power.

The Romanian example, restaged with variations throughout eastern Europe, highlighted lessons Hartnett had learned from books and lectures at Notre Dame. Now they were vividly illustrated by intelligence reports of a desperate sequence of events. The specific themes that would have troubled him most are not difficult to discern because they would be repeated in his writings over the next ten years, namely, the apathy of democratic forces in the face of totalitarianism, and the cynical use of fronts to attain power. As vexing as these developments might have been, however, Hartnett did not devote himself immediately to the anti-Communist cause after leaving the navy in January 1946. Instead he resumed his plans for a writing career.

Back in the New York City area, he freelanced for magazines once again and also wrote pamphlets and newsletters for Father James Keller's spiritual-uplift organization, The Christophers, before landing a job as assistant editor at *Outdoor Life Magazine*. Articles he wrote during this time for *The Sign*, a magazine published by the Passionists order of the Catholic church, reveal that he still held the concerns that arose during his final months in naval intelligence; but he was not yet animated by a great sense of urgency. One contribution outlined the threat posed by the Soviet Union to Turkey, yet for now, two months before Truman asked Congress to provide military aid to Turkey in March 1947, Hartnett conveyed a hopeful attitude and avoided alarmism as he maintained that the United States and Britain had the situation under control. In 1947 he also published two pieces of fiction, sentimental and spiritually instructive tales that both revolved around a classical music theme. One of them — a surprising effort from someone who would soon become such a hard-edged ideologue — was a romantic story filled with wistful yearning about a concert pianist who struggles for years to find the true path, and the true love, that God has charted for him. The other story at least hinted at the coming issue that would dominate Hartnett's life in the 1950s. In "The Way to the Heart," a German orchestra conductor, a survivor of Buchenwald, dismisses warnings from his doctor as he takes on the strain of presenting to the public a new concerto that evokes a struggle against tyranny, "a struggle," he informs his audience, "that is still going on."[5]

More pressing for Hartnett, perhaps, than any other consideration at the time was the practical matter of making more money. He was married now and needed to find work that would support not only himself and his wife but the family they planned on having. He explored another possible source of writing income by taking a course at Columbia University on radio scripting, then, fortuitously, found that he had a family connection that led to an interview with a radio producer in New York by the name of John O. Ives, who worked for Phillips H. Lord, a program packager responsible for two popular crime series, *Gangbusters* and *Counterspy*. In March 1948 he was hired, first as a writer then as Ives's assistant, becoming a supervisor for the *Gangbusters* series. He enjoyed the work of buying stories and consulting with the law enforcement agencies involved in the cases dramatized on the show, and he appreciated the steady, comfortable salary that came with these responsibilities. But soon he seized upon a divisive issue within the production company that took precedence, in his mind, over any comforts the job might offer.[6]

Through a mutual acquaintance, a fellow Notre Dame man named Whit Vernon arranged to meet Hartnett to discuss a problem he was having in the radio industry. Vernon was an actor and, until recently, an active one, appearing in such radio programs as *The Lone Ranger* and *The Big Story* as well as an occasional Broadway show. He came to Hartnett hoping for help in discovering the reasons for his current inability to find radio work, which had begun suddenly and showed no signs of turning around. Hartnett looked into the matter and believed he found a direct correlation between changes in Vernon's fortunes and shifts in his political activities: while Vernon had been involved with the Progressive Citizens of America—later alleged to be a Communist front—his career had flourished; after he backed off from the group's activities, the job offers seemed to vanish. As Hartnett investigated further, he came into contact with a group of right-wing members of the American Federation of Radio Artists (AFRA) known as the Artists' Committee, who told him stories about their struggles within the union against what they considered to be a pro-Communist contingent. Hartnett concluded that there was a blacklist against anti-Communists, not only in radio as a whole but specifically within his own company.[7]

Part of Hartnett's job was to contact the agents for the actors requested by the *Gangbusters* director, William Sweets. He had noticed before that Sweets had a habit of recommending left-wingers, but now Hartnett went a step further to claim that the director was favoring Communist fronters and excluding members of AFRA's anti-Communist faction. Especially galling to him was something he witnessed firsthand in the *Gangbusters* studio. One day early in 1949, just before a broadcast, he saw Sweets recruit actor Roger DeKoven to translate and read aloud for the upcoming

Waldorf Peace Conference a speech that had been written by Cuban Communist leader Juan Marinello. Although he regarded Sweets as a capable broadcast talent, Hartnett decided that the director, a former president of the Radio and Television Directors Guild, was "undoubtedly a very high level commie."[8]

As it turned out, neither Sweets nor Hartnett would work for Phillips H. Lord much longer. After the June 4 broadcast of *Gangbusters*, the company informed Sweets that the sponsors had received a large number of letters protesting the director's involvement in the Lord shows and had decided they would withdraw from the programs if he did not resign. Sweets tried resisting but soon gave in to the pressure and quit both *Gangbusters* and *Counterspy*.[9] Hartnett resigned around the same time. He would write an article about the incident later that year, but only in an interview decades later would he maintain that there was a direct connection between his and Sweets's exit.

His objection to Sweets's activities, he said, was not passive: he translated it into action. He decided he could no longer arrange the hiring of the actors that Sweets recommended. "I said I couldn't do it. Many of them, for example, were sponsors of the May Day parade—that was an open demonstration of party strength," he said. He was also, he later claimed, responsible for orchestrating the letter-writing campaign against Sweets. This, he said, "really threw the egg into the fan." Finally his boss, John Ives, delivered an ultimatum: either he stop the letter-writing campaign and make the necessary calls to hire the actors, or he would have to resign. Unwilling to relent, Hartnett chose to resign.[10] According to his version of events, both he and Sweets had become too controversial for the Phillips H. Lord company to keep on its shows.

The Sweets case quickly became a cause célèbre for the left, a rehearsal for the more pivotal Jean Muir incident a year later. On August 11 the Voice of Freedom Committee and the National Council of the Arts, Sciences and Professions organized a rally for Sweets at the Hotel Abbey in New York City. Among those appearing at the event were actress Hester Sondergaard and writer Millard Lampell, and providing moral support were both the Radio and Television Directors Guild and AFRA, all their efforts meant to amplify the organizers' message that the forced resignation was "a gross injustice against Sweets." Highlighting the event was Sweets himself, who told the audience he had been blacklisted for no other

reason than sponsoring May Day parades and supporting world peace. He
then added, in what *Time* magazine characterized as a party-line moment,
that his loyalty to the United States was never the issue in this controversy
but rather his loyalty "to the ideas of the National Association of Manufacturers."[11] Whatever support he received, and whatever the explanations
he offered, the campaign on his behalf did little to help him. He returned
to his home in Vermont and never worked in broadcasting again.

In a different way the Sweets affair had a profound effect on Hartnett
as well. At this turning point he may have taken to heart a well-known saying of Father James Keller, his superior while at The Christophers: "You,
individually, have a mission to fulfill—a special job to do. You can do
something no other person can do to shape the world in which you live."
His actions certainly seemed to have adhered to this advice as he dedicated himself with great single-mindedness to his new purpose. At a time
when Elizabeth Bentley and Whittaker Chambers were testifying about
Soviet spy networks in America, Hartnett committed himself to exposing
what he saw as Communist infiltration within his own field of professional
experience. He acquired copies of HUAC hearings dealing with the entertainment industry. He gathered copies of Communist periodicals like the
Daily Worker and *Masses and Mainstream*, entertainment publications
such as *Show Business*, *Actors Cues*, and *Players Guide*, as well as letterheads, flyers, and programs for front organizations and events. He also attended Communist-front meetings to acquire firsthand information on
their proceedings and photographed May Day parades to compile a visual
record of those who marched.[12] In his Peter Cooper Village apartment in
downtown Manhattan, he organized all the materials he collected into an
extensive filing system, as if building his own personal intelligence service
on the radio and TV industry.

To bring his information to the public, Hartnett wrote articles with
such titles as "They've Moved In on TV" and "Rascalry on the Air Waves"
to bring attention to such alleged Communist fronters in broadcasting as
Norman Corwin, Ireene Wicker, Zero Mostel, and Everett Sloane. He
also arranged to deliver lectures to conservative community groups. A
short, slim man with owlish features, he might not have presented an imposing appearance, but he offered his audiences an intense belief in his
cause and a detailed presentation of facts based on an encyclopedic memory for the wide array of American front groups and for all those in show

business who might have been associated with them. He would later claim that his new profession "was not of my choice," suggesting that it was thrust upon him by circumstance and necessity.[13]

While developing contacts within New York's anti-Communist camp, he met Theodore Kirkpatrick and began exchanging information with the *Counterattack* staff. It was this relationship that led to his contributions to *Red Channels*, the springboard for his career as the most prominent, and most notorious, of the broadcast Red hunters.

After the Muir incident commanded headlines in September 1950, Hartnett made the most of the *Red Channels* controversy, demonstrating that his anti-Communist fervor was matched by a shrewd knack for self-promotion. He billed himself as the co-author of *Red Channels* and in one article took credit for conceiving the idea for the booklet, though the *Counterattack* publishers maintained that they had come up with the concept at the same time. In January 1951 the unflagging Hartnett also found a way to use the medium he was criticizing by writing an NBC radio documentary called "The Right to Freedom," a program that allowed him to warn the public that Communists were attempting to exploit the Bill of Rights to protect their own activities while intending ultimately to destroy those liberties.[14]

That month Hartnett stepped up his promotion by placing an ad in the *Tablet*, a Brooklyn Catholic weekly, to solicit speaking engagements. "One of the most vital and fascinating talks available today," the ad proclaimed. "Should be heard by all loyal Americans. Exposes the Communist conspiracy to capture motion pictures, the stage, radio and TV. Names (with documented proof) the most influential Communists and Red-Fronters, many of whom YOU ARE SUPPORTING!" To help authenticate this expertise, Hartnett published a typewritten, loose-leaf book entitled *Confidential Notebook (File* 13*)*, an updateable listing of broadcast personnel and their front activities, broader and deeper than *Red Channels*, to be sold for five dollars apiece. His intensified efforts during this time coincided with a growing conviction on his part that the war in Korea was in peril. Unlike his future adversary, John Henry Faulk, who regarded the conflict as an American act of aggression at the behest of Wall Street warmongers, Hartnett feared that the Truman administration was losing its will, that it was undermined by a State Department determined to settle for an unacceptable stalemate.[15]

As he established his Red-hunting expertise, two distinct Hartnett voices emerged. In some cases he could be analytical and relatively cautious, conveying the image of a conscientious researcher. His *Sign* article on anti-Catholic bigotry, for instance, made a case against creeping secularism, which was certainly not likely to please many liberals; still, the piece presented a reasoned conservative argument, as did another article on the anti-Communist credentials of the American Civil Liberties Union, an organization that Hartnett had once belonged to. Even his *Confidential Notebook*, an instrument of the blacklist, at least cautioned its readers that it "is neither stated nor implied that all of the individuals herein named are Communist, pro-Communists, fellow travelers, or anything of the sort. Readers are earnestly asked to remember this, in fairness to all concerned."

At other times, though, Hartnett seemed intent upon being provocative and polarizing, from his use of the term "Commie"—a habit sure to bait many on the left—to likening Communists and fellow travelers to "vermin crawling under a wet rock." He could also conform to the stereotype of anti-Communists as right-wing prigs by writing an article entitled "How Communism Exploits Sex." In a less direct way, he could stir up an already volatile situation by dangling a vague sense of conspiracy. Taking on the Muir affair in an article called "Red Fronts Falling," he declared that the William Morris Agency was involved in the production of Muir's program, *The Aldrich Family*, then went on to list the front associations of "William Morris, Jr." (the quotes are his) and pointed out that the man was a friend of Muir's husband, AFRA attorney Henry Jaffe, without making it clear whether Jaffe's friend was the head of the Morris agency or some other man named William Morris, Jr. Hartnett then distanced himself from the implications he seemed to be making by concluding, "These facts are simply recorded in the interests of complete reporting. No implication is made or intended."[16]

The controversy he courted succeeded in attracting attention, but it could also incite deeply personal confrontations. At the end of March 1952, Hartnett attended a meeting of the American Committee for Cultural Freedom, an anti-Communist organization of intellectuals from both the right and the left. He found that much of the meeting was devoted to debating the proper response to McCarthyism. Max Eastman, a former Marxist who had moved right, rose to defend McCarthy and to declare that "there was no Red Scare," only a legitimate, if sometimes ex-

Throughout the blacklist period, no one became as much of a lightning rod for controversy as Vincent Hartnett, the anti-Red talent consultant for both sponsors and advertising agencies.

cessive, response to a real threat. Taking issue with him was playwright Elmer Rice. Rice had recently taken a stand against *Red Channels* when he had resigned as producer of a TV drama anthology series because the sponsors would not allow him to hire actors listed in the booklet. According to notes on the event compiled by Dwight Macdonald and summarized by William O'Neill, Rice now refuted Eastman by citing the fate of another *Red Channels* listee, Mady Christians. A friend of the actress, he said *Red Channels* had killed her, unaware that Hartnett was sitting nearby. (Macdonald's notes misidentify him as "E. S. Harnett.") The citations on Christians, Hartnett now insisted, were accurate. Further, "it was no business of his how the material was used." He then took the offensive by questioning whether Rice wished "to suppress his right of free speech."

Having dealt with one attendee harboring a personal grievance against him, he quickly found he would have to confront another when a man stood up just two seats away. It was Philip Loeb. The blacklisted actor reiterated his claim that he was not a Communist and now, with the chance to confront a contributor to *Red Channels* face to face, accused Hartnett of ruining his career. Assuming Hartnett had an answer for this, he did not have the opportunity to voice it as he was drowned out by a chorus of shouts and arguments that sprang up throughout the room.[17]

An even more explosive controversy had surrounded Hartnett a year earlier after he delivered a speech to the right-wing Women's Patriotic Conference on National Defense in Washington, D.C. Various Jewish newspapers responded to the speech by accusing him of anti-Semitism.

Papers in Newark, Boston, and Detroit charged that Hartnett had singled out Jews as culprits in the Communist infiltration of show business; the official publication of the American Jewish Congress simply stated that he had made "anti-Semitic remarks." After learning of these accusations a few weeks later, Hartnett defended himself in a form letter that opened with the salutation, "To: My Friends of the Jewish Faith." He maintained, first of all, that the names he mentioned in the speech included the likes of Gene Kelly, Uta Hagen, José Ferrer, Gypsy Rose Lee, and Lena Horne. "Are those names Jewish?" his letter asked. (In a bit of unintentional humor, the list of names he supplied also happened to include Artie Shaw, who was, in fact, Jewish, and whose real name was Arthur Jacob Arshawsky.) Hartnett then took his argument a step further by quoting from his Washington speech: "Don't let anyone persuade you, for example, that, because an actor belongs to certain racial or religious groups that, therefore, he is a Commie. This is nonsense."[18]

Although there is no independent corroboration for the content of Hartnett's speech, there is some reason to believe his version was accurate: the tone he takes in his rebuttal letter is consistent with his articles and other correspondence, which convey an ecumenical Judeo-Christian attitude, a bit patronizing perhaps by later standards but hardly qualifying as Jew-baiting.[19] It's possible that the anti-Semitic charge against Hartnett might have been influenced by the accusers' view of the organization he had chosen to address. At the same event that included Hartnett, the Women's Patriotic Conference on National Defense also featured a speech by the thinly disguised anti-Semite Joseph P. Kamp, and two years

later the group would listen to the words of Robert H. Williams, a rene-
gade pamphleteer whose ideas owed a lot to "The Protocols of the Elders
of Zion." A better charge to make against Hartnett was that he was associating with a suspect group. While it's true that the Women's Patriotic Conference on National Defense was known to hear respectable speakers,
including President Truman, an activist like Hartnett, who held people to
account for mingling with organizations that catered to extremists, should
have been more careful himself in choosing his speaking engagements.
The same could be said for his dealings with the *Tablet*, a paper that, before World War II, had aligned itself with America Firsters, claiming that
Reds and Red dupes in government had manipulated the country into the
conflict, and now in the cold war period regarded Franco as the country's
true friend in Europe.[20]

The episode reflects a larger controversy over the role of anti-Semitism
and religion among the Red hunters. Without doubt, throughout the
1940s and 1950s there were anti-Semites in the anti-Communist movement who equated Judaism with bolshevism and saw an insidious Jewish
influence behind world events. Leading the pack was Congressman John
Rankin, a member of HUAC involved in the investigation of the Hollywood
Ten. Six months before the attack on Pearl Harbor, Rankin had declared
on the floor of the House of Representatives that "Wall Street and a little
group of our international Jewish brethren" were trying to drag the country to war. Another example was Senator Pat McCarran, sponsor of the
1950 Internal Security Act, who was known to pepper his conversation
with the word "kike." Even more overt were Elizabeth Dilling and Gerald
L. K. Smith, who had been charged with sedition during World War II, as
well as Myron C. Fagan, who believed that Communists had overrun the
radio and TV industry thanks to Jewish immigrant executives whose "masters are the same International 'bankers' who control the Hollywood
moguls."[21] Together these figures succeeded in casting a pall over the outlying reaches of the anti-Communist cause, muddying the ideological waters that responsible anti-Communists would have to navigate. But to say
that they represented the entire movement would be a careless charge, for
both anti-Communists in general and the broadcast crusade in particular.

The *Counterattack* partners, for instance, went on record as opposing
Rankin and publicly rejected any affiliation with Fagan.[22] What cannot be
denied, however, is that a great many of the people that *Counterattack*

named as Communists or Communist sympathizers were Jews—a troubling tendency, on the surface at least, following the Nazi horrors of World War II, which raises the question of whether *Counterattack* focused unfairly on Jewish entertainers.

One of the newsletter's researchers, a West Coast representative named Gene Hagberg, clearly displayed an anti-Semitic streak. In one of his memos he gratuitously identified radio news commentator Averill Berman as Jewish, and in another report on Dore Schary he made sneering references to the Hollywood producer's real name of Isidore Scharf.[23] But a perusal of other *Counterattack* internal communications does not reveal this sort of attitude. Even so, the company's activities could be portrayed as bigoted if it had been willing to name Jews on the flimsiest of evidence and to give gentiles a pass despite incriminating information. But, here again, a survey of its public record as well as internal correspondence and reports does not bear that out. If anything, the documents make it clear that the *Counterattack* staff was willing to assume the worst about *anyone*, regardless of ethnicity or religion, and were ready to aim some of their sharpest rebukes at non-Jews, from J. Raymond Walsh, Fredric March, and Dashiell Hammett to Pete Seeger, Earl Robinson, and Jean Muir. Even someone like Ireene Wicker, who incorporated Christian themes into her radio work, was forced to go through a humiliating clearance process.

The anti-Semitic charge against blacklisters might have been less persistent if there had been more Jews involved in the anti-Communist campaign in broadcasting. Although some Jews took part in the effort—among them Alfred Kohlberg, Rabbi Benjamin Schultz, and George Sokolsky—it was another religion that figured much more prominently, both in broadcasting and on the national scene. Commentators on the period have noted that Catholics played a key role in the anti-Communist movement. By no means did they form a monolithic bloc—the liberal, anti-blacklist Catholic magazine *Commonweal* is an obvious exception—but a 1954 Gallup poll showed that 58 percent of American Catholics supported Joe McCarthy, compared to 49 percent for Protestants and 15 percent for Jews. Although various sociological theories have been offered to explain the phenomenon, the events following World War II surely played a crucial role as the Soviets brutally dominated Poland, Hungary, and Czechoslovakia and suppressed the exercise of religion by those countries' largely Catholic populations.[24]

If Catholics did their share to fill the ranks of American anti-communism, some writers maintain that Irish Catholics in particular volunteered to become the vanguard. "In the era of security clearances," Nathan Glazer and Daniel P. Moynihan wryly observed, "to be an Irish Catholic became *prima facie* evidence of loyalty. Harvard men were to be checked; Fordham men would do the checking."[25] On the national stage this could be seen most obviously in the leadership of Joe McCarthy and Pat McCarran. In broadcasting it could be found in the activism of Vincent Hartnett and *Counterattack*'s John Keenan and Francis McNamara. *Counterattack*, especially, seemed to be—like McCarthy—less concerned about Jews than "Harvard men," or, put another way, privileged Protestants. While McCarthy was especially exercised by the likes of Alger Hiss, Dean Acheson, and Owen Lattimore, *Counterattack* often leveled charges of fellow traveling against Reverend Stephen H. Frichtman, Reverend Guy Emery Shipler, and Reverend William Howard Melish.

As for Hartnett, his Catholic upbringing might have influenced his approach toward those who wished to put their Communist affiliations behind them or those who simply wanted to get off the blacklist and back to work. Exposing Reds in broadcasting, he would later say, constituted only half of what he hoped to accomplish. Just as important was his desire to carry on the fight "wherever possible by helping those involved with Communism to break with it." His efforts to assist those who, as he viewed it, wanted to rehabilitate themselves can be seen as his political equivalent of pursuing the religious goal of counseling the wayward. As he would later put it, "I hope God will give me the strength and will to help as many former Communists as possible, and to show them that there is a way out—self-clearance."[26]

Hartnett might welcome political converts, but he believed the burden was on them to prove their sincerity. His thoughts on how Communists and Communist fronters should clear themselves—and he emphasized that it was up to them to make a clean breast of things—seem to parallel the concept of penance, not just a Catholic concept but an Old Testament one as well. As is the case with sinners in spirit, transgressors in ideology could not clear themselves simply by acknowledging past mistakes. What was needed was true, heartfelt remorse, along with a concerted effort and visible evidence that they renounced wrongful ideas and would strike out on a righteous path. Even when Hartnett saw what he regarded as an admirable effort, he might be inclined to ask for something more. When he had the chance to peruse Elia Kazan's affidavit on his Communist past, he noted that the director had dealt with all the points Hartnett himself had raised in his latest installment of *Confidential Notebook*. Still, Kazan needed to dig deeper. "When he has conquered his remaining terror of reprisals from the 'apparat,'" Hartnett wrote at the time, "no doubt he will clear up a few more points which are still unsatisfactory."[27]

In an early foray into the clearance process, Hartnett accompanied Jack Wren and an official of the Catholic War Veterans to Abe Burrows's apartment so that they could hear and appraise the entertainer's explanations for his front associations.[28] Assisting fellow anti-Communists in this way was a matter of duty, to Hartnett's mind, but he was not planning on doing this work strictly on a volunteer basis. He had a growing family to support—he would eventually have six children—and he saw no reason not to provide for them by charging a fee for his expertise and research ability. It would be no different, he believed, than a credit investigator who was paid to evaluate a person's credit risk. By deciding on this course, though, he was sowing the seeds for future controversy, opening himself to charges of mercenary tactics that would have far greater repercussions than similar accusations leveled against *Counterattack*.

Soon after the Muir affair, Hartnett marketed himself in a big way by proposing to help NBC police its programming. The network, he claimed, was allowing suspect guest stars like John Garfield and Gregory Peck to appear on its shows and was airing such questionable programs as *The Magnificent Montague*, a radio comedy produced, written, and directed by *Red Channels* listee Nat Hiken. Especially troubling, the network was about to install Davidson Taylor as its general production executive. Hartnett maintained that Taylor had previously allowed the CBS news and documentary section to be "thoroughly colonized by the Party," employing not only Peter Lyon and Walter Bernstein but Norman Corwin, described by Hartnett as the "Commissar for Radio." Taylor also happened to be responsible for bringing John Henry Faulk to CBS in 1946, though Hartnett made no mention of this. He had collected clippings on the entertainer before compiling *Red Channels* but had chosen not to include Faulk among the listings and still saw no reason to make an issue of his political associations.[29]

Hartnett originally contacted NBC directly to offer his assistance, then asked Alfred Kohlberg to intercede on his behalf; but the network turned him down. Through the rest of 1951 and for much of 1952 he continued to try supplementing his income from writing and lecturing, at one point making his extensive files available for a fee of five hundred dollars. He succeeded in making some headway with Philip Morris, a major broadcast sponsor, when he supplied information that gave announcer Kenneth Roberts "a clean bill of health." Still, progress was slow. At the same time Hartnett tried to establish himself as an independent producer by packaging a show that drew upon his interest in classical music — he proposed to supervise a series that would broadcast operas in English — but ABC-TV decided against the idea.[30] Ultimately his best prospects arose not in broadcast production but within anti-Communist circles, where he struck up a relationship that would eventually propel him to the next level of professional activism.

Most likely he met Laurence Johnson during one of the grocer's frequent trips to Manhattan. As the friendship grew, Hartnett came to know Johnson's allies, including both Francis Neuser of the Veterans Action Committee and John Dungey of American Legion Post 41, and soon became a virtual adjunct to the Syracuse group by supplying his upstate associates with information on writers, actors, and directors who failed to meet their standards of Americanism. He regarded Johnson as an astute patriot with an acumen that transcended his limited formal education. Johnson, meanwhile, was impressed by Hartnett's ability to marshal facts. True, Hartnett's information about director Charles Irving had failed to keep him off Procter & Gamble shows, but that had more to do with what he considered the infuriatingly unreliable sponsor than with Hartnett's research.[31] Other sponsors were more receptive to Johnson's brand of old-fashioned American common sense. With these companies the grocer began to put in a good word for the former intelligence officer.

When Stuart Peabody of the Borden Company made his Syracuse pilgrimage in July 1952, Johnson not only took the executive to task for his company's careless selection of actors but suggested that a well-informed troubleshooter might alleviate the sponsor's problems in the future. A month later Borden acted on the grocer's advice and hired Hartnett as a consultant.[32] It so happened that Hartnett was hired just after he had finished an article for the *American Legion Magazine* that was critical

of Borden's broadcast policies. The timing of the two events was likely a
matter of coincidence, though Hartnett's subsequent decision to revise the
article was not.

After going to work for Borden, he tempered his critique of the sponsor by adding that, despite previous problems, the company had listened
to the protests of the American Legion and "finally took all appropriate
measures to correct the situation." Now Borden had "an effective policy
not only of providing splendid entertainment but also making a positive
contribution to Americanism." Hartnett would later point to similar
changes he had made in the same article to praise actions taken by Pall
Mall, even though he had no connection to that company, and added that
his positive comments about Borden were not based solely on their hiring
him but also on actions taken by the producer and the ad agency involved
in the sponsor's programs. Even so, a conflict of interest hovered over his
actions. Like the *Counterattack* partners, he was unwilling to come to
grips with the issues involved in writing as a journalist about a company
while also accepting work with the same firm as a consultant. For now,
though, the issue received little attention and did nothing to impede his
momentum. Just two months after he began scrutinizing the personnel of
such Borden shows as *Hawkins Falls* and *Treasury Men in Action*, he became a consultant for Lever Brothers—once again with Johnson's help—
and within a year was hired by the ABC network as well.[33]

Hartnett began his stint with Borden by charging twenty dollars for
each person he checked, but as the sponsor's requests increased, he low-
ered the price to five, ultimately his standard fee for all his clients. A follow-up check on a suspect employee would cost another two dollars while
an extensive written report warranted another twenty dollars. Hartnett
now earned a comfortable income from his anti-subversive activities—
more than ten thousand dollars in 1952 and two thousand more the following year[34]—the very fact of which became a sign of avarice to his
enemies. In the view of his allies it was nothing more than a well-deserved
remuneration.

To earn his money Hartnett would begin by confirming the subject's
identity, in case the individual might be confused with someone else with
a similar name, and then would peruse congressional committee transcripts to see if the person had been linked to any Communist causes.
Other sources would be the New York Public Library's theater collection

and references to front activities in his own files. When he was convinced that a person's record was truly damning, Hartnett might call on his Syracuse friends to take action to make sure the sponsor got the message. Some of these protests proved successful—pressure from Johnson and the Veterans Action Committee, for instance, helped remove actor Win Stracke from Borden's *Hawkins Falls*—but others fell on deaf ears. In late 1952, Hartnett compiled a list of twenty-one performers appearing on *Kraft Television Theater* that he deemed unacceptable, and the Syracuse contingent followed up with a protest, but their efforts had little effect and would continue to meet resistance from a sponsor that held its ground against outside agitators.[35]

Hartnett's closeness to the Syracuse group was considered an asset by some of his clients. Broadcasters who were leery of the power wielded by Johnson and his cronies appreciated that Hartnett could influence them and perhaps silence the drumbeat emanating from central New York. But the link could also be a disadvantage, as was the case with ABC, which dropped Hartnett after only a year because the network took a dim view of Johnson's machinations. Hartnett himself may have come to believe that his Syracuse allies could sometimes be a liability, especially when they failed to exercise sufficient caution in their accusations. He once felt compelled to instruct Neuser on the difficulty in pinning down a person's true ideology based solely on his or her front activities. "Never publicly make charges in this field," he wrote, "which you cannot substantiate with some public record."[36]

As stern a taskmaster as Hartnett could be in judging an entertainer's political guilt, he could also, as he saw it, be capable of mercy. He suggested that Lee J. Cobb "be given a break" after the actor had repudiated his Communist past before HUAC, and he recommended the same for Edward G. Robinson, though in this case the pardon came reluctantly. He had compiled a ten-page report on Robinson detailing his Communist-front record and told Johnson that he did not care for the man, but "as a Christian and an American am willing to let bygones by bygones."[37]

The ultimate goal, to his mind, was not to deprive people of their livelihood but to "fracture beyond the possibility of repair the subversive apparatus." In pursuing this aim, few were too insignificant to monitor. Even if news commentators might have been the broadcast employees most likely to influence the political scene, Hartnett agreed with the

Counterattack partners that anyone, even on the entertainment side of the business, could play a role in a time of emergency or could at least contribute funds to the Communist cause. Once Hartnett even lodged a complaint about a woman he had spotted in a crowd scene. Juveniles could also be worthy of attention if the parents had a front record.[38]

Although he prided himself on the precision of his research, Hartnett did not necessarily feel he had been negligent if he failed to acknowledge that a performer had already made a substantial political conversion. He had, for instance, compiled a negative report on actor/announcer Marvin Miller, only later to learn that the performer was now a member of the Motion Picture Alliance for the Preservation of American Ideals, a right-wing, anti-Red organization. "I have no responsibility to go out looking for these things," he wrote Johnson, "when an individual has created by his own public activity an unfavorable public record."[39] As it turned out, Miller continued to work during this period, and we don't know if Hartnett would have taken a different view had the performer been blacklisted. But the episode underscored a central tenet of his approach: the onus, as always, resided with the fronter.

While Hartnett established himself in 1953 as broadcasting's premier Red hunter, world events were shifting dramatically. In March, Stalin, the personification of murderous Communist repression, died of a stroke at the age of seventy-three, and in July the Korean War, the original impetus for the blacklist in radio and TV, finally came to an end. Some might have seen these events as a signal that the world would soon enter a new era, a time of waning tension between East and West. But not Hartnett and his allies. For them the armistice in Korea was not a satisfactory resolution, not as long as the North Koreans still lived under the totalitarian dictatorship of Kim Il Sung. And while Stalin might be dead, the allegiance to Stalinism was not.

Hartnett would not have had to look very far to find an adulation for the dictator that still existed on the home front in America. The African-American educator W. E. B. Du Bois eulogized Stalin as "a great man" who "thought deeply, read understandingly and listened to wisdom, no matter whence it came," who guaranteed that the people of the Balkans would enjoy enlightened self-determination, and who deserved praise for destroying the kulaks, "the rural bloodsuckers," during his forced collectivization campaign. Taking up a similar theme, Paul Robeson wrote in

the *New World Review* of seeing Stalin at a 1937 Moscow recital. He remembered that "the tears began to quietly flow" because here was "a man
who seemed to embrace all. So kindly—I can never forget that warm feeling of kindliness." And just over a month after Stalin's death, Howard Fast
received, with pride, the 1953 Stalin Peace Prize at the Hotel McAlpin in
Manhattan at an event chaired by Reverend William Howard Melish,
whom *Counterattack* had frequently branded a fellow traveler—and, it
would seem, for good reason. In his acceptance speech, Fast lauded the
Soviet Union, the instigator of the Korean War, for its efforts to promote
peace in the face of those "evil men here in America who plan war."[40]

Developments overseas also made it clear that countries living under
Soviet control had little reason for optimism. Perhaps more than any other
event at the time, the Prague purge trials late in 1952 dramatized just how
grim the situation was. After months of interrogation and torture, fourteen
Czechoslovakian Communist leaders were convicted at a show trial on
trumped-up charges of conspiring against the state. Eleven of them were
hanged. Along with the obvious, brutal cynicism of the trials, there was
also a disturbing element of bigotry. Not only were eleven of the fourteen
defendants Jewish, the charges against them included the political transgression of Zionism. In retrospect, the case could be seen as one part of
the larger anti-Semitic policy of the Stalin regime's later years. Later revelations confirmed the original suspicions about the anti-Semitic nature
of the case: a Moscow agent who supervised the proceedings said at the
time that he did not care about the source or reliability of any of the evidence, adding, "Why worry about these Jewish shits anyway?"[41]

Within his own sphere of influence, Hartnett focused not only on suspected Reds on the air but, perhaps more important, their potential control of unions, an objective, he knew, that had been outlined by both
Communist theory and internal party publications. At first, most of the attention of anti-subversives had been fixed on pro-Communist influence in
the Radio Writers Guild, but by the time the McCarran Committee had
published its findings on the union in August 1952, the Radio Writers
Guild, an organization representing a waning medium being overtaken by
television, was already on its way to becoming moribund. Although the
guild had attempted to win jurisdiction over TV as well, a new group
called Television Writers of America frustrated the union's efforts by stak-
ing its own claim to the new medium, and by 1954 the Radio Writers

Guild would cease to exist as a separate entity altogether, absorbed along with the television group into the Writers Guild of America. The broadcast performers union, on the other hand, managed to remain relevant. In 1952 AFRA succeeded where the Radio Writers Guild had failed by taking on TV in addition to radio work. Renamed the American Federation of Television and Radio Artists (AFTRA), it became a primary target of Hartnett's efforts, not only because of its position in the broadcast industry but because of the contacts he had developed within the union, going back to his role in the 1948 William Sweets controversy.

After the Sweets case had introduced him to the issue of pro-communism among radio performers, Hartnett had conducted his own study of AFRA with the help of those actors known as the Artists' Committee. His association with this anti-Communist group spurred his interest in the affairs of the actors union and their effect upon the broadcast industry as a whole. When members of the Artists' Committee consolidated their control of union business, Hartnett acted, as he phrased it, as "vicariously a fellow-combatant."[42]

Playing a lead role in the Artists' Committee were such actors as Bud Collyer, Vinton Hayworth, Ned Wever, Jack Arthur, and Alan Bunce. Hartnett considered them "patriotic, level-headed and unselfish." Others in the union regarded them as vindictive reactionaries who aided the blacklist. Especially offensive to AFTRA liberals was Hayworth, and at least one anecdote suggested a basis for such resentment. When radio comedian Minerva Pious had trouble finding work after her listing in *Red Channels*, Hayworth made it very clear how happy he was with her predicament. Incredulous, union official A. Frank Reel asked him if he wanted "the woman to starve to death." "Yes," was Hayworth's answer.[43] But not all members of the Artists' Committee fit this mold. A conspicuous exception was Bud Collyer.

Better educated than most in his profession, Collyer was a graduate of Fordham Law School and had worked as a law clerk for a short time before deciding he could make a better living during the Great Depression by using the singing and acting talents he inherited from the vaudevillians on his mother's side of the family. He was an FDR New Dealer in those days but by the 1940s became a Republican. Like many others, he was suspicious of the Communists' tactic of prolonging union meetings until they were assured of a majority among those with the stamina to remain in attendance. With his legally trained mind and his ability to memorize Robert's Rules of Order, Collyer did his best to frustrate these maneuvers and became an outspoken opponent of Communist influence. His activism incurred a price. While retaining his signature role as the radio voice of Superman, he found, once he became a leader of the union's anti-Communist faction, that other jobs were harder to find. The antagonism toward him could sometimes be fierce. His son, Michael Collyer, said, "I remember walking across Rockefeller Center with my father— I was seven or eight years old—and someone yelling, 'I hope I'm on the firing squad when we take over and kill you.'" To bypass his job difficulties in radio during the late 1940s, Collyer went to work in the unproven medium of television, where he eventually became best known as a quiz show host for Goodson-Todman Productions.[44]

Vague allegations of anti-Semitism surfaced against some of the Artists' Committee, but the charges clearly did not apply to Collyer, who would later move his family from Pound Ridge, Connecticut, because, his son recalled, "the country club there adopted a policy restricting Jews." As for the blacklist, he did not relish it the way Hayworth did—he once described it as a "rotten practice"—but still he accepted it as one of the regrettable consequences of a polarized era.[45]

Between 1949 and 1951 the union's left wing was able to gather enough support to initiate measures to fight the blacklist. More decisive, though, were the actions of the right-wing Artists' Committee to bring the union into the cold war's anti-Red fight. As early as 1944 they had succeeded in passing a resolution to forbid all political discussion at membership meetings, an attempt to forestall efforts to bring a Communist-front agenda into union proceedings at the expense of pure labor matters. The attempt had been short-lived. Many objected that the rule would stifle free discussion, and within months the resolution was repealed. Events of 1951 revealed just how much had changed in recent years. In August, just over a year after the Korean War had begun, an overwhelming majority of union members approved a constitutional amendment that, in theory at least, would drive Communists out of the organization. Barred from the union would be anyone whose membership in the CPUSA after 1945 was either proven in court or established by federal government agencies, as well as anyone who now joined any organization named by the U.S. attorney general as a subversive group.[46]

Proving membership in the Communist party was extremely difficult, and true Communists could also skirt the new restrictions by steering clear of controversial groups, but the amendment had, at the very least, symbolic significance. Now there could be no doubt that the Artists' Committee and its allies controlled the union and would likely continue to do so for some time. For his part, Hartnett could take satisfaction in the fact that AFTRA had become an anti-Communist stronghold in the broadcast industry. This did not mean, however, that he was about to take anything for granted, especially when, in early 1953, the left wing in both the media and the union began to show signs of renewed defiance.

At the end of January 1953 the *New York Post* published a six-part exposé of blacklisting with a special scathing emphasis on Hartnett's cohort Johnson, described as a collector of Americana who "now collects human scalps." The series' description of AFTRA leaders Vinton Hayworth and Ned Wever as the grocer's personal advisers brought the issue to the floor of the union's membership meeting in March. Hayworth and Wever issued a statement to defend themselves. They did not deny they had met with Johnson but claimed they had done nothing improper in consulting with the man, no matter what the *Post* articles had implied. A contingent of members—among them Jack Gilford, Leon Janney, and Lionel Stander—demanded more of an explanation. Leading the group was blacklisted actress Lee Grant, who argued that the Red hunt had cast a pall over the union and had intimidated many members from speaking their minds. To begin to correct the situation, she demanded that the union condemn Johnson and that Hayworth and Wever provide a complete explanation of their dealings with the Syracuse grocer.[47] For Hartnett, a man determined to guard the barricades against any subversive encroachment, this rumbling of rebellion must have been an ominous development that required ever more vigilance. He began to contemplate a new counteroffensive.

While political turmoil continued to roil his profession, John Henry Faulk could take comfort, at least, in his personal life and career. "I have so much that should rejoice me," he confided to a friend, "a loving wife, three healthy, happy children, an un-explainable, but amazingly successful career." His late afternoon show on WCBS was rated among the most popular New York radio programs, and his yearly salary of $35,000 made it possible to move his family from their apartment on Riverside Drive to larger quarters on West Seventy-ninth Street, just down the street from both Central Park and the American Museum of Natural History. As with any show-business success, though, Faulk's work dominated almost his every waking hour, sometimes as much as fourteen hours a day.[48]

In addition to his WCBS show, he continued to appear on TV panel programs and also became host of a radio game show on NBC called *Walk a Mile*. And his work for WCBS went well beyond his hour on-air each weekday. Of special value to his principal employer was his skill as a pitchman—both over the airwaves and at promotional appearances at local supermarkets—which kept sponsors and local retailers happy and kept the advertising revenues coming in. In its promotional literature, WCBS invoked an image that would likely have appealed to the marketing instincts of Laurence Johnson: "Remember the old fashioned general stores and the friendly proprietor, whose personal recommendations meant so much to the success of a product? Today WCBS radio's John Henry Faulk carries on that tradition. Automatically and with easy conviction he uses tried and true old school selling principles, bulwarked by all tools of modern merchandising."[49]

Faulk's schedule left little time for political activism. This might explain, at least in part, his continued public silence at a time when he was so indignant about cold war policies. When he ventured onto political ground on his radio show, he trod very lightly, restricting himself, as he had to on a commercial program, to tame, folksy observations in the Will Rogers manner. A typical commentary, having to do with political fund-raising dinners—where only five dollars of the total hundred-dollar charge went toward the food—prompted him to point out that a man who "pays $95 to hear a politician speak, Democrat or Republican, must be powerful hard up for entertainment."[50]

Despite Faulk's innocuous public persona, a less guarded comment off the air led federal authorities to take a renewed interest in his political leanings. In April 1952 the FBI received a letter from a former fan of Faulk's who had recently concluded that he might not be as benign as she once had thought. Back in 1948 the correspondent had been such a fan that she wrote letters to the entertainer several times a week. She then had a change of heart when Faulk wrote back encouraging her to support

Henry Wallace for president. She now decided to contact the FBI because she had noticed a newspaper item announcing that Faulk was about to deliver a series of speeches to New York City high schools. She did not think that a supporter of Wallace and his "love of Russia" should have the opportunity to mold young minds. Hoover's office responded by ordering a follow-up inquiry to determine if the Bureau had indeed been correct in removing Faulk's security index card from its files. In May 1953 the New York office arranged for Faulk to come in for an interview.[51]

Faulk explained that he had never been a member of the Communist party, though a Communist had once tried unsuccessfully to recruit him while he was serving in the Merchant Marines. As for Communist fronts, he said he had never been a member of one. If he had ever taken part in a front event, "it was without his knowledge." A good part of the interview concerned his first wife, Hally Wood, who, a year and a half earlier, had been named as a Communist before HUAC by Harvey Matusow. Bureau agents now questioned Faulk about his possible involvement in her activities. He described his marriage to Wood as troubled, partly because of her friendship with radicals in such groups as the People's Educational and Press Association, a pro-Russian circle that Faulk did not approve of. He regarded it as a group of neurotics with "questionable" sexual morals, and put up with them only on a social basis, he now said, as a way to appease his wife and salvage the marriage. The Bureau agents came away from the interview satisfied with the "apparent truthfulness of the subject" and recommended that his case be placed in "a closed status."[52] How satisfied Faulk was with the experience we do not know. Being called into the FBI's New York office, even on a friendly basis, might have alarmed him and discouraged him from making his political views public for fear of becoming a target of Red hunters. Or perhaps the interview angered him by reinforcing his belief that the country really had become a reactionary security state. Most likely the experience provoked a combination of the two responses.

Faulk's thoughts on the current American scene certainly had not changed. An event that struck especially close to home for him was a ceremony held for Joe McCarthy and his new bride by officials from Faulk's native state. Texas governor Allan Shivers drafted for the senator a certificate that read, "Joe McCarthy—a real American—is now officially a Texan." This "Texanizing" of McCarthy spurred Faulk to confide to a friend, "With all the drouth, dust storms and hard times Texas has had to endure, it seems to me this latest plague, not from God, but from Shivers, just about puts us back where we were when old Cabeza de Vaca went hiking across the country naked as a jaybird and eating pricklypear apples." Although cushioned with colorful down-home humor, the sentiment hinted at harder, bitter undercurrents in Faulk's political thinking, a sensibility that characterized the country's cold war policies as an "onslaught against what I consider all that is decent and worthy in American life."[53]

As distressed as he might have been, Faulk continued to keep his head down and left the public debate to others. That would soon change as a new crisis in his profession drew him into the fray.

NINE

Renewed Vigilance

VINCENT HARTNETT and others in the anti-Red camp began to see the need for a new organization as early as 1952. *Counterattack* had done its part, obviously, in leading the fight, but it had never concentrated exclusively on the entertainment industry, always Hartnett's specialized area of expertise. Now, after Theodore Kirkpatrick's departure, the newsletter paid hardly any attention to the subject at all. To correct the situation, Hartnett, Johnson, and members of the Artists' Committee formulated plans for a group that would address the specific concerns of broadcast Red hunters.

Those involved in the new venture began issuing a bulletin in mid-1953, soon after left-wing actors had started to challenge the AFTRA leadership. Although the group's members incorporated their organization in the fall, they did not publicize its formation until December when they announced that Aware, Inc., had arrived "to combat the Communist conspiracy in entertainment communications."

The group reiterated the same concerns originally raised by *Counterattack* and *Red Channels*: the slanting of programs to convey Communist ideas, the infiltration of broadcast unions, the promotion of Communists and fronters within the industry along with discrimination against anti-Reds. If these had been the only ideas that Aware espoused, the group would have offered nothing new. But Aware set itself apart by promising to become a central clearinghouse for information, a "rallying ground" for all those committed to the crusade.[1]

Those who initially rallied round provided both expertise and inside knowledge of the industry. Hartnett, appointed to the board of directors, served as the organization's chief researcher. Joining him on the board were such actors as Vinton Hayworth, William Keene, and Leigh Whipper, who helped form a bridge between the group and AFTRA, a primary focus of Aware's efforts to get subversives off the air. Another actor, Ned Wever, served as first vice president while the position of second vice president was filled by Paul Milton, the radio writer who had testified before the McCarran Committee and had led the anti-Communist group called We the Undersigned, which had attempted to rid the Radio Writers Guild of Communist-front influence. As Aware's president, Godfrey Schmidt lent public stature and intellectual discipline to the top of the organization. A prominent attorney and a professor in constitutional law at Fordham University, he had once served as deputy commissioner of the New York State labor department and as a member of the federal Atomic Energy Labor Relations Panel, and was known for his ability to expound upon the legal and philosophical basis for policing the broadcast industry. Input based more on practical experience came from Aware members Laurence Johnson, Francis Neuser, and John Dungey, experts in the use of economic pressure.

The group supported itself through annual ten-dollar dues from its members as well as donations and admissions to its public events. The money went toward the distribution of information through a membership bulletin, edited by Milton, and through symposiums on the issue of communism, often held on college campuses where Aware hoped to cultivate youthful activists in the cause. Most significant of its activities, as far as outsiders were concerned, was the group's ongoing campaign to monitor those in radio and TV who hired Communists and their sympathizers.[2] All these efforts were inspired by an expanded view of the subversive peril and a broad definition of political evil.

Communist fronters and gullible allies had been targeted before but never quite so explicitly. In a pamphlet entitled "Statement of Principles," Aware made it clear that merely being non-Communist was not enough, that "it is not possible to stand neutral." After discoursing on the deceptive allure of Communist-front causes and their corruption of genuine liberalism, the organization concluded, "One of the real stumbling blocks for those trying to expose the true Communist and confirmed fellow-traveler is the real non-Communist who has never joined Communist fronts, yet defends those who do." This was someone who "opposes 'witch-hunts' even when there are 'witches'" and "decries 'redbaiting' even where there are 'reds.'" The pamphlet did not clarify whether these neutrals would need to do penance in the same way that overt fronters would, but it did place them in the enemy camp.[3]

Although Aware did not, for now, outline an exact procedure by which subversives were to clear themselves, the organization clearly stated that positive acts of anti-communism were required, as Hartnett had advocated in his private consulting work. When it came to the menace of communism, "If you're not fighting it, you're helping it."[4] In time the group's bulletin would name some of those it considered the worst offenders, those most in need of repentance.

Aware's membership over the next few years ranged from 125 to 350. Yet its influence had less to do with the numerical size of the organization than it did with the group's redefinition of the Red hunt for a new era.

The Korean War had been over for five months by the time Aware announced its formation. Welcome as the armistice might have been, the military stalemate did nothing to erase the underlying global conflict. Those who thought the blacklist was strictly a drastic wartime measure, similar to other measures in other wars, could now plainly see that the practice was outliving the overt clash of arms and was extending into the more nebulous cold war struggle. Aware had arrived to marshal the forces and set the rules that would perpetuate the quasi-wartime purge. Presumably, if the blacklist could outlive the Korean War it might persevere indefinitely now that the United States and the Soviet Union were locked in an ongoing confrontation that seemed to have no end in sight. Anyone in broadcasting who needed confirmation that the blacklist was not going away any time soon would find it in a May 1954 decision in the New York courts.

Since filing his lawsuit against the *Red Channels* publishers in December 1950, actor Joe Julian had managed to scrape by in an industry that now had little use for him. He alternated between a diminished number of radio appearances and a series of industrial and institutional films. When his case, the only anti–*Red Channels* libel suit to go to court, finally went to trial in 1954, it did not begin auspiciously for him. On the first day the judge, a liberal-minded and potentially sympathetic jurist named Abraham Geller, disqualified himself because he was a former member of the ACLU, which had once been listed as a subversive organization by the California Un-American Activities Committee, a fact that might at least make it appear that he had a conflict of interest in the case. Eventually Geller would play a key role in deciding the fate of the blacklist, but that would have to wait for another eight years. For now his place would be taken by Irving Saypol, a staunch anti-Communist and the former prosecutor of Julius and Ethel Rosenberg. As his credentials suggested, Saypol was not disposed to give Julian's lawsuit much leeway.[5]

The case had been difficult enough for Julian to assemble even before the judge placed restrictions on it. The actor had admitted he had participated in the two front events listed in *Red Channels* but only as a non-Communist participant; the booklet, he contended, had created the false impression that he was a Red sympathizer. The problem was that few people in broadcasting were willing to take the witness stand and back up his claims. Especially frustrating was the refusal of a talent agent who could have substantiated Julian's assertion that his listing in *Red Channels* had prevented him from getting work. Even so, he was able to enlist no less a personage than Edward R. Murrow, who readily agreed to testify and who also recruited fellow CBS newsman Charles Collingwood to take the stand. Agreeing to act as a character witness was Morton Wishengrad, the writer of "Communism—U.S. Brand," which had starred Julian and would clearly establish his anti-Stalinist sensibilities. On the stand, however, neither Murrow nor Collingwood was permitted by Judge Saypol to vouch for Julian's reputation for patriotism or to comment on the practice of blacklisting. Most damaging of all was Saypol's decision to limit the testimony of Charles Martin, a TV director who had been under instruction not to hire Julian because of his *Red Channels* listing. The judge ruled that Martin's testimony about these instructions had to be stricken because it qualified as hearsay.[6] Without any executives willing to admit they had relayed these orders to the director, Julian was unable to prove that the booklet had damaged his career. After Julian's lawyer presented his case, Saypol granted the defense's motion to dismiss the lawsuit.

Not only had Julian failed to establish a connection between the booklet and his loss of work, Saypol said, but he could not even rightly claim that the book had defamed him. Drawing upon Hartnett's disclaimers in the booklet's introduction, the judge ruled that *Red Channels* had simply reported two activities of Julian's and had never concluded that the actor was a Communist. Julian appealed the decision but with little hope of reversing it.

Ironically, losing the case helped Julian's career. Now that a court had said it was reasonable to assume that *Red Channels* did not brand the actor a Communist, broadcasters were suddenly willing to make that assumption for themselves, as if they had needed the judge to authorize the thought. BBD&O now showed interest in a TV play Julian had written and, provided there were no other potentially embarrassing episodes from Julian's past, wanted to produce it for the *U.S. Steel Hour*. With the help of security officer Jack Wren, the actor recalled, agency executives interrogated Julian and satisfied themselves that they could move ahead. The *U.S. Steel Hour* aired his play in December. "The very next day," Julian later wrote, "I began getting calls for radio acting jobs."[7]

Although the case worked out well personally for Julian, it demonstrated for the industry as a whole that there was little point in confronting the blacklist through the legal system. Finding witnesses to pull the covers off a secretive practice was extremely difficult, and, if Saypol was any indication, the judiciary was liable to give Red hunters the benefit of the doubt. With legal options closed, entertainers who found themselves under a cloud had only one alternative if they wished to keep working, and that was the old, humiliating alternative of wending their way through the back alleys of clearance.

Among those who resorted to the procedure during this period was Vincent Price, who, believing he was being greylisted, volunteered for an interview with the FBI in April 1954, a Bureau report stated, so that he could explain his past involvement with such groups as the Hollywood Independent Citizens Committee for the Arts, Sciences and Professions. The FBI, which had never had any interest in Price, conducted a brief investigation and concluded the obvious, that the actor had no connection to the Communist party. Recollections of the family of John Dungey suggest that Price also traveled to Syracuse and conferred with Dungey to assure his future employment in radio and TV.

Counterattack also continued to play a role in the process. When it raised doubts about Harry Belafonte's associations with Communist fronts and Communist-dominated unions, the singer felt compelled to contact the newsletter and present his side of the story. He denied he was a Communist, maintained he had entertained at front events without knowing their true nature or without participating in their political activities, and dissociated himself from Paul Robeson. A more grueling process was endured by actor William Redfield. Finding himself unemployed after a *Counterattack* piece on him in 1952, he professed his innocence to the newsletter staff, then took a series of actions to clear himself that lasted nearly two years. He composed an affidavit, joined the Americanism committee of his local American Legion post, applied for membership with Aware, conferred with Hartnett, Johnson, and Wren, and finally issued a statement at an AFTRA meeting in March 1954 that attacked an anti-blacklisting resolution, a statement that *Counterattack* reprinted in part two months later.[8]

The supply of people requiring clearance remained steady, thanks to the work of Hartnett and Johnson. Hartnett not only continued to provide his services to Borden and Lever Brothers but acquired another important client in Young & Rubicam, the advertising agency that Johnson had once singled out for being soft on Communists. Hartnett did not confine himself, however, to work strictly for pay. On his own time he attended the Julian trial and, after the case was dismissed, offered to help the actor clear himself of another damaging episode from his past, one that Julian himself was unaware of. It turned out that Hartnett had a snapshot of Julian marching in a May Day parade—or, at least, an indistinct snapshot of somebody vaguely resembling Julian marching in the parade. He made no mention of a fee. As he saw it, this was an act of civic duty and Christian charity. Julian saw it as an arrogant imposition, a false allegation based on grossly inadequate evidence.[9]

Johnson, reaching the age of sixty-five in 1954, began to scale back his activities, at least in his profession as storekeeper, selling his two outlying groceries in Fulton and Oswego, leaving him now with four stores in Syracuse proper. The contraction of his grocery chain did nothing, however, to reduce the awe with which some broadcasters continued to regard him; nor did his advancing age deplete his energy in agitating for his cause. And bad publicity he had attracted had no effect on his fellow true believers. A year earlier, a local veterans council had honored Johnson, as well as the Veterans Action Committee and American Legion Post 41, in a pointed rebuke to the *New York Post* "smear" articles on their activities. And in May 1954 the national convention of the Catholic War Veterans, meeting in nearby Saratoga Springs, showed their appreciation for the grocer by awarding him a national Americanism citation.[10]

As always, the abject cooperation of certain media executives provided invaluable aid to Johnson and Hartnett. That was another lesson of the Julian case. Commenting on the court's decision in the *New York Times*, Jack Gould wrote, "There always will be individuals publishing pamphlets of sundry sorts and indeed their right to do so must be vigorously championed if free speech is to mean anything. Where 'Red Channels' became a serious matter was in its blind acceptance by many sponsors, advertising agencies and networks who, along with Mr. Julian's witnesses, found it convenient to assume the worst about those listed therein." Julian had encountered this reluctance to challenge the blacklist at the very top of the most powerful network. Soon after his troubles had begun, he had written to CBS head William Paley, asking for the executive's advice on how to overcome his employment troubles. Paley's response, Julian said, was to pass the buck to Daniel O'Shea, the network's security officer, who insisted that the actor undergo a demeaning clearance procedure.[11]

If the blacklist was destined to remain in place for the foreseeable future, questions arose not only about entertainers' employment difficulties but about the effect of the practice on the broadcasting product. Did programming deteriorate because a significant portion of the talent pool had been barred? And did the practice also have a chilling effect on the content of shows produced by those who were deemed acceptable? By the mid-1950s the blacklist had been around long enough for there to be an assessment of changes on the broadcast scene.

The most obvious by-products of the cold war were broadcasting's anti-Red melodramas, desperate warning tales of the dire threat that lurked within the unsuspecting American scene, hidden behind cleverly contrived masks of innocence. The dramatized equivalent of *Counterattack*, *I Was a Communist for the FBI* told the true story—or what the show's announcer assured the audience was the true story—of Bureau informer Matt Cvetic, a civil service worker who between 1943 and 1950 infiltrated the Pittsburgh branch of the Communist party. Cvetic had first gained a foothold in the media spotlight through a series of articles on his exploits published in the *Saturday Evening Post*, then parlayed that exposure into a Warner Bros. movie before the Frederic W. Ziv Company brought his story to people's homes via the radio airwaves for a two-year run, beginning in 1952 at the height of the Korean War. Portrayed by Dana Andrews, the radio Cvetic had a hand in foiling virtually every form of Communist conspiracy, from subverting schools and fomenting labor unrest to smuggling military secrets and punishing party deserters—the sort of person who, Cvetic explained, had "stopped being a Red and became a human being." To accent the credibility of its tales of intrigue, the show adopted a quasi-documentary style. But as much as it strove for sober realism, the series was at its most memorable during its closing refrain when it indulged in a flourish of noir-style paranoia: Andrews's Cvetic reflects on his sense of isolation, necessitated by his living a lie as a pseudo-Red, then solemnly reminds the audience, "I walk alone." The line is followed by the sounds of footsteps receding and reverberating down what must surely be a dark, deserted street as could only be imagined by a cinematographer with an expressionistic bent.

From the same production company came another, even more popular first-person exposé, this time on the new medium of television. The hero, once again, was a man who had infiltrated the Communist party for the FBI and had recounted his experiences in print. In the 1952 book *I Led 3 Lives*, a Boston advertising executive named Herbert A. Philbrick related his experiences juggling three identities: "citizen, 'Communist,' counterspy." Contrary to what one might expect of cold war confessionals, the book is not sensationalistic but rather provides a methodical account of everyday life in the Communist party and, at one point, even warns against reckless Red-baiting, particularly the indiscriminate targeting of front organizations, which "is one of the greatest weaknesses of the anti-Communist forces and a source of many injustices." The 1953–1956 TV series was another matter altogether. Pervading it was a sense of anti-Red panic. In the role of Philbrick, Richard Carlson could not walk down a busy, sunlit city street without shooting jittery glances over his shoulder and breaking out in a cold sweat. He did not merely have to contend with ideological rigidity and subterfuge but with the constant, dry-mouth fear of being found out and rubbed out by soulless Commie goons. Harsh black-and-white photography accentuated the sense of grim, dangerous reality, and Carlson's voice-over narration spelled out exactly what the Communists had in mind: "They hate your guts. They intend to destroy you and your family and everything you hold sacred." Sentiments like these endeared the show to Laurence Johnson, who watched the program regularly, and infuriated entertainment-industry leftists like Ring Lardner, Jr., who suggested that the Communist party of Massachusetts might consider suing for libel.[12]

Critics have characterized both *I Was a Communist for the FBI* and *I Led 3 Lives* as symptoms of the era's hysteria, as a distinctive, disturbing phenomenon peculiar to the period. Certainly both shows were outrageously alarmist, but they were hardly unprecedented. Essentially they were cold war equivalents of earlier anti-Axis melodramas, like *Counterspy* and *The FBI in Peace and War*, none of which could be accused of either great subtlety or nuance. In that way, these programs did not represent a drastic shift. Like comparable shows from World War II, the Red-hunter programs represented the official version of events in time of war. They were not, however, the only voices on the air. There was also an occasional dissenting opinion, disguised but not disguised enough to obscure an opposition to the accepted cold war mentality. Not only did the blacklist fail to suppress all leftist commentary, it also failed to exclude all blacklistees from the debate.

Beginning in 1953, the same production team that had created *Danger* launched a new CBS-TV series with a clear potential for veiled political statements. Based on a radio show of the same name, *You Are There* recreated historical events as if covered by a TV news team, with real CBS newsmen such as Mike Wallace and Don Hollenbeck on hand to set the scene and interview players in the real-life drama. As was the case with *Danger*, the writers included blacklistees Walter Bernstein, Abraham Polonsky, and Arnold Manoff working anonymously behind fronts. Seeing themselves as persecuted men of conscience, they were fond of dramatizing the ordeals of martyrs and victims of repression, from Socrates and Galileo to Joan of Arc. Only the unobservant could miss their intent to draw comparisons to the blacklist and congressional probes. The commentary was at its most pointed in the March 29, 1953, broadcast of "The First Salem Witch Trial." Arthur Miller had already seized upon this historical episode as a vehicle for anti-McCarthyism allegory in his play *The Crucible*, and the *You Are There* recreation followed suit by drawing its own analogies for anyone willing to make the connection. The point becomes especially obvious when a New England minister, in response to a reporter's question, ponders the consequences of the Puritans' unrelenting search for the Devil in their midst: "Are we destroying him or are we destroying each other?"[13]

You Are There not only succeeded in injecting a minority opinion into broadcasting's public square, it also carried on a tradition that had once been common a decade earlier. Although it was bankrolled by a sponsor, the show's serious, civic-minded content served as a reminder of the sustaining programming that had contributed to the prestige of broadcasting during the 1940s. It was nearly a lone reminder.

Aside from the advent of television, the most dramatic change in broadcast programming in the 1950s was the absence of nonsponsored shows imbued with a Popular Front sensibility. This was the great lament among those who cherished the so-called Golden Age of radio of the previous decade; it was also the persistent complaint about the new broadcast fare. But was this criticism truly justified? The answer to that question depends to a great extent on how one appraises the earlier Golden Age of the 1940s.

Without doubt the Popular Front spawned some remarkable work, both in radio and in other media, perhaps the best example being Aaron Copland's 1942 orchestral work, "Lincoln Portrait." For other creative types, though, the marriage of politics and art could often lead talent astray rather than nurture it.

Any discussion of radio's Popular Front years naturally revolves around Norman Corwin. His singular importance was something even his detractors acknowledged. For a time, Red hunters like Hartnett tried to establish that Corwin was a linchpin in the Communist conspiracy, even though there was never any evidence to support this contention. More than that, his actions in the summer of 1950 clearly established that he was not a Communist. Until the Korean War, Corwin had been a sponsor of the National Council of American-Soviet Friendship, but the Council's failure to condemn North Korean aggression convinced him to resign from the front group, a decision that no Communist would have made. Still, *Counterattack* never tired of objecting to Corwin's presence on the airwaves. For the newsletter's partners, he posed a danger not only because of his association with front organizations but, perhaps more important, because of his writing skill, which, an internal company report said, could potentially make the party line seem especially enticing.[14]

Politics had not always been the centerpiece of Corwin's work. In such early radio plays as "The Plot to Overthrow Christmas," "Daybreak," and "My Client Curley," he had established his reputation with an extraordinary command of the audio medium that could, depending on the subject, be ingenious, amusing, and whimsical, or highly textured and lyrical. But it was his enthusiastic embrace of Popular Front concerns during World War II that led to his even more elevated stature as radio's great master. Ironically, it is this work that fails to hold up as well as his earlier, less ambitious programs.

While critical praise at the time was effusive for Corwin specials like "We Hold These Truths" and "New York: A Tapestry for Radio," an occasional contrary word could be heard. Commenting on "On a Note of Triumph," Corwin's commemoration of V-E Day, Bernard DeVoto described this work of the "acknowledged master of the art of radio" as "dull, windy, opaque, pretentious, and in the end false."[15] Today DeVoto's words ring more true than the chorus of raves that overpowered his assessment at the time.

Corwin's earlier precision and insight seemed to recede the more he was consumed with his mission to rally the forces against fascism and sing the praises of what the Popular Front called, with unwitting condescension, the Common Man. No longer content with inspired storytelling, he now strained for the rhapsodic as his writing alternated between the trite ("America is all things to all people") and the awkwardly bombastic ("Not they alone, not only little men like they"), all carried along by a wave of portentous musical accompaniment. The rhetoric could become especially windy when narrated by Orson Welles in his most mannered, voice-of-doom delivery. In "Fourteen August," Corwin's celebration of the Japanese surrender, Welles holds forth on the need to mark the occasion by intoning, "So say it tonight with saluting guns, say it with roses, say it with a handclasp, a drink, a prayer, say it any way you want, but say it! SAY IT!" This sort of overwrought iteration—whether on the value of the Bill of Rights or the defeat of fascism—brings to mind a criticism of Leonard Bernstein, another product of the Popular Front era. Writing about the composer's "Mass," Donal Henahan once observed that Bernstein "cannot resist getting down on all fours to sing propagandistic baby-talk to his audience."[16]

Although it didn't indulge in bombast, *You Are There* carried on this tradition in the early 1950s by providing another example of what sometimes happens when talented, creative people become enamored of a mission and message. In the crime show *Danger*, the same production team had created episodes with a quirky sensibility and a deft touch in writing and performance, but when they turned their attention to the political allegories of *You Are There* their efforts lost dramatic vibrancy and became little more than stodgy recitations. And the analogies that supposedly made some of the episodes so important are not necessarily apt. In "The Crisis of Galileo" episode—an apparent allusion to cold war loyalty hearings—the great astronomer must renounce his theories in order to save his life. Given the political beliefs of many who came under scrutiny in the 1950s, the implication here is that Galileo was analogous to American Communists. Although it's true that Galileo and American Communists were equally fervent in their beliefs and equally entitled to espouse those opinions from a civil libertarian perspective, it's difficult to equate a man trying to defend enduring scientific principles with people who clung to the false belief that Stalin was a benign ruler. In another episode, "The First Salem Witch Trial," innocents are sent to the gallows based on nothing but the manipulative ravings of vindictive teenage girls. If this historical event is a true precursor to the HUAC inquiries, we must accept that these characters' transparent antics of feigned demonic possession are essentially no different from the modern-day sworn testimony of people like Allen Sloane and Pauline Swanson Townsend, who were obviously what they claimed to be, namely, former Communists.

By the time *You Are There* premiered, Corwin had left commercial broadcasting behind and never had the chance to champion on television the type of programming he had earlier spearheaded on radio. Some might have regretted this, but they were longing for a broadcast style that did not necessarily make the most of the industry's talent and often diverted it from its true strengths. Critics who have maintained that the blacklist gutted the medium's creativity tend to overlook an obvious fact about broadcasting during these years. True, the industry barred a significant number of people from making a contribution, and we can never know what they might have produced. But it is also true that the early and mid-1950s represented the Golden Age of television—and for reasons that had nothing to do with politics of any kind.

The Golden Age designation needs to be clarified. Only a portion of the programming was truly outstanding, and much of the rest was mediocre if not outright inane. What made this period remarkable was that broadcasters allowed room for excellence. Standing out most of all were the acclaimed drama anthologies that developed the talents of such writers as Paddy Chayefsky, Horton Foote, Ernest Kinoy, Reginald Rose, and Rod Serling. Political or social commentary might have been rare— sponsors, as always, preferred to play it safe—but well-crafted, compelling stories, heightened by the immediacy of live broadcasting, were commonplace. Also memorable were the comedies performed by the likes of Sid Caesar, Jackie Gleason, Jack Benny, and Ernie Kovacs, scripted by yet another memorable list of talent, from Larry Gelbart and Goodman Ace to Neil Simon. Cold war politics failed to halt this surge in quality.

What made this exceptional period possible was the unsettled nature of a medium that was still defining itself. As long as the networks remained unsure how to exploit this new outlet, much of the decision-making was left in the hands of creative executives and producers interested in making the best shows possible rather than stooping to the lowest common denominator. They found ways to produce quality shows despite the restrictions the blacklist placed upon them. At the same time they were not necessarily content to let the blacklisters have their way.

⏷ Many of the independent-minded producers responsible for the best programs during this time—including the likes of Fred Coe, Herbert Brodkin, and David Susskind—were also the same people who continued quietly to make inroads into the broadcast purge. Under Coe's supervision, the Philco and Goodyear anthology series became a constant irritant to those Red hunters who now filled the ranks of Aware, as did *Kraft Television Theatre*, produced by Susskind. At ABC, Brodkin worked with his casting director, Edith Hamlin, to find ways to hire actors like Luther Adler who were under suspicion but still potentially employable if the network and sponsor could be cajoled to clear them. Sometimes banned performers, writers, and directors could be sneaked in through television's back door. A blacklistee might be able to work on a morning show with a small audience because it received little attention from the network brass. Once that was done, a producer could then argue that, with this program credit, the person was now acceptable and could be used on other, higher-profile shows.[17] These efforts to elude the blacklist, however, could work only if the performer was willing to play the game. Not everyone was.

Zero Mostel was known to be especially defiant while barred from working in film or broadcasting. He would make announcements, in no uncertain but certainly scatological terms, that he had no intention of co-operating with anyone to clear himself and would instead go work on the stage. Two writers, Don Mankiewicz and Rex Lardner, thought they might be able to put him back on the air in the lead role for a series based on a Lewis Carroll poem, "The Hunting of the Snark," and man-aged to persuade him to attend a meeting at an advertising agency where they hoped to set up the show. The testy Mostel even followed the writers' instructions by keeping his mouth shut throughout the meeting. "I thought we had the deal set," Mankiewicz recalled, "except that, as the meeting was broken up, Zero, who hadn't been involved in the con-versation at all, took out a newspaper and began to read it, which is a lit-tle disrespectful. But what made it worse was that the newspaper was the *Daily Worker*." Very quickly the deal was dead. "I think Zero just did that as his own little practical joke, or perhaps his revenge for having sat silent for so long."[18]

The best alternative for performers who would or could not obtain clearance was the theater, which mostly ignored the blacklist, much to the dismay of Hartnett, who published an article in the summer of 1953 de-nouncing Broadway as "the last stronghold of show-business Marxists and their supporters." Years later he would say, "Broadway was a lost cause. There was no way you could have leverage on Broadway." With indepen-dent financing and no need for advertisers, theater producers could resist pressure groups much more easily and had no reason even to imagine that a grocer from Syracuse could do them economic harm. For musicians, other alternatives were nightclubs and concerts. Pete Seeger, in particular, was able to cobble together a living through a variety of live venues and music-teaching jobs as well as an occasional appearance on local TV and radio stations that were not especially concerned about potential protests from the American Legion.[19]

For the first three years of the blacklist, the struggle over who was eligible to work was confined primarily to lesser-known performers along with writers and directors who had never been in the public eye. Then, in September 1953, the spotlight fell on television's biggest star of all.

In the second week of September, newspapers across the country relayed a discovery made by a HUAC subcommittee: Lucille Ball, the star of *I Love Lucy*, had registered to vote for the Communist party in 1936. In her testimony before the subcommittee, the star of TV's most popular sitcom had admitted to the 1936 affiliation with the Communists but denied ever joining the party. HUAC confirmed her claims. Still, Red-baiting columnists Jack O'Brian and Westbrook Pegler began to hound her in print while irate citizens sent letters to newspapers to denounce the actress—exactly the sort of groundswell of outrage that had damaged other performers guilty of similar political indiscretions. But that would not happen this time. Both the sponsor, Philip Morris, and the network, CBS, stood by their star, and her series continued without interruption or the slightest drop in popularity.[20]

The incident demonstrated that CBS, the network that was most fearful of blacklist pressure groups, could hold its ground when it felt the situation demanded it remain firm. Helping to make this case different were the hundreds of letters and telegrams in support of Ball, but CBS decisions did not rest solely on the influx or absence of mail. In the past the network had demanded that other actors, like Joe Julian, go through a demeaning clearance process even when there had been no popular outcry against them. No such thing was asked of Ball. When the career of a franchise star was on the line, CBS was willing to ignore potential controversy. And, perhaps more to the point, the Red hunters were powerless to do anything about it. The incident revealed that the blacklisters were not necessarily the unstoppable force that some assumed them to be. As Jack Gould pointed out at the time, one could not "help but wonder if the fear of boycotts is not largely in the minds of those who subscribe to the use of blacklists and private loyalty files of dubious reliability."[21] None of this, though, meant that CBS and the other networks would now make a habit of resisting outside influences. When it came to the employability of less prominent actors, writers, and directors, they continued to seek the safety of avoiding trouble at all cost. In a purely practical sense, they had no compelling reason to buck the blacklist. Even with a certain percentage

of talent banned from the airwaves, there were always more creative people available than there were jobs to fill. As for the principle of standing
up to the unreasonable demands of zealots, many broadcast executives
simply lacked the resolve. And the protests, now coordinated by Aware,
were not about to let up.

Despite resistance by individual producers or any single gesture by
CBS, the cold warriors who had gathered to form Aware continued to influence hiring throughout the broadcast industry. Yet by 1954 some
changes were in the wind. They could be detected, first, in the larger cold
war struggle as President Eisenhower began his effort in the wake of the
Korean War to ease tensions between the United States and the Soviet
Union. The fortunes of Joe McCarthy, the lightning rod for Red-hunting
controversy, had also begun to decline, and television would play a role in
his fall.

When he signed the CBS loyalty oath in 1950, Edward R. Murrow had
suggested that he was biding his time and picking his fights. That time finally came to a close in October 1953. Murrow struck his first serious blow
against what he considered a disturbing age of suspicion when he produced and hosted a program entitled "The Case of Milo Radulovich."
Part of his ongoing documentary series entitled See It Now, Murrow's report focused on a man who had been branded a security risk and
drummed out of the air force reserve on the basis of arbitrary and unfair
proceedings. The program was so effective in making its case that the air
force backtracked and reinstated Radulovich just five weeks later. This
was only the beginning of Murrow's campaign against McCarthyism.
Within a month of the Radulovich report, he produced documentaries on
an Indianapolis ACLU chapter under attack from local right-wing groups,
and a tribute to General George Marshall, who had recently been condemned by Joe McCarthy as an unwitting tool in a vast Communist conspiracy. Although the Marshall report contained no explicit reference to
McCarthy, there could be no mistaking Murrow's contempt for the Wisconsin senator.[22] Before long he would take on McCarthy directly.

Murrow was hardly the first journalist to denounce McCarthy's reckless tactics. Both Drew Pearson and Herb Block at the Washington Post
had taken the senator to task right from the beginning of his anti-Communist crusade, and they were soon joined by the likes of Norman
Cousins, Jack Anderson, and the Alsop brothers as well as Time magazine

and the *New York Post*, which published a seventeen-part series on Mc-Carthy entitled "Smear Inc." Murrow, however, was the first to marshal the visceral power of television in this confrontation.

As much as he opposed McCarthyism out of a sense of fair play and civil libertarian principle, Murrow also had a personal reason. While preparing the McCarthy installment of *See It Now*, the historian A. M. Sperber has written, Murrow dwelled upon the memory of Laurence Duggan, his friend and former State Department official who had committed suicide six years earlier after he had been questioned by the FBI regarding his possible role in the Alger Hiss case. After Duggan's death, Murrow had gone on radio to proclaim his friend's integrity and to deplore his accusers.[23] Now he would confront the mentality that had spawned those charges and still leveled similar allegations against others.

"A Report on Senator Joseph R. McCarthy" went on the air March 9, 1954. Murrow relied heavily on film clips of McCarthy to expose his half-truths and his penchant for bullying and grandstanding. The reporter's eloquent summation included these words: "We will not walk in fear of one another. We will not be drawn by fear into an age of unreason if we dig deep in our history and our doctrine. And remember, we are not descended from fearful men, not from men who feared to write, to speak, to associate and to defend causes that were for the moment unpopular."

The program was greeted with widespread praise for both its skill and its opposition to demagoguery. The broadcast watchdogs, predictably enough, were not nearly as thrilled, even if they were not all unqualified McCarthyites. John Keenan, though obviously a believer in the senator's cause, thought McCarthy had overplayed his hand and become careless in his accusations. Francis McNamara, *Counterattack*'s editor, believed the senator's excesses could sometimes be outright ludicrous. According to McCarthy biographer Arthur Herman, when McNamara "heard on the radio that McCarthy had named [Owen] Lattimore as 'Moscow's top spy,' he laughed out loud." But *Counterattack* still found Murrow more objectionable than the senator. Ten days after the McCarthy program aired, the newsletter devoted an entire issue to condemning the reporter and his work. Hartnett, who otherwise objected to some of McCarthy's abrasive tactics, also weighed in against the Murrow show with a special bulletin. He devoted much of his lengthy essay to analyzing and refuting Murrow's allegations, though never succeeding in getting much beyond an exercise

Edward R. Murrow's exposé of Senator Joe McCarthy on his series *See It Now* signaled a shift in the public's attitude toward anti-Red agitators. *(CBS Photo Archive/Getty Images)*

in splitting hairs. More perceptive was his contention that Murrow distorted the issues through his selection and juxtaposition of film clips, a point also raised by a minority opinion among mainstream critics. Both John Cogley of *Commonweal* and Gilbert Seldes of the *Saturday Review* voiced concerns about this technique, arguing that this sort of manipulation of images could pull any meaning out of any subject, and worried about its implications for future TV journalism. "I am sorry to say," wrote Cogley, "that I truly believe the Edward R. Murrow show has set a potentially dangerous precedent which those who are now applauding it may find good reason to regret in time to come."[24]

Within a week the same documentary method was on display again and once more directed at McCarthy as *See It Now* looked at a witness before his committee named Annie Lee Moss. A clerical worker at the Pentagon, Moss had been judged a Communist and a security risk and had been temporarily dismissed from her job. McCarthy subpoenaed her in the expectation that he would have a fifth columnist within his crosshairs.

As the artfully arranged clips on Murrow's show demonstrated, he made a serious miscalculation. The bespectacled, dowdy Moss, as media historian Thomas Doherty has pointed out, fulfilled white America's conception of "guileless African American servility," the farthest thing from viewers' idea of a cunning agent of a foreign enemy. Apparently the committee had accused the wrong person. Of McCarthy's public relations disasters—and there was an increasing number of them in recent months—this might have been the most devastating, and the mass medium that Murrow had mastered brought the blunder into sharp focus.[25]

In tandem with the first McCarthy report, "Annie Lee Moss Before the McCarthy Committee" presented a damning portrait of the senator and his investigations. But those who questioned whether Murrow's clever use of images might be forcing the issues through a distorting lens would already have had some justification for their fears if they had had access to more complete information about the Moss affair. Four years later, evidence indicated that there had indeed been a member of the CPUSA named Annie Lee Moss residing at the address given by the woman before the McCarthy Committee. Although the evidence is not conclusive, it certainly establishes, as author Arthur Herman points out, that there was at least a legitimate reason to suspect that Moss might pose "a serious security" problem.[26] The Murrow show glossed over potential complexities in the story by relying on edited clips rather than thorough investigative reporting. This was not the only time Murrow failed to take a hard look at possible disloyal activity.

In 1948, when Murrow had broadcast his impassioned defense of Laurence Duggan's good name, his outrage over Duggan's suicide was genuine and his loyalty to a friend admirable, but his facts were wrong. Decades later, decrypted Soviet communications revealed that, between the mid-1930s and 1944, Duggan had in fact been a Soviet agent. He had not killed himself because he was being persecuted. He had killed himself because he was found out. Although Murrow, obviously, did not have access to Soviet documents at the time, it is reasonable to expect journalists to look past the surface of a story and at least investigate the possibility of another, hidden layer of facts. For all of Murrow's fine qualities, and he had many, he also had a blind spot when it came to the subject of Communist infiltration. His reluctance to dig into Duggan's past can be explained by his friendship with the man, but he was just as inclined to accept denials of guilt from Alger Hiss and just as likely to ridicule Hiss's accuser, Whittaker Chambers, whose testimony was later corroborated.[27]

Whatever the faults of Murrow's programs, they succeeded in bringing the persuasive power of TV into the larger critique of a reckless political adventurer and contributed to McCarthy's ongoing decline. Five weeks after the Annie Lee Moss documentary, television played a role once more in the controversy when it broadcast the Army-McCarthy hearings. The purpose of the Senate hearings was to evaluate the recent conflicting charges made by McCarthy and his opponents. The senator alleged that Communists were infiltrating the U.S. Army. His opponents claimed that McCarthy's committee was using these allegations to pressure the army into granting preferential treatment to a recent draftee, G. David Schine, a close friend of McCarthy's chief counsel Roy Cohn. Eventually McCarthy unraveled before the cameras, in the face of Army attorney Joseph Welch's withering rebuke—"Have you no sense of decency, sir, at long last?"—while the medium delivered McCarthy's defining, disastrous moment to the entire country. By December the Senate would censure him for conduct unbecoming of his office.

The Murrow documentaries and the Army hearings coverage demonstrated the potency of television and its ability to influence events. The medium showed its willingness to use that power in tackling controversies in the upper ranks of the federal government, but in another area, much closer to home, the networks remained silent. Ever since the publication of *Red Channels*, broadcasters had granted power to pressure groups, as if they had no weapons at their disposal for fighting against this movement. But, as the later Murrow documentaries made clear, they did have a means of striking back. What if, instead of capitulating, they had made use of their electronic bully pulpit to air investigative reports on *Red Channels* and the Syracuse group? Perhaps they could have neutralized the pressure groups' worst effects. Yet, once again, broadcasters chose safety over confrontation.

The shifting tides that turned against McCarthy at this time also carried a member of his staff onto a new and unpredictable course. Harvey

Matusow, after graduating from his apprenticeship as *Counterattack* underling and Johnson protégé, had been serving on the senator's committee since the spring of 1953 and had assisted in investigations of Communist infiltration into State Department libraries and New York newspapers. He had reached perhaps the highest level a master opportunist could hope for within the Red-hunting field. But the basis for his entrée into the inner circle had always been frivolous, and his lack of substance would soon betray him. It had been his whirlwind romance with and marriage to Arvilla Bentley, a wealthy McCarthy supporter, that had accounted for his job with the senator's committee and his friendship with such anti-Red ideologues as J. B. Matthews and George Sokolsky. By August 1953 his glib charm had lost its appeal with Bentley, and they divorced later in the month. Without his benefactor, he fell out of favor with the anti-Communist elite. Also during this period he left his job on McCarthy's staff.[28]

Matusow would claim that he severed his ties with the McCarthy Committee because of a moral awakening, an increasing distaste for his own hustling ways and the false testimonies he had given in exchange for notoriety. Like just about everything he ever said, this self-serving statement is difficult to accept at face value. Most likely he began seriously to reexamine his life only after his anti-Communist career took a turn for the worse and forced him to reconsider his options. The process took several months. In that time he confided to some that he had made false accusations and let it be known he intended to write a book that would amount to a public confession. Word of the ex-informer's book plans reached New York publisher Albert E. Kahn. He became very interested.

Kahn was a muckraking journalist and author who had been named in 1945 by Elizabeth Bentley as a Soviet agent. Evidence of Kahn's involvement with Russian intelligence has not been definitively verified by Soviet documents, but there is no denying his pro-Soviet inclinations. In 1946 he had co-authored a book entitled *The Great Conspiracy: The Secret War Against Soviet Russia*, which trafficked in party-line smears of Trotsky and cited the forced confessions of the Moscow purge trials as incontrovertible evidence of diabolical plots against the Stalin regime. He was now a partner in a small publishing firm with Angus Cameron, a former editor-in-chief at Little, Brown who had published *The Great Conspiracy* and who had also incurred Arthur Schlesinger, Jr.'s wrath by rejecting George

Orwell's anti-Stalinist parable, *Animal Farm*. In the fall of 1954, with the company Cameron and Kahn in serious financial trouble, the partners believed that a Matusow memoir could both serve a political purpose and keep their firm in business. They decided to contact the former anti-Communist witness but discovered this was no easy task. They left word with Matusow's mother that they wanted to speak to him, but their relayed message went unanswered.

Matusow was going through a period that was erratic even by his own flamboyantly unstable standards. He showed up in Texas, then decided to hit the road. Now assuming an itinerant beat persona, he meandered across the Southwest, taking temporary jobs as a farm worker and dishwasher to sustain himself along the way. Religion also played a role in his new life. Matusow, the Jewish kid from the Bronx, was now a practicing Mormon.

When he drifted into Taos, New Mexico, late in October, he finally returned Kahn's messages. He later claimed he made this call purely as a courtesy. But there was probably a more compelling reason. Matusow had always been adept at latching on to whatever trends might suit his purposes, and perhaps he now sensed that the country's mood was changing, from the sort of alarmism that had embraced his extravagant anti-Red testimonies to a weariness with McCarthyism that just might welcome a tell-all memoir that would discredit the relentless search for Communists in our midst. His associates from *Counterattack* and the Syracuse group might see no reason to change, but Matusow was about to reinvent himself once again. Once he had been a Communist, then an anti-Communist informer and witness. Now he discussed the possibilities for a book that would place him back on the left. Using a plane ticket supplied by Kahn and Cameron, he flew back to New York to begin the writing process.

℞ While McCarthy himself never specialized in investigating the entertainment field, his political demise loomed large in radio and TV as it did in any debate over domestic communism. For opponents of the broadcast blacklist, his censure proved that even the most powerful anti-Red watchdogs could be defeated. For Aware members, it confirmed the belief that their adversaries must never be underestimated. The fate of Mc-

Carthy might have indicated that the country was willing to turn in a new direction, but in other ways it settled nothing. The culture war between right and left continued.

On the local suburban front, the conflict brought Millard Lampell's name back into the news two years after the McCarran hearings had pilloried him and chased him out of commercial broadcasting. First, in February 1954, a group of residents in Scarsdale, a town above New York City, raised a storm of protest when they learned that a sixth-grade assembly in one of their local schools featured a recording of "The Lonesome Train," the folk cantata by Lampell and Earl Robinson. They alerted the rest of their community that both men had been named as Communists in congressional committee reports and highlighted, in particular, Hartnett's testimony about Lampell's position as one of "the most active and capable Communists in the United States." Soon the same controversy over a school's use of the same record erupted in Long Island's Levittown.[29]

"The Lonesome Train," which had premiered over one of Corwin's radio programs in 1944, told the story, in dialogue and song, of the funeral train that transported Lincoln's body from Washington to his home in Springfield, Illinois. During the Popular Front fervor of the World War II years, many might have accepted the piece without question. In the cold war years of the mid-1950s it did not pass without rigorous scrutiny. At one time it might have been viewed simply as a tribute to Lincoln and the Civil War cause—and, by inference, to FDR and the fight against fascism—but now its contrived class-struggle tone was difficult to miss.

Protesters pointed to the contrast that "The Lonesome Train" emphasized between those who sided with Lincoln and those who hated him. His supporters were

A Kansas farmer, a Brooklyn sailor
An Irish policeman, a Jewish tailor;
An old storekeeper shaking his head,
Handing over a loaf of bread

His enemies, on the other hand, included politicians, businessmen, newspaper editors, and cotton speculators, Americans who "didn't like Negroes" or simply "didn't like people."[30] The implication was clear: the good people were sometimes ethnic and were always working class, the bad were capitalists and establishment figures—a predictable dichotomy from a writer with a party-line background. In Lampell's cantata, ideology took precedence over history. The distinction he drew between Lincoln supporters and detractors might have made a tidy political argument, but it ignored inconvenient facts, such as all those economically comfortable people who "helped to save the Union" or those poor ethnics who had rioted against Lincoln's war policies.

All that said, the cantata's class-struggle undercurrent was just that, an undercurrent, not an overt specimen of agitprop, and its historical fallacies could have easily been corrected by any teacher who played the record. The irate citizens of Scarsdale and Levittown failed to make the case that the cantata would seriously distort the minds of their children. This was especially true in Levittown, where the record had been used only in music appreciation classes for lower grades. The protesters were still driven by McCarthyite alarmism. Their opponents spoke out against what they considered right-wing extremism. In Levittown they lost the argument. In 1956, after a protracted struggle, the song was banned from the schools.[31]

In December 1954, while these controversies were still raging, those inclined to sympathize with "The Lonesome Train" defenders could at least take symbolic comfort from another recording, a transcription of a Canadian radio show that mirrored their contempt for the excesses of America's anti-Communist movement. "The Investigator" had aired over the Canadian Broadcasting Corporation the previous May and had been an underground favorite on disk within American left-wing circles for several months. Only now it became available for sale at U.S. record stores. In this satirical fantasy, an inquisitorial congressman—a thinly fictionalized stand-in for McCarthy—dies in a plane crash and is transported "up there," where he continues to interrogate and defame as part of the afterlife's Investigative Committee on Permanent Entry. His fellow committee members are Dr. Titus Oates, the deadly persecutor of English Catholics; George Jeffreys, the so-called Hanging Judge of the Bloody Assizes, responsible for wholesale executions; Cotton Mather, the Salem witch hunter; and Torquemada of the Spanish Inquisition. The congressman quickly assumes control of the committee—he is considered the most able inquisitor of all—and runs amuck in his investigations into the loyalty of the afterlife's most illustrious souls. Before he is done he exiles everybody from Thomas Jefferson and Martin Luther to Chopin,

Beethoven, and Bach. Replacing all these great minds is the consummate nonentity, Otto Schmink.[32]

The radio play, which never misses an opportunity for ham-fisted commentary, is memorable not so much for its satirical qualities, marginal at best, but for what it says about the polarized attitudes of the day. For many in 1954 it was no longer enough to condemn McCarthy for his destructive conspiracy-mongering or ridicule him for his blunders. After enduring his tirades for four years, nothing less would do than to liken him to the worst persecutors in history. Some listeners accepted without question that McCarthy was comparable to Torquemada, a man responsible for having two thousand people burned at the stake. And after four years of the broadcast blacklist, they also accepted another specious assumption, one that Murray Kempton had pinpointed two years earlier, that the blacklist victims were all "flowers of humanity." No one but the most brilliant and inspired is brought before the Investigator, and the same, it seems, could be inferred about the targets of HUAC, Hartnett, and Johnson. A bit of vanity might be at work here. The author of "The Investigator" was former *Life of Riley* scripter Reuben Ship, who had been identified before HUAC as a Communist, had taken the Fifth when he himself appeared before the committee, and was later deported back to his native Canada.[33] According to the thesis of his "Investigator" script, he might have been spared if it weren't for his great talent and intellect.

In broadcasting, liberals and leftists could take satisfaction in their colleague Ship's skewering of the national Red-baiting icon, but they must also have despaired to see Hartnett and Aware still riding high, still unrelenting in their campaign to rid the airwaves of Communists and Communist fronters even after four years of winnowing them out of the industry. The Red hunters saw no reason for complacency, and there was no Murrow exposé of their tactics to galvanize public indignation.

While Hartnett did his part to police the airwaves through his private consulting service, and Johnson used his perceived economic clout to enforce the anti-Communist ban, Aware coordinated efforts through presentations to the public and practical advice to its members. Letter-writing had always been a valuable method of applying pressure, and in October 1954 the organization distributed a detailed memo to its members on how best to craft a message, either of praise or rebuke, and how to maximize its effect on those in radio and TV who might employ the wrong people or express the wrong ideas.[34] In AFTRA, Aware members and allies also continued to maintain an ideological foothold in the industry. Close to a hundred actors in the union belonged to the anti-Communist organization, and even Aware's president, Godfrey Schmidt, could exert an influence on the union as one of its members. Although a lawyer and professor by training, he had joined AFTRA by virtue of his appearances on radio and TV, primarily as a guest commentator on panel shows.

As much as the anti-Communist faction controlled the union, dissenters still put up a fight, and Aware closely monitored their actions. At an AFTRA meeting in March 1954, some members insisted that the union needed to do more to protect actors against blacklisting. The most forceful among the dissenters was Madeline Lee, wife of fellow performer Jack Gilford, who, like her husband, was barred from radio and TV. The situation was so dire, she argued, because actors could be blacklisted "for opposing some of the people who are in this organization, and we oppose them because we are against their policies in this union." The thinly veiled reference to Aware's influence was difficult to miss. At another meeting two months later, Lee took the floor again and went a step further by openly clashing with Aware member and AFTRA officer Vinton Hayworth. Lee declared that the union would never come to grips with the blacklist issue as long as its current officials remained in power because they themselves were "enforcing the blacklisting." Hayworth demanded that she produce evidence to back up her charge. The argument that followed yielded little information but exposed the underlying animosity between the union's right and left camps, one that was certain to flare up at the end of the year when the union held its elections for the local New York board.[35] To maintain their hold on AFTRA, Aware supporters within the union would have to score a resounding win against their challengers.

For Aware, the voting could not have turned out any more satisfying, the latest in what the organization called a series of "clear victories" for forces of "anti-Communism and anti-totalitarianism" within the union.[36] The left-wing opposition, on the outs for years now, was not able to win a single seat on the board. With that loss went any chance of pushing through its demand for forceful action against the blacklist. Aware's officers should have been content. Yet they could not let sleeping dogs lie.

On December 27, just eighteen days after the election, the organization discussed the voting results in the cumbersomely titled News Supplement to Member Bulletin, Aware Publication No. 12. While the newsletter might have chosen to concentrate solely on what it considered a positive outcome, it chose instead to focus almost exclusively, and in obsessive detail, on the defeated opposition. It was not enough that Aware saw its enemies lose. The organization now had to brand its opponents as Communist sympathizers, proving that there truly is such a thing as a sore winner. Based on information in Hartnett's files, the newsletter listed thirteen of the twenty-six opposition candidates and recounted their various associations with Communist-front activities. Included were some of the usual suspects—John Randolph, Lee Grant, Jack Gilford—who were no strangers to these kinds of charges, but also coming under attack were performers like Martin Balsam and Brenda Lewis who had previously not figured prominently among those targeted by Hartnett and Johnson. Not willing to let it go at that, the newsletter then added the names of three others with "less significant records." The very existence of such an opposition slate "demonstrated the need for a full-fledged official investigation of the entertainment industry in New York."[37]

The charges against AFTRA members were not necessarily inaccurate. Even if the evidence is inconclusive, some of those named might have been not only fronters but actual Communists. Yet even from Aware's own perspective, the newsletter's tactics made no sense. McCarthy's demise should have taught broadcast anti-Communists a pragmatic lesson on the dangers of overplaying one's hand. Nonetheless Aware's leadership showed little interest in learning. If the organization had accepted victory with some small measure of grace, it might have been able to consolidate its position in the union even further. By kicking those who were already down, Aware only energized its already outraged enemies and, more important, offended moderate AFTRA members and provoked them into siding with the opposition. If Hartnett and company did not have a real fight on their hands before, they would have one now.

TEN

The Middle of the Road

JUST A MONTH after attacking the AFTRA opposition, Aware set out to show that it had another, more forgiving side, that it was capable of more than just denouncing those who had taken the wrong path. In late January 1955, in what it considered to be an act of Christian mercy and guidance, the organization published a new pamphlet called "The Road Back." It outlined for the first time exactly the organization's ideas of how Communists "and those who helped them or permitted themselves to be put in the light of helping Communism" could clear themselves and return to work. Aware officials might have believed they were now building bridges to those people they had exposed in the past. They failed to see that their advice on doing penance would be regarded as high-handed and overbearing, and not just by Communists but by those who "permitted themselves to be put in the light of helping Communism," and even by those merely friendly to those who had been put in that light.

The pamphlet set the tone of its mission by opening with a biblical excerpt from Acts: "—that they should have a change of heart and mind—performing deeds fitting this change." The idea pervading all twelve pages of the pamphlet was that the responsibility for this sort of change must be assumed by the person who sought clearance, that the "burden of proof must rest on the alleged convert because he is the one responsible for his own acts and for the image of himself which those acts create in the minds of his fellows." In practical terms, within the broadcast industry this meant that performers must do everything possible to prove they had turned over a new leaf, even if they had only joined front organizations, an indiscretion that could make others believe they were Communists. And simply going through the motions to satisfy others was not enough. They had to believe profoundly in their conversion and do whatever it took to convince others they were sincere. "It must," the pamphlet insisted, "be a voluntary surrender to the exigencies of reality, of truth, of love."[1]

To remove any doubt about exactly what was expected, "The Road Back" included a twelve-step program which progressed from internal phases of soul-searching to external acts of contrition. Among the actions an ex-Communist or ex-perceived-Communist might take: write a full statement disclosing past questionable activities, volunteer to an interview with the FBI, write letters condemning communism for publication in newspapers, and support anti-Communist groups. And one more thing to consider: if "the subject's new convictions draw him to, or back to, religion, so much the better." Members of AFTRA could find special significance in step number six, which called for public statements against communism at union meetings. Most onerous of all was the suggestion that self-clearance also involved testifying before congressional committees, an act that would require naming others also involved in the Communist movement. But there was no need to torment oneself about this, the pamphlet explained. "Turning on Communism is not to become an 'informer' in any evil sense. . . . It means 'informing' in the noble sense of warning, educating, counseling."[2]

Now more than ever, Aware, Inc., was perceived as the engine of the blacklist, an organization that codified the rationale for the broadcast purge and promoted the tactics that kept it alive. But the left's resentment was not necessarily directed at the vaguely defined collection of individuals who made up the group; to the minds of many, the group itself was embodied by one man. While others held higher positions within Aware, Vincent Hartnett was the only officer directly connected to *Red Channels*—a fact he himself had emphasized over and over again—and he alone among Aware members operated as a sought-after consultant-for-hire, advising sponsors and networks on the employability of entertainers. The philosophy of Aware reflected his own perspective, and his private activities were a practical extension of the group's purposes. As one AFTRA member put it, Hartnett was "Mr. Aware himself."[3]

Hartnett's hand could be seen in the detailed front records listed in News Supplement Number 12, and his ideas on actively cleansing oneself of any Red taint were clearly mirrored in "The Road Back." The formation of Aware also coincided with greater success in his talent-clearance business. In 1954, Hartnett's income rose to more than sixteen thousand dollars and would increase by another nine thousand dollars the following year; by April 1955 he would be flush enough to move his files out of his apartment and open a business office at 60 West Forty-second Street, complete with an assistant to help handle the increased workload. He was the man to see when blacklist problems arose. In the fall of 1954, actor Everett Sloane met with Aware official Paul Milton to discuss his difficulty finding work, a problem he attributed to confusion between himself and *Red Channels* listee Allen Sloane. When Milton advised him to see Hartnett, he helped foster the idea that the *Red Channels* contributor was Aware's point man in these matters. He further reinforced the notion when he offered similar advice to writer Stanley Silverman and director Robert Lewis Shayon.[4] Other targeted performers didn't need Milton's referral to reach the same conclusion for themselves. The most notorious incident involved actress Kim Hunter.

Hunter had reached a turning point in her career on March 20, 1952, when she won an Oscar for her performance as Stella in the film version of *A Streetcar Named Desire*. By that time, though, her job offers in movies and TV were already beginning to dwindle. A year later, as she was growing desperate, her publicist, Arthur Jacobs, made the most logical move to rehabilitate her career: he sent a letter to Hartnett. He asked the consultant to supply any information he had on Hunter's political activities that might account for her current troubles, adding that he "would be interested in knowing if there would be any costs involved in obtaining this information." In his reply, Hartnett said he had made a cursory examination of his files and discovered that Hunter had been involved in "a number of activities officially cited as Communist-front," but a thorough political appraisal of the actress would require a greater effort. "The fee for such a complete report," he said, "would be two hundred dollars." He explained that the money would pay for his time and effort as well as photographic copies of important documents. He did not insist that he be the one to take on the job—others could also do the work, he said—but he impressed upon Jacobs that the actress would have to find some way to rectify her political indiscretions. "For her country's sake, for her own sake, and for her admiring public's sake, I hope she will do so." In the end, Hunter decided not to hire him or anyone else to assemble a complete review of her political past. Within two weeks of receiving the first letter from Jacobs, Hartnett contacted the publicist again and, in a gesture that suggests he was more zealot than mercenary, offered some free, unsolicited advice: Hunter should refrain from running on the left-wing slate of candidates for the Actors Equity council and should instead endorse the aggressively anti-Communist opposition.[5]

Hartnett continued to project himself to the public and the broadcast industry, sometimes for a fee, often for none. In a series of lectures to both Catholic and community groups, he preached the cause of eliminating Communist infiltration, and to sponsors he volunteered information on questionable actors, writers, and directors, even though these companies had not retained his services.[6] In at least one case he confronted a suspected entertainer directly.

Leslie Barrett was a character actor working in theater, radio, and TV who, in later years of rerun television, would become most recognizable as the pipsqueak pool player with the hulking brute of a friend in the "Bensonhurst Bomber" episode of The Honeymooners. Back in December 1954, though, he was little known at all outside professional acting circles. Still, he managed to keep himself employed and had little reason to fear the blacklist. Then he received, seemingly out of nowhere, a letter from Vincent Hartnett. The letter explained that Hartnett was working on a who's who of the American left-wing theater and wanted information from Barrett concerning a photograph taken in 1952. The photo showed people marching in the May Day parade, an annual event promoted by the Communist party. One of the marchers, Hartnett said, was Barrett. "It is always possible that people who have in good faith supported certain causes come to realize that their support was misplaced," Hartnett wrote. "Therefore, I am writing you to ascertain if there has been any change in your position." If he did not receive a reply, he would "conclude that your marching in the 1952 May Day Parade is still an accurate index of your position and sympathies."[7]

Rattled by this sudden—and, as it turned out, inaccurate—allegation, Barrett contacted his lawyer who then notified Hartnett that the actor had never marched in a May Day parade. Hartnett's response was to chide Barrett for bringing a lawyer into the exchange after Hartnett had merely afforded him "the privilege" of answering his query. As soon as he had thus finished reassuring Barrett that he had no reason to get up in arms, he immediately reinforced his reputation as a relentless ideological blood-hound by asking if Barrett's lawyer, Harvey Klein, was the same Harvey Klein who had once signed a Communist party petition in 1939.[8] If he had deliberately set out to increase Barrett's sense of alarm, Hartnett could not have done a better job. At no time was there any mention of a fee for clear-ing either Barrett or his attorney. Political fervor, once again, was pushing Hartnett on.

Complaints accumulated against Hartnett individually and Aware col-lectively, and fifty-eight members of AFTRA put their grievances down on paper in the form of a resolution and presented it to the local New York board. The document excoriated News Supplement Number 12 for hav-ing "scandalously attacked an entire slate of candidates," and demanded that "Aware, Inc., be condemned for interfering in the internal affairs of our Union."[9] The union board refused to put the resolution on its agenda for the next membership meeting, but that did not prevent a stormy con-frontation when AFTRA members met at Manhattan's Astor Hotel on March 22, 1955.

As soon as the meeting convened, supporters of the resolution protested the board's decision. George Ives, one of the resolution's spon-sors, took the lead in the fight. He read the resolution aloud and, to pro-vide the proper context, also read News Supplement Number 12. Then, in a theatrical moment worthy of his actor's training, he turned to Aware president Godfrey Schmidt and challenged him to "swear to the truth" of the bulletin. Schmidt, the law professor, proceeded to lecture AFTRA mem-bers on the legal implications of the anti-Aware resolution, though he was not greeted with the respectful silence he was accustomed to receiving on the Fordham campus. While peppered by catcalls and boos, he pointed out that Ives had misled his audience by refraining from reading the sec-tion of the original resolution that had accused Aware members of black-mail, a libelous accusation, he said. Turning to those opponents of Aware who had been attacked in News Supplement Number 12, he insisted that these candidates for union office were fair game for public criticism, and that the criticism was warranted. Candidates who were, he said, "foolish enough to be beguiled by Communist propaganda are precisely not the people to be entrusted with office in this great organization." Finally coming to the challenge leveled by Ives, he answered that the Aware newsletter did indeed tell the truth, and "the best proof of it is that none of you will dare, if you feel aggrieved, bring it to court, as you could."[10]

Among those angered by Schmidt's analysis was left-wing activist Lee Grant. The real point, she said, was that lists of actors like the one included in News Supplement Number 12 put people's livelihood in peril and intimidated AFTRA members from running for office. This was inevitable as long as union officers belonged to an organization that included Vincent Hartnett. "I think the fact that our Board members are sitting with a man who is the author of *Red Channels* that helps to put out lists is a shameful, shameful thing and should not be tolerated in our union."[11] The meeting then reached its emotional crescendo when Leslie Barrett rose to speak.

He told his fellow AFTRA members about his experience dealing with Hartnett, the letters he received, and the accusation he felt compelled to refute. Reading from his personal journal, he related the emotional impact of the episode, which made it impossible for him to eat or sleep for several days. He likened Hartnett to "a thug" and characterized his methods as "hoodlum tactics," emphasizing that he was not the only one to regard Hartnett in that way. He paraphrased an AFTRA official who had said that "in all his years of union activity, nothing has made him so sick as this one man." Barrett even suggested that the FBI shared his views. The actor had gone to the Bureau's New York office to lodge an official denial of the May Day allegation, and the agent who interviewed him, Barrett claimed, sympathized with his denunciations of Hartnett. In closing his fifteen-minute speech, Barrett gave his most stinging assessment of the man who had caused him so much distress: "This man represents a dangerous element in this country and the people should be made aware of it. It is as subversive and as much a threat to civil rights and human rights as Communism."[12]

After all the acrimonious debate, a call for calm came from Bud Collyer, one of the more moderate members of the union's anti-Communist faction who had no direct link to Hartnett. Emotional actors were prone to shouting and outraged interruptions, he said, while, on the other hand, "There was an awful lot of good that can be done by just a little bit of love in your hearts."[13] Whatever cooler heads might have hoped, members' hearts harbored little affection and their blood still boiled when the tumultuous three-hour marathon of a meeting finally ended just before midnight. Emotions would not dissipate over the ensuing months. The anti-Aware resolution was now officially placed on the agenda of the next membership meeting in May, and both sides prepared for the fight to come.

Emboldening the left was the publication of an exposé that wreaked havoc within the Red-hunting movement. After coming to New York in October to meet with his new publishers, Harvey Matusow had worked quickly to finish his memoir of life as an anti-Communist informer, and in the process succeeded in finding his way back into the headlines once more. His book, provocatively titled *False Witness*, was released in March, the same month as the debate on the anti-Aware resolution. Matusow's new notoriety initially revolved around affidavits he signed confessing to acts of perjury against a mining union official as well as CPUSA leaders in the Smith Act trials, but opponents of the blacklist in the broadcast industry seized upon other sections of his book: his claim that *Counterattack* was a protection racket; his admission that he had identified performers as Communists without any direct knowledge of their politics; his characterization of Syracuse grocer Laurence Johnson as a "Merchant of Hate."[14]

Buffeted by the Matusow scandal, the right dug in and prepared to strike back. Cold warriors claimed that the compulsive liar's recantations were the real lies. They also questioned the political motives behind the book's publication, pointing out that the project had been financed by the Mine, Mill and Smelters Union, which had been expelled from the CIO on the charge that it was dominated by Communists. Within broadcasting, Aware officials knew that the Matusow book provided ammunition to their enemies and invigorated protests against their anti-Communist campaign. The first tangible result could be seen in Actors Equity, the theater business's equivalent of AFTRA, where the union's council passed a resolution condemning Aware. Hartnett wrote to John Dungey of Syracuse: "Those of us on the spot and in a position to know the facts realize that

Equity is virtually lost, and that we may well lose our solid control of AFTRA."[15] As the next AFTRA meeting approached, Hartnett found a way to influence the debate.

Two years after his first contact with Kim Hunter's publicist, Hartnett was still involved in the actress's career. He was, in fact, instrumental in getting her back on the air. In his capacity as talent consultant for Borden, he recommended that she be allowed to appear in a May episode of the sponsor's show, *Justice*, a legal drama produced by David Susskind. Hartnett's Syracuse allies were not happy with this decision, but Hartnett argued that Hunter deserved a break because she had come out against an anti-Aware resolution in Equity. Even so, he was not ready to let her off the hook entirely. Shortly before the May AFTRA meeting, the actress later said, he called Hunter and explained that her previous actions were not sufficient, that she would be taking an important step toward full clearance by speaking out in favor of Aware at the upcoming actors' meeting. Although she agreed to do something to demonstrate her anti-communism, Hunter balked at this suggestion because she was not, as she told Hartnett, a supporter of his organization. Hartnett then replied that praising Aware was not necessary, but coming out against the anti-Aware resolution would help repudiate her past Communist-front record. Reluctantly, Hunter agreed to send a telegram to be read at the meeting. Writing to Laurence Johnson immediately after this talk, Hartnett predicted that, if Hunter fulfilled her promise, "you will hear the comrades shrieking all the way from New York to Syracuse."[16]

As crucial as the AFTRA controversy was, other matters also commanded Hartnett's attention. One was a mid-April 1955 news item concerning three Texas Broadcasting Corporation radio stations owned, officially at least, by Lady Bird Johnson, but actually run by her husband, U.S. Senator Lyndon Baines Johnson. The stations were about to hire a new vice president of public affairs. His name was John Henry Faulk.

Senator Johnson regarded Faulk as an ideal candidate for the job, combining, as Faulk's biographer pointed out, a local Texan appeal with New York broadcasting experience. For Faulk's part, any doubts he might have had about making such a drastic career move were methodically eliminated by the senator's legendary powers of personal persuasion. Soon

he was not only agreeable but enthusiastic. Although he had come to enjoy New York life, he looked forward to returning to his home state and to
a more relaxed work schedule that would afford him the opportunity "to
get some writing done" and "becoming identified with Texas life again."
The announcement did not create much of a stir within the broadcast industry, but Hartnett viewed it as an alarming development, even though
he had never before shown much interest in Faulk. His concern now was
set off by information he received from Jack Wren at BBD&O, whom Hartnett considered a reliable source. Wren told him that Faulk had once
been a Communist party member. To Hartnett's mind it was a disturbing
turn of events that a powerful member of the Senate might unwittingly
hire a potential subversive. So troubled was he that he called HUAC investigator Donald Appell, a key figure in the Alger Hiss case, to tell him about
the incriminating information and to stress the importance of addressing
the issue. Appell said he would contact Senator Johnson.[17]

Within weeks Lyndon Johnson reneged on his offer, and Faulk found
himself in an unnerving state of limbo, somewhere between the old job
he had left and the new one that no longer existed. Understandably indignant, he contemplated suing the Texas Broadcasting Corporation but
backed off when, by late May, WCBS announced it was taking him back to
continue his late-afternoon program. FBI documents reveal that Johnson's
about-face came after he had requested Bureau information on Faulk and
received a summary of the agency's reports on the performer's alleged
Communist affiliations.[18] What might have motivated him in the first
place to make this request was the tip from Appell. Since Hartnett had
been the one to contact Appell about this issue, he was indirectly responsible for keeping Faulk in New York, where the entertainer would soon
find himself on a collision course with not only Hartnett but Laurence
Johnson and Aware.

When the rancorous May 24 AFTRA meeting began at the City Center
Casino, both sides were prepared with a full complement of speakers to
make their case and harangue their opponents. As Hartnett had hoped,
Kim Hunter came through with a telegram urging AFTRA members to vote
against the anti-Aware resolution, though her statement was hardly an endorsement for the organization. Walking a thin line, she stated that she

did not support Aware but felt the union should defeat the resolution in order to dispel the impression that it might be "protecting and aiding the Communist conspiracy." More enthusiastic members of the Aware faction argued that those named in News Supplement Number 12 were not merely advocates of a contrary political opinion but tools of a Communist effort to infiltrate the union, part of an ongoing campaign originally outlined by Lenin for dominating the labor movement. Despite what some anti-Aware activists might claim, one speaker said, those people who had been named had done much more than merely "married a liberal." Repeatedly the Aware supporters insisted that its newsletter had simply aired the facts, and they challenged those listed to prove otherwise. "If they feel these accusations are not true," Rex Marshall said, "as a member of the Board, I am astonished that none of the individuals who feel themselves unjustly maligned have filed formal charges with the Board, formal charges against the members of Aware."[19]

One person named in the newsletter, Nancy Pollock, stood up to deny the allegations against her, but for the most part the anti-Aware speakers failed to address this challenge. Instead they vented their outrage against the blacklist by branding Aware members as vigilantes who were determined to enforce a stifling political conformity. One speaker went so far as to liken the organization to the Ku Klux Klan. Douglas Gordon delivered perhaps the strongest rebuke to the Aware supporters when he raised the rhetorical questions, "By what right do you make political book on your fellow members? Did the membership vote that you were to be the political arbiters of this union?" Ultimately, in the new political climate five years removed from the storm whipped up by *Red Channels*, this sort of argument proved more persuasive than warnings about creeping communism. The resolution passed by a vote of 197 to 149.[20]

The vote was a dramatic blow to the authority of broadcast Red hunters, but it was not necessarily the final word. Insisting that such an important issue should not be decided only by those attending a New York membership meeting, Aware supporters succeeded in having the resolution placed before the entire AFTRA membership as a union-wide referendum. While union officials prepared the ballots, the conflict spilled over onto the airwaves, the disputed territory itself.

Initiating the clash was a June 15 column in the *New York Herald Tribune* by John Crosby that highlighted Leslie Barrett's brush with Hartnett and called for an end to the entire blacklisting process. Crosby struck a familiar, if not entirely convincing, chord by creating the impression that performers were typically barred from the air for no other reason than their being confused with somebody else or for just having "foreign names." He went after Hartnett in vivid terms, describing his letter to Barrett as "an oily piece of prose" and characterizing him and his allies as a "little wolf pack of vigilantes." Seizing upon an opportunity for controversy, Steve Allen booked both Crosby and Hartnett to appear on the June 21 airing of the *Tonight Show*, and the program lived up to its contentious potential. Crosby was no stranger to televised confrontations with people connected to *Red Channels*. In 1952 he had debated Theodore Kirkpatrick on the show *The Author Meets the Critics*, where he had condemned the *Counterattack* partners as irresponsible purveyors of slander. He had also proved himself capable of slinging loose accusations in the heat of verbal battle. While attacking the competence of Kirkpatrick and his partners, he had maintained that the former FBI agents' experience in the Bureau was meaningless. "Everybody was in the FBI during the War," he had said. "It was a way of getting out of the Army. We have copy boys on our paper who were in the FBI during the War." A few days later Crosby had felt compelled to write a letter of apology to J. Edgar Hoover. Now, as he debated Hartnett, he managed not to offend a powerful government agency, but he was no less emphatic in his denunciation of the blacklist. He repeated his charge that Hartnett and his ilk were blacklisting actors based on mistaken identities. When pressed by Hartnett for either verifiable specifics or a retraction, Crosby countered that he would not name the actor in question because it would leave him open to even greater harm. Hartnett took a dim view of the columnist's remarks and would later file a lawsuit against Crosby for $400,000.[21]

A week after this confrontation, newspapers featured sensational headlines that, for some at least, bolstered the Aware cause. On June 29, Winston Burdett, a CBS news correspondent, admitted before a Senate committee that, between 1940 and 1942, he had been a Soviet agent while working in Europe as a *Brooklyn Eagle* reporter. Although his experiences in Soviet espionage dated back more than a decade, his testimony confirmed some points that Red hunters had been making for years. His story illustrated the Communist penetration of both the media and the unions, the connection between the CPUSA and such insidious figures as Soviet spymaster Jacob Golos, and the ease with which many Communist functionaries had concealed their true ideological bent.[22]

At one time this sort of revelation would have fed a gathering momentum of alarm, but now, in the summer of 1955, the outraged response to the potential for Soviet infiltration was increasingly confined to the true believers. The dominance of their fiercely anti-Red views was not apparent when the ballots on the anti-Aware resolution were tallied at the end of June. The momentum was moving in another direction. By nearly a two-to-one margin, members voted for the resolution, 982 in favor, only 514 against.

Godfrey Schmidt downplayed the importance of the vote, describing it as "meaningless." But clearly the referendum, condemning the organization's "smear methods," signified a major defeat for Aware in what had been the organization's bastion of support. Hartnett certainly was not content to shrug it off. In response to a Jack Gould piece praising the resolution in the New York Times, he wrote a letter to the editor to address what he called "the basic issue." Contrary to claims that Aware was either careless or malicious in its accusations, all its allegations, he said, were based on public records and sworn testimony. He also took offense at Gould's implication that he and Aware were exploiting the anti-communism issue for profit. Again taking a litigious stance against a journalist, Hartnett demanded that the writer "omit possible innuendo and come out flatly and say so, subject to possible penalty under the laws of libel."[23]

Hartnett's combative determination was reflected in a new counteroffensive intended to undo the damage done by the AFTRA resolution. On July 15, Aware News Supplement Number 13 set out to discredit its opposition once again, this time taking aim at those actors who had signed a circular letter in support of the anti-Aware resolution. Escalating their attack, Aware officials no longer contented themselves with perfunctory listings of Communist front associations. For seven of the eight people listed, the newsletter outlined the number of times each had been identified as a Communist before congressional committees.

Although some might have dismissed the accusations as just another smear, the repeated, sworn identification of these people, even if not conclusive, is not so easily explained away. In the case of Elliott Sullivan, for instance, former party members Martin Berkeley, Lee J. Cobb, and Jerome Robbins had all declared that they knew him as a Communist, while information from FBI files—obviously not included in the newsletter—provides corroboration. The reports include observations from informants that Sullivan had been a dedicated party member through the

1930s and 1940s, and an organizer in such transparent fronts as the American Committee for Yugoslav Relief, which conveniently disbanded after Tito broke with Stalin, and the National Council of American-Soviet Friendship, a party-line follower with which he worked into the 1950s. As for actor Lloyd Gough, identified by six former-Communist witnesses, reminiscences by his friends years later would describe him as an ardent, open Communist. Still, even if the allegations were true, there was another compelling reason to regard the Aware newsletter as an exercise in demagoguery: it failed to establish how the eight people listed represented the other 150-odd people who had also signed the circular.[24]

A second phase of the counteroffensive emerged within AFTRA itself. The union's national board, still controlled by Aware supporters, drafted and passed a new union rule that stretched the scope of the organization's constitutional amendment banning Communists from membership. Previously, proof of CPUSA membership had been required before the union could impose punishment. Now AFTRA members could suffer censure, suspension, or outright expulsion if they merely invoked the Fifth Amendment when asked by a congressional committee if they had ever been a member of the Communist party. When the proposed rule was put to a vote at the end of July, the AFTRA membership proved that actors could be a politically fickle lot: after voting two-to-one against Aware just a month before, they now voted four-to-one in favor of the new Aware-supported resolution that would penalize people for exercising a U.S. constitutional right. Perhaps AFTRA members feared that the Aware faction might reassert itself, and they were eager to place themselves on the winning side.

The third phase that provided the climax to the renewed anti-Red campaign followed in mid August when HUAC came to downtown Manhattan to open a series of hearings investigating Communist activities in New York's theatrical and broadcasting world, eight months after Aware had suggested it should do just that. Five of the witnesses had been named in the organization's most recent newsletter. As in earlier hearings, neither side acquitted itself well.

The committee once again seemed more concerned with making headlines than in acquiring information that would lead to useful legislation. And the information this time, regardless of its purpose, was especially scarce. Only one witness, actor George Hall, cooperated with the committee and provided any observations at all about life within Communist groups in broadcasting.

As for the unfriendly witnesses, their refusal to answer questions often came across, again, as disingenuous. Following the usual game plan, uncooperative witnesses like George Tyne and Stanley Prager lambasted friendly witnesses as stool pigeons or indulged in more elaborate descriptions. Elliott Sullivan was especially impassioned on the subject, declaring that these people "have sold their honor and dignity and in fact the best traditions of American life for a mess of pottage, for a job, for a movie contract. I believe all of these people will be judged and are being judged today by the decent people in this country." A stirring statement, to be sure, but one that avoids a central question: were these witnesses telling the truth? When asked if Martin Berkeley had lied when he had identified him as a Communist, Sullivan would only say, "I would challenge your right to ask me that question." By not invoking the Fifth Amendment, Sullivan avoided the obvious implication that he might be concealing something. His answer could be viewed either as an act of principle or as a convenient dodge. Less ambiguous, and less convincing, was a different tack tried by Prager when he portrayed himself as a staunch opponent of thought control. A committee member asked if this meant he opposed thought control exercised by the Communist party. "That is a trick question," was the best reply Prager could muster.[25]

In its four days of well-publicized hearings, the committee produced virtually nothing except intransigence from those it targeted. No matter how specious some of the unfriendly witnesses might have been, people's appetite for HUAC's political theater was fading. In AFTRA, especially, many were either unimpressed with the committee's performance or indignant that it had come to town in the first place to put their fellow performers on the spot. If anything, the hearings inspired AFTRA members to pursue the anti-Aware resistance.

✵ Like many in broadcasting, John Henry Faulk took a keen interest in the HUAC hearings. But unlike most of his colleagues, he was more than a mere observer. Before the hearings, he himself had been subpoenaed for questioning.

The interview took place privately in New York City in early June and was conducted by Donald Appell, the committee investigator who had been contacted by Hartnett. Appell's interrogation went over the same ground as the FBI probes concerning Faulk's alleged associations with the Communist party and front organizations, but in the end the investigator decided that Faulk's case did not warrant a subpoena to bring the performer before the public hearings later that summer.[26] Although the interview led to no further action from HUAC, it became one of several developments that prodded Faulk to take a firm, overt stand within AFTRA as a new set of union elections loomed on the horizon.

Among the other incidents leading to Faulk's new activism had been Leslie Barrett's speech at the March meeting of AFTRA, which had, to Faulk's mind, illustrated the invasive reach of the blacklist machine. Also contributing, according to Faulk's biographer, were the efforts of blacklisted actresses and outspoken union members Lee Grant and Madeline Lee. They met several times with Faulk to brief him on the issues and events that lay behind the Aware controversy. Faulk, already deeply suspicious of right-wing anti-communism, was receptive to the women's concerns, but there was more to these meetings than a simple exchange of information. Mindful of their side's complete failure in the last union elections, the two actresses were on the lookout for a fresh persona who could help win votes for an anti-Aware slate of candidates in December, and they asked Faulk if he would be willing to run for the union board. He readily agreed.[27] His years of quietly nursing his political grievances had finally come to an end.

While spending that summer on Fire Island, a sliver of land just below Long Island's south shore, Faulk found an important ally in his AFTRA crusade. Among his neighbors was Orson Bean, a rising young comedian about to star on Broadway in *Will Success Spoil Rock Hunter?* Faulk impressed Bean as "one of the most charming men in the world," also a highly politicized fellow who "held forth with a messianic fervor" on the machinations of Aware. "Honey," he would tell Bean in his best Texanese, "don't kid yourself. These people are fascists and dangerous. They'll sit there grinnin' like an egg-suckin' dawg, all friendly-like but they'll kill you and they'll kill the country." Bean, who came from a left-wing family, shared Faulk's sentiments and agreed to help him form a slate of AFTRA candidates.[28]

To organize the campaign, Faulk called a meeting of broadcast personalities at his Fire Island home. They began to assemble a list of candidates that would eventually include, in addition to Faulk and Bean, CBS newsman Charles Collingwood, variety show host Garry Moore, actress Janice Rule, talk show host Faye Emerson, and recent cause célèbre Leslie Barrett. In this and subsequent meetings they formulated their platform, one that would distance their slate from the preceding year's failed campaign—which had been condemned by Aware—while still positioning themselves as opponents of the broadcast purge. They decided to call themselves the Middle of the Road slate, meaning they were both anti-Communist and anti-blacklist. By taking this course they were navigating a path too often ignored in the cold war's increasingly polarized debate.

Among intellectuals this path had been championed by Arthur Schlesinger, Jr., and Sidney Hook, and within broadcasting by such writers as Morton Wishengrad and Erik Barnouw. The position had been most recently dramatized by TV scripter Don Mankiewicz in his novel *Trial*, published in January and about to be released in October as a film starring Glenn Ford. Inspired by the Willie McGee case, the book concerned a young Mexican American wrongly prosecuted for the rape and murder of a white teenage girl. The story's hero is one of the Mexican's lawyers, who finds himself caught in the middle between his unscrupulous Communist associate, who is more interested in exploiting the propaganda value of the case than securing an acquittal, and the California Un-American Activities Committee, which reduces anti-communism to vicious, opportunistic Red-baiting. By taking a similar, balanced approach to their own set of issues, AFTRA's Middle of the Road candidates rejected extremism on both sides and offered a true liberal alternative to the union's more strident leftist campaigns that had been associated with Communist fronts and had failed to make headway against the union's right wing.

To maximize their chances for success, it was essential that the Middle of the Roaders avoid any perceived connection with Communist-front activities. At one of the meetings a member of the group insisted that anyone with conceivably questionable past associations should excuse him- or herself from the slate of candidates. Two people at the meeting reluctantly declared themselves off the ticket because of various benefits and committees they had been involved with, and Bean decided he too should disqualify himself. He explained that he had recently performed at a rally against the HUAC hearings that had been sponsored by the Emergency

Civil Liberties Committee, branded by some as a front organization. Faulk quickly reassured him. "Hell, honey, you're as pure as a Baptist minister's six-year-old daughter," he told Bean, and persuaded him to remain on the slate. As for any possible difficulties with his own candidacy, Faulk said nothing.[29]

His silence was, to say the least, puzzling. While it was true that he had never appeared before a congressional committee, he had been questioned by an HUAC investigator, and he had also been called in for an interview by the FBI. He certainly knew that suspicions had been raised about him and at the very least knew that his work for the Southern Conference for Human Welfare could come under scrutiny because the group had been cited as a Communist front in *Red Channels*. The fact that he regarded this characterization as wrong would mean little in the court of public, alarmist opinion. He had also been married to a woman, Hally Wood, who had once been connected to the Communist movement, a link that Red hunters would surely pounce upon if they ever learned of it. Knowing all this, why did Faulk not speak up when his past might jeopardize the prospects for the Middle of the Road slate? The best explanation is that he could no longer resist the impulse to act. After years of suffering in silence as people he regarded as reactionaries waged an "onslaught against what I consider all that is decent and worthy in American life," he must have been champing at the bit to make a stand. Edward R. Murrow had once dissuaded him from taking action, but now he had been courted to lead the anti-blacklist campaign within his union, at a time when attitudes were shifting and the chances of making a difference were promising. He could not let the opportunity pass.

If Faulk was looking for an additional reason to forge ahead, come what may, he would have found one in early September when the newspapers reported that Philip Loeb had killed himself.

Since being pressured off the cast of *The Goldbergs* in January 1952, Loeb had been shut out of television and had returned to his original livelihood of acting on the stage, first in *The Wild Duck*, then in *Time Out for Ginger* both on Broadway and on tour, and, finally in early 1955, in an off-Broadway production of *Three Sisters*. Although his income dropped after his TV dismissal, he still earned between fifteen and twenty thousand dollars a year. Other problems, though, were taking their toll. His son

John had succumbed to schizophrenia after serving in World War II, and during the time when Loeb had been making a generous salary on TV, he had been able to support his son's treatment at a private sanitarium. Now the cost of that care consumed about half his income. As he struggled to maintain his son's private treatment, he was forced to take loans from friends while negotiating with the government on how best to pay off his delinquent back taxes.

By 1954 Loeb was suffering from his own health problems. Cataracts blurred his vision in one eye and might have further impaired his ability to find work. How much the ailment might have been hastened by the unremitting stress is, obviously, a matter of conjecture, but it is a plausible cause considering that he had already been in therapy for psychological problems when these new pressures had begun to overwhelm him. On September 1, four months after the Department of Taxation had issued a warrant for the collection of his back taxes, Loeb checked into room 507 of the Taft Hotel in midtown Manhattan. Later that day, he died from an overdose of sleeping pills.[30]

Although the blacklist alone did not drive Loeb to suicide, no doubt it was a crucial factor and the actor's death provided a clear indication of what it could do to the emotionally vulnerable. Quickly, for people like Faulk, the incident became a rallying point for anti-blacklist activism, the latest in a series of tragedies laid at the door of the broadcast Red hunters. It had all begun in late 1951 with the deaths of Mady Christians and J. Edward Bromberg, and had continued several months later with the fatal heart attack of the blacklisted Canada Lee and in 1954 with the suicide of CBS newsman Don Hollenbeck, who had been branded a Communist sympathizer by columnist Jack O'Brian. The collected grievances, capped by the Loeb suicide, cast the conflict with Aware into ever sharper relief.

In early November the Middle of the Road slate announced its list of candidates running for the New York board and published its platform under the title of "A Declaration of Independents," a document that spelled out its opposition to "Communism and all other totalitarian ideologies" as well as the practice of blacklisting "especially by outside organizations." The centrist position might have assured many in the union that here, finally, was a faction that would steer clear of extremist partisanship. But Hartnett saw only a more sophisticated form of menace.

The Middle of the Road approach, he was convinced, was an insidious ruse with ideological roots in Leninist philosophy. He believed "the idea of middle-of-the-road was a key point of Lenin's argument in *Left Wing Communism, An Infantile Disorder*, that in a union if a Communist bloc, a fraction, running for office or holding office, was identified, their usefulness was virtually eliminated once they were known. So the idea was pull back, withdraw the open Communists . . . and then have a middle of the road group not known as Communists." Hartnett was puzzled by the emergence of Faulk, someone who seemed to have "popped up out of nowhere" to become a major force in AFTRA politics. The Red hunter wasted little time in following up on his concerns. A little over two weeks after the Middle of the Road slate was announced, he wrote a letter to HUAC listing Faulk's various alleged front activities. A week later he sent another note to one of his clients, the Young & Rubicam advertising agency, charging that Faulk had "a significant Communist Front record. I am afraid he is 'using' the liberals."[31]

The union mailed ballots in mid November and received the completed returns by December 8. Three days later the union announced the stunning upset: the Middle of the Road slate had won twenty-seven of thirty-five possible seats. For the first time in years the right wing was no longer in control of the board. Within a month a second vote designated the board's officers, which included Collingwood as president, Bean as first vice president, and Faulk as second vice president. Almost immediately they were forced to confront the latest edition of the controversy that had been racking the union since the publication of *Red Channels*.

On January 17, two days after the union named its new officers, HUAC released a report charging that "radio and television networks continue to use the talents of Communist party members," a situation created in part by the presence in AFTRA of a "militant Communist faction." The issue of blacklisting, the report insisted, was nothing more than a hoax "deliberately manufactured" by Communists. The new AFTRA officers were indignant. Within days Collingwood issued a statement challenging HUAC's findings. "If the committee really thinks," he said, "that the only people in the entertainment industry who are disturbed by the excesses of the blacklisting system are Communists or their dupes, then it is laboring under a misapprehension."[32]

Within Aware, concerns over the new AFTRA administration had already crystallized well over a month earlier when the *New York Herald Tribune* published an interview with Faulk. Identified as the spokesman for the Middle of the Road slate, he had emphasized that opposition to Aware was the slate's "principal platform" and that Aware partisans on the board had "subverted the interests of union members." Meeting on December 15, just three days after the article appeared, the Aware directors discussed what they considered to be Faulk's act of provocation and decided they needed to know more about both him and his fellow Middle of the Road officers. Hartnett, who had already contacted HUAC about Faulk and certainly needed no cajoling to take a closer look, was the logical choice to conduct research on "the worst people in the slate."[33]

Following his standard procedure, Hartnett searched through his files and his collection of congressional reports for incriminating information, and availed himself of some of his best-placed contacts in the anti-Communist movement. He spoke to Appell of HUAC and contacted Ruth Matthews, wife of controversial Red hunter J. B. Matthews, about Faulk's relationship to People's Songs. He also talked to Jack Wren for information on an event that took place at the Jefferson School of Social Science, the CPUSA's adult education center in New York City. Another contact was John Keenan at *Counterattack*. After the formation of Aware, Keenan's newsletter had continued to wane, losing its writer-editor Francis McNamara by May 1954 and finding itself, by 1955, understaffed and scrambling to devise ways to cut costs. Still, as Hartnett knew, the company's files were substantial. Keenan was able to pass along a memo on Faulk's participation in a 1946 event sponsored by the Independent Citizens Committee of the Arts, Sciences and Professions.[34]

Hartnett finished the draft of his report in time to present it to the February 1 meeting of the Aware board, which approved it by a unanimous vote. After being rewritten and edited by Paul Milton and inspected for its legal implications by the organization's attorneys, it was published on February 10 as News Supplement to Membership Bulletin, Aware Publication 16, and was distributed not only to Aware members but also to the press, broadcast networks, and advertising executives.[35]

The newsletter questioned the sincerity of the Middle of the Road officers' pledge to pursue a policy that was both anti-blacklist and anti-Communist. Statements from the new officers directed against Aware and the blacklist were plentiful, the newsletter explained, but they "had no word to say against the many CP fronts that have operated in the entertainment field, and no word against the identified Communists in the union. Silence is sometimes more eloquent than words." Despite the inferences that might be drawn from this accusation, Aware was not suggesting that "the 'middle of the road' slate was a Communist slate," and the bulletin even conceded that Faulk was correct when he told the press that his slate required its candidates to be opposed to both communism and the blacklist. "But how about Faulk himself?" the newsletter asked. "What is his public record?" The results of Hartnett's research then supplied the answer:

> According to the Daily Worker of April 22, 1946, "Jack Faulk" was to appear at Club 65, 13 Astor Place, N.Y.C.—a favorite site of pro-Communist affairs.

> According to the Daily Worker of April 17, 1947, "Johnny Faulk" was to appear as an entertainer at the opening of "Headline Cabaret," sponsored by Stage for Action (officially designated a Communist front). The late Philip Loeb was billed as emcee.

> According to the Daily Worker of April 5, 1948, "John Faulk" contributed cabaret material to "Show-Time for Wallace," revues staged by the Progressive Citizens of America (officially designated a Communist front) in support of Henry A. Wallace's candidacy for the presidency of the U.S. Although Wallace was the officially endorsed candidate of the CP, by no means all his supporters were Communists or pro-Communists. What is in question here is support of any candidate given through a Communist-front setup.

> A program dated April 25, 1946, named "John Faulk" as a scheduled entertainer (with identified Communist Earl Robinson and two non-Communists) under the auspices of the Independent Citizens Committee of the Arts, Sciences and Professions (officially designated a Communist front, and predecessor of the Progressive Citizens of America).

> Vol. 3, Nos. 1 & 2, of the Bulletin of People's Songs (officially designated a Communist front) named Faulk as one who had sent greetings to People's Songs on its second anniversary.

"Johnny Faulk" was listed in a circular as an entertainer or speaker (with Paul Robeson and two others) to appear at "Spotlight on Wallace" to be held in Room 200 of the Jefferson School of Social Science on February 16, 1948. The Jefferson School has been found by the Federal Government to be what it is, the official training school of the Communist conspiracy in New York.

"John H. Faulk" was a U.S. Sponsor of the American Continental Congress for Peace, staged in Mexico City, September 5–10, 1949, as shown by the official "call." The Congress was later described by the HUAC as "another phase in the Communist world 'peace' campaign, aimed at consolidating anti-American forces throughout the Western Hemisphere."

Hartnett also supplied information on Orson Bean and Charles Collingwood, but it was relatively inconsequential: Bean's appearance at the Emergency Civil Liberties Committee rally that he himself had mentioned at a Middle of the Road meeting, and Collingwood's reply to the HUAC report on Communists in AFTRA. Faulk was clearly the primary focus. In the case of all three men, however, the newsletter questioned whether they would be willing to enforce the new national union rule aimed at punishing anyone who failed to cooperate with a congressional committee, in particular those actors who had refused to answer questions from HUAC the preceding August.[36]

One of the reporters to receive a copy of the Aware News Supplement was Val Adams, who covered the broadcast beat for the *New York Times*. Interested in obtaining a quote, he called Faulk at his home on Sunday, February 12, only to learn that the performer had not seen or even heard of the Aware bulletin, released just two days before. As a favor, Adams promised to leave a copy for him at the *Times* reception desk the next morning, initiating a series of events that would occupy Faulk for the next six years.

In later describing his first response upon hearing of the seven allegations against him, Faulk wrote of his outrage at Aware for launching the attack and his fear that he might lose his job with WCBS. He also gave the impression that he was unprepared for such an attack.[37] How he could have been is difficult to understand, given Aware's aggressiveness and the attention Faulk had already received from both the FBI and HUAC. But then he had managed to banish any of these concerns when he agreed to run on the Middle of the Road slate in the first place, and some part of him must have continued to ignore the risks since taking office. In any case, now that he was finally confronted with the allegations, it was specifically his fear about employment that had to be immediately addressed. He moved quickly to gauge the damage he might already have suffered.

That day he met first with his business manager, who stressed the severity of the problem but also suggested two ways of preventing the situation from growing worse: first, to show the newsletter to his supervisors at WCBS before they received it from another source, and second, to gather his allies within AFTRA to help initiate a union response. That same day Faulk consulted with both his immediate superior, Sam Slate, and the WCBS general manager, Carl Ward, and on the night of the next day hosted a meeting of ten fellow Middle of the Roaders in his apartment. The two CBS executives shrugged off Aware's accusations, giving Faulk every reason to believe they were prepared to stand behind him. His AFTRA allies ultimately decided, Faulk later wrote, to propose a resolution "warning employers that AFTRA would investigate any refusal to employ a performer who had been attacked by Aware."[38] Faulk was, for now, reassured.

One of Faulk's closest allies had professional problems of his own to confront. Within days of the Aware newsletter's release, Orson Bean heard from TV impresario Ed Sullivan that his upcoming appearance on Sullivan's variety show had been canceled, and he could expect to remain off the show until he cleared himself of Aware's allegation. He discussed his predicament with both Faulk and Collingwood, who offered ideas on how he might overcome the Sullivan ban without capitulating. Faulk referred him to his own business manager for advice.[39] Around this time, Bean would later claim, he also had a private conversation with Faulk about his friend's listings in News Supplement Number 16.

As Bean recalled it, he asked, "It isn't true, is it, Johnny? You didn't appear at those places, did you?" "Oh, honey," Faulk replied, "what does it matter? Don't you see those people are fascists. If they didn't have something on us, they'd have made something up."[40]

Bean was outraged by this answer. Faulk had been given the opportunity to disqualify himself from the AFTRA election if there had been anything in his past that might be used against the Middle of the Road slate, and he had chosen not to do so. As a result, to Bean's mind, Faulk had made it easy for Aware to attack the slate. "I was very hurt by this," he later recalled, "and felt that both Charlie Collingwood and I and the cause were hurt by his failure to raise his hand and step down from running." For now, Bean would continue to work with Faulk and the rest of the Middle of the Road caucus, but this conversation would remain a source of anger and disappointment.[41]

⟟ The next AFTRA board meeting on March 22 reinforced Faulk's guarded optimism as the union's officers passed the new anti-Aware resolution, though the positive vote came only after stiff opposition not only from known Aware supporters but from some Middle of the Road members who now seemed to be getting cold feet.

The defections from the slate distressed Faulk, but the rancorous meeting was followed by a period of calm undisturbed by discouraging words or actions from his employers. For three weeks Faulk could entertain the notion that the worst was behind him. Then, on April 12, he received a message from Slate to meet him immediately in general manager Ward's office to discuss a "very grave and serious matter."

Ward, Faulk would later recall, told him that Laurence Johnson was "going up and down Madison Avenue, seeing my sponsors and demanding that they withdraw from my show." Faulk was well aware of the grocer from Syracuse and realized right away what this could mean for his show. Ward then explained that Johnson might have already scored a coup. One of Faulk's sponsors, Libby's Frozen Foods, had just dropped out of the show.

Far from the nonchalant attitude he had expressed just a month before, Ward was now clearly rattled. Words on a sheet of paper were one thing, something that could be debated or refuted. But, as always, the threat of economic boycott—even the specter of a threat—was a dire emergency for executives like Ward. He insisted that Faulk take action. The people selling airtime on his show needed definitive reassurance that the show's host was, indeed, a loyal American.[42]

Backlash

THE EARLY MONTHS of 1956 were a time of change in Laurence Johnson's life. On February 25 he sold his remaining four stores in the Syracuse area for one million dollars to the Victory Supermarkets chain of central New York. Although he would serve as a consultant for the new owners, he finally ended his active, full-time involvement in an industry he had helped pioneer some twenty-five years earlier.[1] At the age of sixty-seven he now had both time and money at his disposal as never before and would have to reorder his daily routine to compensate for all the hours he would no longer spend in his stores. He had more time to travel with his wife and to pursue his hobby of collecting Americana and, of course, to save the country from communism.

Aware had extended a special invitation to Johnson as well as to Neuser and Dungey to attend a membership meeting on January 19, where it was announced that its next news supplement would outline the Communist-front record of John Henry Faulk.[2] Taking the allegations to heart, Johnson and his Syracuse cohorts began to see the radio personality as a significant figure in the Communist conspiracy. By March they began to let sponsors know how strongly they felt about the matter.

Among those executives Johnson contacted while making the rounds on Madison Avenue that spring was Thomas Murray of Grey Advertising. Grey handled the Pabst Brewing account, which included Hoffman

Beverages, a *John Henry Faulk Show* sponsor. The encounter demonstrated that the grocer's reputation could still inspire trepidation in high places, even when he was no longer in the retail food business. Calling from his midtown hotel, Johnson went beyond the Aware allegations of front activities and came right out and called Faulk a Communist. It was a "disgrace" that Hoffman sponsored such a person, he told Murray, and warned that the advertising executive "had better get in line because a lot of people along Madison Avenue are getting in line."[3]

Murray, who clearly had not dealt with Johnson before, regarded him as just another private citizen with a complaint—as opposed to the anti-Red powerhouse who loomed in the imagination of some of his colleagues—and he proceeded to make the sensible remark that he was not willing to jettison Faulk on the basis of this sort of information. "How would you like it," Johnson replied, "if your client were to receive a letter from an American Legion Post up here?" Murray, still not sufficiently impressed, said he was a veteran himself and was not willing to believe that Legionnaires would resort to "an obvious blackmail attempt." "Well, you will find out," Johnson warned him. By this time Murray began to surmise that there might be more to this man from Syracuse than he had first imagined. He went to his supervisor, Samuel Dalsimer, and related what had just happened. Dalsimer, who had come up against Johnson before, became alarmed. Murray would have to do something immediately to soothe matters with Johnson, he said. "This could be dynamite."[4]

Murray, as he later recounted, tried ringing Johnson's room at the Park Sheraton Hotel but got no answer. Realizing that he needed to appease the grocer as quickly as possible, he left his office, hailed a cab, and went to the hotel to try tracking Johnson down in person. Murray asked for help from the desk clerk, who was able to point out Johnson standing in another part of the lobby. When Murray approached him and tried to discuss the Faulk matter once again, Johnson said, "After the way you spoke to me, I want nothing further to do with you." He walked off.[5]

Following up on Johnson's warning, Dungey of American Legion Post 41 sent a letter at the end of the month to the president of Pabst Brewing to reinforce Johnson's concerns about Faulk, though in a more guarded manner. Rather than stating outright that the radio personality was a Communist, Dungey stressed the importance of Communist fronts to the larger Red conspiracy, enclosed Aware News Supplement Number 16

containing the allegations against Faulk, and then asked the Pabst executive—as if merely wishing to set the record straight—to confirm if "this is
the same John Henry Faulk who has this WCBS program." Dungey's implications of potential trouble, coming after Johnson's confrontation with
Pabst's advertising agency, could not have been any clearer to the sponsor's officers. Similar letters from Dungey also went to such Faulk advertisers as Nestlé's and Piels Bros. brewery. Hartnett's role in this campaign
was more limited, confined primarily to his consultancy clients, but as
early as February he had sent a letter to an advertising agency that referred
to Faulk's "serious record."[6]

On some occasions Johnson downplayed his connection to the American Legion and emphasized instead his friendship with supermarket
owners, resorting to his well-established tactic of threatening merchandising pressure. As he explained to Faulk advertiser Rheingold Beer, these
unnamed friends of his in the grocery business "would be very happy to
know that Rheingold was sponsoring a Communist"; display space for the
company's product could suddenly become very scarce.[7]

One of Johnson's friends in the supermarket business was not so eager
to go along with this tactic. At the suggestion of a food industry publicist
who was a friend of Charles Collingwood, Faulk met with Lansing Shield,
president of Grand Union Supermarkets, whom he had come to know
through promotional activities for his program, and asked if the grocer
might be able to counteract some of the pressure exerted by Johnson.
Shield did not, like many in broadcasting, regard Johnson as a faceless bo-
geyman known only as "that grocer from Syracuse," but as a respected colleague and congenial acquaintance. When Faulk explained the campaign
that Johnson was waging on the basis of the Aware allegations, Shield was,
Faulk wrote, "amazed to hear that Johnson would do such a thing without
ever having met or confronted me." He told Faulk he would contact Johnson to assure him of Faulk's patriotism. When he was unable to reach
Johnson by phone, he sent him a letter and still did not receive an immediate response.

Shield's letter apparently prompted Johnson to entertain some doubts
about the targeting of Faulk. Shield's respect for Johnson was reciprocated
by the Syracuse grocer, and he decided he needed to confirm the reliability of Aware's information. To accomplish that, during his next trip to
Manhattan he went to see Hartnett at his office on Forty-second Street,

where Aware's research specialist said he had no reason to doubt the allegations, that they were based on solid information. Whatever doubts Johnson might have had now vanished completely. He called Shield to tell him that Faulk was, indeed, a "very dangerous man." Although not persuaded by Johnson's accusation, Shield was nonetheless impressed with his Syracuse associate's determination and was convinced that Johnson would not let up in pressing his claim. He advised Faulk, as the radio personality later recalled, to get "the best lawyer you can find."[8]

Executives at WCBS could not have been entirely pleased with the affidavit Faulk had written to reassure sponsors of his untainted patriotism. True, he swore under oath in the document that he was not now and never had been a member of the Communist party, but he left a crucial question unanswered. General manager Ward had asked the performer to answer the Aware allegations about front activities point by point, yet nowhere in his fourteen-paragraph statement did Faulk make a specific rebuttal. Rather, he stressed his exemplary career, his involvement in AFTRA, and his opposition to blacklisting while restricting his response to the Aware charges to only one sentence: "Frankly, I do not consider the allegations made by Aware of any relevance or importance."[9] Still, for now, and for as long as the station was prepared to stand by him, Ward and Slate made the best of what Faulk had given them and distributed the affidavit to their advertising sales staff.

For his part, Faulk could take satisfaction in the fact that he had not dignified the Aware charges with a direct response—tantamount to crawling, to his way of thinking—but he still bridled at the attack and, perhaps more so, at the campaign currently being waged by Johnson among his sponsors. All this continued to prey on his mind as he saw his career take a turn for the worse, even though his radio show did not seem to be in imminent danger. Some advertisers had canceled but others had taken their place to keep the show fully sponsored. In television, however, he found that job offers for guest appearances suddenly disappeared. He was not exactly being strangled by a blacklist, but a greylist was clearly starting to harry him. Around this time, through his work for AFTRA, Faulk made the acquaintance of a young associate of famed litigator Louis Nizer. Two years earlier Nizer had won a major libel lawsuit for Quentin Reynolds against fellow journalist Westbrook Pegler, and Faulk now began to consider the possibility of initiating a similar legal action. The problem, he knew, was that he had no concrete evidence of a conspiracy to deprive him of his livelihood. So far, his only source of information on the Syracuse group's campaign had been Ward, and the general manager had not been willing to say how he had learned of Johnson's high-pressure calls on Madison Avenue executives,[10] consistent with broadcasters' unwillingness to acknowledge that they were part of a blacklisting process or that the process even existed. At the end of April, though, that situation would change.

The letter that Dungey sent to Pabst was forwarded to Grey Advertising and from there passed along to CBS. Now Slate, the WCBS program director, came into Faulk's office and presented him with a copy of the letter to make it clear to Faulk exactly how determined the Syracuse group had become. With Slate's permission, Faulk was able to keep the copy.[11] Finally he had documentary evidence of the campaign to eliminate his sponsors, evidence that a lawyer could use to begin building a lawsuit.

In Louis Nizer's office the next day, Faulk told the story of the AFTRA conflict, Aware News Supplement Number 16, and the Syracuse group's pressure tactics, and dismissed the seven allegations as either inaccurate or misleading. In the case of five of the alleged Communist-front activities, he said he had taken no part in them; as for the other two, he had participated, but the newsletter misrepresented the purpose of the events. Nizer agreed to represent him in his case of libel, though, the performer recalled, he cautioned Faulk that the process would be long and difficult. It would also be expensive. Nizer was willing to discount his usual fee and to bear the brunt of much of the case's expenses, but the $10,000 retainer was still a daunting total for someone like Faulk. Ultimately he raised $2,500 from various friends while the remainder of the bill was footed by Edward R. Murrow. After the necessary papers were drawn up, the lawsuit was announced on June 19, asking for $500,000 in damages and charging that Aware, Hartnett, and Johnson "conspired and maliciously and willfully participated in a plan and course of action designed to defame and injure the plaintiff in his good name and reputation."[12]

Aware's official answer came in early July. The organization insisted that the allegations against Faulk had been "truthful and accurate" and that any adult who aided Communist causes had "no cause to complain when others disclose the fact of such aid." Hartnett's own personal response was one of stiff-upper-lip determination. "I'm delighted to have these controversies headed for the court," he said. "I will be more than happy to meet any man in court where all these issues can be resolved on a factual basis."[13] Johnson offered no comment. He was away on a vacation in Europe at the time the lawsuit was announced.

For now the case was confined to legalistic wrangling over complaints, answers, and motions between Nizer and Godfrey Schmidt, who served as Aware's chief counsel as well as its president. Faulk, though, could see the first repercussions of his decision within WCBS, where executives were "frightened at my going through with the suit." As he would tell his Texas friends at the time, the station executives "point out that my sponsors have come back and that if I will just forgive and forget, my hide will be safe."[14]

The fact that the Syracuse group's efforts proved ineffective in dismantling the advertising base of the *John Henry Faulk Show* raises the possibility that Johnson's influence was not quite what it had been just a couple of years earlier. Perhaps his retirement from the grocery business made him seem less of a formidable economic force. Another possibility is that the allegations against Faulk were too tenuous, never even purporting to establish Communist party membership at a time when, following Joe McCarthy's political demise, anti-Red passions were not quite so easily stirred. Johnson's decision to go abroad, and set his anti-Faulk efforts aside, might also indicate that even he realized his campaign was failing to gain the desired results.

Despite Johnson's only limited success, Faulk still had to deal with the WCBS executives' skittishness about his legal action. His response to his superiors' fears provides a glimpse into what was most likely his real reason a year earlier for not disqualifying himself from the AFTRA race. As he now related to his friends, he pointed out to his employers that "if Aware Inc. gets off this time, they will do the same thing to somebody else next month and the month after that. The reason they have flourished so long is that nobody would ever wade into them and yank them out into the bright light of day" where the public could see them "in all their rusty gut-ugliness."[15] Someone had to ride out and slay monsters, and Faulk would be the hero of the grand political adventure.

While the ultimate legal confrontation lay somewhere in the distant, uncertain future, Faulk became embroiled in a smaller conflict as the

In the celebrated attorney Louis Nizer, John Henry Faulk found a powerful and eloquent advocate in his libel lawsuit against Aware, Inc. *(Bob Gomel/ Time Life Pictures/Getty Images)*

right and left within his union squabbled over the principal question raised by News Supplement Number 16: would the new AFTRA leadership be willing to enforce the union rule aimed at those who refused to cooperate with congressional investigators? A special committee headed by Faulk put off action until it completed a study of the legal implications of penalizing union members for exercising a constitutional privilege. The right wing, which believed the Middle of the Roaders were simply stalling, attempted to force the committee to file charges under the rule.[16] The experience deepened Faulk's disillusionment with his union activities. Not only was he facing stiff opposition, he saw the Middle of the Road coalition continue to unravel. In mid-May, Orson Bean told him that he was cutting his ties to the Middle of the Road slate in order to avoid further controversy. Others began to side with the opposition. In elections at the close of 1956 the old guard of right-wingers and Aware supporters would regain control of the New York board. By that time the contours of the debate over communism in American life had shifted yet again, thanks to events both abroad and at home.

¶ The first event created shock waves within the Communist movement. In March, American newspapers reported a secret speech delivered by Soviet premier Nikita Khrushchev before the Twentieth Congress of the Soviet Communist party that revealed a catalog of crimes committed by Stalin. The speech forced CPUSA members to confront the truth about their formerly revered leader and instigated a mass exodus from the party. Those who remained were left stranded on the outermost fringes of American political life. Anti-Communists were vindicated; Khrushchev's speech confirmed what they had been saying for years in the face of denials or apologies from many on the left. At the same time, though, the ruination of the CPUSA brought into question the need for the Red-hunting vigilance of governmental agencies like HUAC and private watchdogs like Hartnett and Johnson.

Whatever illusions about the Soviet Union might have been still intact were then demolished in the fall when Russia suppressed the Hungarian revolution, a nakedly brutal act that slaughtered thousands of Hungarians and eliminated any chance of democratic reform in the Eastern Bloc. Despite his denunciation of the Stalinist past, Khrushchev proved that the Soviet regime was still an instrument of murderous, stifling repression. Formerly die-hard Communists found themselves at an ideological dead end. "Doubt solidified into conviction," wrote blacklisted TV writer Walter Bernstein. "This was no longer a Party I wanted to belong to." The only ones who refused to question Russia's actions were the most obstinate party-liners like Paul Robeson, who insisted that the Hungarian revolt was "not a true rising of the people," only an insidious American-instigated plot.[17] In Manhattan and in cities throughout Europe, thousands vented their outrage against the Soviet Union in street demonstrations, a cause not only for conservatives but for more liberal-minded anti-totalitarians as well. Not every professed anti-totalitarian, however, shared this sentiment. Faulk, despite the anti-Communist platform he had adopted in the AFTRA election, was not inclined to join the protests, though his thinking on the issue would not become public until years later.

The Communist movement in America might have been fading fast, but that did not mean that those with a professional stake in rooting out a domestic subversive conspiracy were about to yield their ground. HUAC found another opportunity to assert itself in June 1956 when the Fund for the Republic, a liberal think tank, published the two-volume *Report on Blacklisting*, its first volume devoted to the movie industry, the second to radio and TV.

Written by John Cogley, editor of *Commonweal* magazine, the exposé was essentially a follow-up to the ACLU's *The Judges and the Judged*, better organized and more up to date but suffering from some of the same weaknesses. Perhaps the most valuable of its contributions were detailed sections on the economic pressure tactics of Laurence Johnson and the demanding clearance procedures of BBD&O's Jack Wren, neither of whom had been mentioned in the ACLU book. A principled congressional committee might have used the book's publication as an opportunity for an objective study of the blacklist phenomenon, assessing the strengths and weaknesses of the various perspectives. But HUAC had something else in mind. Its hearings—entitled "Investigation of So-Called 'Blacklisting' in Entertainment Industry"—showcased the committee at its most egregious as it turned the proceedings into a relentless attack on Cogley's book, in effect attacking his right to publish a contrary opinion. The purpose of this strategy was obvious and self-serving: to protect the committee's ongoing mandate to investigate domestic communism. When Cogley appeared at the hearings, the committee had some legitimate grounds for criticizing *Report on Blacklisting*—its reliance on anonymous sources, for instance, and its disinterest in gauging Communist influence in the entertainment business—but the panel went well beyond that to second-guess and browbeat Cogley over virtually every detail of his book. At one point, in exasperation, Cogley shot back, "I wrote the book as I saw fit to write the book. I did not know how you wanted me to write the book."[18]

Among the procession of witnesses called upon to denounce Cogley's work was Vincent Hartnett. He said Cogley "is either woefully ignorant or he is a rogue," and, in an especially agitated moment, went so far as to call him "an ass." At one point, in an allusion to Joe McCarthy that illustrated how far anti-Communists had distanced themselves from the deposed demagogue, Hartnett testified that Cogley "crops evidence like some unscrupulous politicians crop photographs."[19]

In rebuttal to some assertions in the book, Hartnett defended his accusations against Ireene Wicker and his handling of Kim Hunter's request for information, but he was more reflective and less adamant about his exchange of letters with Leslie Barrett. He was clearly defensive about the "interrogating technique" he had used when informing Barrett that he would assume the worst if the actor did not deny any and all Communist sympathies. But this one hint of a doubt in no way meant that Hartnett was backing off from his mission. And despite recent defections from the CPUSA, he still saw a widespread menace. He told HUAC that, according to what he described as his "tabular analysis of records," no more than 5 percent "of the past and present Communists in the entertainment industry have been uncovered." Most vulnerable, he said, were young people entering the field of legitimate theater who saw Communist-front activity as a way to endear themselves to those who could provide job opportunities. Turning to Aware's most immediate concern in broadcasting, he discussed the role of misguided progressives and fellow travelers posing as liberals within AFTRA, maintaining that "while the Communists will carry the ball, you have 5 or 6 alleged liberals who will knock out the opposition."[20] HUAC could not have been more pleased with Hartnett's grim analysis, which seemed to justify the committee's continued existence.

Like HUAC, the Justice Department also had some entrenching to do. The government had relied on Harvey Matusow's testimony in one of the Smith Act trials of CPUSA leaders, a reliance now compromised by the informer's recent admissions. On September 17, Matusow, the compulsive liar and turncoat against the anti-Communist cause, went on trial in federal court for perjury. In yet another curious twist in the bizarre story of his life, the Justice Department did not prosecute him for one of the lies he had recanted but rather for one of his recantations. Following his most recent change of heart, Matusow had sworn in an affidavit and testified in court that federal attorney Roy Cohn had induced him to lie at one of the Smith Act trials. The government now charged that these statements were false. In a trial that lasted only nine days, the jury found Matusow guilty of perjury but also guilty in a larger sense, as the chief prosecutor phrased it, of helping to "discredit the entire fight of the Government and its agencies against the Communist menace."[21] The case provided some collateral benefit for the broadcast Red hunters. Matusow, the one-time *Counterattack* assistant and Laurence Johnson protégé, had renounced his former allies in his book *False Witness*, but now his perjury conviction placed those allegations in doubt as well.

By the close of 1956 the ongoing tug-of-war over the issues of communism and the blacklist revealed that the anti-subversive movement was under pressure but still defiant. Faulk's adversaries in his libel lawsuit were buoyed, in particular, by another recent development with clear implications for their own case. In July, Joe Julian, whose libel case against the *Red Channels* publishers had been dismissed two years earlier, lost his appeal before a higher court. Aware hailed the decision as "a common-sense broadside which shattered the sanctuary from criticism so often claimed by Communist-fronters," a sanctuary, the organization announced, that had been claimed as well by Faulk.[22] But if Hartnett, Johnson, and Aware believed they were now assured of victory, they were seriously underestimating the legal virtuosity and persistence of Louis Nizer. Not about to let the recent decision become an impediment, he deftly maneuvered to create legal distinctions between Faulk's upcoming lawsuit and Julian's failed attempt to fight the blacklist.

⟋ While the outcome of the legal arguments remained uncertain, Faulk could at least take satisfaction in his personal affairs. In December, WCBS offered him a new contract for another five years. Despite all the pressure that had been brought to bear, his radio show seemed secure, even if television jobs were no longer open to him. And so it remained through the first half of 1957. If anything, Faulk was making more money from his radio show than he had before. He was feeling so secure, in fact, that he decided to take his family on a long overdue vacation, leaving the country at the beginning of July to stay for an entire month at the resort town of Ocho Rios on the north coast of Jamaica. Then, the day after he returned to New York on August 5, he received a phone call from his business manager, Gerald Dickler, telling him to come to his office immediately. "When I reached his office," Faulk later wrote, "he stated at once that I had been fired."

Dickler had received the news a week before at a meeting in a midtown hotel bar with Sam Slate, now the WCBS general manager. Slate had insisted that the firing had nothing to do with political pressure; it was based on Faulk's recent drop in the ratings. Dickler had pointed out that Faulk's ratings had not dropped as much as the rest of WCBS's lineup of shows, but Slate stuck to his story. The decision, he said, came from "people upstairs."[23] Faulk was out of his time slot and off the WCBS airwaves altogether.

The process behind this decision has never been sufficiently explained. Conventional wisdom has it that Aware forced Faulk off the air,
and it's certainly true that the organization and its members did their best
to accomplish that: Aware had circulated News Supplement Number 16
throughout the industry, Hartnett had spread the word that Faulk had a
"serious record," and Johnson had pressured advertisers. But that does not
fully explain why WCBS fired Faulk nearly a year and a half after Aware's
newsletter had first publicized the allegations against him. The fact is,
Johnson's tactics—the most effective weapon in the blacklist arsenal—
had failed by mid-1956. Faulk's show had continued to enjoy a full complement of sponsors, the key measure of success in commercial
broadcasting. There was also no evidence of an organized letter-writing
campaign as there had been in the cases of Jean Muir and Philip Loeb.
As long as Faulk's show attracted advertisers and earned respectable ratings, what tangible risk did the station face by choosing to keep him on
the air?

Clearly the original Aware allegations, though an underlying reason,
were not the immediate cause for the firing—if they had been, they would
have succeeded in getting Faulk dismissed months earlier. Instead the station was probably responding to the controversy of the performer's lawsuit.
We know that Faulk's act of defiance aimed at blacklisters had made the
station's general manager immediately uneasy, but others in the company
must have been concerned as well. Slate's remark about "people upstairs"
implicates CBS network executives in the decision. Ultimately the most
plausible explanation for Faulk's firing is CBS's habitual timidity and
panic, the same qualities that had done so much to establish the blacklist
as an institution in the first place. If Faulk had taken the more cautious
route and refrained from legal action, he might have remained on the
air—holding on to his radio show even if greylisted from TV—but the lawsuit's controversy likely proved too much to bear for the timorous corporate culture of CBS.

Faulk now faced the grim prospect of true, industry-wide blacklisting.
The suspicions originally raised by Aware and reinforced by Johnson had
now been certified by the CBS capitulation, attaching an aura of controversy to Faulk that would follow him from one potential employer to another. His hopes were lifted, prematurely it turned out, just a little over
two weeks after the CBS dismissal when a letter arrived from radio station

WCCO in Minneapolis offering him a job. The station's program director, who had previously worked at WCBS, was enthusiastic about bringing Faulk to Minneapolis. He arranged for Faulk to visit, set up a publicity contest to drum up interest in the station's potential new personality, and told Dickler that he could "do big things out here in Minneapolis with Johnnie."[24] A short time later, though, the offer was suddenly withdrawn. The incident signaled the beginning of a maddening pattern.

While major broadcasters like NBC and ABC would not even consider Faulk for employment, smaller companies might show initial interest only to reverse themselves and announce that the deal would not work. One TV packager, for instance, wanted to include Faulk in a revived version of *Leave It to the Girls*, a panel show that had featured him in the past. But then the packagers told Faulk they could not use him because of the controversy that surrounded him. As one advertising executive explained to Faulk, he was even less employable than other blacklistees because of the contentiousness of his lawsuit. Potential employers would not necessarily need to be approached by Hartnett, Johnson, or any of their allies to reach this conclusion. Lester Wolff, owner of an ad agency that produced TV shows, decided he would not be able to hire Faulk because of "some controversy that appeared in the papers."[25] The word on Faulk was clearly well circulated throughout the industry.

At times, though, the link between Faulk's unemployment and his accusers was more distinct. During a period when radio station WOR in New York was considering hiring Faulk, one of the station's executives contacted Hartnett, who asserted that his allegations against Faulk were true. Faulk did not get the WOR job. In the summer of 1958, Faulk accidentally received information that revealed the thinking behind yet another rejection. Once more he had received an offer, this time from KFRC in San Francisco, but in this instance the station mistakenly sent a letter to Faulk that was actually intended for an executive at WOR, which was, like KFRC, a Mutual Broadcasting outlet. "I was concerned before going into this about Johnny's legal problems with Aware, Inc.," the letter stated, "but had been given to understand that these were all cleared up. If this is so, we will definitely be interested in him."[26] The legal problems, obviously, were not resolved, and KFRC withdrew its offer.

By January 1958, Faulk's savings ran out. Over the following year he made only five hundred dollars from broadcast work based on two engagements, an appearance on Jack Paar's *Tonight Show* and a commercial for DuPont. He reached perhaps his lowest point in the spring when, out of desperation, he applied for a job as a sit-in for the quiz show *The $64,000 Question*. A sit-in's job was to take the place of a panelist before going on air while the camera crew checked the lighting on the set. But even this job failed to pan out.[27]

In the midst of his travails, Faulk revealed to his closest friends the sense of mission that motivated him, a belief that was perhaps subconscious when he had first decided to run for AFTRA office but had become overt now that he was suffering from the backlash to his actions. "There is one great and valuable aspect of the thing that I would not confide to anyone but you boys," he wrote in June. "That is, I'm awful glad that it is *me* that they are after, for I consider it an honor to [fight] the scoundrels."[28]

To help with expenses, his wife Lynne took a job in the advertising department of a dress manufacturer. Faulk too looked for work outside the entertainment business. He completed a training course to prepare him to sell mutual funds, and after he found he had no aptitude for this line of work, he learned the ropes of selling the *Encyclopaedia Britannica*, another job he had to quit for the same reason. In December, as his debts mounted, some temporary financial relief came his way via a fund-raising event that included such luminaries as Myrna Loy, Dore Schary, and Eleanor Roosevelt.[29]

Only when he left New York behind did Faulk and his family achieve some level of financial stability, modest though it might have been. Another fleeting job offer precipitated the move. This time the opportunity came from a radio station in his native city of Austin, and when, predictably, the prospect vanished in March 1959, Faulk and his wife decided to relocate to Texas anyway. Faulk obviously had no more professional ties to the city and few reasons to stay, so the Faulks moved to a house in Austin. There, through local contacts, he got a job directing and narrating a promotional film for the Salvation Army, then collaborated with his wife to set up a public relations and advertising agency called John Henry Faulk Associates. Working initially out of their house and then from an outside office, they specialized at first in clients developing Austin shopping centers. In this way they sustained themselves, just barely, while waiting for Faulk's case to go to trial.[30]

During the preparatory stages of the lawsuit, Hartnett's fortunes also began to decline, though by no means as drastically as Faulk's. By 1958, as the demand for his services diminished, he lost the Borden account, once a mainstay of his consultancy business. To minimize expenses, he closed his midtown Manhattan office and moved his files into the four-bedroom suburban home he had purchased two years earlier. The change in political climate was a logical explanation for the drop in business. Hartnett, seeing himself as a victim in this case, believed Faulk's lawsuit was responsible.[31]

While consolidating his business, Hartnett also found it necessary to streamline his legal concerns. His lawsuit against columnist John Crosby was still pending when Faulk had filed his complaint, and Aware attorney Schmidt pointed out, quite sensibly, that Hartnett would have enough to contend with while facing Louis Nizer as an opposing litigator without the burden of an additional legal distraction. Following his attorney's advice, Hartnett dropped the Crosby suit.[32]

All of Hartnett's concentration would be required when he faced his examination before trial. Nizer planned to leave few, if any, stones unturned as he dug for information on the activities of both Hartnett and Aware, no matter how long it took. If Hartnett labored under the suspicion that the lawsuit, as engineered by Nizer, had already made inroads into his life, he would soon confront a far more tangible incursion.

On June 5, 1958, Hartnett's pre-trial examination began. Faulk, who observed the first session, described Nizer's initial manner as "courteous and correct," but as the questioning progressed his queries became more pointed and at times confrontational. He bored into Hartnett's past to substantiate the most complex charge listed in Faulk's complaint, the accusation that the efforts of Hartnett, Johnson, and Aware constituted a conspiracy to defame Faulk and render him unemployable in order to consolidate their own power within the broadcast industry.[33] Such a charge required sustained, intensive questioning, and Nizer was only just beginning to settle in. All told, Hartnett would have to deal with Nizer's dogged interrogation for twenty-three sessions.

The steady pressure had its effect most dramatically when, on June 17, twelve days after his examination had begun, Hartnett made unexpected concessions that appeared at first to alter the course of the entire case.

Nizer, at the time, was questioning him on the nature of the Aware charges against Faulk. "And you never charged him with being pro-Communist," he asked, "I mean a pro-Communist sympathizer?" He was not at all prepared for Hartnett's answer. "I was once sold a barrel of false information," the defendant replied.

When suddenly confronted by this admission, Nizer assumed, naturally enough, that Hartnett was alluding to the original allegations published in News Supplement Number 16. Follow-up questions would have revealed exactly what Hartnett was referring to, but Nizer, as he later explained in his memoir, decided against it. He feared that, if pressed, Hartnett might have second thoughts and retract the admission altogether. Rather than take that risk, Nizer let his assumption stand.[34]

Hartnett had a completely different explanation. His apparent turnaround, he would later claim, was the result, both physically and psychologically, of Nizer's relentless questioning. The experience had worn him down to the point that it had affected his health. "I had to go to the doctor," he said. "They said I was on the verge of a nervous breakdown." During this time, he later testified, he was also treated for hepatitis.[35]

More and more, under the strain, Hartnett had begun to brood about an informer who had presented himself several months after the lawsuit had first been filed. The man had called himself Adams, though that was obviously not his real name. He claimed to be a former Communist party member with reliable information to sell about Faulk, and Hartnett agreed to pay. Adams told him that he had known Faulk in the American Veterans Committee where, Adams asserted, Faulk had been part of a Communist contingent; he also alleged that the performer had taken part in various Communist-front activities. At the time the story seemed to confirm Hartnett's suspicions about Faulk, but now, during his deposition, doubts overcame him. Between the strain of testifying and his physical ailments, Hartnett became "shaky," as he put it, and began to suspect that his informant "was a plant and that he was trying to feed me false information."[36]

This paranoid notion was still on his mind during his critical testimony on June 17. He would always maintain that his "barrel of false information" comment referred only to information he had received from Adams *after* the publication of the newsletter.[37] Although this might be the case, there was likely more to his behavior on June 17 than his second thoughts about a questionable informant-for-hire. His answers to Nizer's questions suggest that his second thoughts were more far-reaching.

Even before his "barrel of false information" comment, Hartnett was already giving ground in his answers. He conceded that Faulk might not have attended the 1946 event at Club 65, cited in the Aware newsletter, and, on broader issues of the blacklist, revealed that he now had a more forgiving attitude, agreeing with Nizer that people should not be barred from working merely because they had joined Communist fronts unwittingly. Following his admission about false information, he went an important step further. Should there be employers interested in hiring Faulk, he would write a letter encouraging them to offer the job, and he would ask Johnson to do the same. He still stressed that Faulk should "make a good public position" to remove questions about his patriotism, but he was willing to do his part in helping the performer get back on the air.

Three days later he was still grappling with the same doubts about the Faulk case. He went to the FBI's Manhattan office and, as if opening up to a confessor, admitted that he might have been taken in by a false informer and "had been entrapped as a result."[38]

The June 17 deposition gave Nizer some hope for a quick resolution to the case, provided that Faulk chose to accept a settlement. Letters from Hartnett and Johnson would probably open doors of employment, but the chances of a payment were less likely: as Nizer later revealed in his memoir on the case, Schmidt informed him that the only defendant with any significant amount of money to offer was Johnson, and he "would not contribute anything to the settlement." In any case, Faulk decided he was not interested. Although encouraged by Hartnett's backtracking, he still intended to take the case to court.[39]

The other side was making some important decisions of its own. Two weeks after Hartnett offered to write a letter on Faulk's behalf, Schmidt resigned from the case and was replaced by Roy Cohn. As Faulk's biographer has put it, the former McCarthy counsel's "first move was to announce that he was leaving for the Far East for several months," effectively postponing further depositions until the end of the summer. During that time Hartnett dealt with the situation in typical fashion: he collected more information. He came upon evidence that he believed substantiated the allegation about Faulk's involvement in the Club 65 event, the topic that had led to Hartnett's concessions during the last examination session. The respite from Nizer's questioning might have also allowed him to regain confidence in his case, which Cohn was prepared to pursue in an aggressive manner. When Hartnett appeared for the next installment of his examination before trial, he took a firm stand once again and, Nizer wrote, "repudiated all the concessions he had made."[40] The legal battle resumed.

Laurence Johnson's deposition, in contrast, offered no great moments of drama and precious few direct answers of any kind. Throughout his testimony he replied in only the vaguest terms, claiming to have little or no memory of the letters and conversations that were brought to his attention. Nizer characterized him as evasive. But George Berger, a lawyer assisting Nizer on the case, took a different view. "He was an old man," he said, "he didn't remember very much and I think that was not feigned," even when he claimed not to recall the circumstances surrounding the documents that were presented to him.[41] The explanation is plausible. At the time of his deposition in 1960, Johnson was seventy-one years old, had been hampered by medical problems, and had suffered a debilitating loss in 1957 with the death of his wife of some forty years.

Whatever the reason for his vagueness, it did not deter Nizer from bringing out the extortionary quality of Johnson's tactics. In particular he focused on the pretense of fair-mindedness that Johnson had assumed while threatening to place Block Drugs products alongside competing products that were announced as not using "Stalin's little creatures."

"At the time you wrote this letter," Nizer asked, "did you expect that Mr. Block would say, 'OK, let's have a poll on my products'?"

"I don't know," Johnson replied.

"In regard to the use of 'Stalin's little creatures.'"

"I don't recall what happened."

"Can't you admit," Nizer insisted, "that you knew darned well he would not agree to that, can't you?"

"He did not anyway."[42]

The pre-trial proceedings dragged on, partly due to time-consuming legal motions and depositions, partly due to Cohn's delaying tactics, intended to pressure Faulk either to capitulate or settle on terms favorable to the defense. In their preparation for the case, Faulk and his legal team had to divert some of their attention to a temporary distraction imposed by the federal government.

¶ Despite the less than stunning results of its last set of hearings, HUAC intended yet again in 1958 to come to New York and investigate the broadcast and theater business. The committee's list of subpoenas included one for Faulk. Nizer, however, succeeded first in securing a postponement, then eventually a withdrawal of the subpoena.[43] The newest probe would have to proceed without Faulk's participation. It is unlikely that his appearance would have helped the investigators to salvage anything from the dreary affair.

If there was actually anything left for HUAC to uncover about the infiltration of the entertainment field, the 1958 hearings failed utterly to discover it. In the last inquiry of 1955 only one witness had been willing to cooperate. Now there was none. The only noteworthy wrinkle to be found this time was the willingness of five unfriendly witnesses to resort to the dubious tactic of denying they were currently Communist party members while refusing to comment on previous membership. In the case of witness Lee Grant, she applied this approach not only to herself but to her testimony about such friends as Morris Carnovsky, Alan Manson, and John Randolph, taking the Fifth when asked about their earlier Communist activities but saying she did not know if they were currently party members.[44] Up to then, Fifth Amendment takers had maintained they had not cooperated because they challenged the committee's right to question citizens about their political beliefs. By taking this selectively uncooperative tack, these witnesses in 1958 were now undercutting the perception that they were refusing to cooperate as a matter of principle. Even so, the tactic invited no public outrage. The public was losing interest.

Sensing that the committee was losing its momentum, Aware did what it could to bolster support by hosting a rally in New York in May on behalf of HUAC, as well as the FBI, another target of the left. Joining Hartnett and Schmidt as speakers was William F. Buckley, the bright young star of the conservative movement and its hope for the future, who might inspire new enthusiasm for the old Red hunters. The event's list of backers, however, included the usual suspects associated with long-standing grievances, from John Keenan and Francis McNamara of *Counterattack* to Johnson and Dungey of Syracuse.[45] The event did little to burnish HUAC's image. Aware, whose fortunes were closely linked to the committee's, was accompanying it on the slide toward declining influence.

Although Faulk was still shut out of broadcasting, the larger radio-and-TV blacklist was beginning to break down. Always porous to one degree or another, it began to crack in significant ways, perhaps most noticeably in June 1958 when NBC cast Jean Muir, the original blacklist cause célèbre, in an episode of *Matinee Theatre*, Muir's first TV appearance since she had been fired from *The Aldrich Family* eight years earlier. Her prolonged absence from the airwaves might have been explained in part by illness and a drinking problem (which, in turn, could be explained by the stress created by her blacklisting). Still, her *Matinee Theatre* appearance was a symbolic breakthrough. Two years later her employability would be reinforced by her performance in an episode of David Susskind's *Witness* for CBS, the toughest of the networks for suspect actors.[46]

The efforts of producers like Susskind and Herbert Brodkin to whittle away at the blacklist continued through the late 1950s, but now they were joined by another producer who had nearly been a blacklist victim himself. Comedy writer-director Nat Hiken had been singled out for attention by Hartnett in an *American Mercury* article and in a letter to NBC, and had been cited in *Red Channels* for sponsoring the Waldorf Peace Conference and two May Day parades. While working on the critically acclaimed *Martha Raye Show*, he came under pressure from Laurence Johnson and needed to act in order to make sure that his work in television would continue. Ultimately, through a politically connected attorney, he arranged to clear himself by publishing a letter in *Variety* renouncing all ties to communism.[47]

Undaunted by his brush with the blacklist, Hiken continued in subtle ways to advocate progressive ideas, through his use of black actors in non-stereotypical roles in his acclaimed series *The Phil Silvers Show*, and through his efforts to bring back onto the air old associates who had been banned from TV. In 1958 he cast fellow *Red Channels* listee Pert Kelton in a TV version of his old radio show *The Magnificent Montague*. Although this attempt to get around the blacklist didn't succeed—the program failed to win a time-slot on the CBS schedule—Hiken was able to get Kelton back on the air the next year in a Phil Silvers special, "The Ballad of Louie the Louse," and he employed the blacklisted director Coby Ruskin in producing and writing another Silvers program in 1960.

The hiring of formerly blacklisted talent was not the only way that the TV industry was becoming somewhat more daring in this period. Programs were now taking on more socially conscious and potentially more controversial subjects that the medium had been less willing to tackle during the Korean War and its immediate aftermath. Rod Serling's 1955 drama "Patterns," for example, cast a harsh light on the world of big business, the heart of 1950s capitalism and the great, abiding American faith of its day. Courtroom dramas such as "12 Angry Men" (1954) and "Judgment at Nuremberg" (1959) dealt with issues of bigotry and moral responsibility while 1956 saw the premiere of the TV play "Massacre at Sand Creek" and the series *Broken Arrow*, both of which offered sympathetic portrayals of Native Americans beset by expansionist and sometimes homicidal white settlers. This emerging sensibility could sometimes nettle those Red hunters most closely involved in broadcasting. A play produced by Brodkin for the *Alcoa Hour*, for instance, drew criticism in 1956 from Hartnett, who divined an insidious message at work in the show. Written by Reginald Rose and directed by Sidney Lumet, "Tragedy in a Temporary Town" told the story of a lynch mob that wrongly targets a Puerto Rican for an assault on a local teenage girl. Hartnett called the play an example, along with the film *The Ox-Bow Incident*, of "parallelism" that could be "used by Communists to insinuate over a period of time by repetition that in most cases the wrong individuals, innocents, have been identified, or, as they say, 'persecuted,' by congressional committees."[48]

Within this new environment of the late 1950s, the aging Johnson receded from the anti-Red crusade and instead absorbed himself in his nostalgic views of the past. In 1958 he sold his country-store artifacts to a theme park in North Carolina, where they would be placed on public display, and in the closing years of the decade contributed articles to the *New York Folklore Quarterly* while working on an anecdotal book-length history that would be a culmination of both his professional interest and his lifelong hobby. It was published in 1961 under the title *Over the Counter and on the Shelf: Country Storekeeping in America, 1620–1920*.

Hartnett, unwilling to give up, did his best to carry the torch into the next decade. As always, few indiscretions evaded his notice. Even the tangential involvement in 1961 of suspected Communist sympathizer Lou Polan in the British monster movie *Gorgo* warranted a letter of concern from him to his faithful co-combatant Dungey. Six months later, in February 1962, he traveled to Dungey's American Legion post to deliver a speech designed to reinvigorate the base of support in central New York that had played such a key role in years gone by. There was no reason for complacency, he argued, because the Red threat in broadcasting was still on the march, especially in the years since 1958 when "Communists have again begun to get high positions in the industry." He pointed in particular to Susskind's *Play of the Week*, being shown on educational TV stations, which featured the likes of John Randolph, Lee Grant, Zero Mostel, and Jack Gilford. "I hope my presence here tonight," he said, "will help the people of Syracuse, under the leadership of the legion, to get back into the fight." Hope he might, but even he was having problems continuing the struggle. Shortly after his Syracuse speech, he received an invitation to appear in Utica at another American Legion post, but he confided to Dungey that his financial situation prevented him from making the trip for the minimal fee offered. Unlike the old days when he would ask only that Legionnaires cover his expenses for the trip, he now required at least $150 to compensate for losses in other areas. "As you know, the events of the past six years virtually wiped out my consultant business."[49]

The only hope for resuscitating the influence of Hartnett and Aware lay in a successful defense against Faulk's libel suit. Aware's attorneys focused on compromising Faulk by seeking information that would corroborate the allegations against him. One of the people they contacted was Faulk's first wife, Hally Wood, who had been involved in Communist activities in the 1940s. The FBI was another source.[50] Especially important to the defense's lawyers was HUAC's Donald Appell, who they hoped would testify about his questioning of Faulk in 1955.

Faulk's legal team, when not filing motions and conducting depositions, worked on assembling its own array of witnesses to help establish the existence of a blacklist conspiracy in broadcasting. Initial efforts produced only a handful of people who were willing to take the stand. Changing attitudes, though, made others bolder, and by 1962 a new momentum brought in an increasing number ready to join the anti-blacklist cause. In time, Nizer's firm gathered more than twenty witnesses. Finding pertinent documents was the other essential element in the case. From the Anti-Defamation League, Faulk's attorneys were able to acquire an especially valuable file of material containing letters written by the Syracuse group to advertising agencies and sponsors.[51] Another, more mysterious windfall came their way in 1962. George Berger was contacted by a man he described as a "turncoat":

> He was kind of a notorious guy. I got a phone call from him, and he said he had papers that would be of interest to me, but he wouldn't come up to the office. I had to meet him on the street, a street corner at midnight. It was cloak and dagger stuff. I met him at midnight on the street corner, and he came up to me, he was wearing a big hat and a beard. It was like out of Orson Welles. And he hands me this shopping bag, and he says, "Good luck," and disappeared. Just turned around and went off into the fog, so to speak. I went back up to the office, and in this shopping bag were copies of correspondence of Aware, Hartnett and others—all in this time period. Not directly related to Faulk but directly related to the whole union battle and what they were trying to achieve [on] the airwaves—high sounding stuff. But it pretty much spelled out the whole theory. He had been a member of this group. . . . But he was well known for other reasons. He had actually done time, too.[52]

Berger did not identify the informant because his dealings with him had been confidential. But one candidate for the part stands out, one who fits the key elements of Berger's description.

Harvey Matusow was a turncoat who had spoken out against his old allies, the Red hunters. He had served time in prison, having just recently completed a three-and-a-half-year sentence in a federal prison for perjury, and certainly qualified as "a notorious guy." Through his connections with *Counterattack*, Johnson, Wren, and associates of the McCarthy Committee, Matusow would have had access to correspondence involving broadcast-blacklist insiders. And as for the contrived, melodramatic trappings of the midnight meeting, he had the self-dramatizing temperament to concoct such a scheme. Yet another factor pointing to Matusow concerns his possible motive. Aside from his recent inclination to support the anti-blacklist cause, he might very well have had a personal reason for dealing himself into the Faulk case. Matusow's perjury conviction had arisen out of accusations he had made against Roy Cohn, and now Cohn, his former nemesis, was representing Faulk's adversaries.

While support for the Faulk case grew in the realm of litigation, some might have also noticed an act of symbolic support on the airwaves, where Faulk was still banned. In 1962, as both sides in the case made final preparations for the impending trial, Rod Serling presented a *Twilight Zone* episode, filmed from his script entitled "Four O'Clock," based on a story by Price Day. It was a thinly veiled morality tale on the blacklist, revolving around a character who bore a distinct resemblance to the liberal conception of Hartnett. The story concerns an obsessed researcher named Oliver Crangle who keeps extensive files in his apartment on all those he considers evil. He rants about the "Communists, subversives, thieves" of the world as he seizes upon people's mistakes to ruin their lives, no matter how innocent those mistakes might have been. In the end, Crangle gets his comeuppance: he is reduced to literal insignificance as he is transformed into a miniature, ineffectual version of himself.

With this piece Serling seemed to be wishing Faulk luck in his quest to marginalize the real Hartnett and his associates. If so, the show was fortuitously timed. It went on the air April 6, 1962. Faulk's lawsuit went to trial just seventeen days later.

T W E L V E

A Case of Libel

FOR YEARS much of the political drama had unfolded in offices, production studios, and meeting halls scattered throughout midtown Manhattan. Now the scene shifted to Foley Square in the municipal district
downtown, where the conflict took on a far more magisterial tone. The
State Supreme Court building projected its solemn presence to any visi-
tor who passed between the structure's Roman Classical columns and entered the rotunda within. Those visitors with a stake in the lawsuit that had
been roiling the broadcast industry would go from there to the second
floor. Given all the anticipation preceding the crucial events about to take
place, many might have shared John Henry Faulk's surprise at their first
glance at the trial's setting, "amazed by the smallness of the courtroom."

The principals from both sides of the case gathered on that warm
spring morning in one central spot. Unlike the usual conception of a
courtroom tableau—with adversaries sitting apart on opposite sides of a
central aisle—both plaintiff and defendant here in the State Supreme
Court building sat at one table: Faulk and his attorneys on the side facing
the judge; the defense team directly across from them, facing the back of
the room. Conspicuously absent was Laurence Johnson. Problems with
his esophagus had grown more acute, and his doctor had concluded that
he should avoid any stress, particularly the duress of taking the witness
stand. That left Hartnett alone among the defendants in the courtroom

this day. (No one represented Aware as a defendant, though Hartnett was one of Aware's directors.) For him and his adversary Faulk, the seating arrangement dictated a forced proximity as they would grapple with the bitter issues that had absorbed them for the last six years, the same issues that had consumed the entire broadcast industry since 1950.[1]

On the broader stage, for all the changes in the twelve years since *Red Channels*'s release, the cold war's basic facts of life had remained stubbornly the same. Ideologically divided Berlin, for one, was just as much a flashpoint as it had been in the years following World War II. In the city where Stalin had once imposed a blockade to try to starve the Western-controlled sector into submission, Khrushchev had just recently, in the preceding autumn, erected a wall to stop the flow of refugees from east to west. And the issue of totalitarian repression in eastern Europe — the great cause of American anti-Communists at the start of the cold war — had dominated headlines again just two weeks before the trial began when Yugoslavian dissident Milovan Djilas was arrested for criticizing the Communist order. Perhaps the most important change was purely a matter of location. For years the focus of cold war attention had been on Korea and Europe. Now, a failed invasion of U.S.-backed exiles at the Bay of Pigs in April 1961 had opened a new front and set the tone for bitter antagonism between the United States and Castro's Marxist-Leninist dictatorship in Cuba. At the same time the involvement of American military advisers in South Vietnam was setting the stage for the next great conflict to come.

The proper response on the home front to these tumultuous world events was an issue still unsettled. The trial in downtown Manhattan, however, promised to resolve that part of the debate involving the proper extent of anti-Communist vigilance in the American media. One change in the way the debate would be conducted should have been obvious right from the beginning. Presiding over the case was Judge Abraham Geller, who had made a brief appearance on the stage of the blacklist drama eight years earlier when he had been designated the original judge in Joseph Julian's libel trial against *Red Channels*. He had recused himself at that time because of his previous membership in the ACLU, once named as a Communist front by the California Un-American Activities Committee, the least reputable of legislative investigators of the CPUSA. This time, though, the liberal-minded Geller remained on the bench. Eight years earlier Julian's complaint had been dismissed quickly by Geller's successor, the fiercely anti-Communist Irving Saypol. This time Aware, Inc., could not reasonably expect the same kind of deference.

By April 23, 1962, the courtroom wrangling over jury selection had already been completed. On this day, after years of charges and counter-charges, cries of communism and fascism, accusations of appeasement and repression, attorneys in the case of *John Henry Faulk v. Aware, Inc., Laurence A. Johnson and Vincent W. Hartnett* would begin their opening arguments.

The first to address the jury was Louis Nizer. In his expansive and eloquent manner, he began by painting a picture of his client—his virtues, politics, and accomplishments. Nizer delineated a portrait of an educated man, a scholar, someone who had been a patriot in time of war and an entertainer in time of peace, with a raconteur's talent that was "a cross between Mark Twain and Will Rogers." Faulk's politics, Nizer went on, were no less principled and wholesome, as one would only expect from such "a good and natural American." Here was a "Southern liberal" who "detested Communism" but who was nonetheless defamed as a friend to Soviet totalitarianism.[2]

Nizer rebutted each of the seven allegations included in Aware's News Supplement Number 16, the charges that constituted the libel directed at his client. He said that Faulk had not attended four of the events listed in the newsletter and denied that he had sent any greetings to People's Songs, as had been alleged. As for the remaining two charges, Faulk had in fact participated in the events, but his involvement, Nizer said, was purely innocent if not downright commendable.[3]

In stark contrast was Nizer's portrayal of the defendants. Hartnett was nothing more than a rank opportunist, whose anti-Communist activities had come about solely because he had lost his job on radio with Phillips H. Lord, a development that had propelled him, in turn, to fall "upon an idea which brought him a great deal of prosperity"—acting as consultant to advertisers, identifying Reds and their like while "charging these sponsors $5 a throw." Johnson, meanwhile, was a "self-appointed and self-anointed" crusader, and Aware a destructive meddler in AFTRA's internal affairs. To compensate for the harm they had all done to Faulk's career, Nizer announced that he was increasing the size of the award he sought, from $500,000 to more than $1 million, in addition to an unspecified amount for punitive damages.[4]

He introduced, at one point, a note of ambiguity about the cause of Faulk's career troubles but passed over it briefly without, perhaps, making any impression on the jury. Almost as an aside, Nizer acknowledged that there had been "sponsors waiting in line" to take the place of those who had dropped out of Faulk's show, conceding, in effect, that Johnson's efforts had failed to accomplish their objective. With this in mind, one would naturally consider CBS's responsibility in derailing Faulk's career, but Nizer explained to the jurors that they should not blame either the network or the sponsors. The lawyer's decision to take this tack must have been a pragmatic one. To spread blame throughout the broadcast industry would diffuse the case Nizer was there to make specifically against Aware, Johnson, and Hartnett. "We may have wished everyone had more courage," he said, "but people are not made as martyrs, and our position is we can understand that sensitivity when a man is so accused."[5]

There was no ambiguity when Nizer denounced the vigilantism and alleged conspiracy of the defendants. The jury had the opportunity, he said, to condemn the practice of blacklisting and make sure that "justice will be done not only for this plaintiff but for a great American cause as well."[6]

When the court reopened after a midday recess, the defense presented its version of events—and the American cause *it* championed.

At one time the Faulk case had promised to be a name-dropping clash of legal titans worthy of a high-concept TV drama, pitting Nizer, the great liberal litigator, against Roy Cohn, the controversial wunderkind of aggressive anti-communism. But Cohn had dropped out of the case, and the defense was now handled by one of his partners in the firm of Saxe, Bacon & O'Shea. Even so, Cohn's substitute was an experienced cold warrior in his own right. Thomas A. Bolan, a graduate, like John Keenan, of St. John's law school, where he had ranked first in his class, had prosecuted Communist party leaders while with the U.S. Attorney's office during the 1950s and had been responsible for winning the perjury conviction against Harvey Matusow. He was just as zealous now in defending the prerogatives of fellow Red hunters in broadcasting and just as vigorous in attacking those, like Faulk, who defied them.

In an attempt to turn the tables on his opponents, Bolan now maintained that the real libel in this case had been committed by Faulk himself, who had described the defendants "as extortionists, as racketeers, and as intimidators, as terrorists." Equally unfounded, Bolan insisted, was Faulk's claim that the defendants had destroyed his livelihood. The entertainer "had made more money" from radio in the two years following the publication of the Aware newsletter than he had in any previous years, and the defendants "had absolutely nothing to do" with the CBS decision to fire him. That was purely a business decision based on falling ratings. Expanding upon this claim, Bolan then made the dubious assertion that none of the defendants had ever applied pressure to any of Faulk's sponsors.[7]

Somewhat confusing the issue was Bolan's acknowledgment that his clients had done all they could in the previous ten years to keep Communists and Communist-fronters off the air—a reasonable goal, as Bolan characterized it. While this might seem to undercut his claim that his clients had not intended to destroy Faulk's career, Bolan used the subject of anti-Red activism to offer a glowing portrait of Hartnett and his qualifications. Hartnett was "an expert in the field of Communism" and "a sincere, dedicated man, who is painstaking in his research." He was also, Bolan promised to prove, "scrupulously honest," as evidenced by his work on Aware News Supplement Number 16, whose allegations were "checked and double-checked," its information "substantially true, from start to finish." Moreover there was nothing in the newsletter that branded Faulk a Communist. It merely "cast doubt on his judgment" and questioned his willingness to enforce the AFTRA rule against the use of the Fifth Amendment before congressional committees. And none of this would have happened in the first place, Bolan maintained, if the defendants had not been "dragged into the picture" by their opponents in AFTRA who had made Aware the central issue of the 1955 union elections.[8]

On one thing the two lawyers agreed: the jurors should pay close attention to the way the principals in the case conducted themselves while testifying. The jury's first opportunity came the next morning when Nizer opened his case by putting Faulk on the stand.

☞ Spectators filled the courtroom on April 24, as they had the day before when Nizer addressed the jury. New Yorkers were eager to see the star performer of the legal profession at work. They now had the opportunity to watch Nizer begin the introductory portion of what would be his client's lengthy testimony by skillfully guiding Faulk through the early years of his life, helping him draw a self-portrait of folksy American decency—though not too folksy. Nizer had advised Faulk to downplay his natural tendency to indulge in humorous Texas colloquialisms in order to convey a properly sober persona for the jury. Faulk, tapping into the more sophisticated, educated side of his character while still projecting an engaging, affable manner, recounted his Austin origins, his education, his master's thesis, his service in World War II, his success in radio and on TV. Nizer methodically solicited evidence of his client's civic-mindedness, and Faulk complied with a long list of speaking engagements—for which he had received no compensation—before a wide range of organizations, from various churches, temples, and high schools to the National Multiple Sclerosis Society, the United Negro College Fund, and the Daughters of the American Revolution. The recitation had its desired effect. The next day, in the first of his series of columns on the trial, Murray Kempton referred to Faulk as "a red, white and blue fellow," and was so impressed with his demeanor on the stand that he saw all but inevitable success for his cause. "He will take his vengeance without rancor," Kempton wrote. "There is a sense that when this one is over, AWARE will never be able to hurt anyone again."[9]

Once this foundation had been firmly laid, Nizer was then ready to move on to the confrontation with Aware, whose attacks might now seem all the more dastardly in light of Faulk's model citizenship.

Faulk told the jury about Leslie Barrett's dramatic speech at the March 1955 meeting of AFTRA in which the actor described the emotional torment caused by Hartnett's accusatory letters. Faulk explained the process and purpose of creating the Middle of the Road slate. He and the other candidates were determined to confront Aware's incursions into their union's affairs while remaining anti-Communist as well. They made sure, Faulk said, that the slate included only people who "had never been called before any committee whatever; that not one whisper had ever been made about any single one of them in one of those smear sheets."[10] Yet for all their diligence and reasonableness, Faulk explained, their victory in the elections was rewarded by nothing but mean-spirited slander from Aware.

In only two instances, he said, did the Aware allegations touch upon the truth. Yes, he had entertained at the 1946 event sponsored by the Independent Citizens Committee of the Arts, Sciences and Professions, but this had been a perfectly admirable first-anniversary tribute to the United Nations, involving such personages as UN secretary-general Trygve Lie and U.S. Secretary of State Edward Stettinius. And, yes, he had in fact contributed sketch material to the 1948 Showtime for Wallace rally, but this had been strictly a work for hire, and he had never been a member of Progressive Citizens of America, the sponsoring organization that had been identified as a Communist front. As for the five other alleged activities, he flatly denied any involvement. In an especially persuasive moment, Nizer produced a letter corroborating Faulk's claim that he had, as he put it, been sick in bed with the flu on the day he supposedly participated in another pro-Wallace event at the Jefferson School for Social Science.[11]

From there, Faulk went on to tell of Aware's attack upon his career, from Laurence Johnson's trip to New York City where he was "playing havoc" on Madison Avenue, to John Dungey's letters to Faulk's sponsors. When the story turned to his life after being fired from CBS, the jury learned the details of the hardships he had endured when he had been forced to take on a late-night radio show for no pay on WBAI as a way to maintain at least some sort of presence in broadcasting while watching his income drop to practically nothing at all. Here again, another letter drove the point home, in this case the letter from KFRC in San Francisco that had been mistakenly sent to Faulk, the one indicating that his confrontation with Aware, not his lack of broadcast credentials, accounted for his inability to land a job at the station.[12]

Throughout six days of direct examination, Nizer made sure to underscore his client's steadfast opposition to communism, contrary to the defendants' efforts to suggest otherwise. Not once, but several times, he asked Faulk to state categorically his views on the subject. On his first morning on the stand, Faulk said he considered communism "a very antagonistic and very destructive philosophy, with which I held no brief whatever, never did and don't presently." Asked again by Nizer that very afternoon, he rephrased and reiterated the same view. On May 1 he was even more emphatic: "As I have testified before, my position has always been unalterably opposed to Communism from earliest memory of knowing anything about it, Mr. Nizer. Neither in utterance nor in action have I in any way, shape or form, given comfort or aid to any Communist cause, or the philosophy of Communism, but to the contrary, have had very strong opinions to the contrary." A few moments later he went a step further, asserting that his stand on the issue had been so far above reproach that he had never even been called before HUAC or any other similar committee. His patriotism and loyalty "had never been questioned by anyone."[13]

⟡ Although the jurors' response at this point was purely a matter of speculation, they had clearly been treated to a persuasively presented conception of Faulk as an ideal citizen of moderate liberal sympathies, a man vindictively maligned with accusations that bore little or no resemblance to reality. Defense attorney Bolan had his work cut out for him if he expected to shatter the edifice constructed by Nizer and Faulk in the jurors' minds. Ultimately he proved to be nothing if not thorough. For nearly six days he kept Faulk on the stand. He failed, however, to put much of a dent in Faulk's story.

Bolan attempted, at length, to downgrade the entertainer's position in broadcasting by trying to get him to admit that he had been known as a mere disk jockey rather than as a humorist and raconteur. He also waded through an intensive examination of the *John Henry Faulk Show*'s schedule of commercials to establish that Faulk's loss of sponsors had little to do with the activities of the defendants. Neither tactic contributed much to the proceedings other than tedium. When Bolan succeeded to some small degree in compromising Faulk's veracity, the impact was minimal. Faulk had tried to create the impression, for instance, that he and his fellow Middle of the Roaders aggressively enforced the union's rule demanding that members cooperate with congressional committees. But Bolan's cross-examination made it clear that the charges brought against an AFTRA member under this rule had been initiated not by the Middle of the Road officers but by their opponents within the union, Aware's allies.[14] Still, this was a peripheral issue involving intramural union conflicts, not a concern that was likely to influence jurors weighing much more basic issues about the alleged destruction of a man's reputation and livelihood.

Of greater moment to Nizer and his associates was another aggressive line of questioning about Faulk's superiors at WCBS. Repeatedly Bolan asked if Faulk regarded Sam Slate and Carl Ward as truthful men, to which Faulk responded that "executives who are very honest men and very good men quite frequently were impelled to take actions and positions that could be described as less than candid let us say." The particular exchange had questionable meaning, but for Faulk's legal team "it was an ominous indication" that Slate and Ward "would be witnesses for the defendants."[15]

A similar concern arose when Bolan challenged Faulk's opposition to communism. "I direct your attention to the month of February, the year 1944," Bolan said, "and ask if you attended a communist party meeting at the home of one Ina May Bull?" Faulk denied that he had. Bolan went on to ask if Faulk had known certain other Austin residents from that period—with the obvious implication that they had been Communists—and asked if he had attended a Marxist study group. In each case Faulk replied in the negative. For the information behind these questions Bolan might have been relying here on leaks from the FBI—most likely through Roy Cohn, who had close relations with the Bureau—and Nizer worried that the people Bolan mentioned might appear as witnesses in an attempt "to denounce Faulk as a Red." He later asked Faulk to make some phone calls to Texas to determine if anyone representing the defense was trying to locate possible ex-Communist informers who might testify against him. Faulk could find no indication that this had been done, and ultimately no such witnesses appeared.[16]

Whatever Nizer's anxieties about this line of questioning by Bolan, the defense's strategy was probably counterproductive. Bolan would be unable to offer any documents or testimony to substantiate his accusations, leaving the jury with no reason to believe the charges. If anything, he seemed to be providing yet another example of a groundless Red-baiting smear, exactly the kind of loose accusation that Faulk claimed had destroyed his career.

When his testimony concluded on May 11, Faulk had good reason to be pleased with his performance on the stand, and anyone other than a staunch adversary was likely to be impressed. But, on close inspection, and with the benefit of hindsight, it is apparent that his testimony left some questions unanswered. Taking into consideration information not presented at the trial—some the defense might have had, some it did not—certain doubts arise about the image Faulk presented of himself.

One question concerned his relationship with People's Songs. Faulk resolutely denied having sent greetings to the group on their second anniversary, as alleged by Aware, despite the fact that his name appeared under the heading of "Birthday Greetings To People's Songs From . . ." in the February–March 1948 issue of the People's Songs bulletin. As long as the defense failed to document this act, as opposed to documenting only his listing, there was no solid basis for refuting Faulk's claim. Even so, Faulk didn't try to say he had no association with the group. He acknowledged that he had taken part in some People's Songs events, but under cross-examination he said the only thing he knew about the group was that "it was an organization that was supposed to spread folk music all over the country," and he "never knew the slightest thing else about them, besides singing folk songs."[17] This must have sounded perfectly plausible to the jury, but only due to a lack of information.

To believe Faulk's assertion, one would have to accept the idea that he was nothing more than a scholarly folklorist, completely insulated from the political realities of the folk-music movement of the 1940s. This was hardly the case. He was politically sophisticated and, as his letters from the period reveal, deeply concerned about the left-wing issues of the day. Could he really have been unaware of the political agenda of activists like Woody Guthrie and Pete Seeger? Did he really not know about the radical leanings of his ex-wife Hally Wood, another People's Songs participant?

About his involvement in the Showtime for Wallace event, another discrepancy emerges. While noting that he contributed material to the event as well as "entertained at one or two more" Wallace functions, he was quick to add, "I didn't speak in support. I went as an entertainer." In saying this he was following through on Nizer's contention, made in his opening statement, that Faulk "voted for Truman. He was not for Wallace, as we will show you."[18] The very idea that someone would entertain at a presidential candidate's rally without supporting that candidate is difficult to accept, especially when the entertainer is as politically minded as Faulk was. Are we to believe, for instance, that he would just as willingly have taken part in a Dewey rally? In any case, the plain truth is that Faulk had been an active supporter of Wallace. Technically Nizer was correct in saying that his client had voted for Truman, but Faulk had switched his support belatedly, and reluctantly, as would only be natural when voting for a man he had likened to a "sick whore."

The question here is why Faulk felt it necessary to distort his 1948 political sympathies. While it is true that in 1962 right-wingers still held Wallace in disrepute, it was also commonly accepted that many liberals as well as Communists had given Wallace their support. Even Aware's News Supplement Number 16 conceded that non-Communists had been involved in the campaign. Perhaps Faulk believed that winning his case required that he distance himself from anything that might possibly be construed as Communist influenced. But this theory is undermined by Faulk's proud announcements on the stand that he had been active in the Southern Conference for Human Welfare, a group named as a Communist front by both congressional committees and *Red Channels*.

Bolan and Hartnett had their own theory: Faulk was concealing something. Faulk's testimony about his 1955 interview with HUAC investigator Donald Appell must have reinforced that suspicion.

Bolan had intended from the beginning to question Faulk about this meeting—and later to put Appell on the stand as well—because he believed he could refute Faulk's testimony that his loyalty had never been questioned. Bolan also intended to bring out what Faulk had told the HUAC investigator—that he had been "devoted to the left-wing causes because of his wife's influence," meaning Faulk's first wife, Hally Wood. Nizer, meanwhile, objected to this line of questioning because it involved a discussion of Wood's political activities, which he considered irrelevant to Aware's allegations.[19] On May 10, Judge Geller allowed Bolan to examine the issue.

When asked about the meeting, Faulk replied that Appell had asked him whether he had been a CPUSA member in Baltimore during World War II, an allegation that Faulk denied. He added that Appell "indicated he believed me, and we have since found out that it was Mr. Hartnett that sent him up to see me and told him that and that he was quite put out with Mr. Hartnett for it." Bolan then broached his primary concern: Had Faulk told Appell that Hally Wood had gotten him involved in Communist fronts? But Faulk denied he had said anything about her influencing him to become involved with People's Songs or any other organizations.[20]

Although these denials were firm, other statements by Faulk were less convincing. At first, for instance, he tried to maintain that his session with the HUAC investigator was not an interrogation at all but only "a discussion." And after he claimed that Appell had believed him, he denied that Appell later served him with a subpoena. HUAC did, in fact, issue Faulk a subpoena in 1958—Faulk himself would later discuss this in his memoir—even if Appell himself might not have been directly responsible.[21] For

Bolan and Hartnett, these two discrepancies, minor though they might have been, must have seemed like an opportunity for discrediting Faulk's testimony. But the defense would only be able to do so once it brought Appell in as a witness. Without him, Faulk's statements would stand unchallenged.

¶ The opening portion of the trial provided more than one encouraging sign for the plaintiff. Not only did Faulk emerge from his lengthy stint on the stand relatively unscathed, the judge's handling of the proceedings demonstrated that anti-Red watchdogs would face a far more rigorous test than they had in the Julian case.

Despite the assertion in News Supplement Number 16 that Aware was not accusing Faulk of being a Communist, Judge Geller instructed the jurors that it was up to them to decide if the allegations were tantamount to calling the entertainer a Communist, pro-Communist, or fellow traveler.[22] Perhaps even more significant, he provided Faulk's legal team ample opportunity to examine the full scope and pervasiveness of the blacklist, regardless of whether the evidence related directly to Faulk. This led to a succession of witnesses who supplied a detailed account of the broadcast purge of the preceding ten years. As an additional benefit, these witnesses also lent an aura of show-business glamour to Faulk's cause.

The first to take the stand was David Susskind, the acclaimed producer and, more recently, host of the TV talk show *Open Mind*. Granted some deference from the court, he was allowed to testify out of turn, in the middle of Faulk's direct examination, in order to accommodate his plans to produce a TV program in England. He explained how the blacklist worked, based upon his experiences dealing with the ad agency Young & Rubicam, a Hartnett client. The agency required that he submit lists of potential actors, one-third of whom would typically be rejected. Once, Susskind said, he complained to his agency contact, David Levy, that he was never given a reason for the rejections. "I can't give you any," Levy explained. "I deplore this practice as much as you do. We're caught in a trap. I have no alternative."[23]

In his testimony's most provocative moment, Susskind recalled the time he had to clear an eight-year-old girl for a part, only to be told that the child was "politically unreliable." This revelation brought an outburst of surprise and laughter from the spectators, so much so that Judge Geller had to demand order in court. The problem, Susskind continued, had been that the girl's father had a suspect political background. Seeing how damaging this information could be, Bolan immediately rose and requested that the judge instruct the jury that no evidence had been offered "that links such testimony with any of the defendants." He could not have been pleased with Nizer's response. Nizer read from Hartnett's examination before trial, in which he had admitted clearing child actors and checking into their parents' political record. This was necessary, Hartnett had said, because "that is part of the tragedy of the communist movement, that even children are brought into the movement at an early age."[24]

Along with firsthand information on the previously secretive blacklist, Susskind's testimony also corroborated Nizer's strategy for isolating Hartnett, Johnson, and Aware as the culprits in the case. Like Nizer, the producer was willing to let ad agencies and sponsors off the hook, asserting they were not responsible for the blacklist phenomenon "because they are, after all, in the marketplace. Their job is to sell products and create good will for their corporation. . . . They are not to blame at all."[25]

Other producers helped establish the role played by Laurence Johnson. Leading quiz-show specialist Mark Goodson related the troubles he had encountered keeping Abe Burrows on his program *The Name's the Same* in the face of a 1952 letter-writing campaign. At first his sponsor, Swanson, had been willing to stand by Burrows, but within a few months the company president decided he would have to fire the comedian after all. The reason was simple: Swanson had gotten a call from Johnson. Himan Brown, producer of such radio shows as *Dick Tracy* and *Inner Sanctum*, illustrated another side of the Johnson phenomenon—the necessity (or, at least, perceived necessity) of showing the grocer proper obeisance. He described the experience of scurrying over to a midtown Manhattan hotel where Johnson had been holding court—beside his errand boy and jester Matusow—in order to hear the grocer's complaints about certain actors appearing on his programs.[26]

Elaborating further along these lines were various radio and TV performers. Bolan asked for a ruling that would exclude more of this sort of testimony on the grounds that it was irrelevant to Faulk's complaint, but Judge Geller allowed Nizer to proceed, deciding that the evidence provided necessary background for the case.

Tony Randall, best known at the time as the co-star in such Doris Day–Rock Hudson films as *Lover Come Back*, described an atmosphere of intimidation perpetrated by Aware within AFTRA, where he was "afraid to be seen voting against the Aware slate." After staying away from union meetings for two or three years, he found that the passage of the anti-Aware resolution of 1955 "brought us out from under the rocks, so to speak." Variety show host Garry Moore failed to bring much hard information to the case, but he may have come up with the trial's best simile. In describing the predicament faced by a targeted performer, he said, "It was a little like fighting with six men in a closet with the light out, and you can't tell who is hitting you."[27]

Everett Sloane, once part of Orson Welles's Mercury Theatre troupe, provided information from the inside of the phenomenon by recounting his efforts to remove himself from a greylist in the early 1950s. He had been told that he was losing work because he was being confused with the writer Allen Sloane, who was listed in *Red Channels*. This assertion that he was purely a victim of mistaken identity would be repeated in a later account of the period as an example of how maddeningly arbitrary the blacklist could be; but the story does not hold up very well. Justifiably or not, Everett Sloane had come under suspicion for his own activities. In 1949, a year before *Red Channels* appeared, Hartnett had mentioned him as a Communist fronter in an article for *The Sign* and later had raised similar concerns about him in a letter to Johnson. But while Sloane's assertion on this score might not have been convincing, his testimony nonetheless helped Faulk's case in a more meaningful way by tying Hartnett into the blacklist process and illustrating the overbearing standards for clearance promoted by both Hartnett and Aware.

Sloane told the jury of meeting Aware official Paul Milton to discuss how he might reopen doors to more broadcast jobs. To demonstrate his employability, Sloane had shown Milton a letter from the Civil Service Commission that vouched for his loyalty. The Aware official was quick to dismiss it. "I take this with a grain of salt," he said, adding that Aware was "more stringent" than federal agencies in judging these matters. He recommended that Sloane meet with Hartnett as a way to discover a more definitive way of clearing himself, to which Sloane responded, according to his testimony, by telling Milton to "Go fly a kite," though his original language had probably been much more colorful.[28]

Other witnesses provided a glimpse into the sort of pressure Hartnett could exert on the lives of performers in his quest to cleanse the airwaves. Radio announcer Kenneth Roberts had been one of many *Red Channels* listees to attend the meeting with attorney Arthur Garfield Hayes to discuss the possibility of suing American Business Consultants. Roberts now told the court that Hartnett had contacted him during this period, informing him that he needed to reassure his sponsor, Philip Morris, about his political record. At the same time Hartnett also requested that Roberts reveal who had attended the meeting with Hayes. The implication was clear: his cooperation with Hartnett could affect his status with Philip Morris.[29]

Much more dramatic testimony of this kind came from Kim Hunter.

Faulk's lawyers had originally asked her in 1960 to testify, but at the time she had not been willing to commit herself to the task; she feared her cooperation with Faulk would "almost certainly put her back on the blacklist." Eventually, in April 1962, she agreed to take the stand, but even then, the night before she was to testify, Faulk and his lawyers had to spend the evening shoring up her resolve. It was not just a fear of the blacklist that made her so reluctant. She was also, Faulk recalled, loath to admit she had "given way under Hartnett's threats, which placed her in an embarrassing position."[30]

Although she might have finally settled on a decision, the decision did not necessarily settle her nerves. From her very first moments on the stand, she was so clearly overcome by anxiety that Judge Geller interceded to try to calm her. He would do so again more than once during her testimony. Struggling to control herself, Hunter told of her early success as an actress, leading to an Oscar for her performance in *A Streetcar Named Desire*, followed by the sudden decline in job offers attributed to unspecified suspicions about her political activities. Even during this early, introductory portion of her testimony, her rattled manner alone conveyed to the jury the trepidation experienced by performers who had found themselves under the Red hunters' scrutiny.

Hunter described her decision to contact Hartnett in order to get more information about the allegations against her. Nizer read to the jury the letter from Arthur Jacobs, her public relations representative, then read Hartnett's reply, in which the talent consultant pointed out that "Miss Hunter's name has been used in connection with a dubious activity as recently as March 1953." Nizer made clear that this sentence referred to

Hunter's small monetary contribution to an effort to reprint a series of *New York Post* articles critical of Johnson.[31] Most important, though, was the revelation that Hartnett had set a price of two hundred dollars for doing the research on Hunter's political record.

For those paying close attention, the letters established that Hartnett had not in fact solicited a fee; instead Jacobs had offered to pay for his time and effort. But a statement from Hartnett's 1956 HUAC testimony, which Nizer now read aloud, had a powerful effect on the jury's perception of the defendant. Commenting on his decision to charge for his services, Hartnett had said, "Here is not Miss Hunter, but a public relations man . . . who makes five G's a year on this. On some accounts his probable retainer is fifty G's a year, and I said I would make a report for him, and I think I would be a complete ass if I did it for nothing." The coarseness of his comment cast a pall over his response to Jacobs's request.[32]

As for the larger issue of the blacklist's effect, Hunter's testimony and the accompanying documents illustrated how Hartnett, the tireless zealot, had meddled in performers' lives, as when he had instructed Hunter to oppose the left-wing faction in Actors Equity and, even more so, when he had asked her to come out against the anti-Aware resolution in AFTRA. Just before the latter conversation, he had approved her appearance on a show sponsored by one of his clients. When he then suggested that she take a stand against the AFTRA measure, Hunter felt, she now testified, "like a donkey with a carrot in front of his nose, that 'You have had a taste of work, now do you want to continue working?'" Once she satisfied Hartnett's request by sending an anti-resolution telegram to the next AFTRA meeting, she found that she "worked quite frequently after that, and to the present day."[33]

℟ As the trial progressed, as days then weeks went by, there was still no sign of Laurence Johnson. On May 15, three weeks into the trial, Judge Geller called Nizer and Bolan into his robing room to discuss the matter.

The judge instructed Bolan that his client's failure to testify, or even to appear, could have repercussions for his case. If Johnson did not show up in court, and Bolan failed to provide adequate explanation for his absence, the jury would be within its rights to "give greater weight to the testimony of the opposition."

Johnson's absence, Nizer pointed out, could also impinge upon the prerogatives of the plaintiff. Nizer explained that, since deposing the grocer before trial, his office had obtained copies of letters from Johnson and might need to put him on the stand in order to confirm the documents' authenticity. He would, naturally, be unable to subpoena Johnson unless Bolan divulged his client's whereabouts, something that Bolan had yet to do. When Nizer expressed disbelief that Bolan had had no recent contact with Johnson, the grocer's attorney maintained that his client "has had no connection with this case from start to finish." Nizer also took issue with the defense's claims that Johnson was too ill to testify, based upon a Syracuse doctor's assessment that such an experience could cause him to become "catastrophically ill." He revealed that he had hired a private investigator to observe Johnson's comings and goings at a time when Bolan had requested an adjournment due to his client's poor health. The detective had learned that Johnson had left his Syracuse home the day the adjournment was denied and had carried his luggage unassisted into a waiting taxi—hardly, Nizer implied, the actions of a desperately ill man. Further, Nizer disputed the medical report that had described Johnson's esophageal afflictions, a report, Nizer contended, that was "an enormously exaggerated series of technical terms which mean nothing."[34]

Judge Geller decided that Bolan must "disclose Mr. Johnson's whereabouts," but the defense attorney had no information to offer. The judge then directed him to provide the information by the end of the day or, at the latest, by the following morning.

That afternoon Bolan was able to learn that Johnson was staying with his daughter Eleanor in Cranston, Rhode Island, in order to be on hand while she went into the hospital for surgery. Later that night, when Bolan succeeded in speaking to him over the phone, Johnson said he was feeling somewhat better but how much better was not clear, leaving open the question of whether he was well enough to testify. Judge Geller was not about to let the question hang much longer. He ordered Bolan to make his client available for a medical exam to be arranged by Nizer.[35]

While it might seem strange that Bolan should have no contact with his client at the time of his trial, it should not have been entirely surprising either. Bolan's actions in recent weeks had suggested some sort of rift, or at least a lack of cooperation, between counsel and client. During preliminary discussions with Judge Geller at the start of the trial, for instance,

Bolan had requested that Johnson be severed from the other defendants in the case. Later, in his opening statement to the jury, he had described Johnson's anti-Communist activities but included no words of personal praise, in contrast to his glowing characterization of Hartnett as a learned expert and a man of scrupulous integrity. Nizer later surmised that Johnson might have harbored ill feeling toward his co-defendants. Having relied on Aware and Hartnett for his information on Faulk, he now "held them responsible for his plight in having been involved in a lawsuit." Another possibility has to do with Johnson's mental condition at the time. Nizer's associate, George Berger, believed that Johnson had been failing and genuinely forgetful during his pre-trial deposition in 1960.[36] Johnson's current negligence in keeping up with the case might have been a symptom of that deterioration. Or perhaps he was simply unwilling, at his advanced age, to come to grips with the distressing chain of events that now confronted him.

With or without Johnson in attendance, Nizer and his associates needed to prove the grocer's role in the attack on Faulk. Witnesses from the advertising business, Johnson's favorite pressure point, were essential to make the case, and it was the first of these witnesses who proved to be most critical.

By taking the stand on May 15, Thomas Murray made good on a pledge of support he had made to Faulk back in the spring of 1956 when he had been the account executive for Pabst Brewing, a *John Henry Faulk Show* sponsor. Now, six years later, he told the jury about the March 1956 phone call he had received from Johnson in which the grocer had branded Faulk a Communist and warned that Murray and Pabst had "better get in line because a lot of people along Madison Avenue are getting in line." Murray also testified that Johnson had threatened that American Legion Post 41 would send a letter to the sponsor.[37] With this, Murray provided unambiguous evidence not only of Johnson's campaign against Faulk's sponsors but also his connection to the Syracuse American Legion post that had pressured those advertisers through the mail. On cross-examination, Bolan tried to legitimize the charges against Faulk by asking if Murray had asked Johnson about the basis of the allegations. Whatever his expectations might have been, the unwelcome response Bolan got was a display of righteous indignation that the jury must have found infectious. "Mr. Johnson had not qualified himself as an authority on such subjects," Murray said. "I thought he should be back wherever he comes from, selling baked beans, to tell you the truth. By what right does a grocer call me up and tell me so and so is a communist, 'Get rid of him.'"[38]

Immediately following this witness was Samuel Dalsimer, Murray's superior at Grey Advertising in 1956, who corroborated the account executive's story and went on to provide an illustration of Johnson's most notorious tactic. Recalling an incident from 1952, he told of his difficulties with the grocer while representing the Block Drug Company, sponsor for *Danger*, perhaps the greatest thorn in the Red hunters' side. Introduced into evidence was a letter from Johnson to Block Drug in which the grocer threatened to run a sales test between Block's Ammident toothpaste and its competitor Chlorident; the sign over the Chlorident display would inform customers that the manufacturer of this product did not employ "Stalin's little creatures."[39] Stories about the grocer from Syracuse that had been circulating quietly over the years—with an occasional mention in liberal media outlets like the *New York Post*—were now becoming part of the public record.

Other advertising executives built upon this record. Not all of them, though, were willing participants. One in particular became part of the plaintiff's case as a result of a phone call during the trial from Harvey Matusow. Whether or not the former anti-Communist informer had been, in fact, the mysterious source of documents for the Faulk team before the trial, he was now willing, as Faulk later recalled, to tell Nizer's office the story of the 1952 meeting at the Hampshire House dining room during which Johnson had pressured the Lennen & Mitchell agency into hiring Matusow as a clearance consultant for *Schlitz Playhouse of Stars*. Being a convicted perjurer, Matusow hardly qualified as "a suitable witness" but Francis Barton, the Lennen & Mitchell executive who had attended the meeting, was a reputable figure in his field, exactly the sort of person who would bring credibility to the story. Barton, however, was not willing to testify. Typical of the attitude that had pervaded advertising for so many years, he was still uneasy about blowing the whistle on the blacklist phenomenon. Eventually he would have to be subpoenaed to compel him to appear in court, but once on the stand he provided a vivid example of Johnson's browbeating tactics and helped establish for the jury that the Faulk affair was not an isolated incident in the grocer's career.[40]

The testimonies of advertising executives, effective as they were, included one curious discrepancy that seemed to pass unnoticed at the time. In testifying about the warnings made by Johnson, Murray explained how actions taken by supermarket operators could impinge upon a manufacturer's sales, specifically by limiting display space for the company's products in stores. "So this," he concluded, "represented a tremendous threat to Pabst Brewing Company, but I mean tremendous." Elaborating on the same theme later that day, Dalsimer said that Johnson could have hurt Pabst "as far as display in his supermarkets."[41] The problem here was that jurors listening to this testimony would never have known that Johnson had sold all his supermarkets a month before approaching these executives about Faulk's sponsor. How could Johnson possibly have reduced Pabst's display space? Whatever direct control he had once had within his little bailiwick in central New York—an overrated consideration to begin with—was now gone. The only advantage left was his alleged influence over other grocers, which, for all Murray and Dalsimer knew, might have been no influence at all. Nizer, obviously, had no reason to bring out these facts, but Bolan could have used the discrepancy to challenge the witnesses' reliability. Still, he made no mention of it. Perhaps Bolan's lack of contact with Johnson accounts for the lapse. Whatever the reason, the failure to note this oversight left a larger issue unexamined: the culpability of advertisers, who often capitulated to Johnson out of reflexive fear of his unsubstantiated clout.

In all, the exhaustive, painstaking testimony presented on Faulk's behalf lasted for a month until May 25, when the plaintiff's case finally rested. The procession of producers, performers, and advertising executives conjured up a striking picture of political vigilantism and an unwarranted attack upon an anti-Communist radio personality who had the temerity to take a stand against the blacklist. Complexities, naturally, had no place in the morality tale crafted by Faulk's legal team, whose job it was to create the most forceful and easily absorbed message possible. The complicity of advertising agencies or of networks could not be allowed to muddy the argument. Nor could the question of whether Faulk would have been just as entitled to compensation had he in fact been a Com-

munist or a habitual Communist fronter. A measure of how well this sim-
plified message was coming across could be gleaned from the media. A
Newsweek report published soon after the conclusion of the plaintiff's case
characterized the testimony as a chronicle of "the dark Middle Ages of the
1950s, away back there when witchcraft was in flower," a period of "ancient history of arbitrary, extralegal blacklisting." The perception of the
anti-Communist crusade as a witch-hunt, as had been promoted early on
by Arthur Miller's *The Crucible,* was beginning to take hold in the public
mind. As for the alleged witch-hunter himself, Hartnett, Faulk did his part
to mold the public's view of him not as a rabid villain but rather as a pathetic figure. "You know, I feel so sorry for him," he told columnist Murray Kempton. "Most of the time he wears that little ribbon in his lapel; I
suppose it means 'honorable discharge.' He wants so much for us to like
him. Poor sad little fellow."[42]

There was a more obvious, more likely explanation for the armed
forces ribbon that Hartnett was so fond of wearing. He was, after all, a
zealot dedicated to serving his cause, not a performer grasping for approval, and the ribbon might simply have represented what it was meant
to represent—pride in his brand of patriotism. For years he had prosely-
tized his patriotic vision with unrelenting determination, and here in the
State Supreme Court building he proved just as tireless now that his conception of God and country was under fire. Winning the jury's affection
was not his goal as much as proving that he was right, that he had always
been right.

Known for years as the keeper of the files for the broadcast purge, Hartnett now aided his defense as a veritable legal assistant, bringing pertinent
documents to court and feeding the appropriate papers to Bolan as the situation demanded. When he had nothing on hand that applied to the
issues currently being raised, he responded as he always had—by un-
earthing yet more information. In the past his talent for assembling facts
had impressed potential clients, helped him secure substantial fees, and
made him an authority within anti-Communist circles. Now he faced a
problem. At his trial there was little room for the kind of information that
had been his specialty.

The obstacles he and Bolan faced first became obvious during the cross-examination of David Susskind. Bolan set out to undo some of the damage incurred during the producer's exposé of blacklisting by underscoring the rationale for barring suspected Communists from the airwaves. With the fruit of Hartnett's years of research at his fingertips, he asked questions designed to establish that blacklistees were not necessarily political innocents.

He asked at one point if Susskind had employed any of the fourteen actors that had taken the Fifth Amendment before HUAC in 1955. Susskind replied that he had, naming Elliott Sullivan as one member of that group. "And this Elliott Sullivan," Bolan said, "had been previously identified as a member of the Communist Party by sworn testimony?" Nizer objected, and Judge Geller sustained the objection. When he faced similar obstructions to his cross-examination, Bolan spelled out the reason behind his questions. He wanted to establish "the right of a private group to advocate that people who take the Fifth Amendment when questioned on Communist Party membership need not or should not be employed on television." The same applied, he argued, for those identified as CPUSA members. The judge was not persuaded.[43]

Unwilling to back off, Bolan then asked Susskind if he considered it "blacklisting to advocate that a person who had been identified as a member of the Communist Party should not be employed in television or radio." Again the question was disallowed. Turning to the judge, Bolan said, "He says he is against blacklisting," referring to Susskind. "I want to find out what blacklisting is here." Judge Geller was not swayed. In one of his most significant statements during the trial, he ruled that "a committee's report of Congress does not constitute an adjudication," effectively ruling out much of the information that Hartnett could provide.[44]

Bolan's frustration continued. Two weeks later it came to a head again when he complained that the judge had allowed testimony on the practice of blacklisting during direct examination but would not allow him to pursue the issue from the defendants' point of view. Once more he was rebuffed. The judge also ruled that the defense could not offer the federal attorney general's list of subversive groups as proof that a given organization was a Communist front, effectively barring yet another source of information from Hartnett's files.[45]

The limits of Hartnett's contributions came up yet again on May 18, during the testimony of Henry Nash Smith, the literary critic and scholar, author of *The Virgin Land,* who was appearing as a character witness for Faulk. With no information immediately at his disposal, Hartnett left the courtroom, according to Faulk, while Smith testified, presumably to place some phone calls, then returned to hand two index cards to his attorney, one of them noting that Smith had signed a petition calling for the abolition of HUAC and the other citing his sponsorship of the Committee to Secure Justice for Morton Sobell, the convicted spy associated with the Rosenberg case. When Bolan tried to question Smith about these associations, the judge called both attorneys to the bench to confer on the propriety of this tactic. Bolan argued that he was merely making the point that Smith was likely to be biased against the defendants, but Judge Geller ruled that he was ranging too far from the libel directed against Faulk.[46] From this point on, Hartnett's research, such a crucial force in the past, such a powerful weapon in the battle of the airwaves, had no place in the trial except as an object of the plaintiff's scorn.

One thing Bolan's early cross-examination did accomplish, at least from a historical if not a legal perspective: he revealed the divide between the two perceptions at odds in this case. After establishing that Susskind had hired Lee Grant in 1958, he asked, "Did you know that she had invoked the Fifth Amendment when she had been questioned as to Communist party membership?" Susskind replied, "That I did not know, and that lay completely beyond my interest."[47]

With so little success in challenging the plaintiff's case, the story that would support the claims of Hartnett, Johnson, and Aware would have to wait until the defense began to call its witnesses. Once Bolan began to present his case, the defendants could finally address the issues they considered central to the lawsuit: the significance of Communist fronts, the individual's right to draw attention to suspicious activities, and the defendants' goodwill in pursuing their crusade—provided, of course, they were allowed sufficient latitude by the judge.

At first, when they opened their case on May 25, they encountered no difficulties. Unlike the plaintiff's team, which had relied so much on the words of show-business personalities, Bolan began with two decidedly unglamorous CBS employees, one a business executive and the other an accountant. More important were the piles of records that accompanied their testimonies and formed the basis for a painstaking review of the frequency of commercials and records of payments for the *John Henry Faulk Show*. For now, Bolan did not address the more personal issues likely to engage the jurors' attention. Only on the next day of court would the jury get to see a face and a personality attached to the defendants' cause, and only then would the fierce antagonism between the two sides become palpable once again.

THIRTEEN

Verdict

FOR THE JURORS watching him take the stand, Paul R. Milton represented a single, specific element in the Faulk case—the defendant Aware. But for those in broadcasting with a long memory, the now fifty-eight-year-old Aware co-founder, going grey and balding, as Faulk described him, was also a reminder of years of ideological struggle. Writers in particular remembered him as the driving force behind We the Undersigned, the anti-Communist caucus within the Radio Writers Guild that had been at the center of the union's fierce conflicts. Those, from both sides, who had taken part in the old battles—and who still nursed old grievances—now had their first chance to see an advocate of the broadcast purge testify under oath on the facts and attitudes that had shaped those events. In the Julian case the media watchdogs had not even been required to present a defense before winning their verdict. Now they would at least have to account for their actions. Milton's old associates attending the start of his testimony on May 28 were hoping for vindication of their shared cause. Old enemies were no doubt anticipating his destruction under a bruising cross-examination.

To create a benign first impression, Bolan began by drawing out the early details of Milton's career, starting with his graduation from Cornell University and his early days as a journalist and author, and leading up to his work as a radio writer for such programs as *The March of Time*,

Counterspy, and *Crime Fighters*. Like Faulk, Milton had been out of broadcasting in recent years, though by his own choice, earning his living in real estate since 1958. When the questions began to tread on the contested ground of Aware and its works, however, Bolan and Milton found their progress quickly stalled by judicial rulings.

Whenever Milton was asked to discuss the purposes of Aware, Judge Geller sustained objections to the questions. Angling for a way around this stance, Bolan then tried to introduce the organization's constitution and bylaws into evidence, only to be stymied by the judge's ruling that the document was inadmissible because it was nothing more than a "self-serving declaration." Bolan met with a similar response when he asked Milton if Aware's officers received any pay for their services. Finally he approached the bench to argue the necessity of his line of questioning: "Your Honor, so far as the jury is now concerned, Aware could have been incorporated into the meat-packing business." Still barring the constitution and bylaws, Judge Geller offered Bolan the chance to submit the group's certificate of incorporation instead, a measure that Bolan regarded as still too restrictive, one that would still not allow him to provide what he considered crucial information. "I submit, your Honor," he said, "where we have a defendant here charged with blacklisting, racketeering and extortion, not to permit me to show how this corporation actually operated is grossly unfair and prejudicial." Judge Geller replied that Bolan could illustrate the inner workings of Aware only as it related specifically to the organization's alleged act of libel, News Supplement Number 16. In the end, Milton's description of the organization's intentions and scope was confined to a listing of the categories of Aware's activities. As for the character of the group and its officers, he would later be allowed to say that the organization never received any money for clearing artists, and never supplied lists of undesirables to networks or sponsors.[1]

Finally Milton discussed his role as principal writer of the newsletter containing the allegations against Faulk. Aware partisans expecting a vigorous defense of the charges heard some justifications from Milton, but once more, to their dismay, they found there were limitations to what could be offered as evidence. Here Bolan hoped to establish that Aware's charges were based at least on reasonable sources, regardless of whether they turned out to be accurate. In commenting on the alleged activities of Faulk involving the Progressive Citizens of America and People's Songs,

Milton explained that his characterization of these two groups as Communist fronts was based on congressional findings—an authority that had already been challenged during the trial. He was allowed only to mention the citations but not any of the details in the findings.[2] A greater challenge awaited when Milton discussed his reasons for assigning front status to the Independent Citizens Committee of the Arts, Sciences and Professions. The dispute over this testimony highlighted the disparity between the two views of domestic communism that had clashed for years.

One of Milton's sources on the Independent Citizens Committee, provided by Hartnett, was an excerpt from the Louis Budenz book *Techniques of Communism*. "As I stated in 1948 before a Senate Subcommittee," Budenz wrote, "the Independent Citizens Committee of the Arts, Sciences and Professions was worked out originally from my office when I was managing editor of the *Daily Worker*." For anti-Communist activists, former CPUSA members turned informers had been a principal source of information throughout the early cold war, and Budenz had been especially important among media watchdogs ever since his *American Legion* article on Communist infiltration of radio. But for those more concerned about Red-baiting than Red infiltration, witnesses like Budenz had always been suspect. Bolan maintained that the Budenz excerpt provided "substantial support" for statements made in the Aware newsletter. Judge Geller's ruling suggested which side of the larger issue he was inclined to favor. Not only did he declare that the excerpt failed to establish definitively in any way that the Independent Citizens Committee was a Communist front, he went a step further by saying that Budenz "doesn't even say that this is a communist front. He says 'was worked out' in the office."[3] In taking this position, Geller seemed to be aligning himself with those who were ready to give such groups the benefit of the doubt, no matter what the basis of the charge might be, as if, in this particular case, it were unreasonable to assume that meetings held at the *Daily Worker* would have been devoted to Communist causes.

Once Bolan finished with his witness, Faulk himself would have to concede one thing: even though Milton's testimony might have been restricted in some ways, his unassuming, sincere manner might have had some value in burnishing the defendants' image. Still, Faulk's supporters had good reason to believe that cross-examination would leave little of that repaired image intact. Nizer would not disappoint them.

Nizer's steady onslaught of barbed questions stung early and often. He succeeded in getting Milton to admit that he knew News Supplement Number 16 might affect Faulk's employment and compelled him to back away from an earlier statement that the newsletter was distributed solely to the news media, forcing him to acknowledge that it also went to sponsors as well as executives at networks and advertising agencies. In an especially combative exchange while dealing with Milton's advice that Everett Sloane contact Hartnett, Nizer said, "And, of course, you knew that if he went to Mr. Hartnett, Mr. Hartnett would charge him for his services, didn't you?" "I did not," Milton answered. Nizer continued to press him on this point, demanding that Milton acknowledge that Hartnett "charged for his services in talking to artists who wanted to clear themselves," but Milton insisted he had "no knowledge that he charged individuals to talk to them." Nizer then brought the confrontation to a head by asking, "Didn't you know that he wanted $200 from Miss Kim Hunter, didn't you hear of that?" When Milton grudgingly admitted that he recalled hearing about this incident, Nizer moved on, satisfied that he had scored his point.[4] He never actually offered evidence that Hartnett had intended to charge Sloane a fee, or, for that matter, that he had ever requested a fee from anyone other than Hunter; but he succeeded in conveying the impression that this was a common practice for Hartnett, even if the exchange with Milton never really rose above the level of speculation.

During almost three days of relentless questioning, Milton continued to backtrack, his credibility unraveled not only by Nizer's incisive cross-examination but by his own penchant for equivocating whenever confronted with inconvenient facts. Often he was cornered into conceding merely minor details. Occasionally, though, his admissions touched upon more critical matters concerning choices he made while preparing the allegations against Faulk and the Middle of the Road candidates. Nizer focused, in particular, on the section of News Supplement Number 16 which stated that the anti-Aware AFTRA ticket "was first reported by the Daily Worker," implying that Faulk and his fellow candidates were the darlings of the Communist press. Milton told the court that, at the time he prepared the newsletter, he had not known that the mainstream press had also given the Middle of the Roaders favorable coverage. Nizer then confronted him with this portion of his pre-trial deposition:

Question: Didn't you know, Mr. Milton, that there had been comments
about the Middle-of-the-Road slate in those conservative, respectable
New York papers, namely, the *New York Times* and the *Herald Tribune?*
Answer: Yes.

Milton admitted that this earlier answer had been correct but not without
a lame attempt to minimize the glaring discrepancy by saying he had mis-
understood Nizer's questions. He then faced further embarrassment when
Nizer read aloud another comment from his deposition regarding Aware's
decision to exclude mainstream references to the Middle of the Road
ticket. "I don't think fairness enters into it," he had said. "We were talking
about connections with communism or communist groups."[5]

Harvey Matusow, whose presence in this lawsuit continued to be felt,
both as a subject for testimony and as an aid to the plaintiff, played a part
in yet another of Milton's gaffes. In addition to contributing to Milton's
unraveling, the episode also supplied a clue to a backstage mystery of
the case. In now typical fashion, Milton made a feeble attempt to deny
that he had once asked Matusow, the convicted perjurer, for information
that could be used against leftist broadcast writers, insisting that he had
engaged only in "social conversations" with the man. This time he was
tripped up when Nizer produced a letter he had written to Matusow asking for exactly that sort of information, along with the envelope that he
himself had addressed.[6] The letter and envelope could only have come
from one source, lending credence to the theory that it had been Matusow who had provided Faulk's legal team with documents immediately
before the trial.

The dramatic high point of Milton's testimony, which would attract
the most pointed press attention, occurred on June 5 when Nizer brought
up the subject of a TV writer named Sheldon Stark. Stark had lost his job
with *Treasury Men in Action* in 1952 after being labeled pro-Communist
in a newsletter that Milton had written for We the Undersigned. Nizer
now got Milton to admit that he had been hired as a writer for the same
show soon after Stark's dismissal. The next day's news reports of the trial
seized upon the sordid scenario that Milton had pressured a man out of
his job so that he could replace him. Adding a possible conspiratorial layer

to the story was the fact that *Treasury Men in Action* had been sponsored by Borden, a Hartnett client. On redirect examination, Bolan was able to repair some of the damage by eliciting from Milton testimony that he had not applied for the *Treasury Men* job but had instead been hired by a friend who was producing the show at the time, and even then had written only one episode. But despite these qualifiers to the story, Bolan failed to dislodge the impression of venal machinations. A letter written by Stark, and published by the *New York Times* ten days after Milton's testimony on this point, helped reinforce this perception while also exemplifying a new, growing consensus about the blacklist. "Those were hysterical times," Stark wrote. "In the three years it took me to catch up with and refute Mr. Milton's false charge I suffered monetary and emotional damage from which, while not as great as that suffered by many, many others, I still bear scars."[7]

Not all of Nizer's cross-examination left Milton in shambles. In one instance, it revealed, at least in retrospect, a certain naiveté that was common among anti-blacklist partisans. When attacking Milton's characterization of People's Songs as a Communist front, Nizer cited the names of some of those people who had sent greetings to the organization on its second anniversary, as Faulk was alleged to have done. Among the names intended to dispel the pro-Communist charge against the group were Burl Ives, Oscar Hammerstein, Leonard Bernstein, and Aaron Copland. Nizer's choice of names in at least two cases was curious. Anti-Communists had long suspected that Copland had once been closely associated with the Communist movement, something that Nizer apparently chose not to believe; but later scholarship would reveal this to be true, even if Copland had not been a CPUSA member. As for Bernstein, while not a party-liner he had displayed at least questionable judgment in some of the activities he patronized, such as the Waldorf Peace Conference and a tribute to composer Hanns Eisler, who would later take refuge in East Germany where he would write that Soviet satellite's national anthem.[8]

While interludes like these might shed some light on how the blacklist debate was evolving at the time, the testimony continued to be dominated by Milton's lapses and his inability to talk his way around embarrassing comments from the past. Columnist Kempton expressed what must have been a common observation when he noted that Milton's testimony was marked not so much by villainy as shabbiness. Kempton had expected the Faulk lawsuit "to be a pleasant spectacle; yet it is oddly sad and pathetic." Milton himself "was here looking far lonelier and more defeated than any of his victims in their darkest time."[9]

🎵 Toward the close of Milton's testimony, one of the defense's best hopes rose to the surface, but only briefly and with little effect on the trial.

In answer to a subpoena from Bolan, Donald Appell, the HUAC investigator, appeared in court on June 5. Bolan had hoped that Appell would testify about his questioning of Faulk in the spring of 1955 and his subsequent conversation with Hartnett about the entertainer's alleged admissions. Presenting this evidence, Bolan maintained, would show that Hartnett had acted without malice, that he had made his charges against Faulk based partly on information from Appell that he believed to be accurate. Judge Geller agreed to accommodate Appell by allowing him to take the stand out of turn in the middle of Milton's testimony, but Appell would answer, in all, only four questions. The first three merely established his identity and the fact that he had been subpoenaed. The fourth concerned his interview of Faulk, at which point he turned to the judge. "Your Honor, as an employee of the House of Representatives, I appear before this Court today under the authority of House Resolution 650 which, with the Court's permission, I would like to read to the Court."

The resolution, passed two weeks earlier, authorized Appell to appear at the trial but ordered him to "respectfully decline to testify concerning any and all matters that may be based on knowledge acquired by him in his official capacity, either by reason of documents and papers appearing in the files of the said Committee on Un-American Activities, including any minutes or transcripts of executive sessions or any evidence of witnesses thereto, or by virtue of conversations or communications with any person or persons, as such testimony is within the privilege of the House of Representatives." Appell, forbidden to testify about the Faulk interview, was then dismissed.[10]

We will never know what impact, if any, Appell would have had on the trial if he had been allowed to testify. If he had described the statements that Faulk had made to him — allegedly admitting that Hally Wood had influenced him into becoming involved in Communist-front activities — he might have led the jury to believe that Hartnett had been reasonable in portraying Faulk the way he did. That was certainly Bolan's contention. Of course, in order to make this sort of impression on the jury, Appell would have had to stand up to Nizer's cross-examination. Nizer's thoughts on Appell's allegations are not known—he did not discuss his strategy for dealing with the investigator in his memoir of the trial. But George Berger, who assisted Nizer in the case, was privy to the law firm's stance on the HUAC interview, based upon what he had been told by Paul Martinson, another lawyer on Nizer's team. "When I came to the firm, Martinson had told me there was such a purported interview but that Appell's notes of that interview were false."[11]

Whatever would have been the outcome of the investigator's testimony once Nizer was done with him, the basic premise of Appell's allegations is not so easily dismissed when squared with another source not publicly available at the time. If Appell had been free to testify, the truth or falsity of his charges would have come down to an inconclusive clash of his word against Faulk's. But the assertion that Faulk had become involved in front activities through his first wife is consistent in certain ways with the report of his May 19, 1953, interview with the FBI. He had told the Bureau at that time, two years before the Appell interview, that in Texas during the early 1940s he had been "in contact" with people who were involved in the People's Educational and Press Association, an alleged Communist front, though his only contact with them "had been at social affairs." He had "disapproved" of his first wife's associations with these people, who had "ideas which favored Russia" and whose morals were "questionable," but had "put up with it because he hoped their marriage could be saved."[12] Even if one assumes that Appell interpreted Faulk's statements to him as severely as possible in order to demonize a tangential relationship with Communist fronters, the basic thrust of the contention jibes with the earlier, more benign version of events found in the FBI report. Without Appell's testimony in answer to Faulk's characterization of the interview, however, the jury was deprived of a chance to assess opposing views in a central issue of the blacklist years, the question of whether a person's association with front groups should be seen as a partnership with Communists, as regrettable naiveté, or as an act of progressive solidarity.

⌥ By June 6 the trial had been going on long enough to bridge a change of seasons. When the confrontation began, New York City had been in the midst of spring. Now it was approaching summer, and yet, a month and a half into the proceedings, the most eagerly awaited act was only about to begin. On that afternoon, Vincent Hartnett finally took the stand. His counsel anticipated that his precise and professional manner would convey a sense of integrity. Opposing counsel looked forward to the opportunity of savaging the record of the man they considered the linchpin in the alleged conspiracy.

Hartnett's introductory comments on his education, war service, and early career took up the remaining hours of the court session that day and continued into the morning of the next. In retracing the path of his life and work, Hartnett was occasionally blocked by Judge Geller's rulings. He was not allowed to elaborate on his expertise in the field of Communist infiltration of broadcasting or to assert that his knowledge was considerable enough for the FBI to request information from him. He did have the chance, however, to rebut one of the most serious allegations against him by denying categorically that he had ever charged a fee for clearing an actor, writer, or producer. Bolan's questioning also allowed him to argue that he had been fair-minded in his investigations. He pointed out that he had, after all, recommended on occasion that certain suspect performers "be given a break" on the basis of "positive favorable information."[13] Throughout, Hartnett's testimony fostered the impression of an orderly mind devoted to a righteous cause, though at the same time he also conveyed a cold, prim formality. In stark contrast to Faulk's easygoing charm, his persona on the stand was not likely to win the hearts of many jurors.

Later that afternoon, as Hartnett cited the sources for his allegations against Faulk, Nizer interrupted Bolan's questioning to challenge his characterization of one of the events that had been linked to his client. Bolan had just produced a brochure entitled "Call to American Continental Congress for Peace," which included the name "John H. Faulk" as one of the event's sponsors, and he quoted from a HUAC report that described the conference as "another phase in the Communist world peace movement aimed at consolidating anti-American forces throughout the Western Hemisphere." Nizer interjected here to read aloud a portion of the brochure's foreword to get across the innocuous nature of the event: "We know the democratic and peace-loving traditions of our continent, and we are sure that our voices will be heard. Peace is the road to liberty and greatness for the Americas." To underscore his point, Nizer then read the names of some of the sponsors, which included a number of clergy as well as the celebrated author Thomas Mann, evidence that the conference had been endorsed by reasonable and respectable people. Once more the divergent views of the front phenomenon were cast in sharp relief when Bolan countered by reading the names of others on the list. One of them was John Abt, a leftist labor lawyer who had been identified by Whittaker Chambers as a Soviet agent (Venona decryptions would later confirm that he had been part of the Communist underground in Washington, D.C.). Another sponsor, historian Herbert Aptheker, was a CPUSA member and an openly pro-Soviet propagandist who, while claiming to be a peace activist, had publicly rationalized North Korea's invasion of South Korea and the Soviet suppression of the Hungarian revolt.[14]

Hartnett's testimony on the sources for News Supplement Number 16 continued into the next day, Friday, June 8, and on into the afternoon before Bolan announced he had no further questions. It was around 3:30 when Nizer rose to begin his cross-examination. While Hartnett braced himself, "Word went out from spectators to friends outside," Faulk later wrote, "that Nizer was about to start his cross-examination."[15]

Nizer's attack initially concentrated, once again, on the claim made in News Supplement Number 16 that the *Daily Worker* had been the first to report on the Middle of the Road ticket. Soon he succeeded in wringing his first admission from Hartnett, that a *Variety* report had in fact preceded the *Daily Worker* piece and that the newsletter had been inaccurate on this point. Hartnett then faced another embarrassment when Nizer produced a letter the Red hunter had written to Young & Rubicam, in which he had claimed that Faulk had "a significant Communist front record," a piece of evidence introduced immediately after Hartnett had finished denying that he had ever volunteered information on the performer.[16] The end of the day's session might have brought him a temporary respite as the court adjourned for the weekend, but he knew that he faced a long and arduous road ahead.

The session on Monday began with a conference in the judge's robing room in which Bolan learned that he might have another reason for being uneasy other than the prospect of an extensive cross-examination. Under discussion was the admissibility of documents to establish a form of defense known as reliance, which could limit the amount of damages awarded to Faulk should the jury find in his favor. This particular bout of legalistic wrangling eventually turned to the charge that Faulk had attended an event at the Jefferson School of Social Science. The information for this charge had come, Hartnett said, from Jack Wren, the advertising clearance officer and former associate of the *Counterattack* publishers; but now Nizer disputed that Wren had ever passed along this tip and added that "if necessary, I will have him here in rebuttal."[17] If true, this desertion from the ranks of one of the Red hunters' most consistent allies could seriously undermine Hartnett's claim that he had acted in good faith when formulating the allegations against Faulk. No matter how steadfast Hartnett was in sticking to his story, a denial from Wren would raise doubt. Troubling as this development was, though, Bolan would have to put off dealing with the problem. More pressing concerns faced him and his client when Hartnett resumed his place on the witness stand.

At times Hartnett was able to hold his own against the withering interrogation. When Nizer suggested, for instance, that the defendant should have regarded Faulk's army service as evidence of patriotic loyalty, Hartnett answered, quite rightly, that military service during those years did not necessarily certify a devotion to America, explaining that "many thousands of Communist Party members served in the Army, or in our armed services, rather, once the USSR became our ally in World War II." His sparring with Nizer, on the other hand, over the issue of Harvey Matusow, the great embarrassment to the anti-Communist cause, did not go as well. Nizer referred to one of Hartnett's file cards that cited Matusow's HUAC testimony as a source and asked if he had ever used any of Matusow's statements in reports to his clients. Hartnett answered that he did not recall doing so, but he was then confronted with an excerpt from his examination before trial in which he admitted using Matusow's congressional committee testimony. Later Hartnett adjusted his defense, trying to draw a distinction between Matusow's act of perjury and his earlier statements. He maintained that the perjurer's conviction for lying under oath "wouldn't necessarily vitiate the prior testimony." Once more, he was upended by his earlier deposition:

> Nizer: Wouldn't you say now that that testimony is certainly very unreliable and under a cloud as to accuracy?
> Hartnett: It is definitely under a cloud.[18]

From there Nizer moved from one topic to another, not necessarily following a chronological or logical pattern, as part of his strategy to keep

Hartnett off balance. Soon he latched onto the issue of fronts. Earlier, when dealing with the American Continental Congress for Peace, he had not succeeded in definitively refuting the Communist-front argument made by anti-Communist groups like Aware, but now he was able to expose a defect in Hartnett's thinking. Making the point that these groups cast a wide net in recruiting supporters, Nizer observed that no less an American icon than Dwight Eisenhower had once been mentioned in HUAC testimony because he had once sent greetings to the National Council of American-Soviet Friendship. He then referred to Hartnett's pre-trial examination, when Nizer had asked if such a listing in the HUAC index would "indicate a doubt about" Eisenhower's Americanism, to which Hartnett had replied it would not. "If he were a performer on radio and television," Nizer had continued during the deposition, "you would list those citations nevertheless, wouldn't you?" "Yes," Hartnett had replied, revealing just how far his methods could take him in his single-minded pursuit of anyone associated with front organizations.[19]

Hartnett quite literally sweated through the day-long grilling as the temperature rose to nearly ninety degrees by mid-afternoon. Finally Judge Geller dismissed the court early, at four o'clock, to provide some relief from the muggy, sweltering air in the un-air-conditioned courtroom. Hartnett's relief lasted only until the next morning when he returned to the stand for the next stage in Nizer's verbal offensive. Much of this day Nizer devoted to dissecting Hartnett's attitudes toward AFTRA, challenging him at one point that Aware "had no business in the affairs of AFTRA at all." To this he got the argument from Hartnett that, as far as the issue of communism was concerned, "any citizens group would have some interest, depending upon its knowledge. Knowledge develops responsibility." While this exchange might have ended in a standoff, Nizer succeeded in wreaking considerable damage when he later returned to the subject of Hartnett's 1955 letter to Young & Rubicam. The letter not only charged Faulk with having "a significant Communist front record" but also suggested that, within the Middle of the Road slate, he was "'using' the liberals." Following up, Nizer demanded, "So you knew when you wrote this that this would have an effect upon the Young & Rubicam agency of hesitating, being reluctant, thinking twice, about hiring John Henry Faulk? You knew that, didn't you, when you wrote it?" After Bolan objected and was overruled, Hartnett answered, "No, I don't believe it even entered my mind." Nizer responded with withering sarcasm: "When you say about an artist who is about to appear on the air that he has a serious record, it never enters your mind that the person who reads that might believe it?" The transcript indicates that there was an outburst of some kind from the audience after this, likely an outburst of laughter. A similar response might have come from the jurors.[20]

Nizer and Hartnett had essentially the same exchange when discussing a similar letter Hartnett had written to the Kudner Agency, except that this time Nizer made a more aggressive effort to corner his opponent. After Hartnett refused once again to acknowledge that his purpose had been to discourage Faulk's employment, Nizer asked if it wasn't Aware's goal to keep pro-Communists off the air. Hartnett agreed that it was. Referring back to the Kudner letter, Nizer then countered that it did "enter your mind that you were fulfilling the avowed purpose of Aware, Inc.?" Hartnett backed off once more. "I think that would really be stretching to say I had that specific thought in my mind as I wrote this," he said.[21] Like the *Counterattack* publishers in the earliest years of the blacklist, Hartnett was taking an ambivalent stance toward the broadcast purge, readily endorsing the blacklist in principle, even if he avoided using that term, but hedging when discussing the phenomenon in practice. In other, less demanding venues, this position might have passed without serious challenge. Each time he reiterated this attitude in court, though, it became less and less credible.

That afternoon Nizer got around to the topic that Hartnett must have known was coming at some point—his admission during his 1958 pre-trial testimony that he had once been "sold a barrel of false information" by an anonymous informant. Determined to connect this admission to Aware's original allegations against Faulk, Nizer stated, "Your information with respect to Exhibit 41 [News Supplement Number 16] came at least partly from an anonymous source that you now designate as having misled you in 1958."

"Came in no manner, shape, or form whatever from an anonymous informant," Hartnett countered, adding later that he received the false information at least six months after the newsletter had been published.[22]

Nizer continued to press the point, maintaining that Hartnett's admission during the deposition had come in response to a question about the Aware newsletter. To substantiate his argument, he read aloud the original question; but nowhere does it in fact refer to the news supplement. Although the confrontation here resulted essentially in a draw, Nizer made more headway a few minutes later in bringing up Hartnett's 1958 agreement—later rescinded—to send letters to broadcasters on Faulk's behalf. Excerpts from the examination before trial made it clear that, in 1958 at least, Hartnett did not regard Faulk's political activities as intentionally pro-Communist and felt that the performer should not remain unemployed on the basis of those allegations. Nizer's purpose in reading these segments aloud was, once more, to connect the "barrel of false information" to the newsletter charges, something that the deposition transcript failed to establish. What the deposition testimony did clarify, however, was that Hartnett's 1958 statements effectively repudiated his earlier actions when he had prejudiced ad agencies against Faulk by asserting that he had a Communist-front record.[23]

Although constantly on the defensive, Hartnett did not lose his composure—"he held up pretty well," Faulk noted—even if at times the strain of maintaining his outward calm began to show. What he also did not lose was his ability to keep his mind trained on the discipline that had dominated his life for almost fifteen years. As always he was watchful, on the alert for developments he considered vital to the areas of American life he monitored. He kept with him a pen and pink cards, and during spare moments during his testimony he kept track of who entered the courtroom—particularly those in broadcasting who had always raised his suspicions—and noted them on his cards.[24]

The presence of mind that he commanded himself to maintain—and that had already been tested—would receive an even greater challenge the next day, June 13, an especially brutal day of questioning. During one brief stretch, Nizer tripped him up twice by introducing statements from his pre-trial examination contradicting his current testimony that the Syracuse group had made little or no use of his information in their efforts to ban certain entertainers from the airwaves.[25] By this time the discrepancies between Hartnett's current testimony and his pre-trial deposition had become a regular source of embarrassment for him. Repeatedly it became clear that he had been more willing a few years earlier to own up to his role in the blacklist and more likely now to claim he could not recall the details of his involvement. One obvious explanation is that it was more important in 1962 to minimize his part in the process, now that the case had come to trial; but that does not explain his earlier candor when he surely must have known that his statements would be used by his opponents as they saw fit. His actions in the late 1950s indicate that Hartnett had, to some extent, been reevaluating his profession, as could be seen in his pretrial willingness to write a letter on Faulk's behalf. Perhaps in the intervening years he had not only regained his determination to stay the course but had also recast and further justified his activities in his own mind.

With or without the examination before trial as a cudgel in his cross-examination, Nizer continued to pummel Hartnett on his career as an anti-Communist watchdog. His interrogation revealed that Hartnett had sent Johnson a report on writer Sheldon Stark, placing the consultant in the process that led to Stark's dismissal from *Treasury Men in Action*, to be followed in turn by the hiring of Milton for the same show. He brought out more details of Hartnett's reports on the political background of juvenile actors. He extracted an admission that Hartnett had frequently exchanged information with the New York Police Department on broadcast talent, and in one instance had informed the police that the Middle of the Road group was "helping communism." Perhaps most devastating of all, Nizer delved into the story of the defendant's article for the *American Legion Magazine* entitled "They're Moving In on TV." He established for the jury that, in an early draft, Hartnett had criticized Borden for allowing Communist fronters on its programs, then, in the article's final form, praised the company—after Hartnett had been hired as the sponsor's talent consultant. Hartnett attempted to minimize this damage by explaining that he had praised Borden for instituting a comprehensive new policy, not just for hiring him.[26] In the minds of the jurors, his explanation paled in comparison to the facts Nizer laid out.

As bad as the substance of his testimony was for Hartnett, his demeanor on the stand exacerbated the damage to his case. Bolan considered his client's answers to be methodical and precise but his testimony to be more problematic than Milton's, which had also been subject to a grueling cross-examination. While Milton was frequently tripped up, he had, Bolan said, "such a pleasant personality I think he went over much better than Hartnett, who was sort of a grim and tight-lipped kind of a guy. You couldn't faze Milton, he'd just shrug it off and smile."[27]

Beginning the following morning, the fifth day of cross-examination, Nizer removed any remaining doubt about the extent of cooperation between Hartnett and Johnson. He outlined, through a combination of documents and questioning, a series of exchanges between the two concerning whether such actors as Win Stracke and Edward G. Robinson belonged on the air. When Nizer asked if actor-director Charles Irving had been fired after Hartnett had supplied information to Johnson, Bolan objected. He argued that Irving had nothing to do with the Faulk case. Even if the purpose was to establish an alleged conspiracy, "the problem is that we can't go into showing what the man's record is." Judge Geller ruled against him. In one instance, while building his case that Hartnett and Johnson were in cahoots, Nizer might have provided one detail too many for his own good. He introduced an element in their relationship that actually spoke for Hartnett's integrity. Interrogating Hartnett about his efforts to assist Johnson in his campaign to pressure Kraft about their use of suspect performers, Nizer asked Hartnett about a letter he had written to the grocer regarding a possible conflict of interest. As Hartnett now explained, he had said in the letter that he did not "want the impression to be created" that Johnson "was drumming up business for me with the Kraft people." The revelation seemed to contradict Nizer's message that Hartnett was an opportunistic mercenary.[28]

On the issue of reliance, Hartnett was not allowed to cite HUAC reports as an authoritative source and had to depend instead on his faith in those people who had supplied information while at the same time defending his own thoroughness as a researcher. For the Independent Citizens Committee event, he explained that he had not actually seen the document that had listed Faulk as a performer but only a memo on the event sent by John Keenan. "In this instance," he asserted, "I felt I could rely on a man of Mr. Keenan's caliber." More difficult for him to explain away was his failure to mention that the event had been attended by such dignitaries as the American secretary of state and England's ambassador to the United States, and that the affair had been a salute to the UN. In discussing the event at Club 65, he was compelled to admit another lapse. He had not checked with any of the event's attendees to see if the advertised performer, "Jack Faulk," had indeed been John Henry Faulk.[29]

Two sources proved especially troublesome for Hartnett. Jack Wren, who, Hartnett said, had told him about the Jefferson School circular containing Faulk's name, now came under attack by Nizer. In a lengthy series of questions, he tried to get Hartnett to admit that he had once accused Wren of supplying inaccurate information to the columnist Fred Wolt-man. Although the results of his questioning were inconclusive, Nizer succeeded in raising at least the possibility that Wren was unreliable. Bolan surely must have been puzzled by this exchange. Earlier, in the judge's chambers, Nizer had intimated that he would call Wren as a re-buttal witness, but now he seemed to be undercutting that possibility by attacking the man's credibility. Not until the end of the trial would Bolan and Hartnett learn exactly what Nizer had in mind. Hartnett faced a greater problem in testifying about Faulk's association with People's Songs: Donald Appell's comments about his interview with Faulk had been crucial, in Hartnett's mind, in corroborating the performer's rela-tionship with the organization, but on the stand he was not allowed to mention the HUAC investigator. Judge Geller reasoned that it would be un-fair to bring up the subject of Appell because the congressional resolution forbidding him from testifying made it impossible for the plaintiff "to question him in rebuttal or reply on that score."[30]

Although Nizer was by no means done, Hartnett was given a tempo-rary reprieve the following day in order to accommodate the schedule of another defense witness. Nizer's earlier suspicion that CBS was cooperat-ing with the defense was now confirmed when Carl Ward took the stand. The former general manager for WCBS radio might have given Faulk a vote of confidence when the Aware allegations had first been published in 1956, but now he was in court to help Aware's case. Specifically Bolan asked him to support the defense's contention that it had been purely business, not Aware's charges, that had driven Faulk off the air. Toward that end, Ward told the court that he had informed Faulk as early as Feb-ruary 1955 that his ratings had begun to slip. Ultimately, though, Ward's testimony did little to help Aware's case, and Faulk's attorneys had little reason to worry once cross-examination was done. Nizer revealed that a second rating service had offered a very different view of Faulk's perform-ance and placed him high among his competitors, which in turn had prompted Ward to decide by May 1955 that Faulk was a valuable part of the WCBS lineup.[31] The defense had failed for now to establish that com-pelling business considerations had driven Faulk off the air, not the Aware allegations. (Still open to question was the culpability of WCBS in Faulk's blacklisting.) All the defense had really accomplished in Ward's day-long testimony was to buy more time for Hartnett as he regrouped for his next encounter with Nizer.

❧ Still unsettled was the state of Laurence Johnson's health. Related questions concerned his intentions about attending the trial or even, at times, his exact whereabouts as he continued to travel between Syracuse and his daughter's home in Rhode Island but never ventured into down-town Manhattan, where his reputation and mission of Americanism were under assault. On June 13, Bolan reported to the judge that his client had again been examined by his physician, Dr. David Jacobowsky of Syracuse, who reaffirmed his earlier diagnosis that Johnson should not be subjected to "mental or emotional strain" due to problems with his esophagus and a condition of "anxiety neurosis." Still skeptical of these conclusions, Nizer pointed out that Johnson was apparently "well enough to travel from Rhode Island to Syracuse and back again" and was likely to be well enough to give testimony, if only he were willing. Judge Geller attempted to resolve the dispute by pressuring Bolan to put Johnson's physician on the stand and ordering once more that Johnson also be examined by a doctor of the plaintiff's choice. Two doctors, each representing a side in the lawsuit, would be able to testify as to the grocer's condition, and each could be cross-examined by the opposition.[32] It would then be up to the jury to decide if Johnson were avoiding the courtroom out of illness or, as Nizer implied, moral cowardice.

❧ Following Carl Ward's testimony, a weekend came and went. That Monday there was yet another day away from the stand for Hartnett as the attorneys spent the entire session entering portions of the pre-trial exami-nation into the record. In all, Hartnett enjoyed a four-day release from tes-tifying before resuming his place in the witness chair on Tuesday, June 19, for what would be his final day of cross-examination. Nizer devoted a great deal of time that morning to a detailed inquiry into Hartnett's finances. As he piled on the minutiae of cash receipts, bank deposits, and tax returns, he ran the risk of burying the jurors in a mountain of tedium—Faulk him-self would later remark that he had trouble staying awake—but by late morning Nizer guaranteed their renewed interest by confronting Hartnett again with an uncomfortable reminder from his zealous past.

From questions about deposited checks, Nizer segued into fees that Hartnett had charged for his reports, then suddenly sprang a question that caught the courtroom off guard.

"Did you ever charge $5 for checking Santa Claus?"

"Checking who?" Judge Geller interjected, not quite sure he had heard right. To demonstrate that he was serious, Nizer produced a document listing broadcast personnel Hartnett had checked, followed by the fee charged for each individual. Immediately after "James Thurber, $20" came the entry "Santa Claus, no record, $5." Hartnett tried to dispel some of the utter absurdity of the entry by pointing out that this Santa Claus was not, as one might assume, the mythical yuletide figure but "a well-known model used by advertisers." As Nizer continued to pepper him with questions, the best explanation Hartnett could offer was that it was "possible that someone was trying to pull my leg on that."[33] In this instance his demeanor on the stand might have helped him: he certainly projected the sort of punctilious, humorless personality that someone might have been tempted to needle with a practical joke.

If there was any consolation here for Hartnett, it was that his cross-examination was nearing an end. He endured the next fifteen minutes of interrogation—and the oppressive heat as the temperature again climbed toward ninety degrees—and finally heard Nizer say, "That is all." After a short break he was delivered, on redirect, to the far friendlier attentions of his own attorney.

The most significant of Bolan's questions were not allowed as he invited Hartnett to tell the court that, after the Aware allegations had been published, he had received additional information on Faulk that confirmed his original assessment of the man's politics. He even tried once more to elicit testimony about the Appell interview, with predictable results. In one area, though, he was allowed some free rein.

Throughout his testimony Hartnett had continued to jot down the names of certain people who had entered the courtroom, especially those who had figured in the battles within AFTRA. The entrance of actor Elliott Sullivan had struck him as especially noteworthy. Over the years Hartnett had included him in *Red Channels* and had listed him in an Aware newsletter as one of those performers named as a Communist by witnesses before HUAC. In court he had noticed Sullivan taking a seat in the spectators section. "I kept taking notes on what was going on, I was a good researcher," he later recalled. "I wanted to keep a record of it. So I thought I saw Mrs. Faulk sitting next to Elliott Sullivan. I said, 'Wow, this [Sullivan] is a toughest-of-the-tough, real core commie.'"[34]

On redirect, Bolan brought up the subject of Hartnett's note-taking, because Nizer had briefly questioned him about it a week earlier, and now Bolan saw an opportunity for his client to state his reasons for the habit. He asked what names Hartnett had noted. "Elliott Sullivan, who was sitting next to Mrs. Faulk," Hartnett answered, "John Randolph, Alan Manson, Jack Gilford, were some of them."

When he heard this exchange, Nizer quickly made a note of his own. "I marked his answer on my pad with several penciled stars," he would later write, "to remind me that this was worthy of recross-examination in depth."[35]

Eager as he was to bring up the subject, Nizer did not introduce it when he first opened his recross. Instead he revisited Hartnett's finances, which had earlier done so much to cast a spell of boredom in the courtroom. This time, though, he used the ponderous interlude to lull Hartnett, his prey, before he decided to pounce. One moment he was asking about some obscure inconsistency between bank deposits and reported income, then he suddenly changed direction:

"You have said that when you were on the witness stand, when somebody came into the room you wrote down the name, and in answer to your counsel's question you gave the name of one person, Mr. Sullivan, and you added he sat right down next to Mrs. Faulk. Did you say that?"

"I did," Hartnett replied.

"Do you see Mrs. Faulk in the court now?"

"I believe she is the lady over here. I am not sure."

"Which lady?" Judge Geller asked.

Nizer turned to the woman Hartnett had indicated. "Will you stand up?" When she rose, he then asked her, "What is your name, please?"

The woman said, "Sofer," then spelled it, "S-O-F-E-R."[36]

Both the jurors and the spectators burst into laughter at this spectacular gaffe. Seizing the moment, Nizer bellowed to be heard above the uproar, "Is that the way you identify people when you also choose . . ." The final words of his accusation were drowned out by Bolan's objection, sustained by the judge. Casting about for some way to explain himself, Hart-nett only made matters worse by saying, "A certain lady was pointed out to me, was described by Mr. Sibley as being Mrs. Faulk." He was referring to John Sibley, the reporter who was covering the trial for the *New York Times*. (Later testimony would refute Hartnett's claim about Sibley's iden-tifying Lynne Faulk.)[37]

In his memoir, Nizer suggests that he did not know if Hartnett would be able to identify Faulk's wife but decided he should take "a gamble." George Berger offers a very different version. "We knew Mrs. Faulk was in Texas," he said. "So it was a very safe question to ask him." Whatever knowledge Nizer possessed at the time, the results of his tactic were clearly devastating for Hartnett. If anyone had missed what the jury would infer from the man's mistake, Murray Kempton spelled it out in his col-umn the next day. "Just how many reports must Vincent Hartnett have made to how many advertising agencies which contained the confident sentence that so-and-so was reported at such-and-such a meeting and that cost so-and-so a job?"[38]

☞ When Hartnett finally left the stand, Faulk and his lawyers had good reason to be confident, but one matter still concerned them. The defense had already called three witnesses from CBS—two business officers to provide information on the financial aspects of the *John Henry Faulk Show*, and Carl Ward to discuss the issue of ratings—and the possibility loomed that other executives were still to come. It was realized later that afternoon when Bolan called to the stand Faulk's immediate supervisor at WCBS, a man the entertainer had once considered a friend and ally.

From the very beginning of his testimony, Sam Slate's demeanor indi-cated how conflicted he was about speaking against Faulk; he was a man "torn between loyalty to his employer and to his dear friend," as Nizer de-scribed it. Repeatedly Judge Geller had to instruct him to raise his voice, but Slate continued to have difficulty making himself heard no matter how hard he tried, as if he were not quite willing to speak the words his situation required. Still, he was here just the same, putting forward the official CBS line, representing the interests of those broadcasters who had made the decision to dismiss Faulk not only from his time slot but from the WCBS lineup altogether. With difficulty Slate described a 1957 meeting with Faulk at which he explained the reasons for his firing. Faulk's ratings, he had told him, had been declining, and WCBS had decided to replace his program with a show hosted by singer Jim Lowe, who had just enjoyed success with a hit record entitled "Dream Doll." The Aware charges had nothing to do with it.[39]

Bringing Slate to the witness stand might have been a coup of sorts for the defense, but his testimony, like Ward's, did little to help Aware's case. Even if his tormented manner had not betrayed him, many of his words would—once they were dragged out of him by Nizer. Under cross-examination Slate was compelled to describe his initial meetings with Faulk after the Aware charges had been published, and went on to imply that the combination of the newsletter and Johnson's efforts might have taken a toll on some of the show's sponsors. Considering the ratings issue in greater detail, he conceded that Faulk's ratings had actually been relatively good, that they had been better between 1955 and 1957 than the station's afternoon ratings overall.[40] In the end, Slate unwittingly accomplished what he might have secretly wished to do: he had helped his old friend more than his current employer.

With, at best, negligible results from Slate's testimony, Bolan finished with the CBS executive on June 20 and brought the defense to its conclusion the next day. There was little left to examine in the case for and against Hartnett and Aware. The case of Laurence Johnson was another matter. Still unresolved was his puzzling absence from the trial and its implications for the jury once they began to deliberate. The issue would come down to, as Faulk would call it, a "duel of doctors."

Before each side brought its physician to the stand, Judge Geller addressed the jury to outline exactly what was at stake in their appraisal of the doctors' testimony. "The rule of law," he said, "is that if a party whose failure to appear at the trial is not proved to be based on a valid legal excuse, does not testify at the trial, the jury is to be instructed that they may be allowed to draw the strongest inference against him which the opposing evidence in the record permits; which means that they have a right to infer that he would not have contradicted proof offered by the plaintiff's witnesses and exhibits concerning matters in which he was stated to have been involved or that he would not have corroborated or supported proof offered by defendants."[41]

Wardner D. Ayer, speaking for the defense, was a small-city doctor from Syracuse, practicing internal medicine with a specialty in neurology.

The plaintiff's expert, Jerome A. Marks, was a specialist in gastroenterology with offices on Manhattan's East Side. On Johnson's basic condition the two doctors agreed: he suffered from a constriction of the esophagus, which could make it difficult to swallow and could lead to regurgitating and vomiting, though the two doctors differed on how to label the disorder. Faulk's witness, Marks, referred to it as achalasia of the esophagus, while Ayer, who thought this a "fussy term," preferred the more traditional name of cardiospasm. The Syracuse doctor also tended to emphasize psychological factors that might have exacerbated the ailment, reporting Johnson's statement that he was plagued by "great nervousness and worry and fatigue." Ayer concluded that drugs would not help Johnson and that testifying in court would endanger his health. Marks, a believer in new drugs to treat the condition, was willing to say "with reasonable certainty that this man would be able to come into court and testify for any reasonable length of time."[42]

The contrasting views of two reputable doctors might seem inconclusive to some, leaving them still undecided as to Johnson's reason for staying away from court throughout the trial. Faulk, however, thought the jurors were inclined to believe Nizer's physician, a prominent specialist in the field relating specifically to Johnson's complaint and more likely to embrace the latest in medical thinking. The conclusion to be drawn from this perspective was expressed by Kempton's pronouncement the next day. He had a new moniker for the man previously known as the grocer from Syracuse. He now dubbed him "Sick Call Larry."[43]

In the final two days of the trial, Faulk's team exercised its prerogative of calling rebuttal witnesses to dispute certain points raised by the defense. One witness provoked outrage among the defendants and presented a startling revisionist view of recent history. On the morning of June 22, Nizer called Jack Wren to testify on Faulk's behalf.

The clearance officer for BBD&O, who now described himself as an "account executive," took the stand for the purpose of answering a single question. Nizer wanted to know if he had ever told Hartnett about Faulk's advertised appearance at an event called Spotlight on Wallace held at the Jefferson School in 1948. "Absolutely not, sir," Wren replied, a complete contradiction of Hartnett's testimony.[44]

Hartnett and Bolan required a short recess to devise some way to discredit Wren's rebuttal. Hartnett told his counsel not only about the conversation he had had with Wren on this subject but also his frequent exchanges of information with the advertising executive over the years, exchanges often documented by correspondence. After more than ten minutes, Bolan was ready to take on the man he considered a turncoat to his client's cause.

He began by trying to show that Wren had essentially been a compatriot of Hartnett's, an ally in the same business of monitoring procommunism in broadcasting. His first question, though, did not elicit the sort of answer he would have wanted the jury to hear. Asked about his duties at BBD&O, Wren said, "Well, my duties, among other things, was to protect our clients against the false charges made that we loaded our shows with Communists, by Vincent Hartnett, who made these charges against us, who wrote poison pen letters behind our backs to our clients, wrote to our officers accusing us of loading our shows with Communists." Bolan pressed on. "Were you known as a security officer?" Wren denied this, but Bolan was not about to let it go at that. Even if he were not relying on Hartnett's word, he could have cited John Cogley's *Report on Blacklisting*, which identified Wren as both a security officer and the most prominent executive of this kind in advertising. Bolan later asked again if Wren was known by this title. "It is not true," Wren answered. "This is a term invented—I never had this title, and I think it was used by John Cogley of the Fund for the Republic. It is a title Mr. Hartnett adores."[45]

By saying this, Wren was painting Hartnett as someone indulging in a cloak-and-dagger fantasy about the business of rooting out Reds in radio and TV. But what he failed to explain was why a liberal blacklist opponent like Cogley, who presumably would have been sympathetic to an advertising executive fending off blacklisters, would have also used the term. Aware advocates were probably not the only ones who found Wren's statements disingenuous. Some anti-blacklist activists must have also been incredulous when they heard him portray himself as a principled bulwark of resistance against the blacklist. Even though they would not have known about Wren's early career as a confidential anti-Communist informant for the FBI or as a researcher for the *Red Channels* publishers during their early days at *Plain Talk*, neither fact would have surprised them, based upon Wren's reputation as a demanding and intrusive clearance officer, a man whom comedian Henry Morgan would describe as the "worst part" of the blacklist process.

Despite any doubts that informed observers might have had, Bolan failed to get Wren to budge in his denial and was unable to convey to the jury the position the advertising executive held in the broadcast industry. He was more successful in challenging Wren's characterization of his relationship with Hartnett.

Early on, the clearance officer denied he had ever consulted with Hartnett in 1955. A few moments later he was willing to concede it was "entirely possible" he sent some notes to him in the early 1950s but only when, as he now reiterated his current line, "Mr. Hartnett was engineering picket lines around our clients' shows, and I had to treat with him as a merchant treats with a racketeer." But he soon contradicted himself by saying he had never sent notes to Hartnett before February 1956. The introduction of several notes sent by Wren to Hartnett then suggested that the correspondence had been more significant, and less one-sided, than Wren now maintained.[46]

When asked if he had ever passed along information on performers' "pro-Communist affiliations," he said, "I don't believe I have given him any such information, to the best of my recollection." He was not able to stand by this statement. Bolan repeated his question later, and Wren gave the same answer but then quickly added that it was "entirely possible" he had supplied information. His explanation, once again, was that he had been reacting to pressure from Hartnett,[47] though by now this sounded self-serving, especially to those familiar with Wren's career as an active anti-Communist.

Bolan hinted at what might have been the real reason for Wren's turning on Hartnett when he asked, "Did you have some personal disagreement with Mr. Hartnett at some time?" "Yes, sir," Wren answered. Many years later Hartnett would relate a story that might explain the rift, as well as shed some light on his compulsion to collect and pass along derogatory information, no matter how ill advised. Someone had once asked him about Wren's reliability, Hartnett said, and he had replied that he considered Wren "an excellent informant." But he had also felt compelled to mention that it had come to his attention that a woman with the same name as Wren's wife "had once signed a CP nominating petition." Learning of this, Wren was furious, Hartnett continued, and "called me, admitted that he and his wife had lived at the address in question, and said testily that he had told his wife never to sign anything."[48] None of this information, though, was presented to the jury.

With this last bit of courtroom confrontation, testimony came to an end that day, Friday, June 22, more than eight weeks after the attorneys had first made their opening statements. The end finally in sight, counsel for both sides prepared for their summations that would begin the following Tuesday.

⟜ Earlier in the week, on Wednesday, June 20, Laurence Johnson had traveled to Manhattan to be examined by Dr. Marks, a trip that constituted his first active participation in the trial proceedings that were putting both his reputation and his fortune at risk. From there he returned to his daughter Eleanor's home in Cranston, Rhode Island, and by Sunday was on the road once more, driving westward along Interstate 95 toward New York State. For some reason, as his route took him into the Bronx that afternoon, he turned off the New England Thruway at Exit 5 and checked into a room at the Town and Country Motor Lodge. One family member believed he was merely making a one-night stopover before continuing the rest of his trip home to Syracuse—though the route is implausible. Unspecified associates of Johnson's, according to a later report, would claim that he made this stop so that he could finally "attend the last days of the trial."[49] If he had in fact intended to leave for Syracuse the next day, he failed to do so. If he had planned on making the trip downtown to the State Supreme Court building, something prevented him from leaving his room.

The outer-borough motel where Johnson now stayed was a far cry from the elegant midtown hotels that had once been his temporary Manhattan headquarters as he patrolled ad agencies and networks some ten years earlier. Similarly, his current physical and mental state was a far cry from his robust condition in those days. Tormented as he was by anxiety, he must have brooded and agonized over the course the trial was taking. And the more he fretted, the more likely his spasmodic esophagus would act up. In this room in the Bronx, cut off from both home and family, he might naturally have switched on the television to find some way to pass the time, perhaps take his mind off his troubles. It's tempting to speculate upon the effect this choice would have had on him.

The airwaves had been, after all, the focus of his concerns about protecting Americanism, and the programs broadcast that evening were just as likely to stir up his anxieties as to settle them. One choice would have been the latest installment of *Open Mind*, a program that would surely have upset the former grocer, hosted as it was by David Susskind, who had testified at the trial against those practices instigated by Johnson and his allies. Trying another option, Johnson might have followed the pattern of so many Americans in those days and tuned in to the *Ed Sullivan Show*. There, however, he would have stumbled upon another reminder, the guest appearance of singer Kate Smith, who at one time had infuriated the grocer because she had featured a leftist lithographer on one of her programs. He would have had no better luck if he watched the *TV Guide* awards show that aired that night, a program featuring Judy Holliday, the actress he had once agitated against but who was now free, despite his past efforts, to appear on-screen in millions of American homes.

We know little about what Johnson did the next day, when he neither left for his long ride to Syracuse nor set out to attend his trial just fifteen miles away. We know he was seen by motel personnel that Monday, but other than that, we can only conjecture that he must have again confined himself to his room. He might have taken comfort in the movie shown on a local station that afternoon, a film called *Woman on Pier* 13, originally titled *I Married a Communist*, a lurid exposé of Communist infiltration of the waterfront unions, released in 1950 when he had just begun to envision his great crusade. As he had been wont to do when watching *I Led 3 Lives*, he would have appreciated the movie's sense of alarm at an insidious, subversive menace, provided of course he was well enough by that time to direct his mind toward the ills he saw plaguing his country rather than his own nagging physical symptoms.

The next day, Tuesday, when the trial's summations began, he failed once again to leave the motel. No one saw him there the entire day.

℟ Bolan began his summation by making a concession designed to wring advantage out of disadvantage. "I hope," he told the jury, "that your decision will not be influenced in any way by what you consider to be the competence of the respective attorneys. This is not a contest of attorneys. If it were, of course, my clients, the defendants, would be seriously hampered because I am no match for the many years of experience, the skill, and eloquence of Mr. Nizer." He implored them instead to consider only the facts. The exceptional length of the trial, he contended, was something the jury should also consider in the defendants' favor. The trial had lasted so long, he said, "because the plaintiff at the outset knew he was not going to be able to prove his case," and it was for this reason that the plaintiff inflated its presentation by bringing in such witnesses as Tony Randall, who had nothing to offer to the charges that the defendants had run John Henry Faulk out of broadcasting.[50]

Bolan's main point was quite blunt: Faulk was a liar. He claimed that Faulk had lied when he said WCBS was happy with his work, had lied about the number of commercials he lost as a result of Aware's allegations, and had lied when he said the Middle of the Road officers had led the way in enforcing AFTRA's rule against Fifth Amendment takers. Also misleading, he said, were Faulk's comments about the affidavits he had submitted to CBS. The entertainer's 1951 loyalty oath, he pointed out, had denied any membership in the Communist party or Communist fronts but was "not a sworn statement." His 1956 statement, on the other hand, was a sworn affidavit but did not include a denial of front activity.[51]

In contrast Bolan offered Hartnett as a model of integrity. In the face of all the talk about racketeering and extortion, Bolan posed the rhetorical question, "is there anything wrong about Mr. Hartnett's getting paid for his work?" Even so, he "never got a penny from any performer for clearing that performer." He was no less scrupulous, Bolan argued, in compiling the allegations that appeared in the Aware bulletin, charges that Hartnett listed not out of malice but out of sincere belief. In determining which organizations should be highlighted in these allegations, Hartnett, like any other citizen, was entitled to consider the findings of HUAC, even if they did not qualify as an official judicial determination. "There have only been a handful of court decisions dealing with Communist fronts, and what procedures do we have for establishing that an individual has been a member of a Communist front? We don't have any."[52]

On behalf of his client who had yet to set foot in the courtroom, Bolan asserted that not "one piece of testimony" connected Johnson to News Supplement Number 16, only testimony on "ancient history," on Johnson's protests against performers from the early 1950s. He reminded the jurors that, due to the rulings of the court, they did not "know the records of the people that Mr. Johnson protested against," and he contended that his client had been within his rights to speak out against these entertainers. In the case of Thomas Murray's testimony, however, the plaintiff had offered evidence that was clearly not "ancient history" but a specific reference to Johnson's role in Faulk's troubles. To minimize this powerful piece of his opposition's case, Bolan resorted to quibbling over Murray's faulty memory of inconsequential details. More pertinent was a fact often overlooked during the trial: Bolan pointed out that Johnson had sold his stores around the time that Aware had made its allegations and could no longer have been "using them as pressure."[53]

As for Johnson's absence from the trial, the jurors should not hold that against him, Bolan said. Not only should they believe the diagnosis of Dr. Ayer, the defense's expert, but they should consider the great emotional toll that cross-examination could exact upon a sickly seventy-three-year-old man. He asked the jury to recall the evident strain of younger witnesses who were accustomed to performing in public, such as David Susskind—"voice rasping, perspiring, shaking"—or, much more evident, Kim Hunter, "a television actress, a movie actress, yet on the witness stand, very shaky, quavering."[54]

The plaintiff's case was at its weakest, Bolan maintained, in its persistent attention to the blacklist, "the biggest smokescreen that has been thrown up in this case, to keep your eyes off the real issue that Mr. Faulk was not damaged" by the Aware accusations. The emphasis on this practice revealed, Bolan said, the true purpose of the plaintiff's lawsuit, which went well beyond the matter of Faulk's employment difficulties. The true aim was "to completely eliminate all private opposition to the employment of Communist Party members, Communist fronters, Fifth Amendment takers in radio and television."[55]

Nizer began his summation the next day, June 27. He wasted little time in demonstrating why Bolan had deferred to his superior experience and ability, regaling the jury immediately with his dynamic gift for oratory that now drew to the courtroom a capacity crowd. Like Bolan, he quickly turned his attention to the length of the trial but took a more positive, lofty approach. There was some compensation for serving on such a protracted trial, he told the jury, "and that is that this is a historic case," not merely confined to the specific charges against these defendants. "There are in the history of litigation just a few of these, sometimes only one in a generation, and I stand here with a very deep sense of responsibility because I have upon me the burden of presenting this case to you," one that "will have significance in the history of litigation nationally and, I think, internationally."[56]

Having placed the lawsuit in a grand context, Nizer then moved swiftly to the attack. He described Bolan's summation as "a very bitter day for us." After all these weeks of testimony, he expected the opposition "to defend themselves, but they didn't have to spill their malice and hate in this courtroom until I felt I was necked in mud yesterday. When a man has no generosity in his heart, he has real heart disease; and I think the defendants yesterday demonstrated the malice with which this case from the first moment has been steeped in." He denounced the defense for calling Faulk a liar. "At the last moment we are libeled again." As he brought what he considered the defendants' offenses into focus, he delineated the historic issue he wanted the jury to consider. He wanted to know if the jurors were "going to permit private vigilantism for profit," a phenomenon embodied by "this gentleman seated here with the thin mouth and the blue suit," referring to Hartnett, the first of several times that Nizer would refer to him in that way. Quick to point out that all Americans should be on guard against communism, he stressed that if anyone had pertinent evidence about this ideological movement, "and he is really a good natured and proper and loyal citizen, he sends it to the governmental authorities. Not this gentlemen," indicating Hartnett once more, "he charged $20 a throw."[57]

The laughter from the spectators that followed this line capped what would be one of the most memorable and persuasive passages from Nizer's summation. What few seemed to remember while engrossed in his words was a moment early on in Hartnett's direct testimony. Bolan had asked him to talk about those times when he had handled requests for information from government agencies, and Hartnett would have elaborated on his cooperation with the government were it not for Nizer's sustained objection.[58]

Nizer spared no superlatives in praising his client, a local radio personality who was now elevated in his lawyer's flamboyant rhetoric to "one of the great stars of our culture." Once more he insisted that Faulk had always been an anti-Communist, "from the first moment that he could understand and breathe," and drove the point home by mocking the very idea that a Communist would have gone out of his way, as Faulk had done, to join the fight in World War II. "This is a fine Communist for you," he wryly noted after recounting how Faulk had signed up for the Merchant Marines after being rejected by the army.[59]

He placed Faulk's tribulations within the context of other such black-list victims as Philip Loeb and Mady Christians, also "great stars," who had been hounded into committing suicide (in fact Christians had died of a cerebral hemorrhage). Although physically surviving, Faulk had nonetheless been figuratively "shipped off to Siberia" by people who had used "Communist techniques under the guise of fighting Communism." And, like Joe McCarthy and other congressional investigators, Nizer said, the defendants "never caught a single Communist."[60]

Describing the motives of the men who had damaged his client, Nizer took pains to make a crucial distinction, stressing that "in this case there was no fanaticism; it was malice." If he had characterized the defendants as fanatics, he would have been implying that they truly believed in what they were doing; but he was determined to portray them as racketeers, typically perceived as horribly cynical, not overzealous. He had already delighted the audience by describing Hartnett as someone who "charged $20 a throw," and there was no denying that Hartnett had made a business of his anti-communism, even if Bolan characterized it as a legitimate enterprise. But Nizer would also strain to extend this charge to the Syracuse group. He claimed that the defense had declined to bring in John Dungey to testify because "we would have found out what his financial arrangement is with Mr. Johnson," though there had been no evidence to suggest that Dungey was making money from his anti-Red crusade.[61] Nor was there evidence to indicate that Johnson had been motivated by financial gain. Describing the defendants as fanatics, imposing their own virtual law, would have been more precise.

Taking his point to its logical conclusion, Nizer discussed the AFTRA battles and Faulk's anti-blacklist stance while running on the Middle of the Road slate. He concluded that the defendants "decided to destroy this man before he destroyed their income, their illegitimate income. That is the reason for the malice in this case." And once more he emphasized, "This isn't even a case of mistaken fanaticism."[62]

Nizer was especially colorful in his series of statements dealing with Johnson's alleged medical problems:

"He is doing fine with this esophagus all this period when he is blacklisting these people, but when he has to come to court and meet this charge, he suddenly gets esophagus trouble."

"Wouldn't you think that Mr. Johnson, if he were half a man—he is ac-cused of all this. Don't you think he'd be eager to come into court if he is innocent, if he didn't do anything wrong?"

"Nothing serious about it [Johnson's condition] incidentally. It's a slight spasm at the end of the colon. I think we all have bellyaches. It's a little bit of that, but this is more advanced."

"The only trouble with him inside is guts, not the esophagus, and he should have appeared here and defended himself and he didn't have the guts to do it. There is nothing the matter with his esophagus."[63]

At around 3:30, as he finished this section of his summation, Nizer asked for a short recess. During that time, Nizer later recalled, Bolan's sec-retary hurried into the courtroom and handed a note to her boss, who then passed it along to Nizer. The note contained some urgent news. It said that Laurence Johnson, the man Nizer had just denounced as a gut-less malingerer, had "just been found dead in a Bronx motel."[64]

After Bolan relayed the message to Judge Geller, the attorneys met with the judge in his chambers to discuss the implications of the news. All they knew at this point was that the body of Johnson, or someone believed to be Johnson, had been delivered to the Jacobi Hospital Morgue in the Bronx. Judge Geller decided, first, that they should verify through the po-lice that the body was in fact Johnson, then determine the proper proce-dure should the story be confirmed. Bolan requested that Johnson be severed from the case, an unwelcome prospect for the plaintiff, which would have removed the one wealthy defendant, the one source for a sub-stantial award for Faulk. Going after the Johnson estate might then require yet another trial. For now, Judge Geller had no opinion. A more immedi-ate problem concerned the jury. Bolan had already spoken to two re-porters about Johnson's death, and their stories had already been filed. To keep the news from prejudicing the jury until he had decided how to pro-ceed, Judge Geller ordered that the jury be sequestered in a hotel that night. For now, until more definitive news about the death arrived, the trial would proceed as if nothing had happened.[65]

Nizer resumed his summation for another half-hour before a second conference was called. By then Judge Geller had received confirmation that the deceased was Laurence Johnson, age seventy-three, of 1202 Broad Street, Syracuse. The staff at the Town and Country Motor Lodge had expected him to check out by that morning and, not having seen him for two days, a clerk had gone to Johnson's room at nine o'clock to present him with his bill. He discovered Johnson in bed, still in his pajamas, with medicine bottles on a nearby night table.

In another conference at the end of the day, Bolan pressed once again for severance and also asked that the jury be informed of Johnson's death in light of Nizer's remarks during his summation, "particularly when he said that people like Mr. Johnson and the defendants make these black-listing charges and then don't have the guts to come in here." Judge Geller made no immediate decision, requesting instead that both sides submit briefs on the legal issues by the next morning. Nizer urged the judge to "keep your mind open" on how to instruct the jury "until we find out the cause of Mr. Johnson's death." He maintained that the cause might have "nothing to do, as I am almost certain, with his esophagus," and that, as far as they knew, Johnson "may have committed suicide."[66]

Between these interruptions Nizer continued with his summation, without knowing exactly how Johnson's death would affect the trial. Johnson might be severed from the case, or the judge might rule the entire proceedings a mistrial. Despite the great uncertainty that now surrounded the lawsuit, he was more than capable of carrying on as he addressed the jury for another hour, though he refrained at this point from further references to Johnson's health.

He reviewed Faulk's final two years at CBS and the series of job offers that evaporated after his firing. In a statement that suggested, perhaps inadvertently, how little the case's evidence related directly to his client's dismissal from CBS, he told the jurors that they "will have to guess what pressures were brought at that time which caused Faulk suddenly to be dropped." However much Nizer expected the jury to connect the dots in a way favorable to his case, he wound up his address with a fervent, compelling appeal on behalf of both Faulk and the higher cause his lawsuit represented. "I place his wife's life and his three children's lives in your hands, very literally, because this man's reputation is either going to be restored by a verdict that will ring to the world, or he will be besmirched all over again." He urged the jury to demand sizable punitive damages in addition to compensatory damages "as a lesson to others to stop blacklisting and free the industry and not destroy people's lives."[67]

The next day Judge Geller announced his decision on the Johnson issue. He would let the jury know about the grocer's death, but he would not sever him from the case and would allow the trial to continue, assigning a temporary administrator of Johnson's estate to look after the dead defendant's interests. "Since this trial has been in progress for more than ten weeks," he said, "and at the time of Mr. Johnson's death or report thereof all evidence was in, there can be no prejudice in permitting it to be completed. To require a retrial would involve great expense to the parties, to the State, and to the City."[68] Although the jurors could still assign compensatory damages to Johnson's estate, they could not impose punitive damages. A financial penalty of this kind was meant to deter the defendant from committing similar offenses in the future, hardly an option now in Johnson's case.

The judge gave his instructions to the jury late that afternoon and at 5:35 announced, "You may now commence to deliberate." The jury conferred for less than an hour before requesting certain documents for closer inspection, then retreated from the courtroom to continue their work. At 10:20 that evening the jury returned once again, this time to pass along a note from the foreman requesting information from the judge: "The jury would like to have a clarification on the subject of awards for punitive damages. Is the jury allowed to award more than the amounts requested by the plaintiff?"[69]

Any doubt about the basic thrust of the verdict was now removed. Neither counsel was especially surprised. As Bolan later put it, "I saw it coming. I was hopeful it might be a deadlock, I didn't think there was a chance of winning." To his mind, the judge's handling of the case had been the determining factor. On the plaintiff's side, Berger believed the outcome could have been predicted from the very beginning. "The trial was over, I thought, in the selection of the jury," he said. He was convinced even then that the jurors would believe Faulk's side of the story.[70]

All that remained was for the jury to decide on the extent of the award. The jury deliberated over this issue for another seventy minutes and arrived in the courtroom at 11:40 P.M. to deliver their verdict. "We, the jury, have arrived at our decision in favor of Mr. Faulk," the foreman said. "We have awarded the plaintiff, Mr. Faulk, compensatory damages in the sum

$1 million against Aware, Inc., Mr. Vincent Hartnett, and the estate of the late Mr. Laurence Johnson. We also have awarded the plaintiff, Mr. Faulk, punitive damages in the sum of $1,250,000 against Aware, Inc. and $1,250,000 against Mr. Hartnett."[71] In all, the damages totaled $3.5 million, to that point the largest libel judgment an American jury had ever awarded.

FOURTEEN

End of an Era

CAPTURING THE SENTIMENTS of many in the media after the verdict was a political cartoon by Herb Block. In a drawing entitled "Nailed," a giant hammer marked "Faulk Case Verdict" pounds a nail through the collar of a black jacket worn by a mole-faced burglar labeled "Blacklisters." From the villain's clawlike hands drop his two favorite implements, a pail of black paint and a battle-ax.

The cartoon set the tone for a host of journalists who celebrated the end of what *Time* called an era of "shadowy terrorism." They applauded the courage of Faulk, who, after years in the wilderness, found a sympathetic audience among a "jury of simple people," as Max Lerner described them, "who found blacklisting revolting despite its cloak of anti-Communist patriotism."

If there was one dispute with the results of the trial, it was that the jury's decision was not far-reaching enough. For commentators like Lerner, Murray Kempton, and Jack Gould, certain key figures were allowed to escape official denunciation altogether. "The strength of the blacklists," Gould pointed out, "never rested with the compilers of the lists; it always rested with those who patronized them"—the networks, the sponsors, and the advertising agencies. The practice thrived, Lerner wrote along similar lines, "mainly because wealth and power do not keep men from being cowards."[1]

While many in the media center of New York City were pleased with the outcome of Faulk's lawsuit, there remained others who championed his adversaries. By the time columnists had rendered their verdict in the southernmost portion of New York State, the upstate city of Syracuse had already paid its respects to one of the men who had been condemned at the trial. The funeral for Laurence Johnson was held on June 30, just two days after the jury had passed judgment on his activities of the preceding ten years. He might have been denounced in a Manhattan court, but Johnson still had his supporters in his hometown.

"A large attendance at the funeral," a local newspaper reported, "and banks of flowers signified the affectionate esteem in which Larry Johnson was held." Among the most faithful, his pallbearers, were John Dungey, his close ally in the American Legion, and Thomas Kenyon, his former merchandise manager and a member of the Veterans Action Committee of Syracuse Super Markets. Johnson was buried in the Savannah-Butler cemetery, near his boyhood home where he had first set his sights on a career as a storekeeper and respected man of his community. A local columnist conceded that Johnson might have done wrong but invoked an allusion to *Othello* when he wrote that, if the grocer "had any fault, it perhaps was that he loved his country 'not wisely but too well.'" Another Syracuse columnist, Joseph H. Adams, suggested that Johnson's downfall came because "he clung to the tried and true, honest, down-to-earth, American traditions as expressed in the old country store he tried so hard to perpetuate." Adams included a poem he had once written for Johnson to commemorate that tradition:

And we wish that now that store somehow
    Could remain a part of our way of life,
That the world could be free of chicanery
    And ceaseless bickering and strife —
That disputes which now make nations snarl
    Could be settled around a cracker-bar'l!

Adams made no mention of the bickering and strife that Johnson himself had instigated in his quest to promote his homespun values.[2]

In part, at least, some of the neighborly sympathy for Johnson must have been stirred by the lambasting he had received in Nizer's summation when the grocer's body had already been laid out in a Bronx morgue.

Early reports had suggested that he had died of natural causes, despite Nizer's conjecture that it might have been a suicide, and the results of the autopsy released later in July confirmed the initial benign conclusion. Johnson had died of "a congenital condition in his esophagus," which led to his choking on his own vomit. His death resulted from exactly those ailments that his doctors had outlined and Nizer had ridiculed.

For those who had not forgotten earlier struggles, Nizer's remarks to the jury—dismissing Johnson's complaints, jeering at his ability to carry on with the rest of his life while not having the courage to face his accusers— should have evoked memories of a clear precedent from the blacklist era. In 1951, *Counterattack* had sneered at J. Edward Bromberg's alleged heart condition that had prevented him from testifying before HUAC but had failed to keep him from appearing in a play. Only months later the actor died of his supposedly bogus heart condition. But in the sharp partisan fervor of the period that still consumed so many people in 1962, Johnson's supporters were not likely to acknowledge the parallel between Nizer's attack and the earlier tirade against Bromberg, which they had probably applauded. Nor would Faulk's supporters have been likely to appreciate the parallel from the opposite direction. Even four years later, when he published his memoir of the case, Nizer would not admit his error, implying that the taking of barbiturates might have somehow contributed to Johnson's death, even though the medical examiner had concluded that medications were not a factor. Murray Kempton stood out among those who had scoffed at Johnson by expressing a slight twinge of regret. Just a week after the end of the trial, during which he had dubbed the grocer "Sick Call Larry," Kempton referred to him as "poor Laurence Johnson." But he still failed to acknowledge in any way that he had belittled the man's illness.[3]

The Johnson estate turned out to be worth much less than Faulk's lawyers had anticipated, amounting to $250,000 rather than the expected millions, and prompting Faulk to accept a settlement from the estate of $175,000. But for the defendants still living there would be more legal wrangling. An immediate attempt to have the verdict set aside was denied by Judge Geller, to be followed by an October 1963 appeal by Hartnett and Aware to the Appellate Division of the State Supreme Court. A month later the appeals court judges decided to reduce the "shockingly excessive" award. "A jury's verdict," Judge Samuel Rubin noted, "must have some relation to reality," and the verdict in the Faulk case was "grossly excessive and most unrealistic." The original total was cut from $3.5 million to $550,000, including punitive damages that amounted to $50,000 to be paid by Aware and $100,000 by Hartnett. The court, however, did not consider the jury wrong for penalizing the defendants, who, the court said, had been "as malicious as they were vicious." Two years later Hartnett and Aware tried to eliminate these damages altogether by taking their case to the U.S. Supreme Court, but the Court refused to consider the appeal.[4]

Within the broadcast industry the blacklist was now going through its death throes. The practice's grip had begun to relax in the last few years, but now the Faulk case had clearly discredited it in the public's eyes. The 1962–1963 TV season, the first in the wake of the Faulk verdict, featured many performers neither seen nor heard on the commercial airwaves for years. Predictably it was the maverick producers who responded the most quickly. On *Car 54, Where Are You?*, Nat Hiken employed Jack Gilford for a guest shot and hired Ossie Davis as a recurring character; and on *The Defenders*, Herbert Brodkin used Frank Silvera, once singled out by Harvey Matusow. The next season, David Susskind cast AFTRA firebrands John Randolph and Lee Grant on *East Side / West Side*. Even when the producers were willing to bring talent back from exile, though, artistic temperament could sometimes be a hindrance.

Howard Fast, the former CPUSA stalwart who had recently renounced his Communist faith, approached the *Defenders* producers about writing an episode, saying he had a story idea, and he wanted, finally, to see his name on television. After the show's executives managed to clear him with the network, he turned in the script; as a novelist, however, he was not accustomed to the TV-writing process and took umbrage when the show's head writer, Reginald Rose, did substantial revisions. "And Howard had a fit," recalled the program's casting director Edith Hamlin. "He said, 'I'm not putting my name on that, that's not my script.' And we're having a terrible fight with Howard, telling him, 'The whole purpose of it is to put your name back on television so people know you're still alive.' He said, 'No, that's not my script, I'm doing it under the name of Mark White.'"[5]

Brodkin's *The Defenders* took perhaps its most significant symbolic step in this process on January 18, 1964, when the series aired an episode entitled "Blacklist." The story by writer Ernest Kinoy dealt with a minor but respected character actor who, after being banned from his profession, has been reduced to working as a clerk in a shoe store. A chance for a return to acting comes his way, but the promoters of the blacklist succeed in applying enough pressure to cancel the offer. One of the blacklisters is an overbearing, retired upstate businessman, clearly modeled after Laurence Johnson; working with him is a female assistant, a fictional stand-in for Hartnett, who manages a clearance racket.

The script's subject was still highly controversial when it was first proposed in 1963, especially for the show's network, CBS, which had played such a prominent role in institutionalizing the blacklist and had figured so importantly in the Faulk case. Network officials might not have gone along with the idea at all were it not for a skillful ploy by one of the series' producers. By first proposing another story idea that was even more taboo, producer Reginald Rose was able to win CBS's approval for the Kinoy story because it seemed less troublesome in comparison. The network, however, demanded one change in the story, which originally focused on the blacklist in broadcasting. Program practices executive Herbert Karlborg told associate producer Robert Markell and story editor David Shaw that the program would have to deal instead with the movie industry because, he blandly asserted, there was no blacklist in TV. That same morning, as it turned out, the producers had to submit the show's cast list for clearance. None of the actors was rejected, but the procedure was still in place.[6]

Whatever trepidations CBS might have had about airing the episode, the industry would reward the network for its decision by honoring the show with two Emmys, one for actor Jack Klugman in the role of the blacklisted actor and another for Kinoy. In retrospect the show, though exceptionally well written and acted, clearly plays it safe on one key issue. The script characterizes its blacklist victim as someone who was originally targeted because of well-meaning involvement with front organizations promoting the Republican cause in the Spanish Civil War. By defining the victim in this unquestionably benign way, the show dodged the tougher civil libertarian issue that would have been posed by the blacklisting of an outright Communist. The program's approach also helped foster the impression that blacklist victims were primarily political innocents.

Soon the broadcast blacklist would become virtually extinct. "After *East Side / West Side* and *The Defenders*," said former CBS executive Alan Wagner, "it was easy. You didn't check anything with anybody," though the formality of submitting names of creative personnel for clearance lingered for several more years. (There was one significant exception: Pete Seeger, one of the few blacklistees who had been an open political propagandist, did not return to the airwaves until an episode of the *Smothers Brothers Comedy Hour* in 1967.) Like the networks, advertising agencies also relaxed their procedures. Jack Wren, the most influential of Madison Avenue security officers and now an embarrassing reminder of a discredited era, faded from the scene during this time without any public acknowledgment of his exit. As fellow BBD&O executive Tom Villante recalled, "I cannot remember anyone ever asking, 'What ever happened to Jack Wren?'"[7]

On the broader cultural scene, evidence of a more widely accepted liberal mentality about the blacklist phenomenon could be found in the 1963 Broadway premiere of *Case of Libel*, an anti-Red-baiting play that was a fictionalized account of the lawsuit litigated by Nizer against columnist Westbrook Pegler. The play was written by Henry Denker, once part of the anti-Communist faction within the Radio Writers Guild who was also an opponent of the political screening of talent. Adding weight to the production's message about the dangers of right-wing smear tactics was the producer's choice of personnel, which included such previously blacklisted actors as John Randolph and Joseph Julian as well as Sam Wanamaker, an actor listed in *Red Channels* who now served as the play's director. Despite this gesture of goodwill, the production did not succeed in avoiding certain ingrained attitudes that had divided the entertainment industry for so many years. Denker recalled meeting for a drink with Wanamaker and the play's star Van Heflin early on in the play's preparation. Eventually the conversation turned to politics. "Sam said something which he expected us to wholeheartedly approve," said Denker, the former anti-Communist partisan. "I can't remember what the hell it was because it wasn't that important, but that's what he expected, because when neither one of us spoke up—we let the thing pass—a pall set in. You could just feel it." Denker believed this led to vindictive behavior on Wanamaker's part, especially in his dealings with Heflin, a particularly insecure actor who required encouragement every step of the way. "On opening night Sam Wanamaker went into his dressing room and said, 'Van, this is a hopeless cause, this play is not going to work. I'm just telling you now for your own good, it's not going to work, forget it.' That's on opening night to an insecure actor!"[8]

In television the new attitudes about old political biases obviously signaled a change in the medium, but they didn't necessarily have the impact on programming that some might have expected. According to one
perspective, the blacklist had depleted broadcasting's creativity and deprived it of some of its finest talent. Yet through much of the 1950s television had enjoyed an especially remarkable period of programming. In the
early 1960s, with previously banned talent now returning to the airwaves,
TV fare, according to this theory, should have improved. Instead, at the
same time the industry's hiring practices became less restrictive, television
became less creative and more formulaic.

As had been the case during the rise of TV's Golden Age, the current
decline had little to do with politics and a great deal to do with the networks' corporate culture. Accounting for much of the change was the
quiz-show scandal of 1959. The revelation that shows like *Twenty-One* had
been fixed not only embarrassed the TV industry but convinced the networks they needed to exercise more control over their programs. Since the
rigged quiz shows had been independent productions, the networks now
stepped in to prevent further scandals by supervising the programs more
closely. They then used the scandal as a pretext to control shows of all
kinds, allowing them to interfere with those independent producers who,
in the past, had been a credit to the industry. Also during this period,
broadcasters decided that their surest route to greater profits was to create
shows that appealed to the least sophisticated segments of the rural markets. The trend was crystallized in the regime of CBS-TV president James
Aubrey, who once declared, "Content is out." True to his word, he went
on to promote such insipid fare as *Mr. Ed*, *The Beverly Hillbillies*, and *Pet-
ticoat Junction*. Golden Age holdouts like Hiken and Brodkin might have
tried to preserve their earlier standards, but they found their ideas increasingly out of favor. The medium rebounded only in the early 1970s
when the networks began to embrace other economic priorities. Ratings
in rural markets were still booming, but viewers there tended to be older
and less affluent. Looking for a new audience that would attract higher-
toned advertisers, CBS initiated a new approach that would appeal to
more urban, more sophisticated viewers with such programs as *All in the
Family* and the *Mary Tyler Moore Show*. Although some shows clearly had
a liberal agenda—particularly *All in the Family* and *M.A.S.H.*—politics
once more were not a key factor.

For John Henry Faulk, changing attitudes in broadcasting after his courtroom victory provided a new lease on life, or so it seemed at first. In September 1962, just over two months after the verdict, he returned to TV for the first time in six years when Mark Goodson, one of his witnesses, hired him as a guest panelist on *To Tell the Truth*. Providing some potential for friction was the presence on the show of Bud Collyer, the series host, an aggressive anti-Communist and onetime opponent of the Middle of the Road slate in AFTRA; but in this case the sparks failed to fly. Never a vindictive man by nature, Collyer welcomed the appearance of Faulk, whom he regarded as a worthy talent.[9] Another guest shot soon followed in a revival of *Leave It to the Girls*, the series that had featured Faulk some ten years earlier, just as his career had been first gathering momentum. The radio airwaves also reopened for him in November when he began hosting *Program P.M.*, a show that ran nightly from Monday to Friday on New York station WINS.

In addition to recovering lost ground in broadcasting, Faulk explored new avenues in publishing and film. He signed a contract with Simon and Schuster to write a memoir about his blacklisting and lawsuit, and this in turn led to a tentative movie deal with independent producers Norman Lear and Bud Yorkin to put his story on film, a project that generated interest in the press when TV comedy star Dick Van Dyke agreed to play the role of Faulk. Faulk himself made his entrée into the movie business with a small role in David Susskind's production of the *All the Way Home* in 1963 and another supporting part the next year in the film adaptation of Gore Vidal's *The Best Man*.

These early steps toward a professional comeback helped compensate for personal troubles that plagued him in the months following the trial. His marriage to Lynne had not been going well for some time, and now, in August 1963, she filed for legal separation, charging him with infidelity. This in itself would have been difficult enough, but the notoriety that had come with his historic libel victory ensured that his troubles would be magnified by public embarrassment as the divorce was dragged through the tabloids. "Wife Charges Faulk Frolicked with 21 Gals and Names Them," salivated a headline in the *New York Daily News*.[10] From there his situation worsened as his return to the entertainment business, which had previously cushioned some of the impact of his personal miseries, soon began to unravel.

Faulk later maintained that job opportunities dried up because of a residual effect from his blacklisting. This explanation leaves certain things unexplained. If he truly was regarded by the entertainment industry as too hot to handle, why did he receive offers in radio, TV, and the movies so soon after his trial? His resignation from WINS in April 1963, just five months after starting his show there, suggests other explanations. At the time, he announced he was quitting the program in order to concentrate on writing his memoir for Simon and Schuster and to pursue opportunities in television.[11] This might have been a public relations cover story concealing the true reason for his departure—such as, perhaps, an inability to get along with his superiors or the show's failure to find an audience. But if there was any truth to the announcement, Faulk's subsequent professional decline might have sprung from an exaggerated estimate of his prospects. After walking away, perhaps prematurely, from a job in the radio industry, which had always been the foundation of his career, Faulk discovered that none of his ventures in publishing or TV led to long-term success. His book, entitled *Fear on Trial*, was published in November 1964, but he did not acquire any other publishing contracts, and the movie project based on the book failed to land financial backing. On TV, while he succeeded in acquiring a part in an episode of Herbert Brodkin's legal drama *For the People*, he could not find steady employment. The same held true for film acting. His respectable but unexceptional performances in *All the Way Home* and *The Best Man* did not immediately lead to other roles. He would not appear in another film for ten years.

During his difficult times in the mid-1960s, politics, as always, commanded Faulk's attention and distracted him to some extent from his professional worries. Sometimes he was exercised enough by the political scene to take action. Especially vexing to him was the 1965 New York City mayoral race. His candidate of choice, liberal Republican John Lindsay, was running against not only a Democratic challenger but also *National Review* editor William F. Buckley. Campaigning for the Conservative party and, more to the point, designating himself as the election's official gadfly, Buckley peppered Lindsay with a merciless stream of caustic and often witty rebukes.[12] So incensed was Faulk by Buckley's remarks that he composed a long letter to the Lindsay campaign outlining what he considered to be his candidate's best strategy.

The key, he maintained, was to expose one of Buckley's past political affiliations. The affiliation he had in mind happened to be of great personal significance to Faulk, none other than Aware, Inc. Claiming that Buckley had denied ever being a member of the organization, Faulk provided a series of photostats and assertions to refute him, including a copy of Aware financial records (subpoenaed during his trial) containing membership information for Buckley from 1956 and a description of a document that showed that he "was a speaker (with Vincent Hartnett and Roy Cohn) at an Aware rally on May 7, 1958." Consumed by his determination to discredit Buckley at all costs, Faulk was apparently oblivious to the similarity between his accusations and the kinds of charges about past affiliations of leftists made by Hartnett ten years earlier. He concluded by saying, "Were I John Lindsay, plagued by the destructive and shocking tactics of William F. Buckley, Jr., I would shut him up before the New York public once and for all, by hanging his membership in Aware, a proven and discredited hate-group, around his neck."[13]

As his entertainment career continued to flounder, Faulk occupied himself with lecture engagements, occasional guest appearances on radio talk shows, and participation in anti–Vietnam War events. The award from his lawsuit did little to help. Of the $175,000 received from the Johnson estate, $100,000 went to Nizer's law firm while much of Faulk's share of $75,000 was, according to his biographer, consumed by debts. The rest of the award had to come from Hartnett, who had no money to spare and would have to pay Faulk a small percentage of his income each year. Eventually Faulk no longer saw any reason for staying in the media center of New York. In 1968 he left Manhattan and, for the second time in ten years, returned to Texas where he settled with his third wife in his hometown of Austin.

☞ To get through the demands of the appeals process, Hartnett needed to rely on favors from friends and compatriots. In this the Syracuse contingent, even without Johnson to spearhead its efforts, proved especially helpful. Eleanor Buchanan, Johnson's daughter, once dubbed the Joan of Arc of Syracuse by the American Legion, contributed six hundred dollars to his legal expenses while John Dungey forwarded checks from both himself and other central New York allies to keep Hartnett solvent at a time when Nizer was attempting to attach both his bank account and his personal property. Help at this time also came from an unexpected source. In May 1965, Hartnett received a letter from Faulk, who had "just learned that some of the monies seized by the Sheriff at the National Bank of Winchester were those of your children." He explained that he had "no desire whatsoever [to] punish your children" and, to rectify the situation, had directed Nizer's firm to reimburse them. The letter included checks for Maureen Hartnett and Vincent Hartnett, Jr.[14]

Hartnett also turned to his religious faith to help him through this period, and in Dungey, a fellow Catholic, he found a kindred spirit. "John," Hartnett wrote to him in 1964, "I've been buoyed up throughout this desperate fight by God's grace and the knowledge that I'm fighting the cause of all who oppose pro-Communist infiltration of TV." Dungey reciprocated with equal fervor. "May God's will triumph," he once wrote, "and the truth on our side finally shine through and awake the American people."[15]

When Hartnett lost his bid to appeal the verdict to the Supreme Court in March 1965, he ran out of legal options and was forced finally to accept his defeat in the courts. Within a few months he also lost Dungey, his supporter and confidant, when the American Legionnaire died of a heart attack at the age of fifty-three. His death fit into the larger pattern of decline within the Red hunters' group.

Aware, Inc., had ceased to exist and, apart from Faulk's fascination with Buckley's connection to the group, was no longer worthy of people's attention. *Counterattack*, the trailblazer for the broadcast purge, had managed to hang on but in a far less pugnacious form, distributed to a far smaller readership. As opposed to its original telegraphic, provocative style, it now contented itself with unexceptional extended essays conveying the conservative perspective on the cold war. The only executive from the newsletter's controversial heyday still attached to the publication was John Keenan. Ken Bierly, after breaking with American Business Consultants to form his own clearance service, had died at the age of forty-two in 1958, and Theodore Kirkpatrick was now ensconced in his apolitical life as personnel manager for John Deere Harvester Works in East Moline, Illinois. Former *Counterattack* editor Francis McNamara, the only one other than Keenan still carrying on the fight, was now serving as staff director for HUAC.

Keenan, the hard-nosed G-man and countersubversive, took a dim view of developments in the second half of the 1960s. He was deeply frustrated over the Vietnam War, taking the then common conservative view that we should either prosecute the conflict decisively or pull out rather than continue what he considered to be the government's prescription for a costly stalemate. Anti-war protesters pleased him just as little. He regarded them as shiftless and spoiled, symptomatic of a society he believed was, as his daughter recalled, "becoming soft." Compounding his sense of disappointment, *Counterattack* did nothing to reverse what he perceived to be the country's lamentable drift as the newsletter staggered on for a few more years, then finally folded in 1973. Shortly before he died three years later, at the age of sixty-five, Keenan instructed his family not to notify the press of his death. He was uneasy at the thought of how obituaries would decry the *Counterattack* legacy. When Kirkpatrick died at age eighty-eight in 1998, he succeeded in passing from the scene without serious attention paid to his Red-hunting days. A local Illinois obituary merely mentioned that he had once been "co-publisher of a newsletter in New York City for several years."[16]

During the mid- and late 1960s, while Keenan was looking askance at America's course, Hartnett must have dealt with his own frustrations, particularly over developments in the broadcast industry. So many of the people he had tried to keep off the airwaves were now appearing on TV, a clear reversal in what he regarded as the battle against the Communist apparatus in the media. Not only that, the converse was also true: some of his allies in AFTRA were finding their careers taking a turn for the worse. "People wouldn't hire people who were the right-wingers who were naming names," said *Defenders* story editor David Shaw. "They became pariahs." Suffering more than others was Vinton Hayworth, perhaps the most vindictive of AFTRA's anti-Communists, who would eventually turn to selling automobile storage batteries at a Hollywood farmers market.[17]

For Hartnett the trend must have been illustrated most dramatically during the Emmy awards ceremony televised on May 22, 1966. Winning the award for Outstanding Writing Achievement in Drama that year was Millard Lampell, a man Hartnett had once designated as a vital "connecting link" between the Communist infiltration of movies, publishing, and radio. When he accepted his award, Lampell told the audience, "Everyone here ought to know, I was blacklisted for ten years."[18] Although this industry recognition for an old bête noire must have been troubling to Hartnett, a *New York Times* article by Lampell three months later must have been outright galling. And he would not have been alone in objecting to the piece. Even a more moderate anti-Communist would have taken exception to Lampell's skewed account of his political past and blacklist experience.

To begin with there was his characterization of his early years, which leaves the distinct impression that he was a sort of second-string Woody Guthrie, a rambling country-boy working-class hero who "bummed freights across country" and eventually left West Virginia to join Pete Seeger in New York City to sing folk songs. In fact he had grown up in Paterson, New Jersey, just west of Manhattan, had attended college, and had worked often as a writer before entering the folk scene. The blacklist, he wrote, caught him by surprise as he found that "quietly, mysteriously and almost overnight, the job offers stopped coming." He claimed he had no idea what the allegations against him were until he appeared before the McCarran Committee in 1952. Leaving aside the fact that *Red Channels* had already specified twenty-one allegations against him two years before this, it is difficult to believe that a former Communist party member would have been surprised that anti-Communists had targeted him. His 1940s membership in the party, naturally, is not mentioned in the article. Instead we are told that the politics that he and the Almanac Singers espoused were nothing more than "a crude, hand-me-down cross between Eugene Debs and the old Wobblies. A primitive folk version of what Franklin D. Roosevelt was saying in his fireside chats." This is a rather surprising claim considering that the Almanacs branded FDR a warmonger, in keeping with Communist policy during the Nazi-Soviet pact period. And, quite unlike freethinking old socialists like Eugene V. Debs, they would regularly receive instructions from composer Earl Robinson on how best to follow the party line. Lampell concludes his account by equating the banning of broadcast talent with the worst horrors of totalitarianism, saying the blacklist experience prepared him for his play adaptation of John Hersey's *The Wall* when he needed to "create the atmosphere of the early days of the Warsaw Ghetto."[19] A new narrative of the ideological struggles of the 1930s, 1940s, and 1950s was in the making, and Lampell's *Times* piece helped disseminate it to an important readership.

The turning tide in broadcasting might have preyed on Hartnett's mind during this period, but he faced more pressing problems that superseded any political concerns he might have had. After years of passing judgment on the employability of others, he now found that his condemnation at the Faulk trial had eliminated any chance of reviving his consulting business and left him with no steady livelihood. It also burdened him with a long series of payments to satisfy the libel judgment. At the age of fifty he had to find a new way of making a living.

Falling back on his college studies in English, Hartnett was able to find work in 1968 as an English teacher at Pelham Memorial High School near his home in the suburbs just above New York City. The new job suited him. At the end of his first year, the school district's report on his performance concluded by saying, "This is high professionalism—competence, commitment, technical skill, absorption in the task at hand, dignity." From the recollections of his colleagues and superiors, a picture emerges of a highly organized professional, efficient and meticulous in his attention to detail, qualities consistent with his previous specialty of methodical, if compulsive, research. Equally unsurprising, the school principal commented that Hartnett was "not particularly charismatic."[20] But what might not have been anticipated, especially by his enemies, was his rapport with his students.

More than one observer remarked on the respect Hartnett showed his pupils. Bill Smith, who was head of the English department at the time and had the best opportunity to observe him, recalled that Hartnett had "a nice way with kids, and liked the interaction, the discussion that went on in the class around a piece of literature." He was known to take the time personally to tutor students who needed help, and also performed well in a cooperative classroom working with the special-education staff to teach children with learning disabilities.[21]

Among his fellow teachers he was known as a pleasant but quiet man who generally kept his own counsel. He conducted himself "at a kind of a remove in that he was not particularly involved with other people in the school," said former principal John Conroy. He believed this was Hartnett's "way of defending himself, keeping people at bay." One teacher,

Jerry Mele, spent more time with him than others, perhaps because he related to Hartnett's religious faith. "I think he would have been a great man of the cloth," he said. "His dedication, his love of God," he said by way of explanation. "He viewed the kids as miracles of our Lord."[22]

His colleagues didn't know, at least at first, why he would keep himself at a distance. They knew nothing about his previous work. One teacher, however, caught a glimpse of a habit of Hartnett's that had earned him both respect and resentment during his talent-consultant days of the 1950s. Frank Orfei recalled a student named Juan from a wealthy Spanish family who especially impressed Hartnett, as he did others, with his intelligence and maturity. "Juan came to me one day," Orfei remembered, "and said, 'Mr. Hartnett told me that he had investigated my family's background and told me that my mother was descended from Czechoslovakian royalty.' Juan was so intrigued. 'Nobody knows about this,' he said. It was just mind-boggling to this kid that he could find out all this information."[23]

It was only a matter of time until someone at the school discovered Hartnett's controversial past. When one of the teachers came across his name in an account of the blacklist period, the news spread quickly among the faculty and caused a mixture of consternation and outrage. Conroy was taken completely by surprise because Hartnett "did not seem like somebody who would have an axe to grind. He was a fairly mild mannered, low-key individual." Others, staunch opponents of McCarthyism, now regarded him as a dangerous person while some simply resented that he had kept his past a secret, that he had flown under false colors. But they expressed none of this directly to Hartnett, confining their comments instead to faculty-room discussion when he was not around. History teacher Orfei was among those reluctant to bring up the subject with him, yet he would not be able resist baiting him on occasion by telling Hartnett that he was teaching his students about the 1950s cold war. "I would say how important it was so that they would understand the period," Orfei said. "But he would just smile and nod his head."[24]

The dust stirred up by the revelation about Hartnett settled over time, but it was agitated again, and more than ever, when Hartnett was portrayed in a major TV movie.

Eleven years after it had first been published, Faulk's memoir of his lawsuit was finally adapted to the screen.

After the failure to film *Fear on Trial* as a vehicle for Dick Van Dyke in the 1960s, Faulk had had no dealings with the film industry until making two appearances in movies shot on location near his Austin home in 1974. The first was a small role in *Lovin' Molly*, Sidney Lumet's well-meaning if unsuccessful adaptation of a Larry McMurtry novel. The second project—far less respectable but far more widely seen—was the nerve-rattling cult favorite *Texas Chainsaw Massacre*, bringing Faulk's image, on display in a single scene, to an altogether different segment of the population than the one that went to hear his high-minded lectures on the blacklist and the First Amendment. His political interests and his involvement with the film industry then became much more closely entwined the following year when Alan Landsurg Productions filmed *Fear on Trial*.

The movie, starring William Devane as Faulk and George C. Scott as Nizer, was aired October 2, 1975, on CBS, the network that had banned Faulk eighteen years earlier. In adapting a story that had taken six years to unfold into one hundred minutes of screen time, the program's scriptwriter naturally took some dramatic license in simplifying and compressing events. Faulk is shown, for instance, watching Murrow's *See It Now* exposé on McCarthy for the first time in 1956, just before his troubles begin, when in fact the documentary had been broadcast two years earlier. More significant to the ongoing reexamination of the blacklist period, the film endorses Faulk's status as a political hero to the exclusion of any complexity.

Not content to portray him as a man unjustly hounded from his profession, the film conceives Faulk as the embodiment of all decent American values, a man who is not even inclined to think uncharitably of his worst enemies. Faulk, who in reality was more than capable of condemning political adversaries in the most colorful fashion, is presented here as a somewhat naive down-home liberal who is willing to consider the bad intentions of his persecutors only when Nizer educates him in man's capacity for evil. Even so, on his first day of trial, he insists on walking over to Hartnett so that he can introduce himself and shake his opponent's hand in a gesture of plain common decency. This simple act of courtesy leaves Hartnett baffled.

In the role of Hartnett the producers cast John Harkins, a fleshy character actor who often played stodgy, unpleasant characters and would develop a small specialty in negative portrayals of anti-Communists. Nine years later he would be cast as Whittaker Chambers in a PBS drama entitled *Concealed Enemies*, which characterized the anti-Communist whistle-blower as a mentally unbalanced fantasist. In *Fear on Trial* he carries out the filmmakers' conception of Hartnett by playing him as an unctuous caricature who preens over his supposed accomplishments, then just as readily slumps in shame when confronted with his misdeeds. Even his attorney can't seem to find a convincing way to place him in a good light. Presenting Hartnett's qualifications as an expert on communism, the Thomas Bolan character can only say that his client has "read many articles."

In broadcasting this film CBS had decided to illuminate an unflattering episode from its own past, yet there was little chance it would place itself under too harsh a light. Before seeing the film, Faulk had conjectured that the network had decided to take on the project so it could control the way it was characterized on screen, as opposed to allowing the film to go to a rival network that "could care less about how CBS looks to the public."[25] The movie's handling of the network's role in the affair confirmed his suspicions. For the most part CBS is conspicuous in its absence. In one of the few instances when the film addresses the role of broadcasters, it points out that all networks had set up clearance boards, as if their approaches were all roughly equivalent, even though CBS had clearly been the most subservient to the blacklisters. And when the character corresponding to Kim Hunter mentions a program that had shut her out, the script makes a point of mentioning that the show's network was ABC, once again diverting attention from the network most deeply implicated in the case.

Historical nuances didn't figure prominently in the immediate assessment of the film. For tackling the subject of the blacklist, critics applauded the adaptation of Faulk's memoir. Harry F. Waters of *Newsweek* called it "a suspenseful morality play." Despite minor reservations, John J. O'Connor of the *New York Times* considered it "absorbing, provocative and generally superior television."[26] The TV industry was no less appreciative, awarding the movie an Emmy for its script in addition to four other nominations. Between them, the praise and the honors helped certify the film as an important and overdue reappraisal of cold war politics. In time the film's attitudes would prove to be a template for future dramatizations of the period. Just as his lawsuit had played a critical role in breaking the blacklist, the TV movie based on Faulk's experience marked a breakthrough in media perceptions of the broadcast purge.

🅡 At Pelham Memorial High School, Hartnett remained tight-lipped while his colleagues discussed the TV movie's revelations, but away from his job he was outspoken about the program's depiction of events. He filed a lawsuit against CBS, asking for $4 million in damages and charging that the network's movie had libeled him in a distorted representation of the trial.[27]

To a great extent Hartnett's complaint hinged on the movie's portrayal of Faulk and its indifference to the contention made by Hartnett and his remaining supporters that the entertainer was something more than an innocuous centrist liberal. This perspective, which had motivated Hartnett when he first attacked Faulk, had never diminished in the minds of the Red hunters. Even in the immediate aftermath of the trial, they had continued to monitor Faulk's activities for signs that would prove their point of view.

In September 1963, for instance, Hartnett had received information from Dungey that Faulk had recently taken part in a reception for the Southern Conference Educational Fund, an organization that had been investigated by the Senate Internal Security Committee as a possible Communist front. This did little to make Hartnett's case as it proved only that Faulk sympathized with the civil rights agenda of a group that might or might not have been infiltrated by Communists. A somewhat more serious investigation was orchestrated a year later by Francis McNamara for HUAC. The committee, considering a series of hearings on the Faulk case, looked for possible connections between the entertainer and the Austin Communist party in the mid-1940s, but the hearings never took place.[28] In 1967, however, a former Aware member came upon more intriguing information.

In January that year the 92nd Street Y in Manhattan held a symposium entitled "Blacklisting, Politics and the Arts," hosted by *Nation* editor Victor Navasky and featuring a panel composed of Faulk, Ring Lardner, Jr., and Millard Lampell. Faulk held forth in his opening remarks about Jefferson, Madison, and the sanctity of the Bill of Rights, burnishing his image as a devout civil libertarian; but he soon let drop a hint that there might be a blind spot in his concern for political liberty. Lampell was denouncing HUAC at the time, describing the committee as part of its era's establishment "whose major drive was to turn foreign policy away from what had been a great alliance in World War II into a Cold War." When the obviously receptive audience applauded, Faulk chimed in with an "Amen," thus siding with a perspective that downplayed the significance of the monstrous repression carried out by Stalin's regime. Even more to the point, in the mind of former Aware member Alan Schneider, who attended the symposium, was Faulk's answer to the final question from the audience.

A man stood up and demanded to know why Faulk had not protested outside the Soviet embassy during the brutal suppression of the 1956 Hungarian revolt. Faulk began his answer by saying that those protests were "very stylish" at the time—as if taking a stand against the slaughter of thousands of freedom-hungry people were a fashion statement—then proceeded to make the cryptic distinction that the Hungarians had mounted not a revolution but a rebellion. Eventually he worked his way to the heart of the matter. He argued that "one has to look at history and understand that the Hungarian army joined Mr. Hitler and marched over the Russian countryside, slaughtering people indiscriminately in World War II, and consequently I don't think the Russians would take a very happy view, realistically—if you want an explanation of my point of view—very realistically of the Hungarians trying to set up a government that they thought might repeat the same process." The Hungarians, he concluded, "were a conquered foe and as I understand it were treated as such."[29]

By implying that the Hungarian freedom fighters were really nothing more than crypto-fascists, Faulk was accepting a rationale for the Hungarian crackdown that even the Soviet apologists at the Monthly Review had been unwilling to swallow at the time, a transparent distortion that had also driven many lifelong CPUSA members out of the party. Somehow Faulk, the devotee of Jefferson and Madison, had found a way to endorse the right of conquerors to impose repressive regimes on their captured subjects.

Four years later an article entitled "Through the Years with the Blacklist," written by Orson Bean for National Review, provided further ammunition to Hartnett and other Aware partisans. The article was an account of Bean's experiences in the AFTRA struggles of the mid-1950s and his year's exile from broadcasting after being named in Aware News Supplement Number 16. He recalled the time, soon after the newsletter appeared, when he had asked Faulk if the allegations against him were true, and had gotten the response, "Oh, honey, what does it matter? Don't you see those people are fascists. If they didn't have something on us, they'd have made something up." To this he added another encounter with Faulk during the trial: "Was the other side right, I asked. 'The point is they didn't prove it,' said Johnny. 'They were sloppy and they were bad detectives, and we're gonna kill 'em.'"[30]

For Aware supporters still keeping the faith, these revelations confirmed their belief that, contrary to the outcome of the trial, Faulk had indeed been involved in Communist-front activities. One right-winger who eventually seized upon Bean's story was U.S. Representative Larry McDonald of Georgia who, on September 20, 1976, incorporated these two episodes in a speech he delivered on the floor of Congress entitled "Blacklisting and John Henry Faulk," a familiar reprise of conservative complaints about Communist infiltration and the blacklisting of anti-Communists in entertainment. Faulk quickly fired off a letter to the congressman, accusing him of unleashing a "savage, utterly dishonest personal attack."[31] The vehemence of this letter, though, was nothing compared to that of the letter he sent the same day to Bean.

Referring to the first of the two alleged conversations Bean had included in his article, Faulk wrote, "I have no idea why you would deliberately fabricate and cause to be published such a *malicious* and patently *false* statement." He then proceeded to reel off a series of facts that he said disproved Bean's story: he pointed out that Bean had been indignant at the first meeting of the Middle of the Road slate when the Aware charges were first outlined; that Bean had spoken to Faulk two days later to relay the news that Ed Sullivan had threatened to blacklist him; and that one week later Bean had discussed with Faulk again the Sullivan situation and their enemies' actions. To this Faulk added that Bean had supported Faulk when his sponsors were under pressure from Johnson. All of which clearly established that Bean and Faulk were allies and friends during this period—but none of which refuted anything in Bean's story. And Faulk did not bolster his credibility when he claimed that, in order to spare Bean embarrassment, he had omitted any mention in his book of Bean's announcement that he would have to drop out of the Middle of the Road coalition for professional reasons. In fact, Faulk had included this episode in Chapter 3.[32]

Faulk called Bean's account of the conversation that took place outside the courtroom "an obscene perversion of the truth!" He could not "conceive of what sort of man you have become to make such a statement." Once again he cited instances of Bean's demonstrating his friendship and support at the time of the incident as a way of proving that the conversation never took place. He ended the five-page letter in a crescendo of outrage, calling Bean "a liar and a scoundrel" and declaring that his "unbridled dishonesty and malice are unpardonable." He demanded that Bean tell Congressman McDonald that the quotes from the *National Review* article were false. "If I do not hear from you in short order," he concluded, "I shall follow another course to expose your malice."[33]

Bean's response three weeks later was much shorter and far less vituperative. He expressed regret that McDonald had used excerpts from his article to vilify his former friend and stressed that he shared Faulk's opposition to blacklisting. "Where we disagree, as I see it," he continued, "is in our concepts of personal responsibility." He recounted the meeting of Middle of the Road organizers at which all possible candidates had been told to reveal any facts from their past "that might be used as ammunition by the blacklisters." Bean and Collingwood had revealed very minor activities that ended up being mentioned in the Aware newsletter, but, Bean now reminded Faulk, "you remained silent." By not speaking up before running for office, Bean wrote, "you provided Aware, Inc. with a juicy target that ultimately enabled them to black-list both you and me (as well as to cause considerable trouble for Collingwood)." He refused to argue over what they had said to each other years before. "I remember them as I wrote about them; you remember them differently." Acknowledging that he had continued to oppose Aware and to stand by Faulk during his lawsuit, he explained that those issues "took precedence over any negative feelings I had toward you. These things are true and it is also true that I felt and feel that you behaved irresponsibly and that this resulted in the black-listers being able to damage my career."[34]

Hartnett's interest in Orson Bean's article had nothing to do with unintentional damage done to the Middle of the Road caucus and everything to do with the piece's implications about Faulk's political past. Bean's version of his conversations with Faulk became part of Hartnett's libel suit against CBS as his attorney argued that the network had ignored this information when preparing *Fear on Trial* for broadcast.[35]

Hartnett came across another piece of information that he thought was also relevant. Roy Brewer, the anti-Communist labor leader in Hollywood, told him that CBS "had destroyed" an important document relating to the case. Years later Hartnett recalled that the document was Faulk's non-Communist affidavit that he had signed to satisfy a provision of the Taft-Hartley Act; but it might also have been the CBS loyalty statement. In either case, Hartnett believed the document "had contained admissions" that would have substantiated his charges against Faulk. Hartnett might have been able to bolster this claim if it had occurred to him to search through an unlikely source. The information buried in the records of the ACLU had not been readily available to CBS at the time the *Fear on Trial* movie was made and would not have factored into the writing of the script, but it would have certainly been welcomed by Hartnett and the Aware holdouts.

In the ACLU files are a large number of documents pertaining to the publication of Merle Miller's *The Judges and the Judged*, which the civil liberties organization had sponsored. One document is entitled "Exhibit 4 / Names of Unidentified Persons Quoted in *The Judges and the Judged*." On page 6 is a reference to an anonymous quote that appears on page 194 of Miller's book: "Anti-Communist employed by CBS said: 'I'm not ashamed of having been a member of the Young Communist League when I was in College. . . . I confessed to Joe Ream . . . but I felt as if the Inquisition had started all over again.'" What comes next is the name of the person who said this: "John Faulk."[36]

Making this information public would have been of interest not only to Hartnett but to many other more moderate observers of the Faulk trial, specifically anyone who remembered that Faulk had testified, "Neither in utterance nor in action have I in any way, shape or form, given comfort or aid to any Communist cause, or the philosophy of Communism, but to the contrary, have had very strong opinions to the contrary."

The revelation is dramatic, but its real significance lies in the larger context of how Faulk presented his politics at the trial. His denial that he had been a Henry Wallace supporter might have been one indication that he misrepresented himself, but his statement in the ACLU files is a striking confirmation and also has implications for other statements he made.

Faulk was clearly not a Communist in the 1940s and 1950s when his activities came under scrutiny, but his youthful flirtation with the Young Communist League makes it harder to believe that he could have been oblivious, as he said he was, to the ideological leanings of the most radical members of People's Songs.

Johnson had undoubtedly been wrong to call Faulk a Communist, and even though the entertainer's name had indeed been used to promote the seven activities listed in the Aware Newsletter, Hartnett had been wrong to imply that Faulk had taken part in all those events. But it's also true that Faulk was unconvincing when he claimed during his trial that he was a staunch anti-Communist. Someone opposed to Soviet-style totalitarianism as a matter of principle would not, as Faulk had done, make the United States the villain when it had resisted Communist aggression in the Korean War, or excuse Russian brutality in Hungary against people fighting for a more democratic system. The term anti-anti-Communist would have been a more appropriate way to describe him.

Striking a politically pure pose helped Faulk win his case, and the trial's outcome, in turn, helped end the blacklist, which was all to the good. In a practical, legal sense, this was the only way to win a decisive verdict. And Faulk's dogged determination to see the lawsuit through was admirable. But the strategy of presenting Faulk simplistically as a maligned mainstream liberal obscured larger issues, namely the rights of not only Communists but those, like Faulk, with unpopular political views to keep working in the face of pressure groups and institutionalized purges.

A libel lawsuit such as Faulk's or the earlier Julian case was not the ideal setting for defending those who might have been accurately accused yet still entitled to work. But even within the limited context of the Faulk trial, the public might have been better served if the defense had been afforded greater latitude in presenting its case, providing a more comprehensive forum for debating the issues. Whatever Judge Geller's legal justification for his rulings, the civic value of the trial would have been enhanced had the defense been allowed to present its evidence on Communist fronts, just as the plaintiff had been allowed to hold forth on the evils of blacklisting. The jury would still have been justified in believing Faulk had been unfairly victimized, but both they and the public would have been given a better chance to weigh the sometimes conflicting values of vigilance and civil liberties.

Revelations about Faulk's politics also underscore the point raised by Bean in his 1976 letter. Regardless of what Faulk might or might not have said in private conversations, there can be no doubt, even though he was not a Communist, that there had been compelling reasons for him to reveal potentially embarrassing activities from his past during the preparations for the AFTRA elections. If he had withdrawn, as common sense dictated, the anti-Aware forces might have been able to dismantle the blacklist practice within the actors union, the great focal point of blacklist activity in the broadcast industry. The Faulk libel suit might not have been necessary.

☞ In order to reverse at least the symbolic value of the Faulk case, Hartnett doggedly pursued his lawsuit against CBS and finally secured a decision in the case years later, in 1986. Once more he was defeated. A state supreme court judge dismissed the lawsuit because, Judge Joseph Owen ruled, it was "nothing more than an attempt to change what plaintiff perceives to be the verdict of history regarding his conduct."[37]

By this time history's initial verdict was already being articulated by a new narrative, promoted early on by the results of the Faulk case and by Millard Lampell's 1966 New York Times piece, now becoming part of both the country's political and pop culture. Helping to pave the way in 1973 was the publication of Stefan Kanfer's book Journal of the Plague Years, to be followed over the next seven years by Lillian Hellman's Scoundrel Time, David Caute's The Great Fear, Larry Ceplair and Steven Englund's The Inquisition in Hollywood, and Victor Navasky's Naming Names. In one way or another, all these authors expounded upon the theme that the blacklist grew out of a groundless hysteria. They tended to belittle the designs of the CPUSA and its involvement in furthering espionage and agents of influence. Little attention was paid to the threat that Stalin posed in Europe and Asia or to the historical context of the Korean War or to comparisons with earlier wartime security measures. The blacklist, we were told in some cases, was intended to suppress dissenters of all kinds, not just Communists and fellow travelers. And some authors insisted that the new heroes in the cause of untrammeled political liberty were the blacklistees themselves, despite the fact that many were Stalinists who had endorsed the Moscow purge trials in 1938 as well as the domestic suppression of Trotskyists in 1941.

On screen, beginning with *Fear on Trial*, there emerged a similar version of history. *The Front*, released in 1976, was directed and written, respectively, by Martin Ritt and Walter Bernstein, who had both been blacklisted while working on *Danger* in the early 1950s. The film tells the story of blacklisted TV writers who must use a front, played by Woody Allen, in order to sell their scripts, just as Bernstein had to do while banned from the airwaves. Unlike some other movies of this type, *The Front* is willing to concede that its blacklisted characters are Communists and fellow travelers as opposed to wrongly accused liberals. But the film, conceived as a comedy, does not pretend to supply a history lesson on the long-standing political struggles that had led up to the blacklist period. Nonetheless the characterizations transmit a very clear message: the radical blacklistees are lovable, quirky iconoclasts while their nemesis, an ex-FBI agent modeled on Hartnett and Theodore Kirkpatrick, is a cold-blooded, nearly robotic inquisitor.

A more serious, and more distorted, foray into revisionism was a 1998 documentary entitled *Scandalize My Name*, a look at the blacklisting of African-American entertainers. The blacklist, the film maintains, targeted anyone who spoke out against racism and "had the courage and enough care to lend their name and talents to help others." The most worthy of these was Paul Robeson, the greatest voice, as interviewee Harry Belafonte puts it, on behalf of "democracy and the rights of human beings." Only the slightest mention is made of Robeson's unflagging and outspoken support of Stalin's nightmarish regime. Belafonte also relates the story of his own brush with the blacklist. When accusations about him surfaced, Belafonte says, he was in danger of being barred from *The Ed Sullivan Show*; but in meeting with Sullivan he refused to dignify the allegations by saying "which is true and which is false because that is not really the issue." Sullivan rewarded his principled stand by agreeing to put him on the program. "This fact and this act," Belafonte says, "forever took me off the blacklist, just Ed Sullivan's endorsement alone gave me that relief." He makes no reference to his approaching the *Counterattack* editors in February 1954 and explaining each of the charges of front activities that had been leveled against him.[38]

The romanticizing of Robeson's politics was accompanied by similar media displays of admiration for Communists and their allies. On the April

8, 1975, telecast of the Academy Awards ceremony, producer Bert Schneider read aloud a message of greetings from the Vietcong ambassador and saluted the "liberation" of South Vietnam, a process that would be completed by the end of the month with the fall of Saigon.[39] Repeating the errors of Soviet apologists in the 1930s, Schneider was, in essence, celebrating the expansion of the latest so-called people's democracy that would bring a stifling Stalinist tyranny to all of Vietnam. Two years later an actual relic of the old Stalinist movement was honored on another Academy Awards broadcast when Lillian Hellman took the stage and received the evening's only standing ovation.

The ready acceptance of this trend by people who had had nothing to do with Stalinism derived from a mentality embodied by Faulk and validated by the outcome of his lawsuit. At his trial, Faulk, the anti-anti-Communist, had been passed off as a Truman Democrat. In years to come his brand of progressivism—the reluctance to criticize Communist regimes and the tendency to find fault first with America—gradually came to pass for mainstream liberalism, as found in the presidency of Jimmy Carter, who repudiated the liberal anti-communism of Truman by dismissing America's "inordinate fear of Communism" and implying that the containment policy was no longer necessary. Faulk himself demonstrated this perspective when he visited Cuba in 1983. He didn't dispute that the country was ruled by a one-party dictatorship, but, he said, "the people seem to love Fidel." He accepted the assertion that "Fidel has had a long standing rule that anyone who does not want to stay in Cuba and help the revolution, is free to leave."[40] In the entertainment industry, this kind of credulity regarding Castro in particular has become common over the years, making admirers of the Cuban dictator out of such celebrities as Oliver Stone and Steven Spielberg and an outspoken advocate out of Harry Belafonte. In more general terms, the influence may also be seen in the scarcity of movies and TV dramas illustrating the repression and atrocities of Communist regimes comparable to dramas exposing World War II fascism.

In the years following the end of the cold war, it would have been reasonable to regard this anti-anti-Communist perspective as something of only historical interest had it not found some way to survive in a different form. Over the years this point of view became so ingrained in certain quarters of the media that it eventually transmuted into a reflexive anti-anti-totalitarianism. Today, while the United States faces a new totalitarian threat posed by the messianic fascism of terrorist groups like Al Qaeda and the murderous dictatorships of Baathists and Iranian theocrats, many in the media are reluctant to acknowledge the true nature of the enemy. Although obviously no supporters of these modern-day fascists, they find ways to minimize their maliciousness, in the same way that some journalists once soft-pedaled the oppression and aggression of the Soviet Union. They refer to terrorists as militants and shy away from detailed reporting on the horrors of Saddam Hussein's regime. In one particular instance of obstinate blandness, the *New York Times* described Mahmoud Ahmadinejad as "the tough-talking Iranian president"—just ten days after he had sworn to wipe Israel off the map.[41]

Through the years Hartnett and the surviving Aware partisans must have gnashed their teeth over the growing willingness to give Communist movements the benefit of the doubt. Yet if they bridled at the fact that public opinion had turned against the anti-Red vigilance they once championed, they had themselves, at least in part, to blame. Their extremism, their eagerness to put people out of work, helped delegitimize anticommunism for many years, prompting people to associate it with vindictiveness and alarmism. Only in the Reagan years of the 1980s would anticommunism return as a popular movement, without the onus of institutionalized purges.

During the 1980s, when the political climate was changing again, Faulk found that his professional opportunities had taken a turn for the better. Between 1975 and 1982 he finally found steady work once more in broadcasting by appearing as a regular performer on the country comedy show *Hee Haw*. Each week he appeared in cowboy hat and Western shirt and jeans, sitting in an old-fashioned country store in the company of good ole boys gathered around the potbellied stove—a setting, ironically, that would have been to the liking of Faulk's old nemesis Laurence Johnson. Here Faulk would rely on his old storytelling persona to drawl an amusing, folksy anecdote. Beginning in 1986 he then branched out by staging a one-man show in Houston entitled *Pear Orchard, Texas*, in which he drew upon his repertoire of impersonations, enacting a series of characters replete with wry humor and political commentary. While enjoying the renewed interest in his storytelling talents, he was, predictably, far less satisfied with the politics of the Reagan administration. He might be willing to cut a dictator like Castro some slack and counsel greater understanding of his policies, but when it came to fervent anti-Communists he continued to spare no invective. Just as he had once called Truman, the originator of the containment doctrine, a "sick whore," he now referred to Reagan, who would help bring about the collapse of the Soviet Union, as a "pus sac on the boil."[42] He won commendations for his advocacy of civil libertarian values, such as the James Madison First Amendment Award, but he showed little interest in attacking leftist totalitarianism.

Faulk died on April 8, 1990, just short of his seventy-seventh birthday. Three months later his admirers filled the house at the Public Theater in Manhattan to pay tribute to his fight against the blacklist, his eulogizers including Joseph Papp, Alan Lomax, Studs Terkel, Kim Hunter, Ring Lardner, Jr., and Tony Randall. Louis Nizer honored Faulk's admirable determination to see his fight through to the end. "When God examines us," he said, "He doesn't look for medals or honorary degrees. He looks for scars, scars suffered doing some good for your fellow man. John Henry Faulk had the scars of suffering for all those years to do some good for the nation." Actor Ossie Davis speculated that Faulk had been born much too late because he would have been "a perfect Founding Father." One curious note was struck that evening when Pete Seeger sought to pay tribute to Faulk's willingness to embrace good causes. Unwittingly he lent some credence to the basic thesis behind the old Aware allegations when he said, "Johnny Faulk was not a Communist, but he worked with all sorts of people, including Communists like me."[43]

Faulk did not live to see the unveiling of secret documents pertaining to Soviet machinations both here and abroad, so we don't know whether these revelations would have had any effect on his views of the cold war. But his nemesis, Hartnett, would live to factor this information into his assessment of the years in which he had played such a controversial role. The Venona transcripts must have confirmed his belief that the country had been compromised by Soviet espionage, and within his own realm of alleged media infiltration, documents corroborated the reliability of Louis Budenz, indirectly buttressing his claims that Communists had targeted the broadcast industry. The decryptions also identified such journalists as Johannes Steel and Cedric Belfrage as Soviet agents. The unsealing of congressional records revealed other information, some of it shedding light on the veracity of certain entertainers who had come under scrutiny in those years. Lloyd Bridges, for instance, who had been mentioned in *Counterattack*, appeared in a 2002 documentary to recount his experiences dealing with the blacklisters who had targeted him solely because, he said, "anyone who was liberal in those days or who did anything to help humanity suffered," a common observation in left-wing accounts of the era. More specifically, he was singled out because of his involvement in the Actors' Lab where, according to Bridges, "there were apparently quite a few Communists." Despite his claim that he was blacklisted merely for being liberal, recently declassified HUAC hearings revealed that he had admitted to the committee that, while attending the Actors' Lab, he himself had been a Communist.[44]

With the release of new information, Hartnett was more likely than ever to stand by his actions of the 1950s, and when he broke his long public silence on his Red-hunting career in 2001, he spoke with characteristic detail and precision in his defense. But over the years he had occasionally entertained second thoughts to one degree or another—not enough, certainly, to dissuade him from his mission but enough to make him reflect on some of its consequences. During his deposition before the Faulk trial, he had expressed doubts about barring unwitting Communist fronters from the airwaves. More recently, in a letter from 2003, in discussing the accusatory letters he had sent to Leslie Barrett, he took great pains to emphasize the context of the episode, "to explain that my opposition to Communism was not some foolish fancy, but the result of experience in World War II and its aftermath, the tragic unfolding of history subsequent to WW II, deep study, and intimate experience in show business." One can read into this insistence on explaining himself a certain uneasiness about the path Hartnett had taken, at least when it came to his handling of Barrett, one of the most inflammatory acts of his career. Except for the one defensive, explanatory note that the "idea was to fight the Party, not the people," at no time, however, did he express any doubt about the correctness of his cause and his reasons for hounding Communist fronters.[45] Evidence indicates he had been right to maintain there was a Communist presence in broadcasting, but his later comments still failed to explain how safeguarding transmission facilities in time of emergency required banning entertainers across the board, from an ex-stripper hosting a quiz program to a rubber-faced comic appearing on a variety show. Going beyond fears of Communist domination of the media, show-business money and prestige placed at the disposal of Communist-front causes might have still been reason for concern. But these activities could have been dele-gitimized, as Arthur Schlesinger would have prescribed, through debate and exposure.

No reservations of any kind would come from the relatives of Laurence Johnson, not from those, in any case, who were willing to talk. His daugh-ter, Eleanor Buchanan, who had played such an important part in the early days of his crusade, fended off requests for comments, as did another of Johnson's daughters. Those relatives who cooperated articulated the family belief that the grocer from Syracuse had been sued by Faulk purely because he was a potential source of money for an award. The family, re-called Johnson's granddaughter Susan Wangerman, was "incensed with the whole idea of my grandfather being tried, and we just thought it was really horrible and he was railroaded and they went for deep pockets."[46]

Hard feelings, and not from the Johnson family alone, have stood the test of time. About Faulk we can only speculate, but given his penchant for castigating his political opposition in the harshest possible terms, he would not have been likely to reconsider old theories about right-wing conspiracies, even in the light of later revelations about the Soviets and their American accomplices. Certainly former Communists in the media have held tight to conceptions of their own political heroism and their en-emies' absolute villainy. In reading their reminiscences, one gets the im-pression they were nothing more than idealistic progressives concerned about the depression and fascism—issues that undoubtedly motivated many to join the Party. But they fail to address the implications of sup-porting one of the most vicious and destructive dictators in history, and they give no credit to those who blew the whistle on Stalin's crimes in the 1930s and 1940s. Even when acknowledging the brutal Soviet legacy, they can indulge in extraordinary euphemisms. Pete Seeger, who had once danced to the tune of the Nazi-Soviet pact, later conceded only that So-viet leaders had indulged in "an awful lot of rough stuff."[47]

From the beginning of the struggles in the late 1930s, rigidity and extremism on both sides exacerbated the crisis that finally came to a head in the *Red Channels* years. Neither side was especially interested in fair play for its enemies. The danger to free speech at one time resided on the left, when Communists smeared all their opponents, attempted to stifle debate, and enforced thought control within their own ranks. And then it emerged full-blown on the opposite side of the spectrum when

anti-Communists employed tactics all too reminiscent of their enemy. Ultimately the greatest abuses in this country were inflicted by those on the
right when they gained the upper hand during the Korean War and
wielded their advantage with little regard for people's rights, including
people's right to be wrong. But at the same time the left provided moral
support to massive totalitarian repression abroad.

If anything could be said for the purges of the early cold war, it is that
they were no more severe than those of World War II and in certain cases
less so. Jobs in the entertainment business came under greater attack in
the 1950s, but other areas did not. The *Daily Worker* continued to publish
throughout the Korean War, even though it obviously sympathized with
the enemy. Pro-fascist publications during World War II, however, were
shut down. And while the McCarran Act theoretically authorized the detention of subversives, FDR's executive orders during World War II led to
the actual roundup of Japanese Americans as well as German and Italian
nationals.

Being a lesser infringement of rights, though, does not make the cold
war blacklist less troubling. It remains a warning tale for other times of
emergency and war, when emotional partisanship runs high on both sides
and the temptation arises to silence the opposition or at the very least to
unleash reckless conspiracy-mongering that poisons the public debate.
On a more hopeful note, the blacklist period, like earlier times of drastic
wartime measures, demonstrates the resiliency of the American system, its
ability to correct itself and return to more levelheaded civil libertarian values. The question is, once polarization and emergency measures take
hold, how long does it take the country to recover? Once the political fab-
ric has been shredded, how quickly can it mend itself?

While the blacklist itself chipped away at civil libertarian values, the
specter of the blacklist in more recent years might have played a role in
preventing similar excesses. To a great extent the 1950s experience sensi-
tized people to the potential for repression. Any hint of blacklist-style tactics has typically been met with cries of McCarthyism, as in the response
to the firing of Danny Glover and Bill Maher in the early years of the War
on Terror. The response seemed to have an effect. In both cases the dismissals remained isolated instances that, unlike similar incidents in the
early cold war, failed to snowball into a widespread, institutionalized practice. Ultimately the firings also failed to cripple the two entertainers' ca-

reers. Other parts of the blacklist legacy, however, have had a less beneficial effect on the country's political climate.

In the last thirty years, many on the left have warned that they are still
potentially at the mercy of right-wing McCarthy-style zealots. If the danger has been as imminent as some have claimed, there is little evidence
that it has succeeded in cowing the opposition. If anything, the dismantling of the blacklist in the 1960s has emboldened the left, sometimes to
the point of vindictiveness. They have not been the least bit shy about
making their own politically correct demands on the media and, in 2000,
in the case of anti-gay-rights radio personality Laura Schlessinger, succeeded in pressuring sponsors from bankrolling someone they consider offensive. In taking this tack they borrowed techniques from anti-Red
pressure groups of the early 1950s, to be soon employed once again by
those on the right in the attacks on Glover and Maher. Some on the left
have also proven themselves capable of creating their own paranoid conspiracy theories—most recently about neoconservative cabals—that are
reminiscent in style, if not content, of overheated tales of Communist infiltration from the early cold war. Joe McCarthy had once blamed the firing of General MacArthur on the insidious influence of presidential
advisers who coaxed Harry Truman into making the decision while plying
him with "Benedictine and bourbon." More recently Ted Kennedy
blamed the Iraq War on another set of unspecified conspirators involved
in a politically motivated fraud "cooked up in Texas." Demagogic name-
calling is another political habit that has remained with us. In recent years
Dick Cheney has been characterized by some on the left as a Nazi in the
same way that Truman's secretary of state Dean Acheson had once been
branded as the "Red Dean" by some on the right. The blacklist should
have provided a sobering lesson on the use of extremist rhetoric, but the
tactic continues to be an option for anyone who believes it can yield partisan advantage.

In looking back on the heyday of the *Daily Worker* and *Red Channels*,
we see the danger of political forces pulling to the extremes. The greatest
failure, though, resided with those in the middle, many of them broadcasters, union officials, and sponsors who maintained they had no choice
in the matter, that they were compelled to give in to pressure groups, as
if courage were never an option. Some in the industry set an admirable
example—Mark Goodson and Charles Russell in their resistance to the

purge mentality of the time, Robert Kintner in taking his stand against empty charges made by the American Legion, and Morton Wishengrad and Jack Gould in their principled opposition to both communism and blacklisting—but few chose to follow. Shortsighted expedience was the order of the day. If the center had resisted the ideological tug-of-war early on and insisted on a sense of perspective and balance, the crisis might not have occurred at all.

Looking back on the 1950s, scriptwriter and novelist Don Mankiewicz concluded that "the great tragedy of the blacklist is that it prevented any serious inquiry into who was conspiring—there were very few people actually conspiring against the United States or working with the enemies of our country." In the absence of careful investigation, partisans indulged in a bitter, open-ended exchange of charges and countercharges. The naive suffered along with the cynically manipulative while judicious whistleblowers labored in the wake of alarmists. For many others, the gathering acrimony clouded issues for years to come.

Notes

FOREWORD

1. Arthur M. Schlesinger, Jr., *The Vital Center* (New Brunswick, N.J.: Transaction Publishers, 1998), 210.

2. Erik Barnouw, *Tube of Plenty* (New York: Oxford University Press, 1975), 122.

1: COMMUNIST SQUAD

1. John Keenan FBI file, Application for Appointment, April 1, 1941, 67-198001-2, and Report, July 10, 1941, 67-198001-16.

2. Kenneth Bierly FBI file, Application for Appointment, October 26, 1940, and Teletype Brief of Investigation, November 23, 1940.

3. Theodore Kirkpatrick FBI file, Application for Employment, May 14, 1942, 67-334276-1; transcript of interview with Theodore Kirkpatrick, Kenneth Bierly, and John Keenan, box 873, folders 1 and 2, American Civil Liberties Union Archives, Seeley G. Mudd Manuscript Library, Princeton University Library, used by permission.

4. Charles Blaisdell, personal interview by author, February 3, 2004; Gino Fopp, telephone interview by author, February 19, 2004; Charles McGroddy, telephone interview by author, August 9, 2004; Keenan FBI file, To: Director, Federal Bureau of Investigation, April 9, 1941, 67-198001-3; Kirkpatrick file, Los Angeles FBI to Director, July 7, 1942, 67-334296-13; ACLU interview.

5. Blaisdell interview.

6. Blaisdell interview; Fopp interview.

7. Blaisdell interview.

8. John Keenan, Jr., personal interview by author, January 7, 2004; Fopp interview.

9. Angela Calomiris, *Red Masquerade* (Philadelphia: Lippincott, 1950); Bierly file, Efficiency Report, March 31, 1944; Kirkpatrick file, Special Efficiency Report, January 13, 1945, 67-334296-58.

10. Keenan, Jr., interview; ACLU interview.

11. ACLU interview.

12. Arthur Herman, *Joseph McCarthy* (New York: Free Press, 2000), 36.

13. ACLU interview.

14. ACLU interview; Keenan, Jr., interview; Kirkpatrick files, J. P. Mohr to W. R. Glavin, October 26, 1945, 67-334296-70; Keenan file, J. P. Mohr to W. R. Glavin, November 16, 1945, 67-198001-67.

15. Kirkpatrick file, Edward H. Tamm to Director, April 18, 1946, and Edward Scheidt SAC to Director, September 6, 1946, 62-8845; ACLU interview.

16. Confidential Memorandum, re: John Quincy Adams Associates, American Business Consultants, Inc., *Counterattack*: Research Files, Tamiment Library/Robert F. Wagner Labor Archives, New York University.

17. Ibid., Theodore C. Kirkpatrick to Rev. William J. Smith, March 13, 1947, *Counterattack* files; ACLU interview.

18. "Communist Pressure on the Radio Industry," *Counterattack* files.

19. Kirkpatrick file, Edward Scheidt to Director, September 6, 1946; Memo, July 8, 1947, *Counterattack* files.

20. Kirkpatrick file, Scheidt to Director, September 6, 1946; Edward A. Tamm to Director, September 11, 1946; D. M. Ladd to Director, October 24, 1946. In the copies of documents from this file that I received from the FBI, Wren's name is redacted in some cases, but his name appears in other documents to make it plain that Wren is the confidential informant hired by *Plain Talk*. Completing the circle are Theodore Kirkpatrick's comments in the interview conducted by Merle Miller, to be found in the ACLU archives. Kirkpatrick makes it clear that Jack Wren, the *Plain Talk* researcher, is the same Jack Wren who went to work for the advertising agency BBD&O.

21. Kirkpatrick file, A. H. Belmont to Director, October 3, 1946, 67-334296-78.

22. Kirkpatrick file, Kirkpatrick to Director, October 17, 1947, 67-334296-102, and John Keenan to Rev. John F. Cronin, October 15, 1946.

23. Kirkpatrick file, Memo to D. M. Ladd, August 19, 1946, and Report by T. Scott Miller, September 18, 1946, 62-8845, and J. P. Coyne to E. A. Tamm, October 25, 1946.

24. Kirkpatrick file, Edward Scheidt to Director, May 20, 1947, 67-334296-89; ACLU interview.

25. Confidential Memorandum, re: John Quincy Adams Associates, *Counterattack* files; ACLU interview; John Cogley, *Report on Blacklisting, II Radio-Television* (New York: Fund for the Republic, 1956), 3.

26. ACLU interview; Theodore Kirkpatrick to Alfred Kohlberg, February 10, 1950, Alfred Kohlberg Papers, boxes 44 and 45, Counterattack folders, Hoover Institution Library and Archives, Stanford University.

27. ACLU interview; Andrew Avery, *The Communist Fifth Column* (Chicago: Journal of Commerce, 1946).

28. Blaisdell interview; Francis McNamara, telephone interview by author, March 20, 2002; Herbert Romerstein, telephone interview by author, March 26, 2004; Transcript, New York State Convention, Communist Party, July 16–18, 1948, *Counterattack* files.

29. ACLU interview.

30. "Kirkpatrick—Average American," flyer, Francis McNamara Collection, Special Collections and Archives, George Mason University; "Communism: How It Works," booklet, Francis McNamara Collection, 17.

31. *Counterattack*, May 16, 1947.

2: SOMETHING IN THE AIR

1. For an appraisal of this period in radio, see Howard Blue, *Words at War* (Lanham, Md.: Scarecrow Press, 2002).

2. Blue, *Words*, 21.

3. *The Propaganda Battlefront*, January 15, March 15, April 10, 1943; John Roy Carlson, *Under Cover* (New York: E. P. Dutton, 1943), 9.

4. Norman Corwin, *Untitled and Other Radio Dramas* (New York: Henry Holt, 1947), 384, 391–392.

5. Erik Barnouw, *Radio Drama in Action* (New York: Farrar & Rinehart, 1945), 170, 180.

6. Norman Corwin, *More by Corwin* (New York: Henry Holt, 1944), 295.

7. "Corwin Heads Radio Division of Independent Citizens Group," *Daily Worker*, May 4, 1945, 11.

8. Michele Hilmes, *Radio Voices* (Minneapolis: University of Minnesota Press, 1997), 271.

9. Robert Taylor, *Fred Allen* (Boston: Little, Brown, 1989), 281.

10. "One World Flight, Moscow," audio recording, Museum of Television and Radio, New York, N.Y.; Corwin, *Untitled*, 399.

11. "The News of Radio," *New York Times*, May 26, 1948, 50; Blue, *Words*, 348.

12. "Communism—U.S. Brand," audio recording, Museum of Television and Radio, New York, N.Y.; Jack Gould, "Communism—U.S. Brand," *New York Times*, August 8, 1948, II, 7; Saul Carson, "Radio: The Network Sees Red," *New Republic*, August 16, 1948, 27–28; Morton Wishengrad to Robert Saudek, August 15, 1948, Morton Wishengrad Papers, 1/17, courtesy of Ratner Center for the Study of Conservative Judaism, Jewish Theological Seminary; Morton Wishengrad to Anton Leader, July 22, 1948, Wishengrad Papers, 1/58.

13. Jack Langguth, ed., *Norman Corwin's Letters* (New York: Barricade Books, 1993), 104; "Broadcast Attacks Inquiry," *New York Times*, November 3, 1947, 19.

14. Keenan, Jr., interview; McGroddy interview; Catherine McCollum, telephone interview by author, February 12, 2004; Blaisdell interview.

15. *Counterattack*, July 25, September 5, 1947.

16. ACLU interview.

17. *Counterattack*, September 5, 1947; January 2, 1948.

18. *Counterattack*, September 19, 1947; October 6, 1950; ACLU interview.

19. *Counterattack*, October 31, 1947; January 9, 1948.

20. *Counterattack*, December 10, 1948; Memo, SH to JB, Subject: Paul Draper, March 26, 1948, *Counterattack* files; "Confidential/Paul Draper," February 11, 1949, *Counterattack* files.

21. Georgi Dimitrov, *The Working Class Against Fascism* (London: Martin Lawrence, 1935), 33, 38, 47.

22. Theodore Draper, *American Communism and Soviet Russia* (New York: Vintage, 1986), 171.

23. Morgan Yale Himelstein, *Drama Was a Weapon* (New Brunswick, N.J.: Rutgers University Press, 1963), 95; "Communist Rally Attended by 15,000," *New York Times*, September 14, 1937, 10.

24. Louis F. Budenz, *Men Without Faces* (New York: Harper, 1950), 216.

25. Paul Robeson, "Land of Love and Happiness," *New World Review*, December 1952, 3; Paul Robeson, *The Negro and the Soviet Union* (New York: New Century, 1950), 3; "I Am Home," *Daily Worker*, January 15, 1935, 5.

26. "The Moscow Trials: A Statement by American Progressives," *New Masses*, May 3, 1938.

27. Don Mankiewicz, telephone interview by author, July 2, 2003.

28. Joan Mellen, *Hellman and Hammett* (New York: HarperCollins, 1996), 107–108, 112; "Theodore Dreiser Gets Peace Award," *New York Times*, June 7, 1941, 5; "Reds Here Shift in Stand on War," *New York Times*, July 27, 1941, 16.

29. "Benefits for Finns Stir Theatre Row," *New York Times*, January 19, 1940, 16; "Actors Widen Split on Finn Benefits," *New York Times*, January 20, 1940, 11; "Finnish War Play Picketed," *New York Times*, May 31, 1940, 21.

30. "Two Producers Ban Theatre Arts Group," *New York Times*, October 23, 1940, 26.

31. Sidney Hook, *Out of Step* (New York: Harper & Row, 1986), 333.

32. Eugene Dennis, "Defeat the Imperial Drive Toward Fascism and War," *Political Affairs*, September 1946, 791–795, 800.

33. "Memorandum for Counter-Attack, Re: Fredric March," *Counterattack* files.

34. McNamara interview; Keenan, Jr., interview; John Keenan to Francis McNamara, December 30, 1949, McNamara collection.

35. "Concert in Greenwich," *Time*, December 15, 1947, 27; "Draper and Adler," *Newsweek*, May 1, 1950, 23.

36. "Budenz Satirical Over 'Innocents,'" *New York Times*, May 16, 1950, 13; "Trials," *Time*, June 5, 1950, 19–20.

37. "Let's Turn the Heat on Martha Deane," flyer, *Counterattack* files; Millard Lampell FBI file, Report, July 18, 1950.

38. ACLU interview; "Most Undesirable," McNamara collection.

3: CULTURAL WORK

1. ACLU interview.

2. ACLU interview; Vincent Hartnett, personal interview by author, November 29, 2001.

3. American Business Consultants, *Red Channels* (New York: Counterattack, 1950), 1, 6.

4. Ibid., 2–5.

5. Ibid., 6–7.

6. ACLU interview; *Red Channels*, 9.

7. ACLU interview; Merle Miller, *The Judges and the Judged* (Garden City, N.Y.: Doubleday, 1952), 100–101.

8. "Town Deserts U.S. for Day in Soviet," *New York Times*, May 2, 1950, 6.

9. Cogley, *Blacklisting*, 14; *Counterattack*, June 23, 1950.

10. John Lewis Gaddis, *We Now Know* (New York: Oxford University Press, 1997), 71–75.

11. "Irwin Shaw Withdraws Peace Play," *New York Times*, August 20, 1950, 81.

12. *Counterattack*, July 7, 1950.

13. *Counterattack*, July 7, 1950; "U.S. Reds Declare Truman Aggressor," *New York Times*, June 29, 1950, 18; "Koreans Free Taejon," *Daily Worker*, July 18, 1950, 1; "Korea," *Monthly Review*, August 1950, 105–118.

14. "Zone of Silence," *Nation*, May 27, 1950, 52; "Zone of Silence," *Nation*, July 8, 1950, 39; Elizabeth Dilling, *Red Network* (Chicago: Dilling, 1934).

15. *Counterattack*, July 28, 1950.

16. ACLU interview.

17. "Purge of Performers," *Newsweek*, September 11, 1950, 51; "The Truth About Red Channels," *Sponsor*, October 8, 1951, 76.

18. "Purge of Performers"; Jack Gould, "TV Play Cancelled in Fight over Actress," *New York Times*, August 28, 1950, 1.

19. Michael Dann, personal interview by author, July 16, 2003.

20. Jack Gould, "Aldrich Show Drops Jean Muir; TV Actress Denies Communist Ties," *New York Times*, August 29, 1950, 1.

21. Ibid.; "Miss Muir Is Ready to Deny Communism," *New York Times*, September 2, 1950, 22.

22. Editorial, "Jean Muir and 'Old Man Atom,'" *New Leader*, September 9, 1950, 30; Editorial, "No Private Censors," *Life*, September 11, 1950, 56; Jack Gould, "General Foods Seeks Radio Unit to Set Policy on Pro-Red Charges," *New York Times*, September 12, 1950, 15.

23. Jack Gould, "Case of Jean Muir," *New York Times*, September 3, 1950, 49.

24. A. M. Sperber, *Murrow* (New York: Freundlich, 1986), 283, 286; Joseph E. Persico, *Edward R. Murrow* (New York: McGraw-Hill, 1988), 251–256; "Zone of Silence," May 27, 1950.

25. Edward Meyerding to George Soll, ACLU archive, Princeton University.

26. Louis Francis Budenz, "How the Reds Invaded Radio," *American Legion Magazine*, December 1950, 14–15, 60–61.

27. John Earl Haynes and Harvey Klehr, *Venona* (New Haven: Yale University Press, 2000), 425–426; Romerstein interview.

28. Haynes and Klehr, *Venona*, 222–223, 234, 250, 261–262, 276–283; Herbert Romerstein and Eric Breindel, *The Venona Secrets* (Washington: Regnery, 2000), 342–344; Romerstein interview.

29. Haynes and Klehr, *Venona*, 77–79, 196, 198–200; Henry Denker, personal interview by author, December 1, 2003.

30. "Labor Ends Bureau Set Up to Aid OWI," *New York Times*, October 5, 1943, 31; Elmer Davis testimony, Hearings Before the Select Committee to Conduct an Investigation of the Facts, Evidence, and Circumstances of the Katyn Forest Massacre, 82nd Congress, 2nd Session (Washington: U.S. Government Printing Office, 1952), 1992–1993, 1995.

31. *Third Venona Release* (Fort George G. Meade, Md.: NSA/CSS, 1996); Haynes and Klehr, *Venona*, 175; Katherine A. S. Sibley, *Red Spies in America* (Lawrence: University Press of Kansas, 2004) 159; *Now!*, April 4, 1946.

32. Haynes and Klehr, *Venona*, 109–111, 237–238, 262, 347–348; "CBS Man Admits He Was a Spy," *New York Times*, June 30, 1955, 1.

33. "Radio—The Voice of Our Mass Agitation," *Party Organizer*, April 1936; "How Can We Secure the Use of Radio?," *Party Organizer*, February 1935; "Foster to Address Symposium on 'Art as a Weapon' Tonight," *Daily Worker*, April 18, 1946, 13; William Z. Foster, "Elements of People's Cultural Policy," *New Masses*, April 23, 1946, 6–9.

34. Harvey Klehr, John Earl Haynes, and Fridrikh Igorevich Firsov, *The Secret World of American Communism* (New Haven: Yale University Press, 1995), 25–26; Harvey Klehr, John Earl Haynes, and Kyrill M. Anderson, *The Soviet World of American Communism* (New Haven: Yale University Press, 1998), 111, 139, 141–142, 148; Edward Jay Epstein, *Dossier: The Secret History of Armand Hammer* (New York: Random House, 1996), 40–41; Transcript, New York State Convention, Communist Party.

35. Stanley B. Hancock testimony, HUAC, 83rd Congress, 2nd Session (Washington: U.S. Government Printing Office, 1954), 4541.

36. Jack Newfield, Budd Schulberg interview, *Tikkun*, May 2000; Alan Wald and Alan Filreis, "A Conversation with Howard Fast," *www.trussel.com/hf/prospect.htm*.

37. "Puppets for Propaganda," flyer, *Counterattack* files.

38. For evidence of Bernay's relationship with Soviet spy Arthur Adams, see Haynes and Klehr, *Venona*, 175.

39. Almanac Singers, *The Almanac Singers: Songs of Protest*, CD audio recording, Prism Leisure, 2001.

40. Martin Bauml Duberman, *Paul Robeson* (New York: Alfred A. Knopf, 1988), 352–354; Louis Rapoport, *Stalin's War Against the Jews* (New York: Free Press, 1990), 109, 115–117.

41. *Voice of Freedom*, May 1948, October 1948.

42. "Would Ban Iron Curtain," *New York Times*, February 9, 1948, 24.

43. People's Radio Foundation pamphlet, *Counterattack* files; V. J. Jerome, *Culture in a Changing World* (New York: New Century, 1947), 60–61.

44. "FM Radio Channel Denied Daily News," *New York Times*, November 5, 1947, 54; "Red Baiters and Radio Baiters," *New Leader*, February 15, 1947, 5; Walter K. Lewis, "Earphones for the Comrades," *New Leader*, March 2, 1947, 5, 19.

45. Ruth Knight testimony, "Subversive Infiltration of Radio, Television and the Entertainment Industry, Part 1," Subcommittee to Investigate the Administration of the Internal Security Act and Other Internal Security Laws of the Committee on the Judiciary, United States Senate (SISS), 82nd Congress, 1st and 2nd Sessions (Washington, U.S. Government Printing Office, 1952), 56; Welbourn Kelley testimony, SISS, 79.

46. Denker interview; Kelley testimony, SISS, 80, 87; Knight testimony, SISS, 58.

47. Denker interview; Jarrico quoted in Mankiewicz interview.

48. Barnouw, *Radio Drama in Action*, 81.

49. Peter Lyon FBI file, Office Memorandum, SAC New York to Director FBI, August 17, 1950, 100-263654-5.

50. Blue, *Words*, 126; Ernest Kinoy, telephone interview by author, June 3, 2003.

51. Lyon FBI file, Report: Robert Crawford Lyon, Jr., July 7, 1950, 100-263654-4.

52. Songs for John Doe circular, courtesy of Ronald Cohen; Lyon FBI file, E. E. Conroy to Director, FBI, January 17, 1944, 100-263654-1.

53. Eric Bentley, ed., *Thirty Years of Treason: Excerpts from Hearings Before the House Committee on Un-American Activities, 1938–1968* (New York: Viking, 1971), 656;

Pauline Swanson Townsend testimony, "Investigation of Communist Activities in the Los Angeles Area," HUAC, 83rd Congress, 1st Session, 957. For information on the CPUSA requirement for transfer cards, see J. Peters, *The Communist Party: A Manual of Organization* (New York: Workers Library, 1935), 108.

54. Lyon FBI file, Office Memorandum, August 17, 1950; Jane Lyon, telephone interview by author, April 14, 2003; Peter Ivy, "On the Air: Two Very Important Matters," *Daily Worker,* October 1, 1943.

55. Lyon FBI file, Report, July 7, 1950, and Report: Robert Crawford Lyon, Jr., March 10, 1951, 100-263654-11.

56. Minutes, Meeting of Radio Writers Guild Eastern Region Council, July 25, 1950, Radio Writers Guild Records, New York Public Library for the Performing Arts.

57. Minutes, Radio Writers Guild, July 25, 1950; Kelley testimony, SISS, 84.

58. Minutes, Radio Writers Guild, July 25, 1950.

59. *Radio Writers Guild News Letter,* October 5, 1950, Radio Writers Guild Collection.

60. Minutes, Radio Writers Guild, May 24, May 27, 1948; Morton Wishengrad to Saul Blackman, May 1, 1955, Wishengrad Papers, 1/55.

61. *Counterattack,* November 10, 1950; Ernie Pyle, "Economics and Social Ethics Interest Hollywood's Radical Actress, Jean Muir, Who Fought Way Back to Stardom," *New York World Telegram,* December 31, 1936, clipping, *Counterattack* files.

62. Erik Barnouw to Sheldon Stark, October 8, 1950, Radio Writers Guild Collection.

63. For information on Sokolsky's relationship to Hart and Smith, see Carlson, *Under Cover,* 466.

4: COMRADES OF THE COMRADES

1. Robert Metz, *CBS: Reflections in a Bloodshot Eye* (Chicago: Playboy Press, 1975), 282; *Counterattack,* July 1, 1949.

2. Kirkpatrick FBI file, SAC New York to Director, FBI, September 27, 1950, 123-3708; Sig Mickelson, interview by Steven H. Scheuer, September 27, 1996, Steven H. Scheuer Television History Collection, Special Collections Research Center, Syracuse University Library; Gary May, *Un-American Activities* (New York: Oxford University Press, 1994), 147, 151.

3. Persico, *Murrow,* 341; Metz, *CBS,* 281; Sally Bedell Smith, *In All His Glory* (New York: Simon & Schuster, 1990), 303.

4. Jack Gould, "C.B.S. Demanding Loyalty Oaths from Its 2,500 Regular Employees," *New York Times,* December 21, 1950, 1.

5. Persico, *Murrow,* 342; Smith, *Glory,* 303.

6. Alan Wagner, personal interview by author, June 9, 2003.

7. Wagner interview; Frank Stanton, interview by David Marc, May 21, 1999, Steven H. Scheuer Television History Collection; Smith, *Glory,* 306.

8. Susan L. Brinson, *The Red Scare, Politics, and the Federal Communications Commission, 1941–1960* (Westport, Conn.: Praeger, 2004), 129–133, 142–155; Susan Brinson, e-mail to author, March 22, 2005; William Robson, interview, ACLU Archive, Princeton University.

9. Jack Gould, "Legion Won't Back Lee Case Charges," *New York Times*, September 14, 1950; "The Accused," *Time*, September 25, 1950, 81.

10. Editorial, *New York Post*, September 13, 1950, clipping, Gypsy Rose Lee Papers, New York Public Library for the Performing Arts.

11. Jack Gould, "Loyalty Probe," *New York Times*, January 7, 1951, 91.

12. Persico, *Murrow*, 342; Minutes, Radio Writers Guild, January 18, 1951; "CBS Dismisses Girl Office Employee for Refusal to Sign Its Loyalty Statement," *New York Times*, January 26, 1951, 15.

13. Kirkpatrick FBI file, L. B. Nichols to Mr. Tolson, February 15, 1949; Cogley, *Blacklisting*, 35.

14. Jack Gould, "TV 'Red Ban' Lifted by General Foods," *New York Times*, September 27, 1950, 32.

15. "Equity Denies Reds Sit on Ruling Board," *New York Times*, July 10, 1940, 15; Kirkpatrick FBI file, E. M. Terrens to F. J. Baumgardner, April 21, 1949; Memo re: Philip Loeb, May 18, 1951, Philip Loeb Papers, Manuscripts and Archives Division, New York Public Library; "The Moscow Trials," *New Masses*; Philip Loeb testimony, "Subversive Infiltration of Radio, Television, and the Entertainment Industry, Part 2," SISS, 82nd Congress, 2nd Session, 197–199; "Bob Reed: Fighter for Freedom," *Daily Worker*, May 22, 1950, 11.

16. "The Truth About Red Channels," *Sponsor*, October 8, 1951; Thomas Doherty, *Cold War, Cool Medium* (New York: Columbia University Press, 2003), 43, 46.

17. Jack Gould, "Actor Is Dropped from Video Cast," *New York Times*, January 8, 1952, 29; "Ousted Video Player Gets 'Goldberg' Fee," *New York Times*, January 25, 1952, 13.

18. Jack Gould, "Network Rejects Protest by Legion," *New York Times*, September 13, 1950, 9; Vincent Hartnett testimony, "Investigation of So-Called 'Blacklisting' in Entertainment Industry," HUAC, 84th Congress, 2nd Session (Washington: U.S. Government Printing Office, 1956), 5304.

19. Ted Poston, "Only Sad Songs for Singing Lady as 'Red Channels' Plays Off Key," *New York Post*, September 11, 1950, 5, ACLU Archive; "Singing Lady Sets Youth Plays," *New York Times*, January 15, 1952, 22; "Radio-TV Notes," *New York Times*, September 23, 1952, 30; Cogley, *Blacklisting*, 34; "News of TV and Radio," *New York Times*, September 27, 1953, 131.

20. Ralph Bell and Pert Kelton to Patrick Malin, October 12, 1952, ACLU Archive.

21. David King Dunaway, *How Can I Keep from Singing: Pete Seeger* (New York: McGraw-Hill, 1981), 152.

22. "News Report," July 12, 1950, *Counterattack* files.

23. ACLU interview; "The Truth About Red Channels," *Sponsor*, October 22, 1951.

24. "Flagstad Here, Defends Record; Has Norse Testimonial of Conduct," *New York Times*, March 15, 1947, 1; "Flagstad Draws 2,700 to Concert," *New York Times*, April 12, 1950, 32.

25. John Crosby quoted in "The Truth About Red Channels," *Sponsor*, October 22, 1951.

26. "'Counterattack' Prints Sequel to Liz Dilling's 'Red Network', Sets Self Up as Radio Censor," *In Fact*, 1.

27. "The Truth About Red Channels," *Sponsor*, October 22, 1951; *Counterattack*, April 14, 1950; ACLU interview.

28. "'Counterattack' Prints Sequel.'"

29. Eugene Lyons, "Red Mouthpiece," *Plain Talk*, March 1947, 3–13; "The Moscow Trials," *New Masses*; examples of Seldes staying close to the party line may be found in *In Fact*, June 3 and August 26, 1940; June 9 and July 14, 1941; June 19, 1950.

30. Miller, *Judged*, 89–91; "Exhibit 4: Names of Unidentified Persons Quoted in Judges and the Judged," box 872, folder 4, ACLU Archive; Kirkpatrick FBI file, L. B. Nichols to Mr. Tolson, February 15, 1949.

31. Walter Bernstein, *Inside Out* (New York: Alfred A. Knopf, 1996), 25; Mona Z. Smith, *Becoming Something: The Story of Canada Lee* (New York: Faber and Faber, 2004), 296; Elijah Wald, *Josh White* (Amherst: University of Massachusetts Press, 2000), 180–184; John Cogley testimony, HUAC, 84th Congress, 2nd Session, 5223.

32. Kirkpatrick FBI file, SAC New York to Director, FBI, June 22, 1949, 62-9189, H. B. Fletcher to D. M. Ladd, July 7, 1949, and H. B. Fletcher to D. M. Ladd, July 19, 1949.

33. Miller, *Judged*, 89–91; Kirkpatrick file, Los Angeles FBI to Director, July 7, 1942, 67-334296-10.

34. "Counterattack's Attack," *Newsweek*, June 30, 1952, 64; "Mr. Counterattack Quits," *Time*, June 30, 1952, 56.

35. "Only Sad Songs for Singing Lady," *New York Post*.

36. Oscar Brand to Counterattack, no date, *Counterattack* files; Inter-Office Memo, TCK to HAM, December 22, 1949, *Counterattack* files.

37. Ibid.

38. Joseph Julian, *This Was Radio* (New York: Viking, 1975), 175–176.

39. Blaisdell interview.

40. Romerstein interview.

41. "How to Keep Reds Off the Air—Sanely," *Sponsor*, November 5, 1951, 32–34, 84–87; "Mr. Counterattack Quits," *Time*.

42. Julian, *Radio*, 168.

5: CONFRONTING AN INSTITUTION

1. Michael C. Burton, *John Henry Faulk* (Austin, Tex.: Eakin, 1993), 4–16, 33; John Henry Faulk, *Fear on Trial* (New York: Simon & Schuster, 1964), 111–112.

2. Burton, *Faulk*, 21–24; Faulk, *Fear*, 111–113; John Henry Faulk to Mr. Bedichek and all the boys, December 31, 1951, box 3Q6, Roy Bedichek Papers, Center for American History, University of Texas at Austin.

3. Burton, *Faulk*, 33, 36.

4. Faulk, *Fear*, 113; "Texas Talk," *Newsweek*, December 29, 1952, 44–45; Louis Nizer, *The Jury Returns* (Garden City, N.Y.: Doubleday, 1966), 253.

5. Burton, *Faulk*, 48, 60–63; Hally Wood FBI file, Report: Harriet Elizabeth Gordon, November 10, 1953, 100-181-324-31.

6. John Henry Faulk FBI file, Report: John Henry Faulk, February 1, 1943, 100-181329-1, and Report: Hallie Faulk, February 16, 1943, 100-3807, and J. E. Hoover to Special Agent in Charge, San Antonio, Texas, April 18, 1944, 100-181329.

7. Faulk FBI file, Report: John Henry Faulk, Harriet Wood Faulk, March 23, 1944, 100-3754, and Office Memorandum, SAC San Antonio to Director, September 30, 1948, 100-3754; Burton, *Faulk*, 34.

8. Burton, *Faulk*, 78–79; "Texas Talk"; "John Henry Faulk," *Variety*, December 26, 1951, clipping, New York Public Library for the Performing Arts.

9. "Programs of the Week," *New York Times*, March 16, 1947, X8; Burton, *Faulk*, 80–81, 91; "Hootenanny," March 10, 1947, RadioGoldindex, www.radiogoldindex.com; "Sing Out Against the Witch Hunters," flyer, *Counterattack* files.

10. John Henry Faulk to Mr. Bedichek, April 6, 1948, Bedichek Papers.

11. "1948 Election Platform of the Communist Party," *Political Affairs*, September 1948, 943.

12. David McCullough, *Truman* (New York: Simon & Schuster, 1992), 646; William L. O'Neill, *A Better World* (New York: Simon & Schuster, 1982), 146, 149, 150–151; Anne Applebaum, *Gulag* (New York: Doubleday, 2003), 441–444.

13. Faulk FBI file, Office Memorandum, SAC San Antonio to Director, August 5, 1948, 100-3754, and Office Memorandum, SAC New York to Director, December 9, 1948, 100-91461.

14. Burton, *Faulk*, 90; John Henry Faulk to Mr. Bedichek, December 2, 1948, Bedichek Papers.

15. Burton, *Faulk*, 91–92; Faulk to Bedichek, December 2, 1948, Bedichek Papers; "Texas Talk"; John Henry Faulk to Bedichek, October 30, 1950, Bedichek Papers; Nizer, *Jury*, 300.

16. Faulk to Bedichek and all the boys, December 31, 1951, Bedichek Papers; Burton, *Faulk*, 100–101.

17. "John Henry Faulk," *Variety*; "John Henry Faulk, Humorist," *Billboard*, February 9, 1952, 16; Trial Transcript, *John Henry Faulk v. Aware, Inc., Laurence A. Johnson and Vincent Hartnett*, 179, 205.

18. Burton, *Faulk*, 87.

19. John Henry Faulk to Mr. Bedichek, September 8, 1950, May 19, 1951; October 30, 1950; November 20, 1951, Bedichek Papers.

20. Faulk to Bedichek, November 20, 1951, Bedichek Papers; "Korea—One Year Later," *Monthly Review*, August 1951, 108–109.

21. Faulk to Bedichek, May 19, 1951, November 20, 1951, Bedichek Papers.

22. Burton, *Faulk*, 87; Faulk to Bedichek, November 20, 1951, Bedichek Papers.

23. Smith, *Glory*, 304–305.

24. Blue, *Words*, 354–355; Julian, *Radio*, 180.

25. Sidney Lumet, telephone interview by author, May 6, 2004.

26. Kirkpatrick FBI file, Scheidt to Director, September 6, 1946; phone message, Wren to *Counterattack*, McNamara Collection; Inter-Office Memo, Subject: Paul Draper, March 26, 1948, *Counterattack* files; Tom Villante, e-mail to author, March 10, 2004.

27. Abe Burrows to Joseph Ream, November 24, 1950, Abe Burrows Papers, New York Public Library for the Performing Arts; Martin Gang to Abe Burrows, November 7, 1951, Burrows Papers; Burrows Statement, May 11, 1951, Burrows Papers; George A. Bolas to Larry Johnson, May 12, 1952, Harvey Matusow Papers, Special Collections, University of Sussex.

28. Martin Gang to Abe Burrows, March 29, 1951, Burrows Papers; Martin Gang to C. Michael Smith, May 21, 1951, Burrows Papers; Gang to Burrows, November 7, 1951, Burrows Papers; Martin Gang to Jack Wren, May 23, 1951, Burrows Papers; C. Michael Smith to Abe Burrows, July 18, 1951, Burrows Papers.

29. Jeff Kisseloff, *The Box* (New York: Penguin, 1995), 423–424.

30. "New NABUG Committee to Seek Facts on 'Blacklist,'" *Stand By*, August 1949, 1, 6; "AFRA, Strongly Unified, Girds for Negotiation; Anti-Communist Action Taken by Convention," *Stand By*, August 1950, 1, 2, 4; "Radio Actors Vote to Bar Communists," *New York Times*, August 9, 1951, 18.

31. From the ACLU Archive, *Judges and the Judged* files: Louis Untermeyer to Patrick Malin, July 1, 1952; Peter Lyon interview; Himan Brown to Patrick Malin, October 20, 1950; Marc Connelly to Patrick Malin, July 14, 1952; Alexander Kendrick to Patrick Malin, October 18, 1950; Howard K. Smith to Patrick Malin, July 18, 1952; Uta Hagen to Patrick Malin, July 1, 1952; L. LeRoy Bannerman, *Norman Corwin and Radio* (University, Ala.: University of Alabama Press, 1986), 219.

32. Ralph Bell and Pert Kelton to Patrick Malin; Cogley, *Blacklisting*, 49.

33. Pat Weaver with Thomas M. Coffy, *The Best Seat in the House* (New York: Alfred A. Knopf, 1994), 238; Kinoy interview; Kisseloff, *Box*, 416.

34. Edith Hamlin, telephone interview by author, April 14, 2003.

35. Mark Goodson, interview (New York: American Jewish Committee, Oral History Library, 1978), New York Public Library.

36. Oliver Platt, "Blacklist," *New York Post*, January 30, 1953, 20; Louis Calta, "Shumlin Acquires Play for New Year," *New York Times*, September 27, 1951, 38; "Drama Mailbag," *New York Times*, November 4, 1951, X3.

37. "Bromberg Silent When Called Red," *New York Times*, June 27, 1951, 9.

38. *Counterattack*, June 29, December 14, 1951.

39. Irwin Shaw, *The Troubled Air* (New York: Random House, 1951), 380.

40. "The Truth About Red Channels," *Sponsor*, October 8, 1951; "The Truth About Red Channels," *Sponsor*, October 22, 1951; "How to Keep Reds Off the Air — Sanely," *Sponsor*, November 5, 1951; *Counterattack*, November 23, 1951.

41. Miller, *Judged*, 211.

42. "Blacklisting Laid to 4 Big Networks," *New York Times*, April 9, 1952, 33; "Air 'Bias' Protest Denied," *New York Times*, June 12, 1952, 20.

43. *Counterattack*, April 11, 1952.

44. Melvin S. Pitzele, "Is There a Blacklist?," *New Leader*, May 12, 1952, 21–23.

45. "Exhibit 4: Names of Unidentified Persons Quoted in *The Judges and the Judged*," ACLU Archive.

46. "Exhibit 5: Report on 2 Right Wingers," *The Judges and the Judged* files, ACLU Archive.

47. Pitzele, "Is There a Blacklist?"

48. Rex Lardner, "The Thought Papers," *New York Post*, April 14, 1952, McNamara Collection.

49. Katherine Weathersby, "New Evidence on the Korean War," *Cold War History Project*, Winter 1998, 176–184; Milton Leitenberg, "The Korean War Biological Weapon Allegations: Additional Information and Disclosures," *Asian Perspective* 24, no. 3 (2000), 156–172.

6: THE BOYS FROM SYRACUSE

1. Edmund Roe Johnson with Laurence Ayres Johnson, *Genealogy of the Descendants of Captain Edmund Johnson, circa 1741–1812* (Lyons, N.Y.: 1954).

2. Ibid.

3. Ibid.; untitled clipping, *Syracuse Post-Standard*, Onondaga Historical Association (OHA).

4. *Genealogy*; Laurence Ayres Johnson, *Over the Counter and On the Shelf: Country Storekeeping in America, 1620–1920* (Rutland, Vt.: C. E. Tuttle, 1961), ix, 122.

5. *Genealogy*; "Food Chain of Johnson Adds Store," April 9, 1941, clipping, OHA; Johnson, *Over the Counter*, ix, 125–126.

6. "Food Chain of Johnson Adds Store"; Johnson, *Over the Counter*, 125–126.

7. "Now Grandma, Were They the Good Old Days?," newspaper clipping, August 25, 1946, OHA; "Syracuse of a Century Ago Still Lives!" newspaper advertisement, OHA.

8. "Magazine Praises Syracuse Grocer," newspaper clipping, September 12, 1941, OHA; "Super-Market Group Honors L.A. Johnson," newspaper clipping, June 24, 1944, OHA.

9. Stephen Mayka, telephone interview by author, February 12, 2004; Mrs. Thomas Kenyon, telephone interview by author, October 15, 2003; Stephen Mayka, telephone interview by author, October 15, 2003.

10. *Genealogy*; "Volunteer Workers," newspaper clipping, October 5, 1943, OHA; Fred Fiske, "Red Scare Linked Faulk, Syracuse," *Syracuse Post-Standard*, April 11, 1990.

11. "Replicas of Drug Store of '60s Highlight Johnson's Museum," *Syracuse Herald Journal*, February 7, 1952, clipping, OHA; Oliver Pilat, "How the Blacklist Works in TV-Radio," *New York Post*, January 28, 1953, 4, 64.

12. "Flattery Advised as Aid to Selling," *New York Times*, May 16, 1950, 53.

13. *Genealogy*.

14. Eleanor Buchanan to J. L. Van Volkenberg, September 13, 1951, box 30, folder 26, George Sokolsky Papers, Hoover Institution Library and Archives, Stanford University.

15. "How the Blacklist Works"; Karl Baarslag, "The Joan of Arc of Syracuse," *National News American Legion Auxiliary*, April 1952, McNamara collection; The Weavers, *Wasn't That a Time*, Vanguard Records, 1993, disk 4.

16. *Genealogy*.

17. Veterans Action Committee flyer, Matusow Papers.

18. Kenyon interview; Hines interview; Mayka interview.

19. Margaret Neuser, telephone interview by author, May 6, 2002.

20. Veterans Action Committee to Liggett & Myers, September 10, 1951, box 30, folder 26, Sokolsky Papers; J. L. Van Volkenberg to Laurence Johnson, September 5, 1951, Matusow Papers; Veterans Action Committee to J. L. Van Volkenberg, September 13, 1951, box 30, folder 26, Sokolsky Papers.

21. John K. Dungey, telephone interview by author, May 9, 2002; Dorothy Dungey, telephone interview by author, May 15, 2002; William Dungey, telephone interview by author, May 16, 2002; flagpole and inscription, personal collection of Dungey family.

22. Dorothy Dungey interview; John K. Dungey interview; "Monthly Box Score," *Spotlight*, March 1952, McNamara collection.

23. "Joint Committee Notes," *Jews Against Communism*, Summer 1952, 2–3, Matusow Papers.

24. Veterans Action Committee to Supermarket, Chain and Independent Operators, Buyers, Merchandisers, March 7, 1952, McNamara Collection; Laurence Johnson to Melvin Block, June 17, 1952, McNamara Collection.

25. Veterans Action Committee to the Directors of the Borden Company, July 1, 1952, McNamara Collection; SP to Francis W. Neuser, July 8, 1952, McNamara Collection; Oliver Pilat, "Blacklist: The Veto Power in TV-Radio," *New York Post*, January 27, 1953, 4, 56.

26. John M. Fox to Laurence Johnson, October 14, 1952, box 66, folder 14, Sokolsky Papers.

27. Laurence Johnson to F. J. Niedermiller, June 26, 1952, box 66, folder 14, Sokolsky Papers; Karl Mundt to Laurence Johnson, February 18, 1954, Sokolsky Papers.

28. Laurence Johnson to Joseph McConnell, October 10, 1953, personal collection of Dungey family.

29. Laurence Johnson to Karl Mundt, February 23, 1954, box 66, folder 14, Sokolsky Papers; Faulk trial transcript, 2442–2444; Veterans Action Committee to Everybody in Retail Foods, April 9, 1952, McNamara Collection.

30. Veterans Action Committee to Supermarket, Chain and Independent Operators; Laurence Johnson to N. H. McElroy, May 8, 1952, McNamara Collection; Howard J. Morgens to Laurence Johnson, May 20, 1952, box 66, folder 14, Sokolsky Papers; Howard J. Morgens to Laurence Johnson, July 1, 1952, box 66, folder 14, Sokolsky Papers; Oliver Pilat, "Blacklist," *New York Post*, January 29, 1953, 25; Johnson to Niedermiller; Francis Neuser to George Sokolsky, box 91, folder 2, April 27, 1953, Sokolsky Papers; Hines interview.

31. Lawrence Myers, telephone interview by author, June 18, 2003; Cogley, *Blacklisting*, 107; "Blacklist: The Veto Power in TV-Radio"; "How the Blacklist Works."

32. Myers interview.

33. Joan Vadeboncoeur, telephone interview by author, June 17, 2003.

34. Myers interview.

35. Myers interview; Cogley, *Blacklisting*, 108.

36. Faulk trial transcript, 2726–2739.

37. "Blacklist: The Veto Power in TV-Radio."

38. Robert M. Lichtman and Ronald D. Cohen, *Deadly Farce: Harvey Matusow and the Informer System in the McCarthy Era* (Urbana: University of Illinois Press, 2004), 17–18; Harvey Matusow, *False Witness* (New York: Cameron & Kahn, 1955), 19–20.

39. Murray Kempton, *America Comes of Middle Age* (Boston: Little, Brown, 1963), 320; Lichtman and Cohen, *Farce*, 19.

40. Lichtman and Cohen, *Farce*, 22–31.

41. Ibid., 40.

42. Robert Lichtman and Ronald D. Cohen, "Harvey Matusow, the FBI, and the Justice Department: Becoming a Government Informer-witness in the McCarthy Era," *American Communist History* 1, no. 1 (2002), 49–61.

43. Matusow, *Witness*, 108.

44. Lichtman and Cohen, *Farce*, 50; Theodore Kirkpatrick to Harvey Matusow, February 14, 1952, Matusow Papers.

45. Matusow, *Witness*, 116–117; "Yogi Berra Ousts Guilford on TV," *New York Journal-American*, June 25, 1952, clipping, Matusow Papers.

46. Matusow, *Witness*, 119–120, 123.

47. Ibid., 123.

48. Laurence Johnson to Harvey Matusow, August 14, 1952, Matusow Papers; Matusow, *Witness*, 123–124; Faulk trial transcript, 3564–3572.

49. Faulk trial transcript, 2697–2706, 2751–2752.

50. Lumet interview; Bernstein, *Inside Out*, 25, 209–210; for references to the Communist background of Bernstein, Manoff, and Polonsky, see ibid., 11, 60, 134, and Patrick McGilligan and Paul Buhle, *Tender Comrades* (New York: St. Martin's, 1997), 46, 483.

51. Melvin Block to Francis Neuser, November 25 (no year), box 91, folder 2, Sokolsky Papers; Lumet interview; Laurence Johnson to Melvin Block, June 17, 1952, McNamara Collection.

52. Lumet interview.

53. Matusow, *Witness*, 177–178, 182.

7: CONGRESSIONAL OVERSIGHT

1. C. P. Trussell, "House Group Asks Spy Death Penalty in Time of Peace," *New York Times*, February 17, 1952, 1.

2. Knight testimony, 49–76; Kelley testimony, 77–88; Paul Milton testimony, SISS, 17–48.

3. Lyon FBI file, Office Memorandum, L. L. Laughlin to D. M. Ladd, September 14, 1951, 100-263654-13.

4. McGilligan and Buhle, 392; Millard Lampell FBI file, Report: Millard Lampell, July 22, 1955, 104-1481, Report on Millard Lampell, September 12, 1950; Office Memorandum, SAC New York to Director, FBI, August 17, 1950, 62-8988, Office Memorandum, L. L. Laughlin to D. M. Ladd, September 12, 1951. Sylvia Richards testimony, HUAC, 83rd Congress, 1st Session, 427.

5. Sam Levenson testimony, SISS, 127–140; Judy Holliday testimony, SISS, 141–186; Burl Ives testimony, SISS, 205–228; Lichtman and Cohen, *Farce*, 58; Will Holtzman, *Judy Holliday* (New York: Putnam, 1982), 155–156.

6. Knight testimony, 64, 66; Milton testimony, 45; "The First Commando," *Cavalcade of America*, radio script, New York Public Library for the Performing Arts; "The First Commando," *Cavalcade of America*, audio recording.

7. Paul Jarrico testimony, HUAC, 82nd Congress, 1st Session, 276.

8. Judith Raymond testimony, HUAC, 83rd Congress, 2nd Session, 4974; Stanley Rubin testimony, HUAC, 83rd Congress, 1st Session, 913.

9. George Hall testimony, HUAC, 84th Congress, 1st Session, 2378; Allen Sloane testimony, HUAC, 83rd Congress, 2nd Session, 3859; Abe Burrows testimony, HUAC, 82nd Congress, 2nd Session, 4477; Haynes and Klehr, *Venona*, 233, 377–378.

10. Burrows testimony, 4478.

11. Sloane testimony, 3863.

12. Owen Vinson testimony, HUAC, 82nd Congress, 1st Session, 4084.

13. Herbert Hill, "The Communist Party—Enemy of Negro Equality," *Crisis*, June–July 1951, 365–371, 421–424; Wilson Record, "The Negro and the Communists," *New Leader*, April 23, 1951, 15–18.

14. "The Communist Party—Enemy of Negro Equality"; Benjamin J. Davis, "New Times," *Daily Worker*, April 8, 1945; Hall Testimony, 2375.

15. Paul Marion testimony, HUAC, 82nd Congress, 1st Session, 4105; Martin Berkeley testimony, HUAC, 82nd Congress, 1st Session, 1606; Rubin testimony, 913, Babette Lang testimony, HUAC, 83rd Congress, 1st Session, 2343.

16. Bernstein, *Inside Out*, 139; Paul Buhle and Dave Wagner, *Radical Hollywood* (New York: New Press, 2002), 265; Leopold L. Atlas testimony, HUAC, 83rd Congress, 1st Session, 945.

17. Richards testimony, 426; Townsend testimony, 962–963; Carin Kinzel Burrows testimony, HUAC, 83rd Congress, 1st Session, 1331.

18. Joseph R. Starobin, *American Communism in Crisis, 1943–1957* (Cambridge: Harvard University Press, 1972), 197–200.

19. Sloane testimony, 3860, 3862–3863.

20. Ibid., 3873.

21. Leonardo Bercovici testimony, HUAC, 82nd Congress, 1st Session, 446; Howard Bay testimony, HUAC, 83rd Congress, 2nd Session, 3881; Waldo Salt testimony, HUAC, 82nd Congress, 1st Session, 269.

22. O'Neill, *Better*, 326–327.

23. Millard Lampell testimony, SISS, 117.

24. Peter Lyon testimony, SISS, 90, 93, 96.

25. *Subversive Infiltration of Radio, Television and the Entertainment Industry* (Washington: U.S. Government Printing Office, 1952), iv; C. P. Trussell, "McCarran Inquiry Unit Says Pro-Reds Rule Radio Guild," *New York Times*, August 28, 1952, 1–2.

26. Kelley testimony, 84–85; "McCarran Inquiry Unit."

27. *Counterattack*, August 29, 1952; Lyon interview; McGilligan and Buhle, *Comrades*, 398–399.

28. Kirkpatrick FBI file, J. P. Mohr to Tolson, March 11, 1952; Edward Scheidt to J. Edgar Hoover, March 13, 1952, 67-334296-132; A. H. Belmont to D. M. Ladd, June 21, 1952, 67-334296-136.

29. Kirkpatrick FBI file, Edward Scheidt to J. Edgar Hoover, August 1, 1952, and Belmont to Ladd, June 21, 1952; Lucille Kirkpatrick, telephone interview by author, October 30, 2003; Theodore Kirkpatrick obituary, clipping, Earlham College Alumni Department.

30. "Mr. Counterattack Quits"; "Counterattack's Attack"; Blaisdell interview.

31. "Cornell Suspends 25 for a Year for 'War' Report on Seized Radio," *New York Times*, May 30, 1952, 17; "The WBVR Incident," *Cornell Daily Sun*, June 6, 1952, 4–5; *Counterattack*, June 6, 1952.

32. Vincent Hartnett testimony, SISS, 13–14.

8: THE PASSION

1. "J. P. Hartnett Dies; Cartier Executive," *New York Times*, May 30, 1937, 18; Vincent Hartnett to author, April 24, 2003.

2. Hartnett to author, April 24, 2003.

3. "Fordham Honors Go to 161 Students," *New York Times*, July 24, 1934, 17; e-mails, Matthew Wilkin, University of Notre Dame records department, to author, November 11, November 17, November 18, 2003; Hartnett testimony, HUAC, 5292.

4. Faulk trial transcript, 4836–4839; Hartnett testimony, SISS, 2–3; Vincent Hartnett to author, August 4, 2003; Hartnett interview.

5. Faulk trial, 4841–4843; Vincent Hartnett, "Turkey Faces the Slav Colossus," *The Sign*, January 1947, 15–17; Vincent Hartnett, "Theme and Variations," *The Sign*, November 1947, 56–58; Vincent Hartnett, "The Way to the Heart," *The Sign*, March 1947, 16–17.

6. Hartnett interview; Faulk trial transcript, 4841–4843.

7. Hartnett interview; Vincent Hartnett, "Red Fronts in Radio," *The Sign*, October 1949, 11–13, 68; Vincent Hartnett to author, September 8, 2003.

8. Hartnett interview.

9. "Sweets States Side in 'Blacklist' Bouncing; Rally Voices Protest," *Variety*, August 17, 1949, 23, 42.

10. Hartnett interview.

11. "Blacklist, the Story Breaks," Voice of Freedom / National Council of the Arts, Sciences and Professions flyer, *Counterattack* files; "Who's Blacklisted," *Time*, August 22, 1949, 81–82.

12. Christophers website, *www.christophers.org/keller.html*; Faulk trial transcript, 4885–4888; Hartnett testimony, HUAC, 5306.

13. Faulk trial transcript, 4846; "Red Fronts in Radio"; Hartnett testimony, HUAC, 5293.

14. Vincent Hartnett, "Red Fronts Falling," *The Sign*, November 1950, 13–15; Jack Gould, "Radio in Review," *New York Times*, February 1, 1951, 34.

15. "Need a Speaker?," advertisement, *Tablet*, January 6, 1951, 10; Vincent Hartnett to George Sokolsky, April 10, 1952, George Sokolsky Papers.

16. Vincent Hartnett, "Every Professor a Pope," *The Sign*, March 1951, 37–39; Faulk trial transcript, 5373; *Confidential Notebook (File 13)*, Robert Donner Collection, Brown Library, Abilene Christian University; Vincent Hartnett to AFRA, September 29, 1950, McNamara Collection; Vincent Hartnett, "How Communism Exploits Sex," *The Sign*, August 1950, 7–9; "Red Fronts Falling."

17. O'Neill, *Better*, 299–301.

18. "Chronicle of Events," *Congress Weekly*, February 5, 1951, 2; Vincent Hartnett to My Friends of the Jewish Faith, March 10, 1951, box 59, folder 3, Sokolsky Papers.

19. For examples of Hartnett's attitude toward Judaism, see "Every Professor a Pope," 38, and Hartnett to Sokolsky, April 10, 1952, box 59, folder 3, Sokolsky Papers. In "Every Professor" he credits Jewish organizations for fighting college admission quotas that had been penalizing Catholic applicants, while also pointing out that Jews had suffered much more. In his letter to Sokolsky, he mentions Jewish contributions to the concept of moral law.

20. "Chronicle of Events"; "Kohlberg Cancels Speech to Women," *New York Times*, January 31, 1953, 18; "The People Awakening," *Tablet*, September 2, 1950, 1.

21. Myron C. Fagan, "Why the People Must—Drive the Reds Out of Radio and TV," pamphlet, Cinema Education Guild, February–March 1957.

22. *Counterattack*, September 19, 1947, and October 6, 1950.

23. "Commentary, Subject: Averill Berman Weeps for North Koreans, Communication No. 360," October 10, 1950, Matusow Papers; News Report, Subject: Isidore Scharf, October 13, 1951, Matusow Papers.

24. William V. Shannon, *The American Irish* (New York: Macmillan, 1963), 381. For a discussion of the role of Catholics in the anti-Communist movement, see Mark S. Massa, *Catholics and American Culture* (New York: Crossroad, 1999).

25. Nathan Glazer and Daniel P. Moynihan, *Beyond the Melting Pot* (Cambridge: MIT Press, 1970), 271.

26. Hartnett interview; Vincent Hartnett to J. Edgar Hoover, June 28, 1955, personal collection of Vincent Hartnett.

27. Vincent Hartnett to George Sokolsky, April 26, 1952, box 59, folder 3, Sokolsky Papers.

28. Hartnett to author, April 24, 2003.

29. Vincent Hartnett to Alfred Kohlberg, December 26, 1950, box 77, Kohlberg Papers; Faulk trial transcript, 5443.

30. Vincent Hartnett to William Brooks, January 2, 1951, box 77, Kohlberg Papers; Miller, 121; Faulk trial transcript, 4946, 6461.

31. Hartnett interview; Faulk trial transcript, 5808–5813, 5872, 5982.

32. Faulk trial transcript, 4873, 5944–5946.

33. Vincent Hartnett, "They've Moved In on TV," *American Legion Magazine*, January 1953, 26–27, 61–63; Faulk trial transcript, 4902–4903, 5830, 5934, 5939–5943; Hartnett interview.

34. Faulk trial transcript, 4898, 4902–4903, 4911.

35. Ibid., 4914–4915, 5626, 5642, 5927, 5979, 5996.

36. Ibid., 5920–5923; Vincent Hartnett to Francis Neuser, April 6, 1954, Dungey collection.

37. Faulk trial transcript, 4955, 5995; Vincent Hartnett to Laurence Johnson, September 25, 1953, Dungey collection.

38. Vincent Hartnett to George Sokolsky, May 19, 1952, box 59, folder 3, Sokolsky Papers; Faulk trial transcript, 5905–5908, 5912–5913.

39. Faulk trial transcript, 5987.

40. W. E. B. DuBois, "Dr. DuBois on Stalin," *National Guardian*, March 16, 1953, 4; Paul Robeson, "To You, Beloved Comrade," *New World Review*, April 1953, reprinted in *Paul Robeson Speaks*, 347–349; Howard Fast, "On Receiving the Stalin Peace Award," *Masses & Mainstream*, May 1954, 35–37.

41. Stephane Courtois, et al., *The Black Book of Communism* (Cambridge: Harvard University Press, 1999), 434.

42. Faulk trial transcript, 4959; Hartnett to AFRA; Vincent Hartnett to author, August 4, 2003.

43. Hartnett to author, August 4, 2003; Rita Morley Harvey, *Those Wonderful, Terrible Years: George Heller and the American Federation of Television and Radio Artists* (Carbondale: Southern Illinois University Press, 1996), 89.

44. Michael Collyer, personal interview by author, May 8, 2003.

45. Ibid.; Harvey, *Years*, 89–91; "March Meeting," *Stand By*, March 1953, 1.

46. Harvey, *Years*, 86; "Radio Actors Vote to Bar Communists."

47. "Blacklist: The Veto Power in TV-Radio"; "March Meeting."

48. Burton, *Faulk*, 104, 106; John Henry Faulk to Mr. Bedichek, October 24, 1953, Bedichek Papers.

49. Faulk trial transcript, 179, 205.

50. Burton, *Faulk*, 101.

51. Faulk FBI file, Director, FBI, to SAC New York, April 23, 1952, 100-181329-23.

52. Harvey Matusow testimony, HUAC, executive session, November 27, 1951, 60–61; Faulk FBI file, Office Memorandum, SAC New York to Director, FBI, June 15, 1953, 100-181329-26.

53. "Texans Give McCarthy Cadillac for His Deeds," *New York Times*, October 22, 1953, 31; Faulk to Bedichek, October 24, 1953, Bedichek Papers; Faulk to Bedichek, November 20, 1951, Bedichek Papers.

9: RENEWED VIGILANCE

1. Aware Statement of Principles, pamphlet, McNamara Collection.

2. Faulk trial transcript, 3981, 3990–3991; Aware Statement.

3. Aware Statement.

4. Aware, Inc., flyer, McNamara Collection.

5. Julian, *Radio*, 181, 187.

6. Ibid., 183–185, 191, 194.

7. Ibid., 199, 202.

8. Vincent Price FBI file, Report: Vincent Price, May 11, 1954, 100-34677; John K. Dungey interview; William Dungey interview; *Counterattack*, January 8, February 12, May 14, 1954; William Redfield to Harry Morgan, August 7, 1952, *Counterattack* files; William Redfield to Office of Counterattack, March 12, 1954; Inter-Office Memo, A. E. Cullen to J. G. Keenan and F. J. McNamara, March 30, 1954, *Counterattack* files.

9. Julian, *Radio*, 200–201.

10. "Vets Council Lauds Anti-Communist Efforts of Several," *Syracuse Post-Standard*, clipping, McNamara Collection; *Genealogy*.

11. Jack Gould, "Case Dismissed," *New York Times*, June 6, 1954, X11; Julian, *Radio*, 178–180.

12. Herbert A. Philbrick, *I Led 3 Lives* (Washington, D.C.: Capitol Hill Press, 1972), 232; *I Led 3 Lives* pilot, Museum of Television and Radio; Susan Wangerman, telephone interview by author, March 23, 2002; Doherty, *Medium*, 143.

13. "The First Salem Witch Trial," *You Are There*, Museum of Television and Radio.

14. *Norman Corwin's Letters*, 125–127; "Report: Norman Corwin," December 1, 1947, *Counterattack* files.

15. Bernard DeVoto, "The Easy Chair," *Harper's Magazine*, July 1945, 33–36.

16. *America at War*, CD audio recording, Radio Spirits, 2001; Donal Henahan, "A Ruptured Duck That Just Will Not Fly," August 15, 1976, 75.

17. Hamlin interview; "John Crosby—Kraft and 'Blacklisting,'" *Spotlight*, August 1955, local history division, local history / special collections, Onondaga County Public Library; Dann interview.

18. Hamlin interview; Mankiewicz interview.

19. Vincent Hartnett, "New York's Great Red Way," *American Mercury*, June 1953, 66–72; Hartnett interview; Dunaway, *Singing*, 159–160.

20. Stefan Kanfer, *Ball of Fire: The Tumultuous Life and Comic Art of Lucille Ball* (New York: Alfred A. Knopf, 2003), 167–174; Doherty, *Cold*, 49–59.

21. Jack Gould, "The Case of Lucille Ball," *New York Times*, September 20, 1953, X13.

22. Doherty, *Cold*, 169–171.

23. Sperber, *Murrow*, 318–319, 430.

24. Keenan interview; McCollum interview; Herman, *McCarthy*, 165; *Counterattack*, March 19, 1954; File 13, Special Supplement, Program Bulletin, March 13, 1954, box 59, folder 3, Kohlberg Papers; Gilbert Seldes, "Murrow, McCarthy and the Empty Formula," *Saturday Review*, April 24, 1954, 26–27; John Cogley, "The Murrow Show," *Commonweal*, March 26, 1954, 618.

25. Persico, *Murrow*, 383–385; Doherty, *Cold*, 181.

26. Herman, *McCarthy*, 336–337.

27. Haynes and Klehr, *Venona*, 201–204; Sperber, *Murrow*, 317.

28. For the information in this section on Harvey Matusow, I relied on two sources: Matusow, *False Witness*, Chapters 17 and 18; and Lichtman and Cohen, *Deadly Farce*, Chapters 6 and 7.

29. William C. Kernan, "Snake in Suburbia's Garden," *Catholic World*, October 1954, 16–23; Joseph F. Maloney, *The Lonesome Train in Levittown* (Indianapolis: Bobbs-Merrill, 1958).

30. "Snake in Suburbia's Garden," 20–21; the full text of "Lonesome Train" can be found in Barnouw, *Radio Drama in Action*, 240–250.

31. Maloney, *Train*, 5, 16.

32. Jack Gould, "Radio in Review," *New York Times*, December 31, 1954, 20; "The Investigator," audio recording, Discuriosities, 1954, New York Public Library for the Performing Arts.

33. Townsend testimony, HUAC, 960; Carin Burrows testimony, HUAC, 1337; Reuben Ship testimony, HUAC, 82nd Congress, 1st Session, 1772.

34. Aware newsletter, October 20, 1954, New York Public Library.

35. "March Membership Meeting," *Stand By*, April 1954, 11–12, 14, and July 1954, 12.

36. "News Supplement to Membership Bulletin, Aware Publication No. 12," December 27, 1954, New York Public Library.

37. Ibid.

10: THE MIDDLE OF THE ROAD

1. "The Road Back," pamphlet, McNamara Collection.

2. Ibid.

3. "May Membership Meeting," *Stand By*, June 1955, 13.

4. Faulk trial transcript, 4157–4162, 4173, 4909–4911.

5. Arthur Jacobs to Vincent Hartnett, May 12, 1953; Vincent Hartnett to Arthur Jacobs, May 15, 1953; Vincent Hartnett to Arthur Jacobs, May 25, 1953, all in box 59, folder 3, Sokolsky Papers.

6. Faulk trial transcript, 4875, 5218–5222.

7. Vincent Hartnett to Leslie Barrett, December 9, 1954, New York Public Library for the Performing Arts.

8. Vincent Hartnett to Leslie Barrett, December 14, 1954, and Leslie Barrett to Vincent Hartnett, December 19, 1954, both in New York Public Library for the Performing Arts.

9. "Referendum Results," *Stand By*, June 1955, 2.

10. "Report on March Meeting of the New York Local Membership," *Stand By*, April 1955, 2–3, 7, 11–12.

11. Ibid.

12. Transcript of Leslie Barrett's speech at March 1955 AFTRA meeting, New York Public Library for the Performing Arts.

13. "Report on March Meeting," *Stand By*.

14. Matusow, *Witness*, 109–110, 117–119.

15. Faulk trial transcript, 5586–5587.

16. Ibid., 2565–2566, 2570–2572, 2581–2582, 5731–5732.

17. Burton, *Faulk*, 108; Hartnett interview; John Henry Faulk to Mr. Dobie, Mody, Mr. Bedichek and Mr. Webb, April 30, 1955, Bedichek Papers.

18. Burton, *Faulk*, 108; Faulk FBI file, Office Memorandum, L. B. Nichols to Mr. Tolson, April 18, 1955, and Office Memorandum, to Mr. Nease, August 19, 1958.

19. "May Membership Meeting," *Stand By*, June 1955, 2, 4–5, 7–8, 13, 16.

20. Ibid.

21. John Crosby, "Enough of Blacklisting," *New York Herald Tribune*, June 15, 1955, clipping, New York Public Library for the Performing Arts; Kirkpatrick FBI file, M. A. Jones to Mr. Nichols, April 11, 1952, and L. B. Nichols to Mr. Tolson, April 15, 1952; Hartnett to Hoover; Vincent Hartnett report on Leslie Barrett, February 28, 1956, personal collection of Vincent Hartnett; Burton, *Faulk*, 125–126.

22. "CBS Man Admits He Was a Red Spy," *New York Times*, June 30, 1955, 1, 8.

23. "Radio and TV Artists Vote, 982 to 514, to Condemn Aware, Anti-Red Group," *New York Times*, July 4, 1955, 23; "Screening TV Artists," *New York Times*, July 15, 1955, 20.

24. "News Supplement to Membership Bulletin, Aware Publication 13," July 15, 1955, New York Public Library; Elliott Sullivan FBI file, Report: Elliott Sullivan, April 30, 1956; McGilligan and Buhle, *Comrades*, 377, 543–544.

25. George Tyne testimony, HUAC, 84th Congress, 1st Session, 2268; Stanley Prager testimony, ibid., 2293, 2296; Elliott Sullivan testimony, ibid., 2333.

26. Burton, *Faulk*, 127–128; Faulk trial transcript, 1474–1487, 4564.

27. Burton, *Faulk*, 126–127.

28. Faulk, *Fear*, 12–13; Orson Bean, "Through the Years with the Blacklist," *National Review*, February 23, 1971, 193–195, 212; Orson Bean, telephone interview by author, January 7, 2002.

29. "Through the Years with the Blacklist," 194; Bean interview; Faulk trial transcript, 2213–2214.

30. Philip Loeb tax statements; Philip Loeb to State Tax Commission, February 27, 1953; Philip Loeb to District Director, Internal Revenue, October 4, 1954; correspondence between Philip Loeb and Dr. Trigant Burrow, all in Loeb Papers.

31. Val Adams, "'Middle-of-the-Road' Candidates Entered in TV Union Election," *New York Times*, November 10, 1955, 71; Hartnett interview; Faulk trial transcript, 849–855, 895–896.

32. Allen Drury, "Reds Held Active in Key U.S. Fields," *New York Times*, January 18, 1956, 14; Val Adams, "Radio-TV Union Hits Red Report," *New York Times*, January 23, 1956, 49.

33. Faulk trial transcript, 4739, 4751, 5007–5008; "'Blacklist' Foes Win in TV Union," *New York Herald Tribune*, December 12, 1955, 7.

34. Faulk trial transcript, 4560, 5012–5013, 5074–5075, 5087–5099, 5123, 5129, 5132, 6082.

35. Faulk trial transcript, 4091, 4145–4146, 4181–4189.

36. "News Supplement to Membership Bulletin, Aware Publication 16," February 10, 1956, New York Public Library.

37. Faulk, *Fear*, 14, 19.

38. Ibid., 20–29.

39. "Through the Years with the Blacklist," 194; John Henry Faulk to Orson Bean, September 29, 1976, box 3E196, John Henry Faulk Papers, Center for American History, University of Texas at Austin.

40. "Through the Years with the Blacklist," 195.

41. "Through the Years with the Blacklist," 195; Bean interview; Orson Bean to John Henry Faulk, October 20, 1976, box 3E196, Faulk Papers.

42. Faulk, *Fear*, 36; Faulk trial transcript, 653–668.

11: BACKLASH

1. "Four Johnson Supermarkets Sold in Reported $1 Million Transaction," *Syracuse Post-Standard*, February 26, 1956, clipping, OHA.

2. Faulk trial transcript, 5863–5865.

3. Ibid., 2342.

4. Ibid., 2343–2345.

5. Ibid., 2345.

6. John Dungey to Harris Perlstein, Pabst Brewing Company, March 31, 1956, reprinted in Faulk trial transcript, a28–a30; Faulk trial transcript, 731, 899.

7. Ibid., 3605–3606.

8. Faulk, *Fear*, 42–43; Faulk trial transcript, 3348–3351, 3354.

9. Faulk, *Fear*, 36–40.

10. Ibid., 36, 41.

11. Faulk trial transcript, 708–711.

12. Faulk, *Fear*, 44–45, 47–48; "Aware, Inc., Sued for Half Million," *New York Times*, June 19, 1956, 59; John Henry Faulk to Dobie, Webb, Mody, and Bedichek, May 30, 1956, Bedichek Papers.

13. "Aware, Inc., Sued for Half Million"; "Aware Answers Charge by Faulk," *New York Times*, July 7, 1956, 33.

14. Faulk to Dobie, Webb, Mody, and Bedichek, May 30, 1956.

15. Ibid.

16. Faulk trial transcript, 1778–1810.

17. Bernstein, *Inside Out*, 254; "'America to Blame for Hungary,'" *Variety*, October 26, 1960, 2.

18. John Cogley testimony, HUAC, 84th Congress, 2nd Session, 5215.

19. Hartnett testimony, HUAC, 5300, 5304, 5310.

20. Ibid., 5294–5295, 5297, 5301, 5305, 5308.

21. David Anderson, "Discredit of U.S. Laid to Matusow," *New York Times*, September 26, 1956, 15.

22. "News Supplement to Membership Bulletin, Aware Publication 19," New York Public Library.

23. Faulk trial transcript, 3540–3545.

24. Ibid., 951–968, 3373–3374.

25. Ibid., 987–988, 992–994, 3635.

26. Ibid., 977, 1003–1010; Burton, *Faulk*, 153.

27. Faulk trial transcript, 1013–1015, 1035, 3377.

28. John Henry Faulk to Boys, June 2, 1958, Bedichek Papers.

29. John Henry Faulk to Boys, July 8, 1958, Bedichek Papers; An End of 1958 Report to Dobie and Bedichek, Bedichek Papers; Faulk trial transcript, 1016–1017; Nizer, *Jury*, 293.

30. Faulk trial transcript, 1018–1031, 1038, 1040; Faulk, *Fear*, 117–122.

31. Faulk trial transcript, 5951; Vincent Hartnett to John Dungey, July 23, 1958, and Hartnett to Dungey, February 26, 1962, personal collection of Dungey family; Vincent Hartnett to author, September 8, 2003.

32. Hartnett to author, September 8, 2003.

33. Faulk, *Fear*, 91–93; Berger interview.

34. Nizer, *Jury*, 284.

35. Hartnett interview; Faulk, *Fear*, 116–117; Faulk trial transcript, 5811.

36. Hartnett interview; Vincent Hartnett to author, January 15, 2002; Faulk trial transcript, 5661–5664.

37. Hartnett interview; Faulk trial transcript, 5661–5664.

38. Nizer, *Jury*, 279–285; Faulk FBI file, United States Memorandum to Mr. W. C. Sullivan, June 29, 1962, 100-181329.

39. Nizer, *Jury*, 287–288.

40. Ibid., 289; Faulk, *Fear*, 97–98; Faulk trial transcript, 6914–6915; Burton, *Faulk*, 155.

41. Berger interview.

42. Faulk trial transcript, 2436–2437.

43. Faulk, *Fear*, 89–90, 94; John Henry Faulk to the Boys, June 2, 1958.

44. Charles S. Dubin testimony, HUAC, 85th Congress, 2nd Session, 2523–2524; James D. Proctor testimony, ibid., 2544–2545; Clifford Carpenter testimony, ibid., 2571–2572; Louis Solomon testimony, ibid., 2592; Lee Grant testimony, 2596–2597.

45. "Unite and Fight," Aware, Inc., flyer, McNamara Collection.

46. "Jean Muir in 'Our Town,'" *New York Times*, March 4, 1959, 35; Bob Chandler, "CBS Pacting of Jean Muir for TV Role Signals End of Blacklist Era," *Variety*, no date, clipping, New York Public Library for the Performing Arts.

47. David Everitt, *King of the Half Hour* (Syracuse, N.Y.: Syracuse University Press, 2001), 74–77.

48. Hartnett testimony, HUAC, 5299–5300.

49. Vincent Hartnett to John Dungey, August 14, 1961, personal collection of Dungey family; "Expert on Communism Cites Reds in TV Field," *Syracuse Post-Standard*, February 14, 1962, clipping, OHA; Hartnett to Dungey, February 26, 1962.

50. John Henry Faulk to Mr. Dobie and Mr. Bedichek, May 15, 1958, Bedichek Papers; Faulk FBI file, Office Memorandum, G. A. Nease to Mr. Tolson, August 20, 1958.

51. Berger interview.

52. Ibid.

12: A CASE OF LIBEL

1. Faulk, *Fear*, 145; Berger interview; Faulk trial transcript, b6.

2. Ibid., b66–b67, b69, b89.

3. Ibid., b92–b99.

4. Ibid., b69–b70, b77, b114–b115.

5. Ibid., b106, b113.

6. Ibid., b118.

7. Ibid., b123, b164–b165.

8. Ibid., b127–b128, b130, b144, b154, b160–b161.

9. Nizer, *Jury*, 253; Murray Kempton, "The Return," *New York Post*, April 25, 1962, 49.

10. Faulk trial transcript, 593.

11. Ibid., 788–795, 1989.

12. Ibid., 653, 734, 1003–1011.

13. Ibid., 68, 176, 777–778, 803.

14. Ibid., 1778–1810.

15. Ibid., 1076–1077; Nizer, *Jury*, 329.

16. Faulk trial transcript, 1860–1865; Faulk, *Fear*, 202–203; Nizer, *Jury*, 335.

17. Faulk trial transcript, 1868–1879; "Birthday Greetings," *People's Songs*, February and March 1948.

18. Faulk trial transcript, b96, 1926–1927.

19. Ibid., 1474–1487.

20. Ibid., 1889–1906.

21. Ibid., 1889, 1892; Faulk, *Fear*, 89.

22. Faulk trial transcript, 604–605.

23. Ibid., 386–391, 394.

24. Ibid., 418–426.

25. Ibid., 536.

26. Ibid., 2987–2990, 2697–2704.

27. Ibid., 2300–2301, 3471.

28. Ibid., 3695, 3699–3713; "Red Fronts in Radio."

29. Nizer, *Jury*, 358–359; Faulk trial transcript, 3196.

30. Faulk trial transcript, 2629; Nizer, *Jury*, 346; Faulk, *Fear*, 215.

31. Faulk trial transcript, 2538, 2636.

32. Nizer, *Jury*, 347; Hartnett testimony, HUAC, 5301.

33. Faulk trial transcript, 2592, 2579.

34. Ibid., 2382–2399.

35. Ibid., 2510, 2517–2522.

36. Ibid., b53, b129–b130; Nizer, *Jury*, 287; Berger interview.

37. Faulk trial transcript, 2339–2343.

38. Ibid., 2367.

39. Ibid., 2427–2428.
40. Ibid., 3564–3572; Faulk, *Fear*, 229, 264; Nizer, *Jury*, 364.
41. Faulk trial transcript, 2346, 2412.
42. "The Name's the Same," *Newsweek*, June 4, 1962, 86–87; Murray Kempton, "Drama in the Courtroom," *New York Post*, May 15, 1962.
43. Faulk trial transcript, 497–501.
44. Ibid., 505–511.
45. Ibid., 1722, 1751–1757.
46. Faulk, *Fear*, 267; Faulk trial transcript, 2889–2897; Nizer, *Jury*, 364.
47. Faulk trial transcript, 503.

13: VERDICT

1. Faulk trial transcript, 3968–3991, 4109–4120.
2. Ibid., 4395–4403.
3. Ibid., 4575–4582.
4. Ibid., 4181–4198, 4166–4168; Faulk, *Fear*, 272–273.
5. Ibid., 4241–4242, 4254.
6. Ibid., 4492–4496.
7. Ibid., 4505–4508, 4790–4792; John Sibley, "Faulk Supported by C.B.S. Official," *New York Times*, June 16, 1962, 32.
8. Faulk trial transcript, 4417; Howard Pollack, *Aaron Copland* (New York: Henry Holt, 1999), 272; Meryle Secrest, *Leonard Bernstein: A Life* (New York: Alfred A. Knopf, 1994), 171–172.
9. Murray Kempton, "Failure's Reward," *New York Post*, May 31, 1962, 49.
10. Faulk trial transcript, 4554–4568; "H. Res. 650," 87th Congress, 2nd Session.
11. Thomas Bolan, personal interview by author, November 27, 2001; Berger interview.
12. Faulk FBI files, Office Memorandum, SAC New York to Director, FBI, June 15, 1953.
13. Faulk trial transcript, 4857–4858, 4907–4909, 4916, 4946–4947, 4955.
14. Ibid., 5020–5024; for information on the CPUSA activities of John Abt, see Haynes and Klehr, *Venona*, 62–64, 340; for examples of Herbert Aptheker publications, see Herbert Aptheker, "The Truth About the Korean War," *Masses & Mainstream*, August 1950, and Herbert Aptheker, *The Truth About Hungary* (New York: Mainstream Publishers, 1957).
15. Faulk, *Fear*, 296.
16. Faulk trial transcript, 5206, 5223–5226.
17. Ibid., 5297.
18. Ibid., 5337–5338, 5394–5409.
19. Nizer, *Jury*, 382; Faulk trial transcript, 5433–5438.
20. Faulk trial transcript, 5558, 5603–5607.
21. Ibid., 5616–5620.
22. Ibid., 5661–5664.
23. Ibid., 5665–5667, 5674–5676.
24. Ibid., 5504; Faulk, *Fear*, 329.
25. Ibid., 5763–5764, 5874–5875.

26. Ibid., 5769–5780, 5908–5913, 5929, 5934–5943.

27. Bolan interview.

28. Faulk trial transcript, 5974–5977, 5982–6002.

29. Ibid., 6018–6019A, 6125, 6128–6130.

30. Ibid., 6098–6104, 6079–6083.

31. Ibid., 6142, 6174–6181.

32. Ibid., 5850–5859, 6032–6039.

33. Ibid., 6497–6499; Faulk, *Fear*, 333.

34. Hartnett interview.

35. Faulk trial transcript, 6538; Nizer, *Jury*, 395–396.

36. Faulk trial transcript, 6572–6574.

37. Nizer, *Jury*, 396; Faulk trial transcript, 6574–6575.

38. Nizer, *Jury*, 396–397; Berger interview; Murray Kempton, "The Lonely Cop," *New York Post*, June 20, 1962, 47.

39. Nizer, *Jury*, 403; Faulk trial transcript, 6637–6646.

40. Faulk trial transcript, 6651–6660, 6738, 6787–6789.

41. Ibid., 6960–6961.

42. Ibid., 6991–6992, 6967, 6982, 7048.

43. Murray Kempton, "Courtroom Sick Call," *New York Post*, June 22, 1962, 53; Faulk, *Fear*, 361.

44. Faulk trial transcript, 7106–7107.

45. Ibid., 7108, 7231.

46. Ibid., 7109, 7113, 7126–7127, 7235–7238, 7248–7249, 7254.

47. Ibid., 7115–7116, 7234.

48. Ibid., 7113–7114, 7381; Vincent Hartnett to author, April 24, 2003.

49. John Sibley, "Faulk Defendant Reported Dead on Eve of Jury's Verdict," *New York Times*, June 28, 1962, 63; Marilyn Giancola interview; Edward Dillon, "Defendant in Libel Trial Is Found Dead," *New York Daily News*, June 28, 1962, clipping, New York Public Library for the Performing Arts.

50. Faulk trial transcript, 7525, 7527–7529.

51. Ibid., 7531–7550, 7664–7668, 7652–7653.

52. Ibid., 7554–7555, 7637, 7657–7659.

53. Ibid., 7596–7599, 7613.

54. Ibid., 7602–7608.

55. Ibid., 7616, 7638.

56. Ibid., 7686–7687.

57. Ibid., 7687–7690, 7694–7695.

58. Ibid., 4907–4908.

59. Ibid., 7702–7703, 7692, 7720–7721.

60. Ibid., 7701–7703, 7847.

61. Ibid., 7698, 7700.

62. Ibid., 7730.

63. Ibid., 7785, 7858, 7861, 7866.

64. Nizer, *Jury*, 441–442.

65. Faulk trial transcript, 7935–7938.

66. Ibid., 7938–7947; "Faulk Defendant Reported Dead."

67. Nizer, *Jury*, 442; Faulk trial transcript, 7872, 7926–7927.

68. Ibid., 8004–8005.

69. Ibid., 8061; Nizer, *Jury*, 450.

70. Bolan interview; Berger interview.

71. Faulk trial transcript, 8063–8064.

14: **END OF AN ERA**

1. Herb Block, "Nailed," *New York Post*, July 3, 1962, 25; "Seven-Year Justice," *Time*, July 6, 1962, 38–39; Max Lerner, "Vigilante Era," *New York Post*, July 3, 1962, 25; Jack Gould, "The Faulk Victory," *New York Times*, July 15, 1962, 73.

2. Ramona B. Bowden, "Large Crowd Attends L. A. Johnson Rites," *Syracuse Post-Standard*, July 1, 1962, clipping, OHA; "Laurence A. Johnson," *Syracuse Post-Standard*, June 29, 1962, clipping, OHA; Joseph H. Adams, "Rambling 'Round," *Syracuse Post-Standard*, July 3, 1962, clipping, OHA.

3. "Johnson Death Ruled Natural," *Syracuse Herald-Journal*, July 24, 1962; Nizer, *Jury*, 447–448; Murray Kempton, "Guilty Party," *New York Post*, July 6, 1962, 35.

4. "Court Lops $3 Million Off Faulk Libel Award," *Syracuse Post-Standard*, November 22, 1963, clipping, OHA; Burton, *Faulk*, 164; "Supreme Court Rejects Appeal in $550,000 Faulk Libel Ruling," *New York Times*, March 2, 1965, 28.

5. Hamlin interview.

6. Robert Markell, telephone interview by author, November 23, 2003; David Shaw, telephone interview by author, May 15, 2003; Wagner interview.

7. Wagner interview; Villante e-mail.

8. Denker interview.

9. Collyer interview.

10. Alfred Albelli, "Wife Charges Faulk Frolicked with 21 Gals and Names Them," *New York Daily News*, August 20, 1963, clipping, New York Public Library for the Performing Arts.

11. Burton, *Faulk*, 167; Matt Messina, "Faulk Leaving WINS," *New York Daily News*, April 8, 1963, clipping, New York Public Library for the Performing Arts.

12. For examples of Buckley's ridiculing of Lindsay, see "Lindsay Is Chided on 10-Point Plan," *New York Times*, August 20, 1965, 27; Sydney H. Schanberg, "Lindsay and Buckley Duel," *New York Times*, October 12, 1965, 1.

13. John Henry Faulk to Robert Lindsay, October 12, 1965, John Henry Faulk Papers.

14. Vincent Hartnett to John Dungey, September 23, 1963, and Vincent Hartnett to John Dungey, May 20, 1964, both in personal collection of Dungey family; John Henry Faulk to Vincent Hartnett, May 5, 1965, personal collection of Vincent Hartnett.

15. Vincent Hartnett to John Dungey, May 20, 1964, and John Dungey to Vincent Hartnett, December 3, 1963, both in personal collection of Dungey family.

16. John Keenan, Jr., interview; McCollum interview; Theodore Kirkpatrick obituary, clipping, Earlham College alumni division.

17. Shaw interview; E. G. Marshall interview, Steven H. Scheuer Television History Collection, Syracuse University.

18. Val Adams, "Bill Cosby of 'I Spy' Series Wins TV Emmy," *New York Times*, May 23, 1966, 68. Lampell is usually quoted as saying, "I think I ought to mention I

was blacklisted for ten years," but I have chosen "Everyone here ought to know, I was blacklisted for ten years," as was reported on the spot by the *Times*.

19. Millard Lampell, "I Think I Ought to Mention I Was Blacklisted," *New York Times*, August 21, 1966, 109; McGilligan and Buhle, *Comrades*, 392–393; Barnouw, *Radio*, 241.

20. Dennis A. Lauro, Jr., Assistant Superintendent for Instruction and Personnel, Pelham Public Schools, to author, November 24, 2004; W. J. Russell to Dr. McKinney, First Year Probationary Report, June 18, 1969, personal collection of Vincent Hartnett; John Conroy, telephone interview by author, November 24, 2003.

21. Dr. Knueppel to Dr. McKinney, "Tenure Year Report," January 11, 1971, personal collection of Vincent Hartnett; Conroy interview; Bill Smith, telephone interview by author, November 7, 2003; Jerry Mele, telephone interview by author, November 14, 2003; Charles Wilson, telephone interview by author, November 17, 2003.

22. Conroy interview; Mele interview.

23. Frank Orfei, telephone interview by author, December 11, 2003.

24. Conroy interview; Orfei interview.

25. John Henry Faulk to David Halberstam, September 5, 1975, John Henry Faulk Papers.

26. Harry F. Waters, "CBS on Trial," *Newsweek*, October 6, 1975, 95; John J. O'Connor, "TV: CBS Dramatizes John Faulk's 'Fear on Trial,'" *New York Times*, October 2, 1975, 58.

27. "McCarthy Era Figure Loses Libel Suit Against CBS," *San Francisco Chronicle*, January 21, 1986, 36.

28. John Dungey to Vincent Hartnett, September 17, 1963, personal collection of the Dungey family; Faulk FBI file, To F. J. Baumgardner, March 16, 1964, 100-181329, and SAC, San Antonio to Director, FBI, April 3, 1964.

29. "Blacklisting, Politics and the Arts," January 11, 1967, audio recording, 92nd Street Y; Alan Schneider, personal interview by author, November 27, 2001.

30. "Through the Years with the Blacklist."

31. John Henry Faulk to Larry McDonald, September 29, 1976, box 3E196, John Henry Faulk Papers.

32. John Henry Faulk to Orson Bean, September 29, 1976, John Henry Faulk Papers; Faulk, *Fear*, 29–30.

33. Faulk to Bean.

34. Orson Bean to John Henry Faulk, October 20, 1976, John Henry Faulk Papers.

35. Bolan interview.

36. Vincent Hartnett to author, July 20, 2006; "Exhibit 4, Names of Unidentified Persons Quoted in *The Judges and the Judged*," ACLU Archive, Princeton University.

37. "McCarthy Era Figure Loses Libel Suit Against CBS."

38. *Scandalize My Name, Stories from the Blacklist*, videorecording, 1998, Starz Encore Entertainment.

39. Stephen Farber, "The Man Who Brought Us Greetings from the Vietcong," *New York Times*, April 29, 1975, 30.

40. Cuba article, unpublished manuscript, 1983, John Henry Faulk Papers.

41. Dexter Filkins, "Chalabi, in Tehran, Meets with Iranian President Before Traveling to U.S.," *New York Times*, November 6, 2005, 1.

42. Burton, *Faulk*, 178.

43. Jeremy Gerard, "John Henry Faulk Is Eulogized in a Gathering at Public Theater," *New York Times*, July 11, 1990, D19.

44. Ronald Radosh and Allis Radosh, *Red Star Over Hollywood* (San Francisco: Encounter, 2005), 84–85.

45. Hartnett to author, August 4, 2003; Hartnett interview.

46. Giancola interview; Wangerman interview.

47. Eric Breindel, "Stalinist Follies," *Commentary*, October 1982, 46–49.

Bibliography

COLLECTIONS

Abe Burrows Papers, New York Public Library for the Performing Arts.
Alfred Kohlberg Papers, Hoover Institution Library and Archives, Stanford University.
American Business Consultants, Inc. *Counterattack*: Research Files, Tamiment Library / Robert F. Wagner Labor Archives, New York University.
American Civil Liberties Union Archives, Seeley G. Mudd Manuscript Library, Princeton University.
American Jewish Committee Oral History Collection, Dorot Jewish Division, New York Public Library.
Francis J. McNamara Collection, Special Collections and Archives, George Mason University.
George Sokolsky Papers, Hoover Institution Library and Archives, Stanford University.
Gypsy Rose Lee Papers, New York Public Library for the Performing Arts.
Harvey Matusow Papers, Special Collections, University of Sussex.
John Henry Faulk Papers, Center for American History, University of Texas at Austin.
Leslie Barrett Correspondence and Ephemera, Special Collections, New York Public Library for the Performing Arts.
Luther Adler Papers, Special Collections, New York Public Library for the Performing Arts.
Morton Wishengrad Papers, Ratner Center for the Study of Conservative Judaism, Jewish Theological Seminary Library.
Philip Loeb Papers, Manuscripts and Archives Division, New York Public Library.
Radio Writers Guild Records, Special Collections, New York Public Library for the Performing Arts.
Roy Bedichek Papers, Center for American History, University of Texas at Austin.

Steven H. Scheuer Television History Collection, Special Collections Research Center, Syracuse University.

BOOKS

American Business Consultants, *Red Channels*. New York: Counterattack, 1950.

Applebaum, Anne, *Gulag: A History*. New York: Doubleday, 2003.

Bannerman, R. LeRoy, *Norman Corwin and Radio: The Golden Years*. University, Ala.: University of Alabama Press, 1986.

Barnouw, Erik, ed., *Radio Drama in Action*. New York: Farrar & Rinehart, 1945.

Barnouw, Erik, *Tube of Plenty: The Evolution of American Television*. New York: Oxford University Press, 1975.

Barson, Michael, and Steven Heller, *Red Scared!: The Commie Menace in Propaganda and Popular Culture*. San Francisco: Chronicle Books, 2001.

Bentley, Eric, *Thirty Years of Treason: Excerpts from Hearings Before the House Committee on Un-American Activities, 1938–1968*. New York: Viking, 1971.

Bernstein, Walter, *Inside Out: A Memoir of the Blacklist*. New York: Alfred A. Knopf, 1996.

Billingsley, Kenneth Lloyd, *Hollywood Party: How Communism Seduced the American Film Industry in the 1930s and 1940s*.Rocklin, Calif.: Forum, 1998.

Blue, Howard, *Words at War: World War II Radio Drama and the Postwar Broadcasting Industry Blacklist*. Lanham, Md.: Scarecrow, 2002.

Brinson, Susan L., *The Red Scare, Politics and the Federal Communications Commission, 1941–1960*. Westport, Conn.: Praeger, 2004.

Budenz, Louis F., *Men Without Faces: The Communist Conspiracy in the United States*. New York: Harper, 1950.

Buhle, Paul, and Dave Wagner, *Hide in Plain Sight: The Hollywood Blacklistees in Film and Television, 1950–2002*. New York: Palgrave Macmillan, 2003.

Buhle, Paul, and Dave Wagner, *Radical Hollywood: The Untold Story Behind America's Favorite Movies*. New York: New Press, 2002.

Burton, Michael C., *John Henry Faulk: The Making of a Liberated Mind*. Austin, Tex.: Eakin, 1993.

Calomiris, Angela, *Red Masquerade: Undercover for the FBI*. Philadelphia: Lippincott, 1950.

Carlson, John Roy, *Under Cover*. New York: E. P. Dutton, 1943.

Caute, David, *The Great Fear: The Anti-Communist Purge Under Truman and Eisenhower*. New York: Simon & Schuster, 1978.

Cogley, John, *Report on Blacklisting: II Radio-Television*. New York: Fund for the Republic, 1956.

Corwin, Norman, *More by Corwin*. New York: Henry Holt, 1944.

Corwin, Norman, *Untitled and Other Radio Dramas*. New York: Henry Holt, 1947.

Courtois, Stephane, et al., *The Black Book of Communism*. Cambridge: Harvard University Press, 1999.

Dilling, Elizabeth, *The Red Network*. Chicago: Dilling, 1934.

Dimitrov, Georgi, *The Working Class Against Fascism*. London: M. Lawrence, 1935.

Doherty, Thomas, *Cold War, Cool Medium: Television, McCarthyism and American Culture*. New York: Columbia University Press, 2003.

Draper, Theodore, *American Communism and Soviet Russia*. New York: Vintage, 1986.

Duberman, Martin Bauml, *Paul Robeson*. New York: Alfred A. Knopf, 1988.

Dunaway, David King, *How Can I Keep from Singing: Pete Seeger*. New York: McGraw-Hill, 1981.

Epstein, Edward Jay, *Dossier: The Secret History of Armand Hammer*. New York: Random House, 1996.

Faulk, John Henry, *Fear on Trial*. New York: Simon & Schuster, 1964.

Foster, William Z., *Toward Soviet America*. New York: Coward-McCann, 1932.

Gaddis, John Lewis, *We Now Know: Rethinking Cold War History*. New York: Oxford University Press, 1997.

Glazer, Nathan, and Daniel Patrick Moynihan, *Beyond the Melting Pot*. Cambridge: MIT Press, 1970.

Harvey, Rita Morley, *Those Wonderful, Terrible Years: George Heller and the American Federation of Television and Radio Artists*. Carbondale, Ill.: Southern Illinois University Press, 1996.

Haynes, John Earl, and Harvey Klehr, *Venona: Decoding Soviet Espionage in America*. New Haven, Conn.: Yale University Press, 1999.

Herman, Arthur, *Joseph McCarthy: Re-examining the Life and Legacy of America's Most Hated Senator*. New York: Free Press, 2000.

Hilmes, Michele, *Radio Voices: American Broadcasting, 1922–1952*. Minneapolis: University of Minnesota Press, 1997.

Himelstein, Morgan Yale, *Drama Was a Weapon*. New Brunswick, N.J.: Rutgers University Press, 1963.

Hook, Sidney, *Out of Step: An Unquiet Life in the 20th Century*. New York: Harper & Row, 1987.

Houseman, John, *Run-Through*. New York: Simon & Schuster, 1972.

Johnson, Edmund Roe, with Laurence Ayres Johnson, *Genealogy of the Descendants of Captain Edmund Johnson*. Lyons, N.Y.: 1954.

Johnson, Laurence A., *Over the Counter and On the Shelf: Country Storekeeping in America, 1620–1920*. Rutland, Vt.: C. E. Tuttle, 1961.

Julian, Joseph, *This Was Radio: A Personal Memoir*. New York: Viking, 1975.

Kanfer, Stefan, *Ball of Fire: The Tumultuous Life and Comic Art of Lucille Ball*. New York: Alfred A. Knopf, 2003.

Kanfer, Stefan, *Journal of the Plague Years*. New York: Atheneum, 1973.

Kempton, Murray, *America Comes of Middle Age*. Boston: Little, Brown, 1963.

Kessler, Ronald, *The Bureau: The Secret History of the FBI*. New York: St. Martin's, 2002.

Kisseloff, Jeff, *The Box: An Oral History of Television, 1920–1961*. New York: Viking, 1995.

Klehr, Harvey, John Earl Haynes, and Fridrikh Igorevich Firsov, *The Secret World of American Communism*. New Haven, Conn.: Yale University Press, 1995.

Klehr, Harvey, John Earl Haynes, and Kyrill M. Anderson, *The Soviet World of American Communism*. New Haven, Conn.: Yale University Press, 1998.

Koch, Stephen, *Double Lives: Spies and Writers in the Secret Soviet War of Ideas Against the West*. New York: Free Press, 1994.

Kraditor, Aileen S., *Jimmy Higgins: The Mental World of the American Rank-and-File Communist, 1930–1958*. New York: Greenwood, 1988.

Lamphere, Robert J., and Tom Schachtman, *The FBI-KGB War: A Special Agent's Story*. New York: Random House, 1986.

Langguth, A. J., ed., *Norman Corwin's Letters*. New York: Barricade, 1994.

Lichtman, Robert M., and Ronald D. Cohen, *Deadly Farce: Harvey Matusow and the Informer System in the McCarthy Era*. Urbana: University of Illinois Press, 2004.

Lyons, Eugene, *The Red Decade: The Stalinist Penetration of America*. Indianapolis: Bobbs-Merrill, 1941.

Maloney, Joseph F., *The Lonesome Train in Levittown*. Indianapolis: Bobbs-Merrill, 1958.

Massa, Mark Stephen, *Catholics and American Culture*. New York: Crossroad, 1999.

Matusow, Harvey, *False Witness*. New York: Cameron & Kahn, 1955.

May, Gary, *Un-American Activities: The Trials of William Remington*. New York: Oxford University Press, 1994.

McCullough, David, *Truman*. New York: Simon & Schuster, 1992.

McGilligan, Patrick, and Paul Buhle, *Tender Comrades: A Backstory of the Hollywood Blacklist*. New York: St. Martin's, 1997.

Mellen, Joan, *Hellman and Hammett*. New York: HarperCollins, 1996.

Metz, Robert, *CBS: Reflections in a Bloodshot Eye*. Chicago: Playboy Press, 1975.

Miller, Merle, *The Judges and the Judged*. Garden City, N.Y.: Doubleday, 1952.

Navasky, Victor, *Naming Names*. New York: Viking Press, 1980.

Nizer, Louis, *The Jury Returns*. Garden City, N.Y.: Doubleday, 1966.

O'Neill, William L., *A Better World: The Great Schism: Stalinism and the American Intellectuals*. New York: Simon & Schuster, 1982.

Persico, Joseph E., *Edward R. Murrow: An American Original*. New York: McGraw-Hill, 1988.

Peters, J., *The Communist Party: A Manual on Organization*. New York: Workers Library, 1935.

Philbrick, Herbert A., *I Led 3 Lives*. New York: McGraw-Hill, 1952.

Pollack, Howard, *Aaron Copland*. New York: Henry Holt, 1999.

Powers, Richard Gid, *Not Without Honor: The History of American Anti-Communism*. New York: Free Press, 1995.

Radosh, Ronald, and Allis Radosh, *Red Star over Hollywood: The Film Colony's Long Romance with the Left*. San Francisco: Encounter, 2005.

Rapoport, Louis, *Stalin's War Against the Jews*. New York: Free Press, 1990.

Reeves, Thomas C., *The Life and Times of Joe McCarthy*. New York: Stein and Day, 1982.

Ribuffo, Leo, *The Old Christian Right: The Protestant Far Right from the Great Depression to the Cold War*. Philadelphia: Temple University Press, 1983.

Romerstein, Herbert, and Eric Breindel, *Venona Secrets: Exposing Soviet Espionage and America's Traitors*. Washington, D.C.: Regnery, 2000.

Schlesinger, Arthur M., Jr., *The Vital Center*. New Brunswick, N.J.: Transaction Publishers, 1998.

Secrest, Meryle, *Leonard Bernstein: A Life*. New York: Alfred A. Knopf, 1994.

Shaw, Irwin, *The Troubled Air*. New York: Random House, 1951.

Smith, Mona Z., *Becoming Something: The Story of Canada Lee*. New York: Faber and Faber, 2004.

Smith, Sally Bedell, *In All His Glory: The Life of William S. Paley, the Legendary Tycoon and His Brilliant Circle*. New York: Simon & Schuster, 1990.

Sperber, A. M., *Murrow: His Life and Times*. New York: Freundlich, 1986.

Starobin, Joseph R., *American Communism in Crisis, 1943–1957*. Cambridge: Harvard University Press, 1972.

Tanenhaus, Sam, *Whittaker Chambers*. New York: Random House, 1997.

Wald, Elijah, *Josh White: Society Blues*. Amherst: University of Massachusetts Press, 2000.

Weaver, Pat, with Thomas M. Coffy, *The Best Seat in the House: The Golden Years of Radio and Television*. New York: Alfred A. Knopf, 1994.

INTERVIEWS BY THE AUTHOR

Bean, Orson, January 7, 2002.
Berger, George, August 26, 2003.
Blaisdell, Charles, February 3, 2004.
Bolan, Thomas, November 27, 2001.
Coleman, Allen J., November 30, 2003.
Collyer, Michael, May 8, 2003.
Conroy, John, November 24, 2003.
Dann, Michael, July 16, 2003.
Daugherty, Jean, June 17, 2003.
Denker, Henry, December 1, 2003.
Dungey, Dorothy, May 15, 2002.
Dungey, John K., May 9, 2002.
Dungey, William, May 16, 2002.
Esce, Joseph, October 15, 2003.
Fopp, Gino, February 19, 2004.
Giancola, Marilyn, May 14, 2002.
Hamlin, Edith, April 14, 2003.
Hartnett, Vincent, November 29, 2001.
Hines, Alva, October 15, 2003.
Keenan, John, Jr., January 7, 2004.
Kenyon, Mrs. Thomas, October 15, 2003.
Kinoy, Ernest, June 3, 2003.
Kirkpatrick, Lucille, October 30, 2003.
Lumet, Sidney, May 6, 2004.
Lyon, Jane, April 14, 2003.
Mankiewicz, Don, July 2, 2003.
Markell, Robert, November 23, 2003.
Mayka, Stephen, October 16, 2003.
McCollum, Catherine Keenan, February 12, 2004.
McGroddy, Charles, August 9, 2004.
McNamara, Francis, March 20, 2002.
Mele, Jerry, November 14, 2003.
Montagne, Edward, July 15, 2003.

Myers, Lawrence, June 18, 2003.
Neuser, Margaret, May 6, 2002.
Orfei, Frank, December 11, 2003.
Polera, Rocco, November 13, 2003.
Randall, Tony, March 13, 2002.
Romerstein, Herbert, March 26, 2004.
Schneider, Alan, November 27, 2001.
Shaw, David, May 15, 2003.
Smith, Bill, November 7, 2003.
Vadeboncoeur, Joan, June 17, 2003.
Wagner, Alan, June 9, 2003.
Wallace, Don, September 11, 2003.
Wangerman, Susan, March 23, 2002.
Wilson, Charles, November 17, 2003.

Index

ABC (American Broadcasting
    Company): anti-Communist
    influence on, 80–81, 174–175;
    anti-Communists challenged by,
    74–76
Abraham Lincoln Brigade, FBI
    investigation, 8
Abt, John, 292
Academy Awards, 342–343
Ace, Goodman, 195
Acheson, Dean, 171, 349
ACLU: anti-Communism, 166; FCC
    petition, 112; *Judges and the Judged,*
    The (Miller), 111–115, 243, 339;
    records, 339; as a subversive
    organization, 187, 199
Actors' Equity, 48–49, 79, 217, 274
Actors' Lab, 346
Actors. *See* Movie actors; Theater;
    actors by name.
Adams, Douglas, 23
Adams (informer), 250

Adams, Val, 232
Adler, Larry, 30, 39, 107
Advertising: Faulk, 181, 248. *See also*
    Advertising agencies.
Advertising agencies: blacklistee
    careers in, 248; blacklist
    involvement, 104–106, 127, 130, 133,
    137–138, 235–238, 256–257, 270–271,
    277–278, 292, 294–295, 318, 323. *See*
    also Sponsors.
AFRA (American Federation of Radio
    Artists), 106, 162, 163, 178. *See also*
    AFTRA.
African-American celebrities: casting,
    254, 321; dramatic portrayal of
    blacklistees, 342. *See also celebrities*
    by name.
AFTRA (American Federation of
    Television and Radio Artists),
    178–180, 208–210; anti-Communists
    post-blacklist, 329; Aware
    condemnation, 214–218, 219–221,

AFTRA (*continued*)
224–234, 241, 264, 266, 272, 286–287,
294; congressional hearing
mandate, 232, 241; HUAC hearings,
224–227; Middle of the Road
officers, 226–234, 241, 264, 266,
286–287, 292, 294, 297, 310, 313, 325,
337–338, 341. *See also* AFRA.
Ahmadinejad, Mahmoud, 344
Aldrich Family, The, 49–50, 166
Allen, Fred, 20, 25, 61–62
Allen, Steve, 221
Allen, Woody, 342
Almanac Singers, 60, 144, 330
Alsop brothers, 199
American Business Consultants, 16,
37–41, 87, 90–92, 155–156;
accusations of, 85–88, 273;
blacklists, 42–46, 79, 82, 127–128.
See also Bierly, Kenneth M.;
Counterattack; Keenan, John G.;
Kirkpatrick, Theodore C.; *Red
Channels.*
American Communist party. *See*
CPUSA.
American Continental Congress
for World Peace, 31, 232, 291–292,
294
American Jewish League Against
Communism, 52, 126–127
American Legion: Americanism
committees, 189; anti-Communist
activities, 45, 54, 74–76, 103,
125–126, 174, 236, 256, 276
American Legion Magazine: Budenz
article, 54–58, 64, 65–66, 154, 285;
Hartnell article, 173–174, 297;
Lumet photo (purported), 140
American-Soviet Music Society, 97
American Writers Congress, 31

American Youth for Democracy, 30,
135
Americanism, 119, 159, 189;
communism as, 32
Ammident toothpaste, 140, 277
Anderson, Jack, 199
Andrews, Dana, 191
Animal Farm (Orwell), 204–205
"Annie Lee Moss Before the
McCarthy Committee," 201–202
Anti-anti-communism, 114–115,
318–324; anti-anti-totalitarianism
and, 343–344; books, 191, 204–205,
217, 325–326, 341–342; credibility,
113–114, 243–244, 341–342;
journalism, 52, 76, 77, 84, 88–89,
180, 190, 199–200, 220–221, 222, 232,
288, 330–331, 334, 341; movies,
325–326, 332–335, 342–343; plays,
192–193, 323; television
programming, 199–203, 221, 255,
258, 321–322; unions, 180, 217. *See
also* AFTRA; anti-McCarthyism.
Anti-anti-totalitarianism, 343–344,
348
Anti-Catholicism, 166
Anti-communism: books, 49; boycotts,
121–123, 125; credibility, 279, 341–342;
FCC, 74; former Communists,
54–58; media portrayal, 26, 318,
321–324, 329–331, 332–338, 341–343;
pageants, 45; post-blacklist careers
and, 329; right-wingers, 69–70, 337;
union resolutions, 106. *See also*
American Business Consultants;
American Legion; Aware; Catholic
church; HUAC; Jewish organizations;
Loyalty oaths; McCarthyism;
Veterans; *anti-Communists by
name.*

Anti-Defamation League, Faulk trial
testimony, 256–257
Anti-fascism: entertainment industry,
34–35; political activism, 24; radio
programs on, 22–24; World War II
era, 22–24, 348
Anti-McCarthyism: plays on, 192–193;
in print, 112, 199–200; programs on,
27, 192–193, 199–203; radio
community, 40. *See also* Anti-anti-
communism; McCarthyism.
Anti-Semitism: anti-communism and,
17–18, 49, 155–156, 168–170, 179;
Communists and, 34, 60–61, 177
Anti-war protests, 48, 60, 242, 329
Appeals in libel suits, 320–321, 327–328
Appell, Donald, 219, 224–225, 230, 256;
Faulk v. Aware trial, 269–270,
289–290, 299, 301
Aptheker, Herbert, 292
Arens, Richard, 153
Army. *See* U.S. Army.
Army-McCarthy hearings, 203
Arthur Godfrey and Friends, 125
Arthur, Jack, 178
Artists' Committee, 5, 178–180. *See
also* Aware.
Artists' Front to Win the War, 24
Aubrey, James, 324
Author Meets the Critics, The, 221
Authors League of America, 66–68
Avery, Andrew (Sam Horn), 16
Aware, Inc., 184–186, 199, 208–241,
284, 295, 311; AFTRA condemnation,
214–218, 219–221, 224–234, 241, 264,
266, 272, 286–287, 294; Buckley
involvement, 327; credibility, 222,
237–238, 261, 264–265, 284, 285–303,
305–306, 310; decline of, 253, 328;
defense testimony of, 283–289;

Faulk and, 224–225, 230–241,
245–247, 249–252, 256–317, 320–321,
336–337; HUAC rally, 253; McCarthy
and, 205–206; newsletters, 215–216,
219–221, 230–231, 233, 238, 241,
249–250, 261, 263, 269, 270, 284, 286,
292, 295–296, 336–337. *See also*
Hartnett, Vincent; Johnson,
Laurence A.
Ayer, Wardner D., 304–305, 311

Bach, J. S., 207–208
Ball, Lucille, 198
Balsam, Martin, 210
"Banks of Marble, The," 122–123
Bannerman, R. LeRoy, 107
Barnouw, Erik, 69, 76, 226
Barrett, Leslie, 164, 214–215, 216,
220–221, 225–226, 243–244, 346
Barrow, Erik, 64
Barson, Michael, 31, 35
Barton, Francis, 277–278
Bay, Howard, 153
Bay of Pigs, 260
Bean, Orson, 225–227, 229, 232,
233–234, 241, 336–338, 341
Beethoven, Ludwig von, 207–208
Belafonte, Harry, 188–189, 342, 343
Belfrage, Cedric, 58, 345
Bell, Ralph, 90–91, 107
Benny, Jack, 20, 195
Bentkover, Jack, 67
Bentley, Arvilla, 141, 204
Bentley, Elizabeth, 56, 164, 204
Bercovici, Leonard, 153
Berg, Gertrude, 78, 79–80
Berger, George, 251, 257, 276, 290,
303
Berkeley, Martin, 222, 224
Berlin blockade, 4, 46

Berman, Averill, 170

Bernay, Eric, 60

Bernstein, Leonard, 194–195, 288

Bernstein, Walter, 87, 139, 150, 172, 192, 242, 342

Berra, Yogi, 137

Berry, Alfred, 103

Bierly, Kenneth M., 5–19, 27–31, 37–41, 88, 90–92, 328; accusations of, 85–88; blacklisting by, 42–46, 83; CBS viewed by, 71; clearance consultancy, 145; Kenby Associates, 92. *See also* American Business Consultants; *Counterattack*.

Birkhead, L. M., 22, 53

"Blacklist" (Kinoy), 321–322, 325–326

"Blacklisting, Politics and the Arts," 335–336

Blacklists, 42–70, 78–92, 103–115, 123–134, 184–210; advertising agency role, 104–106, 127, 130, 133, 137–138, 235–238, 256–257, 270–271, 277–278, 292, 294–295, 305–306, 318, 323; Aware, 123–134, 184–190, 199, 205–206, 208–218, 219–234, 259–282; breakdown of, 254–255, 256, 321–324; careers affected by, 81–83, 89–92, 102, 107–110, 145, 152, 155, 163–164, 166–168, 178, 186–188, 227–228, 232–241, 270–279; civil liberties, 52–54, 70, 78–79, 80, 106, 115, 335–336, 348–350; cold war, 184–210; *Confidential Notebook (File 13)* (Hartnett), 165, 166, 172; congressional contributions, 145–146, 154–155; criticism of, 48–49, 51–54, 110–115, 230–231; defiance of, 108–109, 129–133, 139–140, 175, 179, 180, 196–197, 215–218, 232–233, 254–255, 256,

321–324; dramatic depictions, 321–322, 332–335, 342; Faulk lawsuit testimony, 270–282; greylists, 108, 238, 272; health effects, 109–110, 167, 227–228, 250, 254, 320; history leading to, 54–68; HUAC investigations, 243–244; legacy of, 347–350; licensing of stations, 74, 112; movies, 92, 133; programming effects, 190–197; protests, 84, 163; radio, 42–46, 53, 71–72, 163, 233, 234, 238–241, 245–247; sources, 44, 174–175, 176, 231–232; sponsors and, 50–54, 70, 78, 79–80, 85, 104–106, 109, 123–134, 198, 234–241, 251, 256–257, 262, 263, 265, 266–279, 297, 298, 304, 318; survivors, 107–110, 192–193; television, 48, 49–54, 68–70, 78–82, 103–115, 138–140, 175, 179, 180, 195–197, 233, 247, 322–323, 329; unions and, 106–107, 178. *See also Counterattack; Red Channels.*

Blaisdell, Charles, 8, 90–91, 156

Block Drug Company, 139–140, 251, 277

Block, Herb, 199, 318

Block, Melvin, 139–140

Bolan, Thomas A., 262–263; dramatic depictions, 334; *Faulk v. Aware,* 262–263, 266–270, 274–276, 278–290, 291–293, 297–299, 300–303, 306–308, 310–311, 315–316; tactics, 266–267, 281–282

Books: anti-anti-Communist, 152, 191, 204–205, 217, 325–326; anti-Communist, 49; blacklists, 42–49, 165, 166, 172; CPUSA publishers, 58

Borden Company, 127–128, 129, 173–174, 189, 218, 249, 287–288, 297

Boycotts, anti-Communist, 121–123, 125

Brady, Thomas, 85
Brand, Oscar, 89–90
Brewer, Roy, 339
Bridges, Lloyd, 345–346
Brinson, Susan L., 74
Broadcasting: anti-Communist
    defiance, 108–109, 129–133, 139–140,
    175, 179, 180, 196–197, 215–218,
    232–233, 254–255, 256, 321–324; anti-
    Communist subservience, 128–129,
    133–134, 173–175, 189, 190, 203;
    Counterattack campaign against,
    27–31, 40–41, 61, 83, 85; HUAC
    investigation, 72, 142–143, 198;
    industry magazines, 44, 111;
    McCarthy's fall and, 205; union
    actions, 77, 177–180. *See also* AFTRA;
    Radio; Sponsors; Television.
Broadcasting magazine, anti-
    Communist editorials, 44
Brodkin, Herbert, 108, 196, 254, 255,
    321, 324
Brodsky, Joseph, 55, 58
Broken Arrow, 255
Bromberg, J. Edward, 110, 228, 320
Brooks, Van Wyck, 36
Brown, Himan, 107, 138, 271
Brynner, Yul, 139
Buchanan, Eleanor, 121–123, 275, 308,
    327, 347
Buchanan, John A., 121–122
Buckley, William F., 253, 326–327
Budenz, Louis Francis, 39, 54–58, 64,
    65–66, 144, 154, 285, 345
Bull, Ina May, 267
Bunce, Alan, 178
Burdett, Winston, 58, 221
Burrows, Abe, 28, 105–106, 127, 142,
    147, 172, 271
Burrows, Carin Kinzel, 151

Burton, Michael C., 94
Bury the Dead (Shaw), 47
Business, fellow travelers, 18

Caesar, Sid, 195
Calomiris, Angela, 9
Cameron, Angus, 204–205
Canadian Broadcasting Corporations
    (CBC): anti-anti-Communist
    broadcasts, 207–208
Car 54, Where Are You?, 321
Careers: CPUSA influence, 148,
    162–163, 178–180. *See also* Careers
    affected by blacklists.
Careers affected by blacklists: CPUSA
    and, 152, 155, 163–164; defiance of
    blacklists, 108–109, 129–133, 139–140,
    175, 179, 180, 196–197, 215–218,
    232–233, 254–255, 256, 321–324;
    dramatic depictions, 321–322;
    finances, 178, 227–228, 248, 256;
    firing, 245–247, 263, 265, 287–288,
    299–300, 303–304, 315–316; hiring,
    104–106, 138, 145, 172–176, 189, 197,
    213–214, 218, 249, 250, 256, 270–271,
    272, 277–278, 286, 291, 294–295, 334;
    return of blacklistees, 321–324,
    329–330; smaller stations, 247;
    survivors, 107–110, 192–193; theater
    as a refuge, 197–198, 217–218,
    227–228; writers, 139, 155, 192–193,
    287–288, 329–330. *See also*
    Clearance.
Carlson, Richard, 191–194
Carnovsky, Morris, 253
Carroll, Nancy, 51
Carson, Saul, 26, 51
Carter, Jimmy, 343
Cartner, Hermione, 118
Cartoons on anti-Communists, 318

Case of Libel, 323
"Case of Milo Radulovich, The," 199
Castro, Fidel, 260, 343
Catholic church: anti-Catholicism and, 166; anti-Communist activities, 11–12, 54, 102; anti-Communist influence, 170–172, 211–212, 328; Catholic War Veterans, 50, 105–106, 172, 190; organizations, 159, 161, 164; Protestants and, 171
Catholic War Veterans, 50, 105–106, 172, 190
Caute, David, 341–342
CBC (Canadian Broadcasting Corporation), anti-anti-Communist broadcasts, 207–208
CBS (Columbia Broadcasting System): anti-blacklist dramas, 321–322, 332–335; blacklists, 71–78, 75, 93, 103–104, 109, 124–125, 127, 138–139, 190, 198–199, 233, 234, 238–241, 245–247, 254, 262, 263, 265, 299–300, 303–304, 322; Faulk and, 96–97, 100–103, 219, 233, 234, 238–241, 245–247, 262, 265, 266–267, 281–282, 299–300, 333; Hartnett v., 335, 338–339, 341; internal employee investigation, 103–104; liberalism, 71, 104, 172; loyalty oaths, 71–78, 75, 93, 102, 104, 199, 238, 310, 339; security measures, 76, 190
Censorship: CPUSA and, 62; World War II, 22, 52–53, 348
Ceplair, Larry, 341–342
Chambers, Whittaker, 56, 164, 203, 292, 334
Chaplin, Charlie, 130
Chayefsky, Paddy, 195
Cheney, Dick, 349
Chess, Stephen C., 50

Chiang Kai-shek, 101, 102
Chicago Tribune, fascist front charges, 22
Children's entertainment, Wicker, 80–81
China, Nationalist, 12, 102
Chopin, Frederic, 207–208
Christians, Mady, 109–110, 167, 228, 313
Christophers, The, 161, 164
Civil liberties: blacklisting and, 52–54, 70, 78–79, 80, 106, 115, 335–336, 348–350; Fifth Amendment, 152–153, 253, 280, 281, 310; freedom of speech, 190; libel suits and, 187–188, 340; Mundt-Nixon bill, 68, 70; radio shows on, 165; U.S. policies, 102; War on Terror, 348; World War II, 22, 52–53, 348
Civil rights. *See* Civil liberties.
Civil Rights Congress, 39, 48
Clamage, Edward, 74
Clearance: advertising agency departments, 104–106, 138, 197, 270–271, 294–295, 305–306; Aware pamphlet, 211–212; consultants, 145, 172–176, 189, 213–214, 218, 249, 250, 256, 271, 272, 277–278, 286, 291, 300–303, 310, 312; hiring policies, 104–106, 138, 145, 172–176, 189, 197, 213–214, 218, 249, 250, 256, 270–271, 272, 277–278, 286, 291, 294–295, 334; research techniques, 174–175, 176; voluntary, 188–189, 211–218, 272
Clergy, fellow travelers, 18–19
Cobb, Lee J., 65, 175, 222
Coe, Fred, 196
Cogley, John, 87, 108, 201, 243–244, 306
Cohen, Ronald D., 135

Cohn, Roy, 203, 244, 250–252, 257, 262, 267, 327

Cold war, 4, 260; blacklisting and, 184–210, 260; *Counterattack* views, 28; Eisenhower policies, 199; programming and, 190–196; teaching about, 332. *See also* Korean War.

Collectivization program, 34

Collingwood, Charles, 21, 77, 187, 225–226, 229, 232, 233, 234, 237, 338

Collins, Richard, 146–147

Collyer, Bud, 178–179, 216–217, 325

Collyer, Michael, 179

Columbia Pictures, blacklists, 92

Columbia Workshop, The (Corwin), 21–22

Comedies (radio), 20; McCarthy satire, 207–208; monitoring, 28–29. *See also* Comedies (television).

Comedies (television): Golden Age, 195; post-blacklist era, 324, 344. *See also* Comedies (radio).

Comintern (Communist International) Seventh World Congress, 31–32

Commercialism: radio, 24–25; television, 324

Committee for the First Amendment, 27

Commonweal, Cogley articles, 201

Communism: media portrayal, 8, 10, 23, 45, 309, 343. *See also* CPUSA; USSR.

"Communism—U.S. Brand" (Wishengrad), 26, 92, 187

Communist fronts: entertainers and, 30–41, 44, 89–90, 189, 222–223, 226–227, 231–232, 264–265, 269, 284–285, 290, 294, 335; liberals and, 33–38, 44, 47, 70, 91–92, 147, 154; McCarran Act, 70, 143, 348; propaganda and, 61–62; protests organized by, 84, 226–227, 230; resentment of, 122; unions, 22; youth organizations, 135, 136, 140, 339, 340. *See also* Popular Front.

Communist International (Comintern) Seventh World Congress, 31–32

Communist party (U.S.). *See* CPUSA.

Communist Political Association. *See* CPUSA.

"Communist Pressure on the Radio Industry" (Keenan, Kirkpatrick, and Bierly), 13

Concealed Enemies, 334

"Concerning the Red Army" (Rosten), 23

Confidential Notebook (File 13) (Hartnett), 165, 166, 172

Conflict of interest: Aware defendants, 274, 286, 287–288, 297, 300–303, 312; clearance consultants, 172, 174, 274, 286, 291, 297, 298, 300–303, 310, 312, 313; libel suit jurors, 187. *See also* Credibility.

Congress of American Women, 30

Congressional hearings, 142–157; blacklists derived from, 145–146, 154–155; Fifth Amendment, 152–153, 253, 280, 281; friendly witnesses, 146–147; legal admissibility, 280, 285, 293, 298; self-clearance and, 212; Southern Conference Educational Fund, 335; union cooperation mandate, 232, 241; writers, 142, 146–147, 153–155, 208. *See also* HUAC; McCarran Committee; McCarthy, Joseph.

Connolly, Marc, 107
Conroy, John, 331
Consumers Union, 31
Copland, Aaron, 193, 288
Cornell University, radio prank, 156–157
Corwin, Norman, 18, 21–24, 107, 195; anti-blacklist activities, 27; broadcasts produced by, 25, 60, 66, 107, 143–144, 206; criticism of, 194; politics, 36, 71; Popular Front and, 148, 164, 172, 193–195
Cotten, Joseph, 133–134
Coughlin, Charles, 23
Counterattack, I Was a Communist for the FBI, 190–191, 192
Counterattack, 16–19, 25, 90–92, 155–156, 230, 328, 329; ABC and, 74–76, 80–81; anti-broadcasting industry campaign, 27–31, 40–41, 42–70, 71–72, 78–92, 103, 127, 142, 156–157, 189, 342, 345–346; anti-Semitism, 169–170; Bromberg attack, 110, 320; CBS and, 71–73, 74, 77; credibility, 49, 85; criticism of, 49, 83–88, 91, 110–115, 155–156, 217, 221; finances, 88, 156, 230; Johnson and, 127; libel suits against, 30–31, 38–41, 90–92; McCarran Committee hearings, 145, 154–155; Matusow and, 136–137; Murrow viewed by, 200; Popular Front and, 36–41, 193–194; protests agitated by, 83, 85; racketeering charges, 84–88; Stockholm Peace Appeal and, 48; support of, 84, 122. *See also* Bierly, Kenneth M.; Keenan, John G.; *Plain Talk*; *Red Channels*.
Country stores, 117, 119
Cousins, Norman, 199

CPUSA (American Communist party): anti-war protests, 48, 60; Comintern Congress influence, 30–32; cultural commission, 59–70, 148, 162–163, 178–180, 330; defectors, 54–55, 135, 146–147, 150–151, 285, 321, 336; ideology, 56, 148, 229; infiltration of, 9, 17, 190–191; Popular Front, 32–38, 66, 147–150, 193–195; Progressive party and, 98; propaganda, 59–60, 147; racism, 149; radio commission, 55–70, 147; restrictiveness of, 150; revolutionist tactics, 38–41; secrecy of, 42; Trotsky murder, 56; weakening of, 242–243; writers influenced by, 59, 63–64, 66–68, 69, 150–151, 206–207; youth organizations, 135, 136, 140, 339, 340
Crangle, Oliver, 258
Credibility: anti-anti-communism, 113–114, 243–244, 341–342; anti-communism, 279, 341–342; Aware, 222, 237–238, 261, 264–265, 284, 285–303; blacklistees, 69, 261, 263, 264, 265–270, 310, 312, 335–340, 343; *Counterattack*, 49, 85; evidence sources, 280, 285, 292–293; Faulk, 261, 263, 264, 265–270, 310, 312, 335–340, 343; friendly witnesses, 54–55, 56, 135, 146–147, 150–151, 217, 244, 285, 293; Hartnett, 249–250, 261, 310, 313; Johnson, 261, 305–306, 310–311, 313–314; Murrow anti-McCarthy programs, 202–203; unfriendly witnesses, 34, 146–147, 224. *See also* Clearance; Conflict of interest.
"Crisis of Galileo, The," 195
Critics, on anti-Communist radio shows, 26

Cronin, John F., 11–12
Crosby, John, 84, 220–221, 249
Crucible, The (Miller), 192–193, 279
Cuba, 260, 343
Cultural commission (CPUSA), 59–70
Cvetic, Matt, 190–191

Daily Worker, 33, 348; as a blacklist
    source, 44, 231–232, 292; Budenz's
    editorship, 54, 285; civil rights stand,
    149; Korean War articles, 48
Dalsimer, Samuel, 130, 236, 277, 278
Danger, 138–139, 149, 192, 195, 342
Dann, Michael, 50–51
Darkness at Noon (Koestler), 150
Da Silva, Howard, 48
Davidson, Jo, 33
Davis, Benjamin J., 81, 89, 149
Davis, Bette, 36
Davis, Elmer, 57, 65
Davis, Ossie, 321, 345
Deane, Martha, 40
Deaths, 109–110, 167, 227–228, 315, 316,
    319–320, 328, 329, 345
Debs, Eugene V., 94, 330
Defectors: from the CPUSA, 54–55, 135,
    146–147, 150–151, 285, 321, 336; from
    the USSR, 62
Defenders, The, 321–322
Dehn, Adolph, 128
De Koven, Roger, 47, 162–163
De Kruif, Paul, 34
Democratic socialism, 94
Denker, Henry, 57, 63, 67–68, 323
Dennis, Eugene, 38
Depression: political activism, 3;
    political influence of, 20, 22, 25,
    26–27
Devane, William, 333
DeVoto, Bernard, 194

Dewey, John, 34
Dewey, Thomas F., 99
Dickler, Gerald, 245, 247
Dilling, Elizabeth, 49, 169
Dimitrov, Georgi, 32
Djilas, Milovan, 260
Documentaries: anti-McCarthyism
    programs, 199–203; methods, 201,
    202. *See also* Historical programs;
    Memoirs; Sustaining programs.
Doherty, Thomas, 202
Downs, Bill, 77
Dramas: anti-anti-Communist,
    192–193, 199–203, 221, 255, 258,
    321–322, 323, 325–326, 332–335,
    342–343; anti-Red melodramas,
    190–192; Golden Age, 196; left-wing,
    192–197, 207–208; monitoring, 28–29
Draper, Paul, 30, 39, 53
Draper, Theodore, 32
Du Bois, W. E. B., 176
Duelos, Jacques, 38
Duggan, Laurence, 102–103, 200, 202
Dulles, John Foster, 101, 102
Dungey, John, 125–126; American
    Legion involvement, 125–126, 173,
    256; Aware involvement, 185, 235,
    236–237, 239, 253, 313; Faulk and,
    265, 335; Hartnett and, 173, 217–218,
    255–256, 327–328, 335; influence of,
    134, 188
DuPont Corporation, 248

East Side / West Side, 321–322
Eastman, Max, 166–167
Educational radio shows, 21, 22
Egotism, anti-Communists and, 131,
    134, 137, 138
Einhorn, Nathan, 58
Einstein, Albert, 33

Eisenhower, Dwight, 199, 294
Eisler, Hanns, 288
Eldridge, Florence, 30
Electronics Corporation of America, 57
Emergency Civil Liberties Committee, 226–227, 230
Emerson, Faye, 109, 225–226
Emmy awards, 329–330, 334
Englund, Steven, 341–342
Entertainment business: anti-Communists post-blacklist, 329; anti-fascism, 34–35; *Counterattack* purge campaign, 29–31; CPUSA infiltration, 43–44, 58, 163–165, 222–223, 229–230, 242, 244, 330, 337, 345–346; entertainers and Communist fronts, 89–90, 189, 222–223, 226–227, 231–232, 264–265, 269, 284–285, 290, 294, 335; fellow travelers, 18, 44–45; HUAC investigations, 27, 29, 31, 72, 103, 110; Korean war's effect on, 47–48, 50, 53–54, 67, 156, 193; Popular Front and, 33–38, 66, 147–150, 193–195; unions, 48–49, 77, 106–107, 177–180. *See also* Movies; Music; Radio; Television; Theater.
Evidence, source admissability, 280, 285, 291, 292–293, 298
Experimental radio shows, 21–22
Extremism: dangers of, 347–350. *See also* Left-wingers; Middle of the Road; Right-wingers.

False Witness (Matusow), 204–205, 217, 244
Fascists: modern-day, 343–344; as traitors, 22; U.S., 102, 114. *See also* Anti-fascism.

Fast, Howard, 59, 151, 177, 321
Faulk, Henry, 94
Faulk, John Henry, 93–103, 264; AFTRA involvement, 224–227, 229–234, 241, 337–338, 341; Aware lawsuit, 172, 224–225, 230–241, 245–247, 249–252, 256–318, 336–337; career development, 96–97, 99–101, 101, 180–182, 218–219, 325–327, 333, 344, 345; CBS firing of, 245–247, 263, 265, 299–300, 303–304, 315–316, 339; credibility, 261, 263, 264, 265–270, 310, 312, 335–341, 343, 345; damages awarded, 316–317, 320–321, 327–328; FBI investigation, 95–96, 99, 182–183, 219, 224–225, 290; HUAC and, 219, 224–225, 253, 269–270, 289, 335; memoir, 325–326, 332–335; *Nation* symposium, 335–336; politics, 93–99, 101–103, 165, 182–183, 325–326, 344–345
Faulk, Lynne, 248, 302–303, 325
FBI: American Business Consultants and, 87, 221; anti-Communist activities, 5–11, 14, 57; dramas on, 190–191, 192; Faulk investigation, 95–96, 99, 182–183, 219, 224–225, 267, 290; Hartnett viewed by, 216; information sources, 105, 135–136; Lampell investigation, 144; Loeb investigation, 78–79; Lyon investigation, 64–65; *Plain Talk* and, 14–15; Price investigation, 188; public viewed by, 10–11; Sullivan investigation, 222–223
FCC: ACLU petition against, 112; anti-communism, 74
Fear on Trial (Faulk), 326, 332–335
Feffer, Itzik, 61

Fellow travelers: business, 18; clergy, 18–19; entertainment, 18, 29–30, 44–45; organizations, 30, 33. *See also* Communist fronts.

Ferrer, José 127, 130, 168

Fifth Amendment, congressional testimonies and, 152–153, 253, 280, 281

Finances: blacklists and, 80, 227–228, 248, 256; *Counterattack*, 88, 156, 230; damages awarded Faulk, 316–317, 320–321, 327–328. *See also* Financing.

Financing: anti-Communist publications, 11–12, 17–18; CPUSA, 58. *See also* Sponsors.

Finland, 35–36

Firings: blacklisting, 78–80, 245–247, 263, 265, 287–288, 299–300, 303–304, 315–316; War on Terror era, 348–349

Flagstad, Kirsten, 84

FM radio, 62–63

Folk music, 60, 82, 89–90, 96, 97, 330; anti-Communist attitudes, 122, 131, 143–144, 206–207, 230, 231, 261; People's Songs, 97, 267–268, 284, 288, 299, 340

Foote, Horton, 195

Fopp, Gino, 9

Ford, Glenn, 226

Foster, William Z., 58, 64, 147, 150–151

"Four O'Clock," 258

Fox, John M., 128

Frankenheimer, John, 139

Frankfurter, Felix, 49

Franklin, Zalmond, 56

Freedom of speech, 190

Frichtman, Stephen H., 171

Friendly witnesses, 54–55, 56, 135, 146–147, 150–151, 217, 244, 285, 293

Friends of Democracy's Battle, 22, 53

Front, The, 342

Fronts: for blacklisted writers, 139, 155, 192–193, 342. *See also* Communist fronts.

Gailmor, William S., 28, 57, 61

Galileo, 195

Gangbusters, 162

Garfield, John, 34, 44, 172

Garland, Judy, 33

Gary, Sam, 60

Gebert, Bill, 56

Gelbart, Larry, 195

Geller, Abraham, 187, 260–261, 270, 273, 274–276, 280, 284, 285, 289, 340; Hartnett testimony, 291, 294, 298, 299, 303; Johnson testimony, 300, 314–315; Slate testimony, 303–304; verdict, 320–321

General Foods, 50–51, 52, 78, 79–80, 86

Germ warfare, 115

German-American Bund, FBI investigation, 8

Germany, Berlin blockade, 4, 46

Gilford, Jack, 108, 124–125, 137, 180, 210, 256, 321

Glazer, Nathan, 171

Gleason, Jackie, 81–82, 108, 195

Glover, Danny, 348

Godfrey, Arthur, 125

Goldbergs, The, 78–80, 86

Golden Age: radio, 20–25; television, 193–196, 324

Golos, Jacob, 147, 221

Goodson, Mark, 108–109, 271, 349–350

Gordon, Douglas, 220

Gough, Lloyd, 223
Gould, Jack, 26, 52, 77, 84, 190, 198, 222, 318, 350
Gouzenko, Igor, 10, 62
Grant, Lee, 139, 180, 210, 216, 225, 253, 256, 281, 321
Great Conspiracy, The: The Secret War Against Russia, 204
Great Depression. *See* Depression.
Great Fear, The (Caute), 341–342
Greece, communism in, 98
Grey Advertising, 130, 235–238, 277
Greylists, 108, 238, 272
Grocery stores: country stores, 117, 119, 255; merchandising agreement cancellations, 129, 278; storekeepers community role, 117–118; supermarkets, 118–119
Groza, Petru, 160
Gurian, Waldemar, 159–160
Guthrie, Woody, 60, 97, 268, 330

Hagberg, Gene, 170
Hagen, Uta, 107, 168
Hall, George, 149, 223
Hall, Gus, 48
Hamlin, Edith, 196–197, 321
Hammer, Armand, 80
Hammer, Victor, 80
Hammerstein, Oscar, 288
Hammett, Dashiell, 31, 35, 82, 170
Harkins, John, 333–334
Hart, James, 67
Hart, Merwin K., 29, 69
Hartnett, Joseph Patrick, 158; Wren and, 305–308
Hartnett, Maureen, 328
Hartnett, Vincent, 43–44, 54, 157–183, 167, 184–185, 255–256; appeals, 320–321, 327–328; background, 158–160, 291; Barrett pursuit, 214–215, 216, 243–244, 264, 346; CBS sued by, 335, 338–339, 341; clearance consultancy, 172–176, 189, 213–214, 218, 249, 250, 256, 271, 272, 273–274, 286, 291, 298, 300–303, 310; convictions of, 159, 161, 164, 171–172, 296–297, 328, 332, 335, 346; credibility, 249–250, 261, 262, 264–265, 273–274, 279, 286, 289–295, 297, 300–303, 305–306, 310, 312, 313, 346–347; criticism of, 166–168, 208, 212–218, 261; Crosby lawsuit, 221, 249; dramatic depictions of, 322, 332–335; Dungey and, 173, 217–218, 255–256, 327–328, 335; Faulk and, 230, 247, 249–252, 256–262, 269, 270, 271, 272, 273–274, 276, 279–281, 285, 286, 289, 290, 291–303, 305–308, 317, 320–321, 327, 335, 338–339; Hiken attack, 154; HUAC testimony, 243–244, 274; influence of, 190, 208, 213, 218–219, 249, 272–274, 329–330; Johnson's partnership with, 173, 298, 310–311; Murrow criticized by, 200–201; research skills, 174–175, 176, 296, 301–302, 332; Sloane denounced by, 272; speaking career, 164–165, 214, 221, 253, 256, 327, 346; support of, 263; teaching career, 331–332; theater denounced by, 197, 217–218; union investigations, 177–180; writing career, 160, 161–162, 165–166, 297
Hayes, Arthur Garfield, 273
Haynes, John Earl, 56
Hays, Arthur Garfield, 49, 90
Hays, Lee, 60
Hayworth, Vinton, 178, 180, 185, 329

Health: blacklist effects, 109–110, 167, 227–228, 250, 254, 320; Johnson testimony and, 275, 300, 304–305, 308–309, 311, 313–315, 320

Hee Haw, 344

Heflin, Van, 323

Heller, Abraham A., 55, 58, 64

Heller, Steven, 31, 35

Hellman, Lillian, 34, 341–342, 343

Henahan, Donal, 194–195

Herman, Arthur, 200, 202

Hersey, John, 330

Higley, Philo, 154

Hiken, Nat, 108, 172, 254–255, 321, 324

Hilmes, Michele, 24

Hilton & Riggio, 138

Hiring policies, 104–106, 138, 145, 172–176, 189, 197, 213–214, 218, 249, 250, 256, 270–271, 272, 277–278, 286, 291, 294–295, 334

Hiss, Alger, 103, 171, 200, 203

Historical programs, 192–193. *See also* Documentaries; Memoirs.

Hoffman Beverages, 235–237

Hollenbeck, Don, 77, 192, 228

Holliday, Judy, 44, 92, 144–145, 309

Hollywood Anti-Nazi League, 34–35

Hollywood League for Democratic Action, 35

Hollywood Ten, 27, 29, 55

"Honeymooners," 81–82, 108

Hook, Sidney, 37, 47, 226

Hoover, J. Edgar, 6, 8, 43, 71, 221

Horn, Sam, 16, 39, 85

Horne, Lena, 168

Houseman, John, 28

House Un-American Activities Committee. *See* HUAC.

"How Communism Exploits Sex" (Hartnett), 166

"How the Reds Invaded Radio" (Budenz), 54–58, 64, 65–66

HUAC: as a blacklist source, 44; broadcast industry investigation, 72, 142–143, 198; Cogley attack, 243–244; criticism of, 229, 336; decline of, 253; Eisenhower and, 294; Faulk and, 219, 253, 269–270, 289, 335; Fifth Amendment tactics, 153, 253, 280, 281; Matusow involvement, 136, 141, 145; movie investigation, 27, 29, 31, 32, 65, 103, 110, 142; New York hearings, 223–224, 253; peace movement viewed by, 291; protests of, 97, 226–227, 232; racism in, 29; radio programs on, 27; testimony refusal, 289, 299; theater investigation, 223–224, 253; writer investigations, 142, 146–147, 208

Hughes, Langston, 44

Humor, CPUSA and, 147–148

Hungary, 242, 336

Hunt, Marsha, 48

Hunter, Kim, 213–214, 218, 219–220, 243, 273–274, 311, 334, 345

Hussein, Saddam, 344

Hutchins Agency, 85–86

I Led 3 Lives (Philbrick), 191–192, 309

I Married a Communist, 309

I Remember Mama, 109

Ideology, CPUSA stress on, 56, 148, 229

Independent Citizens Committee of the Arts, Sciences and Professions, 24, 25, 36, 38, 231, 264–265, 285, 298

Indictments. *See* Libel suits.

In Fact, 85

Infiltration, 43–44, 58, 163–165; army, 203; of the Communist party, 9, 17,

Infiltration (*continued*)
190–191; entertainment business,
43–44, 58, 163–165, 222–223,
229–230, 242, 244, 330, 337, 345–346;
movies, 55; newspapers, 58, 221–222;
organizations, 31–41; radio, 43–44,
54–58, 142–157, 162–163; television,
43–44, 54–58, 142–157; unions, 8–9,
13, 26, 58, 63, 66–68, 79, 143, 145,
154, 177–180, 221, 229–230. *See also*
Popular Front; Spies.
Inquisition in Hollywood, The (Ceplair
and Englund), 341–342
Intellectuals, Popular Front tactics,
33–38, 147–150
Internal Security Act, 70, 143
International Publishers, 58
"Investigations of the So-Called
'Blacklisting' in Entertainment
Industry," 243–244
"Investigator, The," 207–208
Irish Catholicism, anti-communism
and, 171
Iron Curtain, The, 62
Irving, Charles, 130–131, 173, 298
Ives, Burl, 28, 144–145, 288
Ives, George, 214–215
Ives, John O., 162, 163
Ivy, Peter, 55, 66, 154

Jacobowsky, David, 300
Jacobs, Arthur, 213, 273–274
Jacobson, David, 86, 87–88
Jaffe, Henry, 166
Janney, Leon, 180
Jarrico, Paul, 64, 146–147
Jefferson School of Social Science,
232, 265, 293, 298
Jefferson, Thomas, 207–208
Jeffreys, George, 207

Jerome, V. J., 55, 58, 79
Jewish organizations: anti-Communist
activities, 12, 52, 126–127. *See also*
Anti-Semitism.
John Henry Faulk Show, 100, 101,
235–241, 266, 276, 282
John Quincy Adams Associates,
13–16
Johnny's Front Porch, 96–97
Johnson, Edmund, 116–117
Johnson, Eleanor, 121–123, 275,
308, 327, 347
Johnson, Francis Marion, 117
Johnson, Lady Bird, 218–219
Johnson, Laurence A., 116–141, 125,
142, 189–190; Americana, 119, 121,
255; Aware involvement, 185,
208–210, 218, 249, 250, 253, 259, 272,
296, 297, 298, 304; credibility,
237–238, 261, 305–306, 310–311,
313–314; criticism of, 180, 190, 217,
313; death of, 315, 316, 319–320;
dramatic depictions of, 322; estate,
320–321; Faulk v., 247, 249–252, 259,
271, 272, 274–279, 300, 304–305,
308–309, 310–311, 313–315, 316, 317;
grocery career, 117, 119, 129, 235, 255;
Hartnett's partnership with, 173,
298, 310–311; health problems, 275,
300, 304–305, 308–309, 311, 313–315,
320; influence of, 128–129, 133–134,
173–175, 189, 190, 208, 234, 236, 240,
243, 251, 271, 276–279; radio
involvement, 121, 123–134;
reputation, 120, 237, 261, 347;
support of, 134, 189–190, 319–320,
347; television preferences, 192,
308–309; veterans group, 123–124,
127, 130, 139–140, 156, 173, 175
Johnson, Lyndon Baines, 218–219

Joint Anti-Fascist Refugee Committee, 24, 31, 39
Joint Committee Against Communism, 50
Journal of the Plague Years (Kanfer), 341–342
Journalism. *See* Newsletters; Newspapers; *publications by name.*
"Judgment at Nuremberg," 255
Judges and the Judged, The (Miller), 111–115, 243, 339
Julian, Joseph, 90, 91–92, 186–188, 189, 190, 245, 260–261, 323

Kahn, Albert E., 204–205
Kamp, Joseph P., 168–169
Kanfer, Stefan, 341–342
Karlborg, Herbert, 322
Kazan, Elia, 110, 172
Keenan, John G., 5–19, 27–31, 37–41, 88, 90–91, 159, 171, 253, 328–329; accusations of, 85–88; blacklisting by, 42–46, 83–84, 230, 298; CBS viewed by, 71; Kirkpatrick's departure and, 156; McCarthy viewed by, 200. *See also* American Business Consultants; *Counterattack*; *Red Channels.*
Keene, William, 185
Keller, James, 161, 164
Kelley, Welbourn, 63, 66–67, 143, 154–155
Kellogg, blacklisting and, 80–81
Kelly, Gene, 168
Kelton, Pert, 81–82, 90–91, 107–108, 254
Kempton, Murray, 112, 114, 208, 264, 279, 288–289, 303, 305, 318, 320
Kenby Associates, 92
Kendrick, Alexander, 77, 107

Kennedy, Ted, 349
Keynote Recording Company, 60
KFI loyalty oath, 72
KFRC, Faulk and, 247, 265
Khrushchev, Nikita, 242
Kinoy, Ernest, 108, 154, 195, 321–322
Kintner, Robert, 74–76, 350
Kirkpatrick, Theodore C., 5–19, 27–31, 37–41, 37, 88–89, 221, 328, 329; ABC and, 76; accusations of, 85–88, 221; blacklisting by, 42–46, 83–84; CBS and, 71, 73; departure from American Business Consultants, 155–156; Hartnett and, 165; Matusow and, 136–137. *See also* American Business Consultants; *Counterattack*; *Red Channels.*
Klehr, Harvey, 56
Klein, Adelaide, 85
Klein, Harvey, 214
Klugman, Jack, 322
Knight, Ruth Adams, 63, 67–68, 143, 146, 154–155
Koestler, Arthur, 150
Kohlberg, Alfred, 12, 16, 50, 170, 173
Korean War, 46–48, 103, 115, 156, 176, 177, 186; criticism of, 48, 67, 101–102, 165, 193; *Daily Worker* articles, 48; entertainment industry effects, 47–48, 50, 53–54, 121–124, 129, 156; USSR's role, 46, 101–102, 115, 176, 177, 292
Kovacs, Ernie, 195
Kraft foods, 298
Kramden, Alice, 81, 108
Kudner Agency, 294

Labor. *See* Unions.
Labor Short Wave Bureau, 57, 65
Labor Youth League, 135

La Guardia, Fiorello, 49

Laird, Stephen, 58

Lambertson, William, 78

Lampell, Millard: anti-blacklist activities, 163, 341; blacklist effects on, 155, 206–207; CPUSA involvement, 151–152, 153, 157; McCarran Committee, 143–144, 153; *Nation* symposium, 335–336; post-blacklist, 329–331; songwriting, 60, 143–144, 206–207

Lardner, Rex, 84, 114, 197

Lardner, Ring, Jr., 192, 335–336, 345

Lattimore, Owen, 56, 171, 200

Lawrence, Mark, 110

Lawson, John Howard, 55, 59, 151

Lawsuits. *See* Libel suits.

Leader, Anton, 26

League of American Writers, 35

League of Women Shoppers, 31

Lear, Norman, 325

Lee, Canada, 228

Lee, Gypsy Rose, 44, 53, 74–76, 168

Lee, Madeleine, 225

Leech, John L., 38, 68–69

Left Wing Communism, An Infantile Disorder (Lenin), 229

Left-wingers: CBS, 71–72; as Communist allies, 79, 144; CPUSA views, 150–151; extremism, 347–348, 349–350; movie industry, 69; news commentators, 13–14, 71–72; organizations, 25; programming by, 192–197, 199–203, 207–208; radio community, 3–5, 13–14, 24–28; *Red Channel* list effects, 107; Texas, 93–94, 267, 290

Lennen & Mitchell, 138

Lerner, Max, 318

Letters: accusatory, 198, 214–215, 216, 243–244, 255–256, 264, 273–274, 292, 294–295, 306, 346; Faulk to accusers, 337–338; Faulk v. Aware testimony, 256–257, 265, 277, 287, 288; letter-writing campaigns, 208–209, 271; supportive, 66; to editors, 288; to sponsors, 78, 109, 127, 236, 239, 256–257, 277

Levenson, Sam, 144–145

Lever Brothers, 174, 189

Levine, Isaac Don, 12, 15–16, 52

Levittown, folk music controversy, 206–207

Levy, David, 270

Lewis, Brenda, 210

Libby's Frozen Foods, 234

Libel suits: against *Counterattack*, 30–31, 38–41, 90–92; against *Red Channels*, 186–188; appeals, 320–321; civic value, 340; evidence considered admissible, 280, 285, 291, 292–293, 298; *Faulk v. Aware*, 238–241, 245–247, 249–252, 256–317, 336–337; Hartnett v. CBS, 335, 338–339, 341; Hartnett v. Crosby, 221, 249; uselessness of, 187–188; U.S. v. newspapers, 22

Liberals: anti-anti-communism, 114–115, 191; Communist fronts and, 33–38, 44, 47, 70, 91–92, 147, 154; Moscow purge trials and, 34, 79, 341–342; Stalin defended by, 33–34, 35, 97, 98–99, 176–177, 242, 341–342, 343, 347. *See also* Left-wingers.

Licensing of stations, blacklists and, 74, 112

Lichtman, Robert M., 135

Lie, Trygve, 265

Life: Muir blacklisting response, 52; Veterans Action Committee and, 130

Lincoln, Abraham, 206–207

Lindsay, John, 326–327

Loeb, John, 227–228

Loeb, Philip, 53, 78–79, 86, 106, 107, 145, 168, 227–228, 231, 313

Lomax, Alan, 96, 97, 102, 345

"Lonesome Train, The" (Lampell and Robinson), 206–207

Lord, Phillips H., 162, 163

Lowe, Jim, 304

Loyalty oaths: CBS, 71–78, 75, 93, 102, 104, 238, 310, 339; KFI, 72

Ludwig, Salem, 139

Lumet, Sidney, 104, 139–140, 255, 333

Luther, Martin, 207–208

Lyon, Don, 131–132

Lyon, Peter, 64–68, 107, 143, 146, 153–154, 155, 157, 172

MacArthur, Douglas, 22, 101, 102, 349

Macdonald, Dwight, 47, 167

McCarran Committee, 143–146, 153–157, 185, 330

McCarran Internal Security Act, 70, 143, 348

McCarran, Pat, 143, 169. See also McCarran Committee; McCarran Internal Security Act.

McCarthy Committee, 204–205

McCarthy, Joseph, 40, 201, 349; campaigns, 141; criticism of, 102–103, 243, 313; fall of, 199–203, 205–206; McCarthy Committee, 204–205; satires, 207–208; support of, 170, 182–183; televised hearings, 201–203. See also HUAC; McCarthyism.

McCarthyism: American Committee for Cultural Freedom debate, 166–168. See also Anti-communism; Anti-McCarthyism.

McCullough, Hester, 30, 39, 50, 107

McDonald, Larry, 337, 338

McGee, Willie, 63, 226

McNamara, Francis, 39, 156, 171, 200, 230, 253, 328–329, 335

Magnificent Montague, The, 108, 172

Maher, Bill, 348

Maltz, Albert, 150

Mankiewicz, Don, 34–35, 197, 226, 350

Mann, Thomas, 33, 292

Manoff, Arnold, 139, 192

Manson, Alan, 253

March, Fredric, 30, 33, 69, 170

Marinello, Juan, 163

Marion, Paul, 150

Markell, Robert, 322

Marketing: anti-Communist concepts, 140, 251, 277. See also Advertising; Advertising agencies.

Marks, Jerome A., 305, 308

Marshall Plan, 61

Marshall, George, 199

Marshall, Rex, 220

Martin, Charles, 188

Martinson, Paul, 290

"Massacre at Sand Creek," 255

Mather, Cotton, 207

Matinee Theatre, Muir performance, 254

Matthews, J. B., 204, 230

Matthews, Ruth, 230

Matusow, Harvey, 134–141, 203–205; credibility, 217, 244, 293; Faulk v. Aware, 257, 262, 277, 287, 293; testimony, 145, 244, 321

Mayka, Stephen, 120

Meadows, Audrey, 82

Mele, Jerry, 331–332

Melish, William Howard, 18–19, 171, 177

Mellen, Joan, 35

Memoirs, 204–205, 217, 325–326, 332–335, 342

Menjou, Adolphe, 134

Menuhin, Yehudi, 36

Meredith, Burgess, 81

Metz, Robert, 71

Michael, King of Romania, 160

Mickelson, Sid, 72

Middle of the Road slate, 226–234, 241, 264, 266, 286–287, 292, 294, 297, 310, 313, 325, 337–338, 341

Militarization of the U.S., 101–102

Miller, Arthur, 21, 192–193, 279

Miller, Marvin, 176

Miller, Merle, 17, 111–113, 339

Milton, Paul: Aware involvement, 185, 213, 230; Aware trial testimony, 272, 283–289, 297; conflict of interest, 287–288, 297; McCarran Committee testimony, 146, 154–155; radio career, 283–284; We the Undersigned, 143, 185, 283, 287

Mine, Mill and Smelters Union, anti-anti-communism, 217

Minton, Bruce, 147

Minute Maid, 128, 129

Monthly Review, 48, 102

Moore, Gary, 225–226, 272

Moore, Sam, 150, 154

Morgan, Henry, 106, 109, 306

Morgens, Howard, 130–131

Morris, William, Jr., 166

Moscow purge trials, 34, 79, 341–342

Moss, Annie Lee, 201–202

Mostel, Zero, 164, 197, 256

Motion Picture Alliance for the Preservation of American Ideals, 176

Movie actors: blacklists, 92, 133; left-wingers, 69; Popular Front and, 33–38. *See also* Movies; *actors by name.*

Movies: anti-anti-Communist, 325–326, 332–335, 342–343; anti-Communist analogies, 255; HUAC investigation, 27, 29, 32, 65, 103, 110, 142; infiltration, 55; Middle of the Road movies, 226; Spanish Civil War portrayed by, 8; USSR portrayed by, 10. *See also* Movie actors.

Muir, Jean, 49–54, 68–70, 72, 78, 163, 166, 170, 254

Mundt, Karl, 128

Mundt-Nixon bill, 68, 70

Mundy, Meg, 81

Murray, Thomas, 235–236, 276–277, 278, 310–311

Murrow, Edward R., 21, 75, 201; anti-McCarthy programming, 199–203, 333; Faulk and, 100–101, 102, 227, 239; libel suit testimony, 187; liberal politics, 71; loyalty oaths and, 73, 77, 199

Music: anti-Communist influences, 82, 131; anti-nuclear, 83; CPUSA influences, 60, 82, 89–90, 194–195; folk music, 60, 82, 89–90, 96, 97, 122, 131, 143–144, 206–207, 230, 231, 261, 267–268

Myers, Lawrence, 132

NAACP, CPUSA viewed by, 149

Naming Names (Navasky), 152, 341–342

Nation, 49, 335–336

National Committee to Win the Peace, 30

National Council of American-Soviet Friendship, 62, 294

National Council of the Arts, Sciences and Professions, 84, 163

National Negro Congress, 38

Nationalist China, 12, 102

Navasky, Victor, 152, 341–342
Nazis: FBI investigation, 8; Hollywood Anti-Nazi League, 34–35; U.S. sentiments, 22, 35. *See also* World War II.
NBC (National Broadcasting Company): blacklist policies, 108, 130, 172–173; Muir controversy, 49–54, 68–70, 72, 78, 163, 166
Neuser, Francis, 124, 134, 139, 173, 175, 185, 235
Neuser, Margaret, 124
New Deal: Communist party views, 32; political influence of, 20, 22, 25, 26–27
New Leader, 51–52, 54
New Masses, 58, 147, 150
New Republic, 26, 51
New World Review, 176–177
New York City: FBI headquarters, 7–8, 14; HUAC hearings, 223–224, 253; mayoral race (1965), 326–327
New York Daily News, 22, 45, 325
New York Herald Tribune, 84, 220–221
New York Police Department, Hartnett and, 297
New York Post: anti-blacklist series, 180; anti-Communists critiqued by, 76, 84, 88–89; anti-McCarthyism and, 112, 199–200
New York Times: anti-Communist radio show reviews, 26; anti-Communists critiqued in, 52, 77, 84, 190, 222, 232, 288, 330–331, 334, 341; mock Communist putsch description, 45
News (print). *See* Newsletters; Newspapers; *publications by name*.
News (radio): *Counterattack* campaign against, 27–31; left-winger, 71–72, 77; pro-Communist slants, 13–14, 57,

61–62, 65, 172; union reportage, 57; World War II coverage, 22–24
News Supplements (Aware), 215–216, 222, 230–231, 233, 241; *Faulk v. Aware* trial evidence, 238, 249–250, 261, 263, 269, 270, 284, 286, 292, 295–296, 336–337; HUAC Communist citings lists, 301–302
Newsletters, Aware, 215–216, 219–221, 230–231, 233, 238, 241, 249–250, 261, 263, 269, 270, 284, 286, 292, 295–296, 336–337
Newspapers: anti-McCarthyism, 199–200; Communist infiltration, 58, 221–222; libel suits, 22. *See also* Newsletters.
Newsweek, anti-anti-Communist articles, 279, 334
Nizer, Louis, 95, 238–241, 241, 245, 253–257, 261–262, 263–266, 268, 280, 345; Appell testimony, 289–290; dramatic depictions of, 333; Hartnett and, 249–252, 271, 291, 292–303, 328; Hunter testimony, 273–275; Johnson and, 252, 320; Milton testimony, 286–289; Pegler case, 323; summation, 311–314, 315–316; Wren testimony, 304–306
North, Joseph, 147
Note-taking by Hartnett at trial, 296, 301–302
Novick, Sam, 57
Now! (Bailmor), 57

Oates, Titus, 207
Oaths. *See* Loyalty oaths.
Oboler, Arch, 21
O'Brian, Jack, 198, 228
O'Connor, John, 334
"Old Man Atom," 83
O'Neill, William L., 153, 167

One World Flight (Corwin), 25
Orfei, Frank, 332
Organizations: Catholic, 159, 161, 164;
    Communist infiltration of, 30–41;
    fellow travelers, 30, 33; Jewish, 12,
    52, 126–127; left-winger, 25. *See also*
    Communist fronts; Veterans;
    organizations by name.
Orwell, George, 204–205
O'Shea, Daniel T., 104, 190
Over the Counter and on the Shelf:
    Country Storekeeping in America
    (Johnson), 255
Owen, Joseph, 341
OWI, infiltration of, 56–57, 64
Ox Bow Incident, The, 255

Paar, Jack, 248
Pabst Brewing Company, 235–237,
    239, 276–277, 278
Paley, William S., 71, 74, 190
Pall Mall, 174
Pamphlets, Aware, 211–212
Panel shows, 100, 109, 247, 248, 325
Papp, Joseph, 345
Parker, Dorothy, 34
Party Organizer, 58
Passport for Adams series (Corwin), 23,
    66
"Patterns" (Serling), 255
Pauling, Linus, 36
Peabody, Stuart, 127–128
Peace movements, 31, 47, 48, 63, 84,
    162–163, 232, 291–292
Pear Orchard, Texas, 344
Pearson, Drew, 199
Peck, Gregory, 172
Pegler, Westbrook, 198, 238–239, 323
Pelley, William Dudley, 34
People's Artists, 89

People's Educational and Press
    Association, 290
People's Radio Foundation, 5, 62
People's Songs, 97, 267–268, 284, 288,
    299, 340
Persico, Joseph, 77
Phil Silvers Show, The, 254
Philbrick, Herbert A., 191–192
Philco, 85
Philco Television Playhouse, 85
Philip Morris, 173, 273
Pious, Minerva, 178
Pitzele, Melvin S., 112–113
Plain Talk, 11–16, 52, 306
Plays, anti-anti-Communist, 192–193,
    323
Pledges, anti-Communist. *See* Loyalty
    oaths.
Polan, Lou, 255–256
Poland, USSR's takeover, 4, 57
Police, Hartnett information
    exchange, 297
Political activism: anti-Communist,
    29–31; anti-fascist, 24, 31, 34–35;
    depression, 3; depression
    influences, 20, 22, 25, 26–27, 32;
    radio community, 3, 5, 20, 24–25,
    181, 183; socialist, 94, 95. *See also*
    Organizations; Protests.
Pollock, Nancy, 220
Polonsky, Abraham, 139, 192
Popular Front, 32–41, 66, 147–150,
    193–195
Prager, Stanley, 224
Prague purge trials, 177
Price, Vincent, 188
Print media. *See* Books; Newsletters;
    Newspapers; *publications by name.*
Prisoners of war, USSR treatment, 23
Private Files of Matthew Bell, 133–134

Proctor & Gamble, 130–131, 173

Producers, blacklist defiance, 196–197

Programming: anti-anti-Communist, 199–203, 221, 255, 258, 321–322; anti-Red melodramas, 190–192; blacklist effect, 190–197; Golden Age, 20–25, 193–196, 324; leftist, 192–197, 199–203; left-wing, 192–197, 199–203, 207–208; post-blacklist, 324

Progressive Citizens of America, 25, 231, 265, 284

Progressive party, 25, 98

Propaganda (CPUSA), 59–62, 147

Protestant-Catholic hostilities, 171

Protests: anti-blacklist, 84, 163; anti-war, 48, 60, 329; *Counterattack* agitation of, 83, 85; Flagstad pickets, 84; HUAC, 226–227, 232; Muir appearance, 50–54; USSR actions, 242

Puppets for Propaganda, 59–60

Pyle, Ernie, 69

Quisinberry, Perry, 23

Quiz shows, 324

Racism, 149; actions against, 94; anti-communism and, 18; CPUSA, 149; HUAC, 29; television, 254, 321; World War II broadcasting on, 22. *See also* Civil liberties.

Racketeering, *Counterattack* and, 84–88

Radio: anti-Red shows, 190–191; blacklist defiance, 131–133, 179, 180; blacklists, 42–46, 53, 71–72, 163, 233, 234, 238–241, 245–247; civil liberties broadcasts, 165; *Counterattack* campaign against, 28–31, 40–41; CPUSA infiltration, 43–44, 54–70, 142–157, 162–163; FM radio, 62–63;

folk music broadcasts, 97, 131, 143–144, 206; Golden Age, 20–25, 193–196; importance of, 19, 24, 43, 45–46; sustaining programs, 21–25, 64, 107, 194, 196; televisions' effect on, 4, 24. *See also* Radio community.

Radio community: anti-communism, 26; anti-fascism, 3–4, 20; anti-McCarthyism, 40; blacklists, 42–46, 53, 71–72, 77–78, 103–115, 163; HUAC and, 72; left-wingers, 3–5, 13–14, 24–28; loyalty oath protests, 77; political activism, 3, 5, 20, 24–25, 181, 183; USSR supported by, 3–4, 23, 25–26, 66. *See also* AFTRA; Radio; Radio Writers Guild.

Radio and Television Directors Guild, 48–49, 163

Radio Writers Guild: anti-blacklist activities, 48–49, 77, 131, 323; anti-Communist caucus, 66–68, 283, 323; Communist infiltration of, 63–64, 69, 107, 143, 154, 177; demise of, 177–178; investigations of, 142, 143, 154–155

Randall, Tony, 272, 310, 345

Randoph, A. Philip, 149

Randolph, John, 127, 139, 210, 253, 256, 321, 323

Rankin, John, 29, 169

Raphaelson, Samson, 81

Ray, Anne, 142

Raymond, Judith, 147

Reagan, Ronald, 344–345

Ream, Joseph H., 71, 72–73, 77–78, 103–104

Rearn, Joe, 339

Red Channels, 43–70, 78, 79, 80–82, 102, 106–109, 129, 220, 227; blacklistees, 78, 79, 254, 272, 273,

Red Channels (*continued*)
301, 323, 330; blacklists, 42–70, 78–92, 103–115; criticism of, 48–49, 51–54, 84–88, 91, 105, 107, 112–115, 167–168, 190; Hartnett and, 165, 212–213; libel suits, 90–92, 186–187; loyalty oaths and, 72, 73; protests, 50–54, 76, 90–92; support of, 84, 122; survivors, 107–110. *See also Counterattack.*

Red Fascists. *See* CPUSA.

"Red Fronts Falling" (Hartnett), 166

Red Network, The, 49

Red Scared (Barson and Heller), 31, 35

Redfield, William, 189

Reed, Bob, 79

Reel, A. Frank, 178

Reinnarma, 152

Religion. *See* Catholic church; Jewish organizations.

Remington, William, 72

Report on Blacklisting (Cogley), 243–244, 306

"Report on Senator Joe McCarthy, A," 200

Research for clearance, 174–175, 176

Reynolds, Quentin, 13, 238–239

Reynolds Tobacco Company, 109

Rheingold Beer, 237

Rhodes, Peter, 57

Rice, Elmer, 110, 167

Richards, Sylvia, 144, 150–151

Riesel, Victor, 10, 84, 138, 140

"Right to Freedom, The," 165

Right-wingers: anti-communism, 69–70, 337; anti-Semitism, 17–18, 49, 155–156, 168–170, 179; as conspirators, 347; *Counterattack* views, 29; extremism, 347–348, 349–350; as traitors, 22. *See also* Left-wingers.

Ritt, Martin, 127, 139, 342

"Road Back, The" (Aware pamphlet), 211–212

Robbins, Jerome, 222

Roberts, Kenneth, 173, 273

Robeson, Paul, 18, 33, 60–61, 176–177, 189, 232, 242, 342–343

Robinson, Earl, 143, 170, 206, 231, 330

Robinson, Edward G., 3, 44, 175, 298

Robson, William, 21, 25, 27

Roche, Estelle, 158

Rodman, Howard, 154

Romain, Jerome Isaac (V. J. Jerome), 59

Romania, Soviet takeover, 160

Romerstein, Herbert, 56, 91

Roosevelt, Eleanor, 33, 60

Roosevelt, Franklin Delano: anti-Communist views, 39; Communist party view of, 32, 60, 330; League of American Writers denunciation, 35; World War II internal policies, 348

Rose, Reginald, 195, 255, 321, 322

Rosenberg trial, 187, 281

Rosten, Norman, 23

Royle, Selena, 90–91

Rubin, Samuel, 320–321

Rubin, Stanley, 147

Rule, Janice, 225–226

Ruskin, Coby, 254

Russell, Charles, 139, 349–350

Saboteurs, Nazi, 8

Salt, Waldo, 153

Santa Claus, clearance checks, 301

Sarnoff, David, 108

Saturday Review, Murrow critiqued by, 201
Saypol, Irving, 187, 260–261
Scandalize My Name, 342
Scarsdale, folk music controversy, 206–207
Schary, Dore, 170
Schine, G. David, 203
Schlesinger, Arthur, Jr., 204–205, 226, 347
Schlessinger, Laura, 349
Schlitz, 138
Schmidt, Godfrey, 185, 214–215, 222, 240, 250, 253
Schmink, Otto, 208
Schneider, Bert, 343
Schoenbrun, David, 77
Schools, music played in, 206–207
Schulberg, Budd, 59
Schultz, Benjamin, 50, 52, 170
Schuster, Bernard, 56
Scientific and Cultural Conference for World Peace, 47
Scott, George C., 333
Scott, Hazel, 53
Scoundrel Time (Hellman), 341–342
Seabrook Farms, 133–134
Secrecy of CPUSA, 42
Security measures. *See* Clearance.
See It Now, 199, 201, 201, 333
Seeger, Pete, 60, 82, 97, 170, 197, 268, 323, 330, 345, 347
Seldes, George, 85–86, 87
Seldes, Gilbert, 201
Serling, Rod, 195, 255, 258
Sevareid, Eric, 21, 77
Seymour, Katherine, 63
Shaw, Artie, 131, 168
Shaw, David, 322, 329

Shaw, Irwin, 47, 110–111
Shayon, Robert Lewis, 21
Sheen, Fulton J., 54
Sherwood, Robert E., 36
Shield, Lansing, 237–238
Ship, Reuben, 142, 208
Shipler, Guy Emery, 18–19, 171
Shirer, William L., 21, 53
Shivers, Allan, 182–183
Sibley, John, 303
Sign, 166
Sillen, Samuel, 79
Silver Shirts, 34–35
Silvera, Frank, 321
Simon, Neil, 195
Slate, Sam, 233, 238, 239, 245, 266–267, 303–304
Sloane, Allen, 148, 151–152, 213, 272
Sloane, Everett, 164, 213, 272, 286
Smith, Bill, 331
Smith, Gerald L. K., 70, 89
Smith, Henry Nash, 281
Smith, Howard K., 21, 28, 107
Smith, Kate, 309
Smith, L. K., 169
Smith, Lynne, 97
Smith, Mona Z., 87
Smith, Sally Bedell, 73
Sobell, Morton, 281
Social consciousness: television, 254–255, 258. *See also* Civil liberties; Political activism; Protests.
Social Justice, 23
Socialism, 94, 95
Sokolsky, George, 69–70, 84, 138, 170, 204
Sondergaard, Hester, 163
Songs for John Doe, 60, 65

Southern Conference Educational Fund, 335
Southern Conference for Human Welfare, 227, 269
Soviet Union (former). See USSR.
Spanish Civil War, 8
Spellman, Francis, 11
Sperber, A. M., 200
Spielberg, Steven, 343
Spies: anti-Communist, 9; dramas, on, 190–192; Nazi, 8; Soviet, 10, 56–57, 62, 72, 147, 202–203, 204, 221–222, 281, 292, 345–346. See also Infiltration.
Spiritual radio shows, 21
Sponsor, blacklist critique, 111
Sponsors, 121; blacklists and, 50–54, 70, 78, 79–80, 85, 109, 123–134, 198, 234–241, 251, 256–257, 262, 263, 265, 266–279, 297, 298, 304, 318; clearance measures, 104–106, 138, 145, 172–176, 189, 197, 270–271, 272; letters to, 78, 109, 127, 236, 239, 256–257, 277; loyalty oaths and, 73. See also Advertising agencies.
Spotlight, 126, 130
Stalin, Joseph: anti-Semitic purges, 60–61; collectivization program, 34; death of, 176; Khrushchev exposes, 242; liberals' defense of, 33–34, 35, 97, 98–99, 176–177, 242, 341–342, 343, 347; Moscow purge trials, 34, 79, 341–342; radio portrayals of, 23; takeovers by, 4, 35–36, 45, 57, 160–161, 170
Stander, Lionel, 180
Stanton, Frank, 72, 73–74, 75
Stark, Sheldon, 67, 287–288, 297
Starobin, Joseph, 151
Steel, Johannes, 13, 28, 57, 61, 345

Stettinius, Edward, 265
Stockholm Peace Appeal, 31, 48, 63
Stone, Harold, 80
Stone, Oliver, 343
Storekeepers, community role, 117–118
Stracke, Win, 175, 298
Strand, Paul, 34
Stritch, Samuel Cardinal, 12
"Subversive Infiltration of Radio, Television and the Entertainment Industry" (McCarran Committee), 143
Suicides, 227–228
Sullivan, Ed, 45, 53, 233, 309, 342
Sullivan, Elliot, 222–223, 224, 280, 301–302
Supermarkets, 118–119
Susskind, David, 308–309, 311; blacklist defiance, 108, 218, 254, 256, 281; Faulk v. Aware testimony, 270–271, 280, 281; movies by, 325; television shows by, 196, 218, 256, 326
Sustaining programs, 21–25, 64, 107, 194, 196. See also Historical programs.
Swanson, 271
Sweets, William, 53, 162–164, 178
Syracuse anti-Communists, 116–141, 235–241, 296, 327–328. See also American Legion; Dungey, John; Johnson, Laurence A.; Neuser, Francis.

Tablet, 169
Taft-Hartley Act, 27
Taylor, Davidson, 96, 172
Techniques of Communism, 285
Television: anti-anti-Communist programs, 199–203, 221, 255,

258, 321–322, 332–335; anti-Red dramas, 191–192; blacklist defiance, 139–140, 175, 179, 180, 196–197, 254–255, 256, 321–324; blacklist effects, 195–197, 233, 324, 329; blacklists, 48, 49–54, 68–70, 78–82, 103–115, 138–139, 247, 322–323; CPUSA infiltration, 43–44, 54–58, 142–157; Emmy awards, 329–330, 334; Golden Age, 193–196, 324; importance of, 43, 202–203; panel shows, 100, 109, 247, 248, 325; post-blacklist programming, 324; quiz show scandals, 324; radio affected by, 4, 24; social consciousness in, 254–255, 258, 321–322. *See also* networks by name.
Television Writers of America, 177–178
Terkel, Studs, 345
Texas, left-wingers, 93–94, 267, 290
Texas Broadcasting Corporation, 218–219
Texas Chainsaw Massacre, 333
Theater: Actors' Lab, 346; anti-anti-Communist plays, 192–193, 323; as a blacklistee refuge, 197–198, 217–218, 227–228; communism portrayed in, 45; front organizations and, 35–36, 40; HUAC investigation, 223–224; unions, 48–49, 79, 217, 274
Theatre Arts Committee, 35–36, 39, 79
There Shall Be No Night (Sherwood), 36
"They're Moving In on TV" (Hartnett), 297
Third violin theory, 28–29, 83, 175–176
This Is War (Corwin), 23
"Through the Years with the Blacklist" (Bean), 336–337

Thurber, James, 301
Tiffany Network. *See* CBS.
Time magazine, 199–200
Toast of the Town, 53
Todd, Betty, 72
Todman, Bill, 108
Tonight Show, 221, 248
Torquemada, 207
Totalitarianism: anti-anti-totalitarianism and, 343–344, 348; FBI training, 7. *See also* Anti-fascism; Fascists; Stalin, Joseph.
To Tell the Truth, 325
Toward a Soviet America (Foster), 147
Townsend, Pauline Swanson, 65, 151
Trachtenberg, Alexander, 55, 57, 58
"Tragedy in a Temporary Town" (Rose), 255
Treasury Men in Action, 287–288, 297
Trial (Mankiewicz), 226
Trials. *See* Congressional hearings; Libel suits.
Trotsky, Leon, 56
Troubled Air, The (Shaw), 110–111
Truman, Harry, 99, 345, 349; communism policies, 98, 101–102, 161, 165, 343
Turkey, USSR and, 161
Tuttle, Frank, 110
"12 Angry Men," 255
Twelve-step clearance programs, 211–212
Twilight Zone, 258
Tyne, George, 224

Unfriendly witnesses, credibility, 34, 224
Unions: anti-anti-communism, 180, 217; anti-Communist control, 29, 178–180; anti-Communists critiqued

Unions (*continued*)
by, 77; blacklist supporters, 178;
Communist infiltration, 8–9, 13, 22,
26, 58, 63, 66–68, 79, 143, 145, 154,
177–180, 221, 229–230; congressional
hearing mandate, 232, 241;
entertainment industry, 48–49, 77,
106–107, 177–180; radio broadcasts
by, 57; radio personalities involved
with, 3, 4; Taft-Hartley Act, 27;
theater, 48–49, 79, 217, 274. *See also*
ACLU; AFRA; AFTRA; Radio Writers
Guild; *other unions and guilds by
name.*
United Nations Radio, 107
United Nations tribute, 264–265, 298
United States: indictments of native
fascists, 22; loyalty programs, 72;
militarization, 101–102; newspapers
sued by, 22; radio programs
sponsored by, 23; Truman policies,
98; USSR allied with, 10, 23. *See also*
Cold war; Congressional hearings;
FCC; HUAC; Korean War; Marshall
Plan; U.S. Army; Vietnam War;
World War II.
Untermeyer, Louis, 48, 107, 109
U.S. Army: Army-McCarthy hearings,
203; Communist members, 203,
293; militarization of the U.S.,
101–102
USSR (Union of Soviet Socialist
Republics): anti-Semitic purges,
60–61, 177; celebrity endorsement
of, 33, 60–61, 98–99, 336, 340,
341–342, 343, 347; collectivization
program, 34; Comintern, 31–32;
CPUSA support, 48; FBI policies,
7–19; Hungarian revolution, 242,
336; Korean war role, 46, 101–102,
115, 176, 177, 292; Moscow purge
trials, 34, 79, 341–342; Prague purge
trials, 177; radio programs on, 23,
25–26; spy operations, 10, 56–57,
62, 72, 147, 202–203, 204, 221–222,
281, 292; support by U.S. citizens,
3–5, 23, 25–26, 33–34, 35, 66, 97,
98–99, 176–177, 242, 292; takeovers
by, 4, 35–36, 45, 57, 160–161, 170,
242, 260, 336, 343; U.S. alliance
with, 10, 23; Yugoslavian repression,
260

Vadeboncoeur, E. R., 132
Vadeboncoeur, Joan, 132
Van Dyke, Dick, 325, 333
Venona transcripts, 56, 57, 292, 345
Vernon, Whit, 162
Veterans: anti-Communist activities,
50, 105–106, 123–124, 127, 130,
139–140, 156, 173, 175, 189–190. *See
also* American Legion; Veterans
Action Committee.
Veterans Action Committee of
Syracuse Super Markets, 123–124,
127, 130, 139–140, 156, 173, 175,
189–190
Veterans of World War II of Johnson's
Organizations, 123–124. *See also*
Veterans Action Committee.
Vietnam War, 329
Villante, Tom, 323
Vinson, Owen, 148
Vishinsky, Andrei, 160
Voice of Freedom Committee, 5, 13,
28, 40, 61–62, 163

Wagner, Alan, 74, 322–323
Waldorf Peace Conference, 84,
162–163, 288

Wallace, Henry, 25, 97, 98, 99,
    114, 182, 231, 232, 265, 268–269,
    305, 339
Wallace, Mike, 192
Walsh, J. Raymond, 28, 170
Wanamaker, Sam, 323
Wangerman, Susan, 347
"War of the Worlds" (Welles), 19
Ward, Carl, 233, 234, 238, 239,
    266–267, 299–300, 303
Washington Post, anti-McCarthy
    articles, 199
Water, Harry F., 334
WCCO, Faulk job offer, 246–247
We the Undersigned, 143, 185, 283, 287
Weaver, Pat, 108
Weavers, 82, 122–123, 131
Welch, Joseph, 203
Welles, Orson, 3, 13, 19, 44, 194, 272
Weltfish, Gene, 114
Wever, Ned, 178, 180, 185
What Makes Sammy Run?
    (Schulberg), 59
Whipper, Lee, 185
White, Josh, 60, 81, 87
White, Mark (Howard Fast), 321
Wicker, Ireene, 80–81, 88–89, 164,
    170, 243
William Esty Agency, 109
William Morris Agency, 166
Williams, Richard L., 130
Williams, Robert H., 169
Wishengrad, Morton, 26, 52, 68, 187,
    226, 350
Woltman, Fred, 299
Women's Patriotic Conference on
    National Defense, 168–169
Wood, Hally, 95, 96, 97, 182, 227, 256,
    268, 289, 290

WOR, Faulk blacklist and, 247
World War II: censorship, 22, 52–53,
    348; CPUSA propaganda efforts,
    60–62, 194; League of American
    Writers views, 35; radio coverage,
    22–24, 26; sedition charges, 22. See
    also Marshall Plan; Nazis.
WPAT, Faulk show, 99
Wren, Jack: advertising career,
    105–106, 306; background, 14–15;
    credibility, 299; criticism of, 243;
    disappearance of, 323; exonerations
    by, 145, 172, 188; Faulk v. Aware
    testimony, 305–308; FBI informer
    role, 15, 105; investigations by, 176,
    219, 230, 293, 298–299, 305–306;
    Matusow and, 138
Writers: awards, 329–330; blacklists,
    139, 155, 192–193, 287–288, 329–330,
    342; congressional investigations,
    142, 146–147, 153–155, 208; CPUSA
    pressure on, 59, 63–64, 66–68, 69,
    150–151, 206–207, 330; Golden Age,
    196; loyalty oaths, 77; Popular front
    and, 147–148, 193–195; style affected
    by ideology, 194–195. See also Radio
    Writers Guild.
Writers Guild of America, 178

Yankees, blacklists and, 137
Yorkin, Bud, 325
You Are There, 192–193, 195
Young & Rubicam, 130, 189, 270, 292,
    294
Young Communist League, 140, 339,
    340
Youth organizations, Communist
    fronts, 135, 136, 140, 339, 340
Yugoslavia, Soviet repression, 260

A NOTE ON THE AUTHOR

David Everitt was born in New York City and studied at the State University of New York at Buffalo. After working as a magazine editor, he became a full-time writer whose articles have appeared in the *New York Times*, *Entertainment Weekly*, *Biography*, and *American History*. His book *King of the Half-Hour* explored the golden age of television comedy. Mr. Everitt is married with two children and lives in Huntington, New York.